# WILD WEST Women

## Fifty Lives That Shaped the Frontier

### EDITED BY
# ERIN H. TURNER

TWODOT®

GUILFORD, CONNECTICUT
HELENA, MONTANA

**A · T W O D O T® · B O O K**

An imprint and registered trademark of Rowman & Littlefield

Distributed by NATIONAL BOOK NETWORK

Copyright © 2016 by Rowman & Littlefield

British Library Cataloguing-in-Publication Information Available

**Library of Congress Cataloging-in-Publication Data Available**

ISBN 978-1-4930-2333-2 (paperback)
ISBN 978-1-4930-2334-9 (e-book)

∞™ The paper used in this publication meets the minimum requirements of American National Standard for Information Sciences—Permanence of Paper for Printed Library Materials, ANSI/NISO Z39.48-1992.

# Contents

CONTENTS

CONTENTS

# Preface

For more than twenty years, TwoDot books have been telling the stories of the women who shaped the history of the West, from the brilliant and accomplished physicians who couldn't find work in the East but brought their skills to the frontier, to the daring and talented entertainers who found their way to the make-shift stages and elaborate opera houses that provided respite from the back-breaking work of Manifest Destiny. In these pages are fifty stories of women like them whose part in history has become part of our national memory and whose contributions have often been unsung.

These are immigrants, Native Americans, second-generation Americans, larger-than-life characters, unassuming wallflowers, social workers, entrepreneurs, nuns, pilots, artists, cowgirls, photographers, homesteaders, and of course, teachers, suffragists, doctors, nurses, lawyers, and politicians. All were truly remarkable, in spirit, determination, integrity, and perseverance, regardless of how much (or little) they accomplished in their lifetimes. These are all women with grit, who gripped the reins and settled in for the ride, uninhibited by how rough it would prove to be, and their stories should inspire current and future generations.

# ALASKA WOMEN

# NELLIE NEAL LAWING

## (1873–1956)

### The Legendary "Alaska Nellie"

A petite, vivacious woman with curly gray hair hurried over to the tourists who were scrambling off the train.

"Welcome to Lawing, at Mile 23," she called. "How was your boat trip? What do you think of Alaska? Come on, I know you want to see my museum, and we don't have all day!"

The group followed as the woman walked briskly down a path that led to an old two-story cabin on the bank of Kenai Lake. Entering the large room, the travelers gasped with amazement at the array of Alaskan wildlife displayed on every wall and in every corner.

"Alaska Nellie" began telling her stories. "Yep, I killed 'em all myself," she proudly announced. "That big brown bear? My pet bear, Mike, was lost, and I went running into the woods to find him. 'Round a bend was the biggest, meanest bear I ever saw, standing over poor little Mike's dead body! I turned and ran for home, but he followed me and I just barely got the barn door open in time to run in and pull it behind me—but he slammed into it and scratched my arm and broke my three fingers and bruised my knee, see...."

She pulled back her sleeve and showed the crowd her scars. "Then I waited 'til it got real quiet, slipped into the house, got my gun, and went after him. I saw him on the ridge the same time he saw me. He reared up and I sent a bullet into him, hit him in the foot, then another hit him in the leg. Had to shoot him six times 'fore he keeled over!"

It was a good story, and it got better every time she told it. She could have told a similarly exciting tale about any item in the room.

Nellie Trosper was born in Missouri on July 25, 1873, the eldest of ten surviving children. As a child, she fished, hunted, trapped, and did farm work alongside her brothers. She dreamed of going to Alaska to hunt moose and bear, and often told her parents she would live there one day and drive a sled dog team.

Nellie left school before she was fourteen to help her mother with the family. Although she worked away from home for a short time in Missouri, she returned when her mother grew ill. After her mother died, she stayed on to help until her father remarried. Finally, at the age of twenty-seven, Nellie left home for good.

Her journey to Alaska had many twists and turns along the way. She worked at railroad restaurants in Wyoming and Colorado, before beginning work at a boardinghouse in Cripple Creek, Colorado. Eventually she ran a boardinghouse of her own there. She met and married Wesley Neal, a mine assayer, but after a short time of happiness, the marriage began to disintegrate.

"My home life was made unbearable by that demon, rum, which destroys the best in man," wrote Nellie. She left her husband, and Cripple Creek, to continue the westward journey that would lead her, at last, to Alaska.

It was July 3, 1915, when Nellie Neal arrived in the land of her heart's desire. She was forty-two years old. As she sat in her hotel room in Seward that night, she penned this poem:

*After many solemn years had fled,*
*By an unseen force I had been led*
*To the land of my sweet childhood dreams,*
*Where the midnight sun on the ocean gleams.*

With her boardinghouse experience, she soon found work at the Kenai Gold Mine, where she was hired to cook and drive the freight wagon. When the train stopped to unload supplies at Roosevelt, on the edge of Kenai Lake, she was delighted with what she saw. Writing about it later, she recalled, "This place seemed very familiar to me and I hoped that I might some day come back here and make my home."

Nellie's childhood hunting and trapping skills came in handy, as she was often able to secure fresh meat for the hungry miners. On one of her trips into the wilderness, she came upon an abandoned miner's cabin and a plan began to form in her mind. When the mine crew stopped work and moved into Seward for the winter, Nellie had other ideas.

In Seward she purchased a sled and supplies, and then, very early on a crisp December morning, she set out from Seward, following the railroad track. As she had no dogs, she "necked" the sled—that is, pulled it herself, by way of a strap around her shoulders. After traveling for twenty-three miles, she came to Roosevelt and spent the night with the roadhouse proprietors, Mr. and Mrs. Roberts. The next day she covered the remaining seven miles, using snowshoes for the first time in her life. She arrived at the little abandoned miner's cabin where she would spend the winter and began to make her new quarters hospitable. In writing about this experience, Nellie quipped, "If one has never tried cutting wood while on snowshoes, he should really try it as a new outdoor sport."

For the next three months, Nellie ran trap lines, prepared the collected pelts from rabbit, fox, ermine, mink, and lynx, and developed plans for her future. On a clear, cold Christmas Eve, she was awestruck at first experiencing the shimmering, glowing curtain of colors that were the Northern Lights.

When Nellie returned to Seward in the spring of 1916, the US government had purchased the Alaska Railroad and planned to extend the tracks from Seward to Anchorage. Nellie applied to run an eating house on the construction line and was awarded a contract for the roadhouse at Mile 45—she was the first woman to be so selected.

The contract provided that she would be allowed to purchase supplies from the government commissary, have free freight by rail, be paid fifty cents per meal, and charge a dollar per night for lodging. She would collect vouchers from the employees and turn them in each month for payment.

So Nellie set up business at Mile 45, renaming the roadhouse there "Grandview." Ever resourceful, she made a sign for the building using blue letters cut from an old coat and sewn onto white canvas. She assumed there would be ample business opportunities for at least three years.

At that time, the train from Seward came to Mile 40, at Hunter. From there the mail and other supplies had to come by wagon in summer and by dog team in winter. Nellie knew she would need kennels and a cookhouse for dog food, so she proceeded to cut trees and saw them into logs for the buildings. By the time winter arrived, the kennels were ready. She acquired a dog team for her sled and became an expert musher.

Soon Nellie could traverse the forty-five-mile trip from Grandview to Seward on snowshoes in a day, and had braved many a heavy blizzard with her dog team and sled. Stories about her prowess on the trail began to circulate, and her exploits were touted around roadhouse kitchens all over the territory. But it was during her second Alaska winter that the stories about Nellie began to take on legend status.

By then the track had been extended past Grandview for several miles. In November she heard that the train was stuck over the summit in a snowstorm two miles away at Mile 47.

"Every available man has been sent here to help dig us out, and there are at least fifty men here now who have been working feverishly since early morning and without food," the roadmaster told her by telephone. He had attached his portable unit to a telephone line to make the call.

When the train failed to arrive after several hours, Nellie began cooking ham and eggs for sandwiches, frying doughnuts, and making coffee until she had enough for fifty men. She packed it in a washtub, loaded it on her sled, and set out through the storm. When she reached the train, the men were exhausted and hungry. The food gave them the energy they needed to finish digging out the train, which finally returned to Grandview, taking eighteen hours to travel seven miles. There would be no more trains over the summit until spring.

On January 20, 1917, a day that the mail was to come by dog team from Tunnel to Grandview and then on to meet the train at Hunter, there came a wild, blowing snowstorm. By two o'clock it was totally dark, and the carrier had not yet arrived at Grandview. Nellie contacted Tunnel and was told the carrier had left five hours earlier. After waiting another five hours, Nellie knew something was wrong. She donned her parka, hitched her dogs to the sled, threw in a rabbit-skin robe, shovel, lantern, and snowshoes, and was on her way to the rescue.

With the snow swirling around her, Nellie made her way along the railroad track, sometimes having to put on her snowshoes and travel in front of the dogs to break the trail through the snow, or shovel their way through a huge snow-drift. At last, the dogs plunged up and over the last drift to where they found the carrier's dogs and the carrier, huddled in his sled, nearly frozen. She helped the man onto her sled and struggled to rouse the dogs from where they had bedded themselves down in the snow.

When she reached Grandview, she nursed the carrier's near-frozen hands, feet, and face, provided him with hot drinks, and settled him to sleep. Then Nellie returned to the mail sled, hitched her dogs to it, and trailed her own sled behind it. When she got back to Grandview and saw that her "patient" was still sleeping, she decided to take the mail on to its next delivery stop at Hunter. By the time she returned to Grandview, it was seven o'clock in the morning!

The next Christmas, Nellie received a great surprise. As a reward for her valiant rescue, a group of pioneers in Seward sent her a necklace of solid gold nuggets, with a larger nugget pendant set with a diamond. The accompanying note read:

> To Nellie—from oldtimers
> Who on snowshoes broke down the trail;
> Who fought the elements to take through the mail.
> They struggled on without food or rest—
> To rescue the perishing they did their best.

The necklace was her most prized possession and she wore it the rest of her life. Two years had seen the extension of track so that the Alaska Railroad now reached from Seward to Kern Creek, twenty-six miles north of Grandview. Nellie purchased the roadhouse at Kern Creek, overlooking Turnagain Arm, and when hunting season came, she started on her collection of Alaska wildlife trophies. The first moose she killed had thirty-eight-point antlers with a sixty-eight-inch spread. She took down two mountain sheep in one day, and her first bear had a hide measuring seven feet from nose to tail. It was at Kern Creek that she had her little pet bear, Mike. Nellie's encounter with the big brown bear that killed him gave her ample storytelling material for many years.

After her three-year contract with the railroad ended, and after an unsuccessful foray into the mining business, Nellie found herself again running a roadhouse. She managed to procure another contract, this one at Dead Horse Hill, or Mile 248, halfway between Seward and Fairbanks. She saw it as another good opportunity, and anticipated a need for the housing and feeding of workers for some time to come.

In the winter of 1922, Nellie and one of the construction workers became sweethearts. Kenneth Holden had come to Alaska from Seattle. His mother and his cousin, Billie Lawing, remained there, waiting for him to send for them once he was settled. Kenneth was charming and witty, and he played the piano and sang beautifully. He and Nellie became engaged the night before he went off on a construction job. He entertained at a party that night, and his last songs were "Somewhere a Voice Is Calling," and "The End of a Perfect Day." Kenneth died in an accident on that job, and Nellie was heartbroken. She bought the piano on which he had played his final melodies and traveled to Seward with his coffin, which was put on a ship to Seattle. His mother died soon after, and his cousin began a correspondence with Nellie.

In July 1923, President Warren G. Harding traveled to Alaska to drive in the Golden Stake signifying the completion of the Alaska Railroad. His entourage, including his wife and Herbert Hoover, stopped overnight at Dead Horse Hill. Harding wanted to meet "Nellie Neal," whose signature had graced those expense vouchers sent to Washington, DC. It was chilly when morning came around, so Nellie served breakfast on the table in the warm kitchen. When she noted an expression of disapproval from one of the guests, she said, frankly, "Presidents of the United States like to be comfortable when they eat, just like anybody else." The president and the secretary agreed wholeheartedly.

With the completion of the Alaska Railroad came the expiration of Nellie's Dead Horse Hill contract. She was looking for a new project when she received a letter that offered the fulfillment of her dream.

Mrs. Roberts, from Roosevelt, the beautiful spot on Kenai Lake with which Nellie had been so taken years earlier, was willing to sell her property. Mr. Roberts had died and she wanted to return to the States. Nellie was on the next train to meet her and sign the papers.

The log building was perfect for Nellie's long-desired trophy room. Her collection by now included dozens of moose, bear, sheep, and other game, as well as a number of birds. She spent hours arranging the displays as she had always seen them in her mind.

Shortly after her arrival at Roosevelt, she received a letter from Billie Lawing in Seattle. Having lost both his cousin and his aunt, he was particularly lonely. He wanted to come to Alaska and marry Nellie. She, too, was feeling the need for companionship, and so she agreed to marry him. They met in Seward and were wed on the stage of the Seward Theatre on September 8, 1923, right after the show.

About their return to Roosevelt, Nellie wrote, "When Billie entered the trophy room, he was speechless with surprise."

Nellie was now truly living her childhood dream. She and Billie renamed the location Lawing, and Nellie was appointed postmistress. They made many improvements to their property, and soon Lawing was a recreation destination for Seward residents, as well as tourists. The twice-weekly train stopped for ten minutes so that Nellie could take visitors through her "Wildlife Museum." On Kenai Lake, Billie operated a thirty-six-foot cabin cruiser, christened the *Nellie Neal*. For thirteen years their idyllic spot on the edge of the lake gave them joy. Then in March 1936, Nellie's Billie died of heart failure while cutting ice from the lake.

Nellie continued to entertain tourists, both long-term cabin guests and ten-minute train visitors. Her extensive garden provided fresh vegetables even early in the season, since she started the seedlings in a hothouse. To provide fresh fish for the table, Nellie rigged a line that dropped right out her kitchen window into the lake. It was attached to a bell so that when a fish took the hook, the line pulled on the bell and Nellie knew dinner was on the other end. Many celebrities stayed at Lawing, including silent film star Alice Calhoun, who became a good friend.

In 1930, Nellie finished the autobiography she had started years earlier and took the manuscript by bus to New York City, in search of a publisher. On her trip she personally presented four Alaska potatoes to President Franklin D. Roosevelt. Her return trip took her to California, where she visited Alice Calhoun. Alice found someone to help Nellie "polish up" her manuscript.

In 1940, MGM released a short documentary on Nellie, calling it *In the Land of Alaska Nellie*, and her famous nickname was established. That same year Seattle's Chieftain Press published her book, *Alaska Nellie*. On a book tour across the country, she attended President Roosevelt's third inauguration as a special guest. She was a shameless self-promoter and sold hundreds of copies of her book to the public on book tours, to tourists who stopped at Lawing, and to soldiers whom she entertained with stories at the Seward USO. Most of the copies sold by her were autographed, "Sincerely, Alaska Nellie."

Nellie lived the rest of her life in Lawing. The trains slowed their service from Seward in the late 1940s. Still, tourists, coming by bus and automobile, continued to visit Alaska Nellie's famous wildlife museum. As the buildings fell into disrepair, there were fewer overnight guests, but Nellie continued to provide excellent home-cooked meals. She invited neighbors and trappers to join her for Christmas, with colored lights blazing on trees in the snow, and a great feast.

One old-timer remembered:

> *There were all kinds of roasts—bear, moose, caribou, reindeer. There were vegetables, cakes, pies—even hardtack for the Swedes. We joked and told stories while we ate and drank until we could hold no more. Then came the dance with the old phonograph wheezing out "Bye Bye Blackbird" and "Roll Out the Barrel." Nellie was my partner most of the time. She was tall and slim and danced like a bird. She was in her sixties but only looked about twenty-three.*

On January 21, 1956, Nellie was honored in Anchorage with "Alaska Nellie Day." Scarcely four months later, she died at home in Lawing, on May 10, at the age of eighty-two.

Nellie Trosper Neal Lawing came to Alaska and became a legend. She was known for her exploits and storytelling, and in 1942 a letter addressed only to "Nellie, Alaska," was delivered to her promptly. Her life personified the independent, able-bodied, and sometimes outrageous spirit of the pioneers who helped build Alaska.

# ETTA EUGENIE SCHUREMAN JONES

⁓❧⁓

## (1879–1965)

### Native Village Teacher and WWII POW

Etta looked out over the attractive little village of Attu, where she and Foster had spent barely a year of their final assignment for the Alaska Indian Service (AIS). They had come to open a new school on this farthermost island of the Aleutian Chain. The AIS had been looking for a husband-and-wife team in which the wife would be the teacher and the husband would operate an important station for the Weather Bureau. Etta's excellent teaching record and Foster's radio and Morse-code skills made them perfect candidates. Although both were sixty-two years of age, they accepted the positions. It seemed that one more challenging assignment would be just the thing to round out their careers before retiring.

Etta had felt perfectly safe on Attu, even though they were closer to Japan than to the mainland of Alaska. The strongest radio signal they received was actually from Tokyo. But now they were personally feeling the effects of the Japanese attack on Pearl Harbor six months earlier. The natives of the other Aleutian Islands had all been evacuated to locations in southeast Alaska, and the ship that would take Etta and Foster Jones and the forty-five Aleut natives off of Attu was expected any day.

On that morning, June 7, 1942, Etta was making final preparations for the move, and Foster was sending out his eleven o'clock weather report. The natives were returning to their homes after the Sunday church service.

Suddenly one of them pointed to the hills above the village. They could see hundreds of soldiers swarming down the snow-covered mountainside toward the village. The soldiers slipped and slid, holding their rifles above their heads, screaming and yelling. Once they reached the village, the soldiers began shooting bullets and throwing rocks. The people of Attu quickly barricaded themselves inside their homes. Etta hastily gathered all the papers that she could find, letters and reports, and thrust them into the stove. Foster added four words to his morning weather report, "The Japs are here!" Then he smashed the radio.

Etta Schureman was born in Waterbury, Connecticut, on September 30, 1879, the second of four children. Marie was the youngest. Etta received her diploma and teaching certificate from Connecticut State Normal College in

1900, and helped to finance Marie's education. She then graduated from the Pennsylvania Hospital Training School in Philadelphia and worked in nursing and social work.

It was Marie who wanted to spend a year in Alaska. She had taught in Montana, far from her East Coast home, and now was teaching in New York. But she wanted adventure, and begged her sister, Etta, to accompany her to Alaska, where Marie would apply for a teaching position.

Etta was reluctant to leave her comfortable nursing job in Pittsburgh, a cosmopolitan city rich in culture, and go to a place so far away and so wild. Finally, after much consideration, she agreed to go along, on one condition: Marie had to understand that Etta would return to Pennsylvania after one year, even if Marie chose to stay. But at the end of the year it was Marie who returned to the hustle and bustle of the city, and Etta who remained in Alaska, where she would teach for almost twenty years.

By the time Marie convinced her to take the Alaska journey, Etta was forty-two years old, and Marie was thirty-nine. That the two women would travel alone the 3,500 miles to the territory of Alaska indicated their determination and self-confidence.

In the summer of 1922 the sisters boarded the train that would carry them across the country to Seattle, where they would take a steamship to Juneau, Alaska. There, at the Office of the Commissioner of Education, Marie accepted a position teaching at Tanana, where the Tanana River joined the Yukon, just south of the Arctic Circle. So on they went, first by ship to Seward, then on an overnight train to Nenana.

In Nenana they were introduced to travel in Alaska. There was no regular passenger boat, but a commercial boat would be taking supplies to Tanana and would give them passage. After checking with the boat every day about when departure would be, they were told, "Oh, you'll get used to Alaska ways. It isn't a question of hour and minute; it isn't even a question of what day. Just take it easy."

They arrived in Tanana on August 20 and had just a few weeks to get settled before freezing weather and snow arrived by October. They were lucky to rent a compact little log cabin, one of the few in town with a second story, for fifteen dollars a month. Everyone was very helpful, bringing a gasoline stove, cutting wood for the heater, fixing storm windows and doors, and providing lots of advice.

Particularly helpful was Foster Jones, a prospector and miner who had joined the gold rush of 1898 and been in Alaska ever since. By 1922 he and his mining partner, Frank Lundin, had settled in Tanana and were involved in civic and social activities there.

While Marie taught at the government school for white children, Etta got a job at the post office. According to Frank, one day he and Foster walked into the post office and Foster, indicating Etta, said to him, "I'm going to marry that girl."

On Easter Sunday, April 1, 1923, Foster Jones made good on his prediction. Etta had found more happiness than she dreamed possible on her adventure trip to Alaska.

Marie was not enamored of the Great North. She couldn't get used to the silence, the weather, the strange foods, or, especially, the isolation. So she returned to her home in the lower forty-eight and Etta took over the teaching job in Tanana that fall.

Etta loved Alaska. She and Foster enjoyed the summers of fishing, camping, and berry picking. But the winters were best. They traveled by dogsled to visit friends, and to go on winter picnics to woodcutters' camps. Etta had her own three-dog sled team, but she wrote that she was a "softie" with the dogs, "not a good trainer, so they were not obedient."

After teaching in the school for white children for five years, Etta applied to the Alaska Indian Service, stating, "I wish to be more actively associated with the Natives." She was accepted to teach twenty-four Athabaskan students in Tanana.

Two years later Foster was also accepted to teach in the AIS. He was assigned to Kaltag, an Inupiat Eskimo village 327 miles from Fairbanks, while Etta was transferred to Tatitlek, 450 miles south of Kaltag, near Valdez! These posts came with the caveat "This transfer is not for the convenience of the employee," which meant that the AIS at least covered the cost of the moves. Fortunately, at the end of the school year Etta and Foster were happily reunited when both were transferred to Old Harbor, on Kodiak Island.

The school was a home, was nestled among vibrant green hills, with views across the water of snow covered vistas and glaciers. The village itself was neat and clean. The school building was perfect, with good heating and lighting, more than adequate rooms and storage, and even plumbing and playground equipment.

Etta was impressed with the Alutiiq natives in Old Harbor and particularly enjoyed the services and music from their beautiful Russian Orthodox church. At Christmastime she wrote to her mother and Marie about the traditions. The first celebrations were "Starring," in which the participants traveled from house to house, singing carols, with the procession preceded by someone carrying and rotating a giant star. Next came the "Masking," during which participants traveled from house to house wearing masks and the hosts were supposed to guess who was behind the masks, to the great delight of all.

Etta and Foster were well received by the students and their families. They enjoyed a mild winter and spring, and looked forward to another year of berry picking and other pleasant activities.

Part of the salary they received from the AIS included a year's worth of supplies for their use and for the school. A typical order would include twenty or twenty-five cases of canned fruits, vegetables, and dried and condensed milk, and many cases of assorted meats. Added to that would be at least 575 pounds of various dry goods such as flour, rice, coffee, and oats, several bottles or cans each of such items as ketchup, honey, molasses, salad oil, and vinegar, plus assorted spices and other condiments. An order might also include something for the community Christmas tree, for example, twelve pounds of French mixed candy, twelve pounds of satin mixed candy, ten pounds of cube sugar, and twenty pounds of pipe tobacco.

After they had already placed their order in the summer for the following school year, Etta and Foster were notified that they were being transferred to start a new school in the Yup'ik Eskimo village of Kipnuk, which was located on Kuskokwim Bay off the Bering Sea, one hundred miles southwest of Bethel. They decided just to leave everything they had ordered for the use of the new teacher who would come to Old Harbor, and pick up everything they would need in Kipnuk when they arrived in Bethel.

Etta and Foster were selected to be sent to Kipnuk because of their experience and expertise. When the plans were made for this position, the commissioner of Indian Affairs wrote, "Please bear in mind complete isolation, difficult water supply, great destitution of natives, and necessary native health program in making your selection. Practical man whose wife is a nurse is the best combination for this place."

Etta wrote many letters to her mother and to Marie while she was teaching in Alaska. There was constant reference in them to the difficulty of sending and receiving mail, as there was no regular service and delivery depended upon when boats or planes would arrive and leave. Mail to and from Kipnuk was an especially difficult situation, as it was extremely remote. With every opportunity for sending and receiving mail, there were usually several letters at a time, both going out and coming in.

On the trip from Old Harbor to Kipnuk they stopped at Nushagak and Etta wrote:

> *There will be an airplane here in a few days which will*
> *take this, and if I get a chance to write from Bethel, I will.*
> *Otherwise, don't look for letters too often. I hope to goodness we*
> *find letters from you at Bethel. We left orders at Kodiak to have*
> *them forwarded. They will go by way of Anchorage and should*
> *have reached there long before we do. You can imagine how*
> *hungry I am for letters.*

And from Kipnuk: "I will write occasionally and keep a letter handy in case I have a chance to send it."

The trip from Bethel to Kipnuk took six days, on a flat-bottomed boat that traveled down the Kuskokwim River and around the edge of the bay. They made a stop at Kwigillingok, where they met Bess and Gus Martin, Moravian missionaries. The Martins would remain their close friends. At Kwigillingok they were also introduced to the shortwave radio, which would give them much pleasure, as well as needed communication. Foster mastered the radio immediately and soon constructed one of his own.

Kipnuk had none of the mountainous grandeur they had seen in other parts of Alaska. In fact, it was flat tundra, with only a small hill that could still be seen though ten miles away. When they arrived, their house was not finished, so they lived in a tent until it could be occupied.

The Eskimos were very primitive. They came into Kipnuk only in the winter and prepared a new house each year. The houses were dugouts, covered with sod and moss over a driftwood frame, with a smoke hole in the top and a wooden door against the storms. Their diet was primarily fish, supplemented with walrus, seal, ducks, and geese.

In winter they wore warm parkas made mostly from reindeer skins. Shoes were rags wrapped around the feet, then dry grass for insulation, all covered by a boot with seal-skin sole and tops of reindeer hide.

There was no chief, just groups of people who moved from village to village. It was not even definite that if a new school were built in Kipnuk that the same Eskimos would be back the next year to attend it!

The first year of their stay in Kipnuk was spent getting to know the Eskimos and understanding their way of life. The natives were cheerful and friendly, and seemed eager to have the new school. When the building was ready for the next year, adults, as well as children, were encouraged to come to school. The school had thirty-three seats, but sixty-four students enrolled, so it was necessary to have the youngest come in the morning and the older in the afternoon. Etta and Foster gave all the children English names, as the Eskimo names were unclear to them. They also had to guess at the children's ages, as birth dates were not noted. Etta would try to figure out birthdays by asking the mothers if the children were born "when snow was on the ground, when the ducks came, or when berries were ripe, then give a wild guess at the year." The government enrollment forms required names and birth dates for each student.

At the beginning the Eskimos knew no English and Etta knew about "3 Eskimo words." Everything was an English lesson, from calling roll with their new names, to naming objects and gesturing to show verbs. As none of the students had ever attended school before, Etta had to put together a whole new curriculum that would work in the context of Eskimo daily lives. The lessons were practical ones, with Etta teaching the girls to sew and Foster doing carpentry with the boys. The students were very good with their hands, learned writing quickly, were exceedingly artistic, and were excellent in mathematics.

During the five years that Etta and Foster spent in Kipnuk, they had many unusual experiences. One of the Eskimos gave them a piece of walrus meat. The outside was so tough it couldn't be cut even with a razor. Finally they scalded it and boiled it for several hours. Foster said it "tasted like a mukluk smells." Shortly after that, another visitor offered them a piece of walrus, "But just having disposed of the other piece his offering was kindly refused." However, as Etta wrote, "When we were cooking onions last winter the children held their noses at the smell in great disgust, so our eating in some ways is as offensive to them as theirs is to us."

The shortwave radio that Foster had built was an integral part of their life in Kipnuk. They used it not only for news exchanges with neighboring villages, but also for entertainment. Etta wrote in one letter that she had to "bring it to a close" because it was time to hear *Amos 'n' Andy*. Sometimes they invited the villagers to listen to the radio in the schoolroom. Etta also noted that she and Foster were learning Morse code.

In 1937 Etta and Foster requested a transfer, hoping to return to Old Harbor. They were grateful to receive the letter from the director of the AIS granting their request. Claude M. Hirst wrote, "We feel that people who have done the kind of work that you have at Kipnuk the past four years should be recognized in a request of this kind." By that time they had actually been in Kipnuk for five years.

Etta and Foster were happy to be back in Old Harbor. Etta delighted in the view of the mountains and bays. She wrote about watching the whales and the whalers, even visiting the nearby whaling station that was still operating when they arrived. The next three years were spent pleasantly. Etta enjoyed her teaching and participated in the social activities and events of the village.

In the spring of 1941 the Joneses were again contacted by the AIS regarding a transfer, this time to Attu. They accepted, planning for it to be their last assignment, and they were happy with their choice. Etta wrote in a letter, "We like Attu. It grows on one, and the people are fine." She described a "church holiday" where all the little girls wore white dresses, white shoes and stockings, and white hair bows, and the boys wore little blue suits and white caps. In her last letter home she asked for some seeds, or cuttings from houseplants. But nothing could prepare her for the horrors of the invasion and the next few years of her life.

After the Sunday morning invasion, the Japanese soldiers separated her from Foster and took him away for questioning. They were sure he was a spy and that his weather reports were in code. During the interrogation he was killed, and Etta was then shoved into the room and forced to watch them behead him. One week later she was transferred to a Japanese ship and taken as a prisoner to Yokohoma, Japan.

Her prison was not a POW camp with barbed wire, but the Bund Hotel, which had formerly catered to Western guests. After spending a month alone there, she was amazed one day to see a group of women who were speaking English coming into the hotel. They were seventeen Australian nurses and one older woman, a British national, who had been captured in Papua New Guinea, and after a horrendous six-month ordeal at the hands of their Japanese captors had been transported to Yokohama and the Bund Hotel. One of the nurses later wrote, "There was this dear little sad lady who told us later she had never been so happy in her life as when she heard us speaking English. From that moment on, she became one of us." She introduced herself as Mrs. Etta Jones. "We were young (twenty-five to thirty-five years old), and she was always Mrs. Jones to us."

After a month at the Bund Hotel, the nineteen women were transferred to another seemingly suitable place, the Yokohama Yacht Club. Although it may have at one time been an elegant facility, it became an inhospitable prison for them. The women had been able to see in the harbor large black boats with white crosses on them, which they had hoped were prisoner exchange ships. American and European missionaries from China had been loaded onto them, and the women were sure that they would be next. But they were not taken to them, and the ships disappeared.

For the next two years the women were kept at the Yokohama Yacht Club, sleeping on straw mats in what had been the ballroom. They were fed poorly and mistreated by a series of guards who would alternately give them things and take them away. The Japanese winters were harsh, so the women were allowed to use four yards each of a thick fabric to sew something for themselves. They were forced to knit small silk bags for Japanese soldiers, and to fold and glue envelopes for use by the army. They discovered that the glue had a taste, and some of them, from hunger, actually ate the glue.

Although their health began to fail, the women tried to keep up their spirits. They sang, wrote poetry, and used journals that they were able to hide from being confiscated by their captors. When Etta had been ordered to pack her things for leaving Attu she had managed to bring some colored paper, stationery, crayons, pencils, and scissors. The women used these items, and whatever else they could find, to make cards and gifts for one another on birthdays and at Christmas.

After two years in Yokohama, the prisoners were again moved. This time they were driven outside of the city to the small rural slum of Totsuka. There they were ensconced in a group of dilapidated buildings that had once been a hospital for tuberculosis victims. Although they were able to divide up into small rooms, their beds were again pallets on the floor. The women were forced to carry water for themselves and for filling the villagers' large bathing vats, as well as carry wood up the hill for the kitchen of their lodgings. That winter was extremely harsh, and the women had no warm clothes and no heat in their buildings.

In the spring of 1945 the Allies bombed Tokyo, and signs of escalation encouraged the prisoners. In July they were finally visited by the Red Cross, who brought boxes of food and supplies, along with the news that the war had been over in Germany for two months. At last the war came to an end, when Japan surrendered on August 15. Still the women waited for rescue. At last, on August 31, 1945, a convoy of American soldiers found them and they were truly free.

Etta was the first American woman prisoner of war to be freed. Until the Red Cross had visited the Totsuka prison in July, no one at home knew what had become of either Etta or Foster. Since that June day in 1942, many letters had been exchanged among her family, the AIS, and the Secretary of the Interior regarding their fate and that of the Attuan natives. No definitive information was available.

When Etta returned to the United States, she traveled to Chicago to visit her older sister, Nan, and niece, Elinor, arriving there on her sixty-sixth birthday. Then she visited Foster's family in St. Paris, Ohio, before traveling on to Margate, New Jersey, where her brother lived. She bought a house there, but when her brother died, she moved to Bradenton, Florida, where her friends from Alaska, Bess and Gus Martin, also lived.

Etta never returned to Alaska, where she and Foster had enjoyed an idyllic life together. She wrote a long memoir of their time there, but did not ever write about anything that happened after his death. Upon her return from Japan, she was often asked to speak about her experiences. She was always happy to share about her years in Alaska, but did not talk about any of her later trials. In 1957, Etta traveled for five months in New Zealand and Australia, where she reunited with the women who had been her companions during those dark war days. She wrote to her niece, Elinor, "We had a hilarious time, for there was no gloominess connected with this reunion."

Etta Jones died at her home in Bradenton, Florida, on December 12, 1965, at the age of eighty-six.

In September 1942, the forty remaining Attuan natives had been taken to Otaru, on the west side of Hokkaido Island in Japan, where they endured unimaginable hardship as prisoners. Twenty-one of them, mostly children, died in Japan. After the war, the nineteen remaining Attuans were not allowed to return to Attu. Some settled in Seattle, some went to a boarding school in Sitka, Alaska, and the rest settled on the Aleutian Island of Atka.

Foster Jones's body, which had been buried by two Attuans near the old Russian church, was exhumed and now lies in the Fort Richardson Post Cemetery in Anchorage, Alaska.

# FLORENCE BARRETT WILLOUGHBY

❧

(1886–1959)

### Alaska's Storyteller and Author

"And then, with the quickness of a thunderclap, everything changed. Chilled air slapped her face. Swash of waters, blasts of exhausts, the hunters' gladsome chorus reverberated between Stygian walls that shot up on either side, blotting out the valley, the stars.

"She caught her breath. 'We've plunged into the Big Canyon!' And, galvanized into alertness, she stepped out on deck."

Florence Willoughby pushed back from her typewriter and read what she had just written. She remembered the exhilarating feeling of running the wild Stikine River with legendary Captain Syd Barrington, when doing field research for this book, *River House*. Of course, unlike her fictional heroine, she had not made the trip in the dark, in a storm, and trying to get an injured man to the doctor in Wrangell in time to save his arm!

Florence had been working on this particular passage all day. After several rewrites of the chapter, she felt it was finally perfect. Writing was hard work.

In the 1920s, '30s, and early '40s, Florence's pen name, Barrett Willoughby, was well-known to readers of adventure, romance, and travel literature. Her vivid language brought to life the characters, both fictional and real, that filled her novels, biographies, and travelogues. Her subjects were of exceptional interest to her devoted readers in the "lower forty-eight." Barrett Willoughby wrote about Alaska, the place she always considered home.

Florence Barrett was born in Wisconsin in May 1886. There are no official records for verification, but that is the date found in the 1910 census of Katalla, Alaska. Both of her parents had immigrated to the United States. Her father, Martin Barrett, came from Ireland in 1854 at the age of eight. Her mother, Florence Clink, was born in Germany in 1867 and moved to Wisconsin as a young girl.

Martin was an adventurer and had been on his own since his early teenage years. He had worked on steamships that plied the Mississippi River, and sought gold in mining camps across the Rocky Mountains and all up and down the West Coast. But in 1883 he had made his way to Wisconsin and had decided to settle down, marrying Florence Clink, who was seventeen years old and twenty-one years his junior.

Their first child, Laurence, was born a year later, followed by a daughter, Florence, named after her mother. Shortly thereafter the Barretts moved to Washington state. In 1892 little Frederick was born, completing the family.

Martin had not lost his taste for adventure, however, and the search for gold still had its allure. He acquired a schooner, the *Tyee,* and set forth to search the shores of Alaska. On board were not only a crew of two and a captain, but also Martin's wife, who shared his adventurous spirit, and their three little children.

Gold had been mined all along the coast of southeast Alaska since the 1870s, so the Barretts traveled that area, searching in all the logical spots. They spent quite a bit of time around Sitka, where young Florence enjoyed exploring and playing with the native and Russian children who lived there. These were some of the experiences that she would feature in her future stories.

One of the family's adventures turned out to be a bit more hazardous than they had anticipated. In September 1896, Martin sold the *Tyee* and had the new owner drop off the Barrett family and Captain Belmont to prospect for gold on Middleton Island. Arrangements were made that the schooner would return to pick up the group in a few weeks. For some reason, the *Tyee* did not come back to get them, and they remained marooned on the island for ten months.

Middleton Island is directly south of Anchorage in the Gulf of Alaska, seventy-five miles from the coast. It is only three and a half miles long and half a mile wide. Although in later years it became home to the Middleton Island Air Force Station, at that time not only was it isolated, but it also provided very little in the way of survival resources. The family barely made it through the winter, living in a small tent braced against the elements with driftwood and rocks. They ate the rations they had brought with them, including waterlogged flour, and gathered limpets and whatever else washed ashore that could be consumed. In June a passing cannery tender finally rescued them.

Now the Klondike gold rush was beginning and Martin jumped right into it, spending the next half dozen years living in and mining around Dawson, Yukon Territory. While the Barretts were living in Dawson, their older children, Lawrence and Florence, boarded during the winter at Catholic schools in Seattle. Florence was enrolled at the Academy of the Holy Names there, and may also have attended a Catholic convent school in San Francisco for a time.

Martin was apparently successful in his mining endeavors, for in 1903 he was able to purchase a general store, hotel, and restaurant in the newly founded town of Katalla, on the coast south of present-day Cordova. Both of those small towns hoped to attract the railroad and other investments to their area.

Florence was happy to be back living in Alaska with her family, and made use of her typing skills as a clerk of the Commissioner's Court for Kayak Precinct in Katalla. Katalla was a busy, boisterous place then.

One of the men drawn to adventure in Katalla was Oliver Willoughby, who came from Port Townsend, Washington, to explore land and management opportunities in the district. Oliver's older half-brother, Charles, also from Washington, was a well-known sea captain who had mined successfully in Alaska and then settled in Katalla.

Oliver and Florence often met in social situations, and she was attracted to this older, outgoing, tall, and handsome man. Florence and Oliver were married in January 1907. Following in her mother's footsteps, she was not quite twenty-one years old, and he was thirty-eight, almost twice her age. But he was an adventurer and storyteller, like her father, and Florence adored her father.

This was a happy time for Florence. She was active in the community and often entertained ladies with literary programs in her home. Ollie had a lumber business in town, and did exploration for coal and oil development. Just before their first anniversary, Florence delivered a stillborn son. Florence had always wanted children, but that pregnancy would be her last.

Florence continued to be content in her Katalla home, still entertaining her friends. She loved to hike out in the backwoods, and had bonded deeply with the North Country. She spent much of her time outdoors, despite the often-bad weather that was the norm in that part of Alaska. In fact, it was the bad weather that eventually sealed the fate of the little town. Storms raged through from the Gulf of Alaska in 1907 and 1908. Ships could not dock, so they could not load or unload their goods. The Alaska Syndicate railroad that had laid eight miles of track outside of Katalla decided to move all of its facilities to Cordova. Perhaps the death knell came in 1909, when the town newspaper, the *Katalla Herald,* shut down.

The Barretts and the Willoughbys stayed on, trying to make a go of life in Katalla. Ollie still had the lumberyard, and still surveyed for coal and oil in the hills. He traveled more often now to Port Townsend, seeking investors. Florence was his business contact in the north. But the town's population continued to shrink.

In 1912 Florence's father, Martin, died from a heart attack at the age of sixty-six. Florence was devastated. Sadly, only three months later, her younger brother, Frederick, died of tuberculosis in Spokane, Washington.

Then, surprisingly, four months after Frederick's death, Florence's mother eloped to Valdez with Oliver Willoughby's older half-brother, Charles. Now there were two Florence Willoughbys in Katalla—not only were they mother and daughter, but also sisters-in-law!

Florence (Mrs. Oliver) kept herself busy, as the town grew smaller and duller. She continued to take care of any business of Ollie's that needed to be addressed, even asking advice from her new stepfather. But Ollie's trips back to Katalla became fewer and fewer. Soon it became clear that he was spending time with other women, and eventually this led to a rift in the marriage.

Florence spent her remaining time in Katalla wisely. She took a correspondence course in writing and began sending out articles to various magazines. Her first sale was a household hint for which she was paid fifty cents. In the next few years Florence wrote as the Katalla correspondent for the short-lived *All-Alaska Review*, published a story in a magazine for boys that earned her $2.50, and contributed several small articles in other publications. It was in 1916 that she received national exposure when *Sunset* magazine published three of her articles in its "Interesting Westerners" feature, publishing two more the following year.

Florence's relationship with Ollie continued to deteriorate and in 1917 he filed for divorce and the judgment was granted. Although divorced, the two remained on friendly terms. (After all, he was still her step-uncle.) There was nothing now to keep her in Katalla, so on an impulse she rushed into a second marriage with a local coal worker, Roger Summy. The couple moved to Anchorage, where Florence's brother, Lawrence, lived with his wife and baby daughter. Soon Lawrence moved his family to Wyoming, where unfortunately he was shot and killed by a former lover.

Florence admitted that marrying Roger had been a mistake. He was a heavy drinker and stayed away from home for long periods of time. Soon she returned to Katalla, separated from her husband and disillusioned with marriage. She realized that she was at a crossroads in her life and determined to pursue her dream of writing.

January 1920 found Florence once more using the surname Willoughby, and living in San Francisco. Now she could devote herself to her career. This is probably when she decided to shave a few years off of her age. Since there was no actual proof of her birth date, she just intimated, when asked, that she was about five (sometimes ten) years younger than she actually was. She also did nothing to negate the opinion that she was born in Alaska, and she referred to her mother as "a blond English lady." It was not favorable at the time to be German.

Florence got a secretarial job that enabled her to pay the rent and work on her own projects after hours. She wanted to write about Alaska, to show the side of her beloved state that was not evident in the popular, masculine stories by Jack London and Rex Beach. Their stories focused on the gold-rush era, the schemes and wild adventures experienced by the miners and promoters, and portrayed Alaska as wild and cold and forbidding. Florence's Alaska was one of spring, summer, and fall, fishing and hiking, "a land of bright courage and joyous living, where everybody had an awfully good time," as she described it years later in a radio interview.

Florence greatly admired the illustrated novel *Wilderness*, written by Rockwell Kent. She wrote him, "For you, of all the adventurers who have gone to Alaska, are the only one to interpret the Spirit of the North." She noted also, "*Wilderness* is to me as the Psalms of David."

Kent forwarded her letter to his publisher, George Putnam, who wrote back to her and requested some of her writings. In 1922 Putnam published Florence's first book, a romantic novel, *Where the Sun Swings North*. She used her pen name, Barrett Willoughby, for this novel and all her subsequent works.

This novel was based on the winter that her family was marooned on Middleton Island. The child in the story was named "Loll," after her older brother. Although she relied on her memory for the emotional impact of the book, she used the diary her mother had kept during that time for descriptions of actual events. Although the novel is fictionalized, in another book, *Gentlemen Unafraid*, Barrett tells the true story of that adventure.

The experience was incorporated in what became her basic romantic-novel plot. There was usually a young woman who was spending a season in Alaska, either visiting from California or returning after many years away. There was a handsome manly hero, a woman of questionable character, some kind of "Irish father figure," and a villain. The settings were in a particular area of Alaska and dealt with an aspect of that place.

Many of Barrett Willoughby's stories incorporate native Alaska people in their plots. Although her attitude toward them might be considered "politically incorrect" today, it was consistent with the thinking of her time. But her interest in them and her research into their customs and beliefs illustrated her respect for their way of life.

Barrett's next book, *Rocking Moon*, also published by Putnam, came out in 1925 and was instantly successful. It had three printings in the first month and was the first Alaska novel to be made into a movie filmed on location. The setting for this story is a small island near Kodiak Island, and the plot centers on a fox farm. *Where the Sun Swings North and Rocking Moon* were so successful that Grosset and Dunlap republished them together under the title *The Fur Trail Omnibus*.

*The Trail Eater: A Romance of the All-Alaska Sweepstakes* followed in 1929. Its action focuses on the dogsled races that were the forerunners of the famous Iditarod race, and it is set in Nome.

*Spawn of the North*, appearing first in 1930 and then published two years later by Grosset and Dunlap, was possibly Barrett's most popular romantic novel. It was serialized in *Cosmopolitan* magazine before publication, and had three printings before the scheduled release date. In 1938 it was made into a movie starring George Raft, Henry Fonda, Dorothy Lamour, and John Barrymore, names well-known then and still remembered today. This novel has a more complicated plot, involving the fall salmon run in Ketchikan, fish pirates, conflicting loyalties, and violent Alaska storms.

*River House* was published in 1936. This story is set in a hunting lodge up the Stikine River from Wrangell, on the southeast Alaska coastline. Circumstances bring the young heroine from San Francisco to the lodge, where she finds herself having to spend the long winter. In the end, she must decide between "civilization" and "The-Land-of-Don't-Give-a-Damn." This novel, too, was serialized in a magazine before its book form, and had three printings in its first month of publication.

Barrett's redheaded niece, her brother Lawrence's daughter (and her namesake, Florence Barrett), was the inspiration for her next novel, *Sandra O'Moore*, published in 1939. Set in and around Sitka, the story is an exciting tale of spies, stolen valuables, and smuggling.

*Golden Totem* was Barrett Willoughby's last full-length book, published by Little, Brown and Co. in 1945. The plot, set near Juneau, revolves around a gold mine, an unscrupulous owner selling worthless stock, wild adventure, and true love.

Barrett also wrote nonfiction. She continued to write articles for *Sunset* magazine, the *American Magazine*, the *Saturday Evening Post*, the *Alaska Sportsman*, and even *Reader's Digest* throughout her career. Many of the articles then became chapters in her nonfiction books.

Putnam published *Gentlemen Unafraid* in 1928. In it Barrett wrote factually about six Alaska pioneers, including her father, and their family's time on Middleton Island. Also in the book is dogsled racer "Scotty" Allan, who became the model for her hero in *The Trail Eater*, which came out the following year.

*Sitka, Portal to Romance*, published in 1930, is part travelogue, part history, and part memoir. Barrett wrote of a visit to Sitka, on Baranof Island in the Inside Passage, with a friend, Kay. In a chatty style, Barrett tells the Russian history of Sitka as she guides Kay around the sites and reminisces about spending time there as a child.

In *Alaskans All*, which appeared in print in 1933, Barrett again tells the stories of some fascinating pioneers. She got to know each of her subjects, writing their stories from the notes she took during her time with them. She camped with Father Bernard R. Hubbard, the "Glacier Priest," and flew with pioneer pilot Ben Eielson. She spent hours interviewing Arctic adventurer Louis Lane, hotelier Harriet Pullen, and legendary newspaperman "Stroller" White.

Almost half of Barrett's final nonfiction book, *Alaskan Holiday*, is just that: the story of several weeks that she and a friend, identified only as "Zoe," spent on the island of Kodiak, west of the Alaska Peninsula in the Gulf of Alaska. The other chapters touch on such diverse subjects as the seal harvesting on the Pribilof Islands, the native and Russian treatments of their dead, biographical studies of a lighthouse keeper, a Matanuska Colonist, and Klondyke Kate, the "Belle of the Yukon." It also includes a very funny but hair-raising account of a night spent lost in the forest, sheltered in an old bear hunter's "haunted" cabin.

Barrett Willoughby's nonfiction works were not academic studies and contained no indexes, dates, or bibliographies. They were meant to entertain and inform, and did both admirably. They were further enhanced by dozens of spectacular black-and-white photographs that gave extra meaning to the text.

Although Barrett Willoughby did all of her writing while comfortably settled in her residence in California, she was no armchair author. Every summer, and parts of many winters, she traveled to Alaska, where she researched the topics of her coming books and actually experienced much of the action that became her plots or articles.

For example, when her plot centered on the salmon industry in *Spawn of the North*, Barrett spent time in Ketchikan, learning all she could about the salmon run. She studied how the traps were built, how they worked, and everything that was involved in getting the fish from the water to the canneries, and into the cans. She learned about fish pirates, and listened to the workers on the docks and in the bars to get the vernacular correct. Here her upbringing helped—she had grown up around rough talkers, and could use "man-talk" with the best of them. In fact, some of the early reviewers of her books commented on the good use of masculine dialogue that "Mr. Willoughby" wrote into "his" plots. She had purposefully chosen a pen name that was not gender specific, so that until her work was proven there would not be criticism just because she was a woman.

It was important to Barrett that her books reflect the Alaska that she knew and had loved since she was a child. The attitude still prevailed in the "lower forty-eight" that Alaska was wild and cold, with snow and ice everywhere. She wanted her readers to see what she saw—an Alaska that was warm, sunny, and inviting; where people traveled around the territory by airplane, as well as dogsled, and were well read and listened to the same music on the radio as their counterparts in the States.

To bring a story to life the way she wanted, Barrett focused on the logistics of her writing. While doing her research in Alaska she carried her diary with her every day and tried to write two thousand words a day in it. Then she returned to her desk in California to put the books or articles together.

She told an interviewer, "I write every day from 9 to 4 and it's hard work. One can't make one's living writing if one waits for inspiration!"

As she worked out the plot of a novel she would examine each character in depth, and sometimes the characters themselves would direct the plot and the story line would change. She confided to "Stroller" White that she had rewritten her first novel eight times, and another book eighteen times.

Barrett also continued to take writing classes, and was always open to ways she could improve her already captivating style.

She was inundated with requests from would-be writers to read and critique their work, but she learned to return their manuscripts unopened. However, remembering the kind interest taken in her by Rockwell Kent, she was not averse to giving advice to young writers who took the time to write to her. Wilna Lee Ury wrote to her from Seward asking for information to do a report for school. Barrett sent her a clipping and a list of her books, and wrote:

> *Your letter of December 1, 1935, was delayed in reaching me. I hope my answer will get back to you in time for your report on an author.*
>
> *It was good of you to select me for your theme.*
>
> *All these books are about Alaska and Alaskans. I do not write about anything else, you know. One day I shall write a novel about Seward.*
>
> *I have lived there and think it one of the most beautiful spots in the North.*
>
> *I get many letters from high school students all over the United States, but yours is the only one I have had from my own Alaskans.*
>
> *My best wishes to you, little Sourdough.*
>
> *Sincerely yours,*
>
> *(signed) Barrett Willoughby*

As Barrett Willoughby's name became well-known and her career blossomed, her personal life had its ups and downs.

Barrett's mother, Florence, and her stepfather, Charles Willoughby, finally left the nearly deserted Alaska town of Katalla and moved to San Francisco. They apparently lived with Barrett for the rest of their lives. Charles continued to be involved in various business ventures, none of them particularly successful, and several of them subsidized by Barrett. Florence sometimes accompanied her daughter on her research trips back to Alaska in the summer.

When Barrett had first arrived in California she did secretarial work for a well-known author and critic, Frederick O'Brien. Through him she met and socialized with some famous names of the day, such as novelist Fannie Hurst and writer Edna Ferber, and enjoyed the new social life she found there.

She met a young University of California engineer, Robert Prosser, who was eight years younger than she (but who probably didn't know that). The two were married in October 1927, and Barrett dedicated *Gentlemen Unafraid* to "Robert H. Prosser, a Gentleman Unafraid." The marriage was happy, albeit short. Less than ten months after their wedding, Robert died of complications during sinus surgery while they were traveling in Philadelphia.

While doing research in Wrangell for *River House*, Barrett met a boat operator, Captain Larry O'Connor, who followed her back to San Francisco. He became sort of a secretary to Barrett, and began to manage some of her affairs. They were subsequently married in Reno in 1935, and moved to a secluded little house in San Carlos, just south of San Francisco. Barrett's father-in-law, Charles Willoughby, died in 1938, and her mother continued to live with her and manage the household.

O'Connor was also a writer, and he and Barrett enjoyed reading and critiquing each other's efforts. When either of them had something published they would celebrate with a little trip or a party. But Larry was not very successful in his writing, so Barrett set him up with a furniture store. Not only did he run off with the bookkeeper, but he had also managed to lose a great deal of her money in ill-planned financial dealings. After her divorce in 1942, Barrett moved with her mother to Southern California and hoped to regain her financial standing with another novel.

*The Golden Totem*, published in 1945, was Barrett's last book. It was, fortunately, another best seller. However, insight into her life at this time might be gained by its dedication: "To a cheerful, disenchanted lady—myself."

During the next ten years Barrett did very little writing. Her mother died in Southern California during that time, and Barrett relocated back to San Francisco. Although her correspondence indicates that she had lots of ideas of books to come, she published only one more article, in *Good Housekeeping* magazine in 1956.

Barrett Willoughby died in Berkeley, California, in July 1959, at the age of seventy-three. Her last bit of fiction writing was on her death certificate. She was listed as having been born in Alaska in 1900, of an English mother.

All of Barrett Willoughby's books are long out of print, although some that are out of copyright are available on the Internet. It is still possible to find one in a library or a used bookstore. The search for a romance novel with a lurid dust jacket enticing the reader to look inside, or for a travelogue on old Alaska, is well worth the time spent, when the treasure is found. Barrett's remarkable vocabulary, compelling writing, and spellbinding plots still captivate readers who want to know what Alaska was like in those vibrant days about which she wrote.

# ANFESIA SHAPSNIKOFF

## (1900–1973)

### Attu Weaver and Aleut Culture Keeper

On June 3, 1942, Japanese planes attacked the US military base at Dutch Harbor on Amaknak Island, on the north side of Unalaska. For two days bombs fell, and when it was over, thirty-five men had been killed. In the village near the base, there were no casualties among the local residents, who had taken refuge in air-raid shelters as instructed. This attack came almost exactly six months after the Japanese bombed Pearl Harbor.

On the seventh of June, Japanese forces invaded Attu, the westernmost island of the Aleutian Chain, a mere 750 miles from Japan. They captured forty-five Aleut natives and the government schoolteacher, whose husband was killed in the invasion. The prisoners were taken to internment camps in Japan.

Shortly thereafter, the US Navy evacuated the residents of Atka and burned their village to save it from Japanese occupation. Next, the Pribilof Islanders were evacuated, as were the residents of five smaller villages. The people of Unalaska knew that their turn would come and they prepared as best they could.

Several men from the community packed belongings from the Church of the Holy Ascension. Father Dionecious removed items from the altar while Anfesia Shapsnikoff's son, Vincent Tutiakoff, kept a careful inventory of everything being crated. Because Anfesia was a reader for the church, she was responsible for packing the books and packed sixteen boxes.

The SS *Alaska* took the people from their homes. Each person could carry only one suitcase of belongings. Family heirlooms, photographs, and other items of irreplaceable value were hidden in their homes before the doors and windows were shut and locked. Reluctantly, Anfesia left behind the precious violin of her first husband, Michael Tutiakoff.

The ship deposited them in Wrangell, in southeast Alaska. From there they were moved to Burnett Inlet, a wilderness area between Wrangell and Ketchikan, where they found themselves surrounded by a forested world completely foreign from the wide-open landscapes of their homeland. There, they struggled to maintain their very existence in deplorable conditions. Many of the elderly died in that place, far from home. Although the Japanese troops were defeated the following year and there were no more hostilities in the Aleutians, it was three long years before the residents of Unalaska were returned to their island on April 22, 1945. Their homecoming was not a joyous one; they found their homes uninhabitable and ransacked, their valuables pilfered, and their church damaged.

"When we came [back] to Unalaska," Anfesia recalled, "we were happy and we were sad at the same time. Some of the homes were already deteriorating, windows broken, doors kicked in, personal belongings were gone. It made you feel like crying whenever someone got to go inside of their homes." The Aleut community had suffered severe blows, both physically and psychologically, from which it was unlikely they would completely recover.

Anfesia was born in Atka in 1900. When she was six years old, the family moved to Unalaska, then called Iliuliuk. Anfesia and her two brothers attended the Russian school there, where she learned to read Russian, as well as her own Aleut language. She also took classes at the government school, where she was taught English, along with such skills as cooking and sewing.

Anfesia was not a perfect student and told stories about having to kneel in front of an icon because she had not done her lessons. In later years she recalled that she had not been at all interested in learning to weave at school, as her mother, who was an expert Attu basket maker, wanted her to do. But her aunt was her teacher and would not let her say no, so she learned!

Anfesia's father died while she was a young teenager. When she was seventeen years old, Michael Tutiakoff, Anfesia's teacher in the Aleut language class, escorted her to choir practice in the winter, because her mother would not let her go out alone after dark. It was the next year, 1918, when Michael spoke to his father, telling him he would like to get married. He gave his father Anfesia's name, which his father gave to the chief, Alexei Yatchmenoff, so that the marriage could be arranged. This was the native way, and the bride and groom usually did not know each other before the wedding.

As Anfesia slyly described it:

> And so, when mother got word, she went and told my godmother and I had one step ahead of them, because I had already talked this over with Mike Tutiakoff before this all happened. He got my okay before he went and asked his father to marry me. The Chief and the rest of the people didn't know about that. So, I went one step ahead of them. Anyways, it was a good marriage.

Soon after wedding plans had begun, Anfesia's mother, her aunt, and Michael's father were among forty-four residents who died during the devastating flu epidemic that swept through Unalaska between May 26 and June 13,

27

1919. Therefore, the chief finished the arrangements for the marriage and the wedding took place soon thereafter.

Anfesia and Mike raised one daughter, Martha; three sons, Vincent, Tracy, and Philemon; and an adopted son, Timothy. Another daughter, Mayme, died in infancy.

The first year of their marriage, Mike worked at a whaling station on Akutan, then cooked for sulfur miners on Akun. After that they returned to Unalaska, where he worked for the church and received a small salary. The family lived a subsistence lifestyle, in the native way. Anfesia referred to it as "going out and hustling for food." Ducks and seals were plentiful, and from a boat they could drop a line anywhere, anytime, and catch fish from the numerous codfish grounds in Unalaska Bay. They gathered sea urchins and clams along the beach. In the summer and fall, berries were plentiful in the hills, and gardens produced vegetables. The family worked hard. Anfesia said, "If we didn't put up our winter supply, why, then the children went hungry."

Mike was becoming more of a leader, both in the Aleut community and the Russian Orthodox Church. He had been the church secretary for many years and had helped the priest and teachers at the Russian school.

In 1932, he became a deacon and he might have gone on to become a priest. But in January 1933, he traveled with the bishop aboard the ship the *Umnak Native*. The vessel broke apart during a violent storm, and Michael Tutiakoff drowned.

The next few years were difficult for Anfesia and the children. The Unalaska Sisterhood and Brotherhood helped them with food; friends also shared provisions. Anfesia fished from the beach and sometimes caught enough salmon to exchange with Pribilof Islanders for seal meat. And, of course, she picked berries for jams and pies, and grew potatoes. Help came when Chief Alexei Yatchmenoff once more arranged a marriage for her. In February 1937, Anfesia married Sergie Shapsnikoff, a widower.

Sergie not only provided for Anfesia and her children, but he and she adopted two more children, Kathryn and Gregory. The children called him "Friend."

About that time, the bishop of Alaska, Bishop Alexei, visited the Aleutians. When he came to Unalaska, he blessed Anfesia as a reader in the Church of the Holy Ascension, a position that elevated her standing in the community. As a reader, she was called on to communicate with the many outsiders and officials who began to swarm the island as construction began on Dutch Harbor, the military facility on Amaknak Island. She had also become an expert weaver of baskets in the Attu tradition, as her mother had been before her.

Then came the war and evacuation.

After their return home from southeast Alaska, Anfesia's community came together and began reassembling the pieces of their disheveled lives. Anfesia's second husband had drowned while fishing to provide food for the family, only one of the numerous casualties of the evacuation.

Although her son, Vincent Tutiakoff, was officially the chairman and recording secretary of the church committee, it fell to Anfesia to write letters for the committee. With her command of English, she wrote about missing church papers and other items, and about church property and repairs. Father Dionecious had not come back to Unalaska, so she was called on to conduct church services and to assist visiting priests.

In 1947, Vincent drowned at the age of twenty-five. He was an officer in the Orthodox Brotherhood and had been in line to become a church leader. Anfesia became quite ill with tuberculosis of the spine but recovered, despite dire predictions from her doctors.

The next two decades brought the burgeoning king crab industry and another influx of people and commercial building to Unalaska. Although the companies did hire local help and brought money into the community, the aftereffects continued to destroy the Aleut native way of life. When Anfesia was a little girl growing up in Unalaska, she could drink clean water right from the creek, pick berries from the hills, and gather clams, mussels, and sea urchins on the beach. Because of pollution from the canneries and the ruins from the war, these simple pastimes were no longer easily accomplished.

Anfesia also recognized that the young people weren't interested in pursuing the subsistence lifestyle, even if it were still possible. Many of them had turned their eyes Outside. They wanted jobs and the things that money could buy. She intensified her efforts to pass on the Aleut language and her skill of basket weaving to the next generation. By working with visiting linguists and anthropologists, she hoped to ensure an accurate preservation of her people's language and traditions.

Anfesia's grandson, Vincent—known to his family as Buddy—eventually moved in with her. In 1956 she again became ill, and had to go to the hospital in Anchorage. Buddy stayed at the Baptist mission in Kodiak until she was able to return three months later.

Anfesia had been communicating with the historical society in Kodiak, and after she recovered from her illness, she traveled there and gave the first of many basket-weaving classes. Her first class in 1957 consisted of nine students, and she returned to give classes there off and on for several years.

One summer she was giving a class in Kodiak during the historical society's outdoor theater production of the *Cry of the Wild Ram*. The historical drama celebrated Alaska's Russian heritage, particularly the Russian colony on Kodiak. Anfesia was recruited to perform in the play.

"I'm the Aleut they found," she said, laughing.

She was supposed to squat down and weave a basket. Of course, to be authentic to the time, she couldn't wear her glasses, so decided to weave a fish basket because the weave was larger. As she still couldn't see well enough to weave, her class members would work on it some each day until they finished it for her.

"It was in display in Anchorage and it looked real nice and it was bought afterwards," she reported when telling the story.

In 1959, Alaska Governor William A. Egan put Anfesia in charge of the Alaska booth at the Oregon Centennial in Portland. She took her "demonstration" basket, which she used in her classes, and was delighted when Senator John F. Kennedy held it in his hands and spoke with her. During the next few years, she traveled and gave talks and demonstrations in California and Arizona.

In the summer of 1967, Anfesia was invited to speak to the Resurrection Bay Historical Society in Seward as part of their Alaska Centennial Celebration. She told the group it was the first time she had given her presentation in Alaska. From Seward she traveled to Anchorage and Juneau, speaking, giving basket-weaving demonstrations, and, in Anchorage, even appearing on television.

From Anchorage she wrote to Margaret Hafemeister in Seward, "Busy, busy. I didn't know it would turn out this way, but I am wanted here and there. . . . Seems as if everyone knows me here, even the priest."

As part of the statewide Alaska Centennial Celebration in 1967, Anfesia was given the Governor's Award for perpetuating native arts and crafts through her basketry.

But even as the state was praising her, it was creating another tragedy in her community. That summer a social worker came to Unalaska bearing a list of about twenty children who were to be removed from their homes and raised in more "civilized" conditions. This was an affront to the Aleuts, and Anfesia took it personally.

She protested the policy and wrote to her friend Ray Hudson, "I have written Juneau and told them what is happening. . . . I let them know Unalaska could keep neglected children too like elsewhere so they could know of their native ways, so Aleuts could be restored. . . ."

The welfare of Aleut children had always been one of Anfesia's primary concerns. She served several terms on the Unalaska City Council and was on the city's first Board of Health. In that capacity she contributed to the organization of the Iliuliuk Family and Health Services, incorporated in 1971 and still the primary health agency for the community.

Anfesia deeply lamented the declining interest of her people in speaking Aleut and maintaining their traditions. Hoping to preserve as much as possible, Anfesia went to the University of Alaska in Fairbanks, where she taught Aleut dancing as well as basket-weaving, and recorded songs and stories. In fact, one of her last trips was to Fairbanks to work with the Alaska Native Languages Program, developing the Atka and Unalaska dialects.

Back in Unalaska, she gave basket-weaving classes from her home. She spoke to students about her childhood and native customs, and she sang to them and told them traditional stories. A booklet encompassing her childhood Christmas memories was distributed to Unalaska schoolchildren at Russian Christmas in January 1972.

For several weeks, beginning in November 1969, she inserted in the Unalaskan newspaper an item in Aleut. Underneath the first one it said in English, "If you don't understand this, learn it! And ask what it means." For the second and successive weeks, she included the translation for the previous week.

The item for the week of November 17 read:

*Iig^akun tutalix aqaning waya malgakun ang^achin*
*aqatalgaqangin–Ulux^waya galix tanax ama angachisin*
*sulakyn. Malix miimiin tununalgilix. Tunuxtan.*

Anfesia wrote Aleut in the Cyrillic script developed in the 1820s. This rendition is written in Roman letters. Each little cap goes above the letter preceding it. Here is the translation for the item:

*Things I heard of long ago are happening. Unknown people are*
*coming, taking over our land and the things we made our living*
*with. So let's get together and prevent these, by speaking up.*

Those long-ago predictions were certainly beginning to come true in 1970. The US government planned to sell the land that it had claimed to build military facilities on Amaknak Island and surrounding the village. Anfesia blamed the military for much of the pollution of traditional fishing grounds. She would not stand by and let them take away the land, too. She had served on the Board of Equalization, and feared that the Aleuts would be forced to pay taxes on the land where they lived.

In January 1971, the government sale was stopped by a civil lawsuit on behalf of Anfesia Shapsnikoff, Nick Peterson, and Henry Swanson, the eldest residents of Unalaska. In December President Richard Nixon signed the Alaska Native Claims Act. The land for sale on Amaknak and Unalaska Islands now belonged to the Aleut people.

In December 1972, although ill and growing weaker, Anfesia supervised the cleaning of the interior of the Cathedral of the Holy Ascension in preparation for Christmas services. She had done this many times before as a member and officer of the Sisterhood. She recognized the importance of this church, both as a place of worship and as a building of great historic significance. The cathedral is on the National Register of Historic Places and is a National Historic Landmark.

The following January, Anfesia baptized her great-grandson, Vincent Michael Jr., although she was too weak to lift the baby the customary three times and had to perform the baptism in her home. She continued to weaken and died on the airplane taking her to the Native Hospital in Anchorage on January 15. She is buried in the church graveyard beside Alexei Yatchmenoff.

Anfesia's influence in the Aleut community endures after her death. Children she instructed in the teachings of her church have become important members of the congregation. Her passion for Aleut culture has infused various Aleut organizations, and her willingness to serve on civic boards has inspired others to follow her example. The basket-weaving classes continued to flourish in Kodiak, and in 2005 Hazel Jones, who was one of Anfesia's students in the early 1970s, taught the class. Anfesia received many awards and honors, including honorary lifetime memberships in the Resurrection Bay Historical Society and Kodiak Historical Society, and a special certificate from Bishop Theodosius for her long and outstanding service to the Orthodox faith.

Three weeks after her death, "Senate Concurrent Resolution No. 24 in the Legislature of the State of Alaska, Eighth Legislature—First Session: Honoring Anfesia Shapsnikoff" was read into the record on February 6, 1973. It concluded:

> BE IT RESOLVED *by the Alaska Legislature that it expresses its most profound sense of loss as a result of the death of this truly remarkable "Little Grandma" but affirms its belief that, because of her devotion to her people, her culture, her community, and her state, generations of Alaskans for years to come will be indebted to Anfesia Shapsnikoff and she will always be revered as a truly great Alaskan.*

# ARIZONA WOMEN

# LOZEN

(183?–1889)

### "A Shield to Her People"

A few stars still glimmered and blinked as salmon brushstrokes streaked across the eastern sky. The fall rains had brought a good spring to southern Arizona. The desert willows were bright with flowers, and the yucca blooms stood tall, like white waxed beacons among the mesquites. A coyote yipped, another answered.

The horses were clustered near camp. One stood apart, watching, listening, an equine sentinel, while the others dozed.

Only one human stirred. A slight young woman unwrapped herself from her blanket and walked silently to higher ground. She extended her arms, threw her head back, and sang, while turning slowly in a circle:

> *Upon this earth*
> *On which we live*
> *Ussen has Power.*
> *This Power He grants me*
> *For locating the Enemy.*
> *I search for that Enemy*
> *Which only Ussen, Creator of Life*
> *Can reveal to me.*

This morning, her palms were cool and remained the color of normal flesh. She was relieved. All too often lately, her hands turned hot, purple even—and always when facing the approaching foe.

She didn't understand this ability of her body to locate the enemy, but it wasn't her role to understand or question. Her role was to protect her People.

The sun edged over the distant lavender mountains. People stirred in the camp below her.

Lozen walked back down the hill to let them know they were safe.

For now.

Lozen, an Apache warrior, scout, and medicine woman, is almost as much of a challenge for contemporary historians as she was for nineteenth-century soldiers. Not only did the Apaches leave no written record of her, but the white men of the time were unable to imagine that any woman could have held as powerful and vital a role—so they never mentioned her.

Some experts believe that Lozen's role has been magnified beyond reality to the point of making her a myth. Other sources say the Apaches deliberately underplayed Lozen's importance as a way to protect her. The records that do exist are oral—historians' interviews of adult Apaches recalling their childhoods spent with the famous chiefs, Geronimo, Cochise, Victorio, and others. Again and again these eyewitnesses mention Lozen. One, James Kaywaykla, wrote that the last free Apaches would have been captured years earlier except for her ability to locate the enemy. He remembers Chief Victorio saying, "Lozen is as my right hand. Strong as a man, braver than most, and cunning in strategy, Lozen is a shield to her people."

One historian points out that Kaywaykla was only three or four and questions if he could have remembered these words—while another says Lozen can claim the title of "America's greatest guerilla fighter."

What is clear is that Lozen's story roams over more than just the Arizona Territory. The Apache tribe is usually divided into six groups: Western, Chiricahua (pronounced *cheer-ee-kah-wah*), Mescalero, Jicarilla, Lipan, and Kiowa.

The Western Apaches occupied both eastern Arizona and western New Mexico and included the Warm Springs (also known as the Chihenne) and White Mountain bands. The Chiricahua lived in southwestern New Mexico, southeastern Arizona, and the adjacent Mexican states of Chihuahua and Sonora. The Mescalero still reside east of the Rio Grande in southern New Mexico.

All the Apaches were in the Southwest long before state and national boundaries. Topographical landmarks mattered far more to them than the arbitrary political lines drawn in the desert by white men. All the "Indeh" (the People) were nomadic, and they easily covered thousands of miles on horseback, often spending summers in the Arizona mountains and winters in central Mexico. The Chiricahua and Chihenne bands were closely related, often intermarried, and frequently traveled through each other's territories without acrimony.

Lozen was born into the Warm Springs band, sometime in the early 1830s, probably in southern New Mexico. The band considered Ojo Caliente, between what are now Silver City and Socorro, to be its spiritual home and where they felt closest to Ussen, the Creator of Life. It's a beautiful area of high desert with islands of mountain ranges and a surprising number of volcanic hot springs.

Not much is known of Lozen's family except that she was the younger sister of Chief Victorio, who was born in 1825.

Although the women did most of the food-gathering and cooking, Apache girls had the same training as boys: They learned to hunt, ride, and fight, since the band might need every individual for defense. There was nothing squeamish about these women—if a family member was killed, the perpetrator was caught, brought back to camp, and turned loose among the angry women, who beat, stabbed, or stoned the assailant to death.

Lozen was small in stature, but physically gifted, and soon proved to be a faster runner than most of the boys, as well as a better marksman and equestrian. She was far more interested in warrior skills than cooking, and quickly earned her name, which meant "Dexterous Horse Thief" in Apache.

A formative event in the childhoods of both Victorio and Lozen took place in the spring of 1837 and marked the beginning of animosity between the Apaches and white settlers. The Warm Springs band was lured to a fiesta by the residents of Santa Rita, in the northern Mexico state of Sonora. Led by a Kentucky bounty hunter, John James Johnson, the "party" turned into a massacre, and among those killed was the leader of the band. As a result, Mangas Coloradas (Red Sleeves) became the new Warm Springs chief.

He soon realized Lozen had a talent even more valuable than stealing horses. Since the ceremony she performed allowed her to detect enemies, he invited her to participate in raids. According to one source, only promiscuous women went with the warriors, but Lozen's responsibilities were to protect the men and fight with them. She also never married. Legend has it that the chief of an unidentified Eastern band passed through, stopping off to visit the Warm Springs camp. According to James Kaywaykla's grandmother,

> Lozen was too young for marriage, but she had seen this chief and no other man ever interested her. She put marriage from her mind and rode beside her brother as a warrior. She lives solely to aid him and her people. And she is sacred . . . , she is respected above all living women.

By 1861, relations between the whites and the Apaches were deteriorating fast, but Mangas Coloradas still believed that surely the land could support both cultures. He arranged a meeting to reason with the mining community in Pinos Altos, New Mexico, and planned to guide the miners to other gold-bearing sites in exchange for allowing his band to live on their ancestral lands.

He quickly lost interest in the peace process when the miners captured, tied, and whipped him before his sons could come to his rescue. That same year, the peaceful Chiricahua chief Cochise, son-in-law of Mangas Coloradas, was falsely accused of kidnapping a white child. The white soldiers reacted by killing Cochise's brother.

To both the Chiricahua and the Chihenne, war was the only honorable response. Victorio, accompanied by another Warm Springs leader, Nana, along with Lozen, led many successful raids against the white settlers. By now Lozen had proven herself on her three apprenticeship raids, and often advised Victorio about the most effective strategies. She was the only woman ever allowed in councils though she was apparently shy and said little in public.

At first it seemed as if their raids had been victorious. The soldiers marched away, and Lozen's ceremony was no longer needed. Little did the Apaches know that the soldiers were embroiled in a bigger battle and had been summoned East to fight in the Civil War.

The next summer the white men reappeared in even greater numbers, and this time they brought cannons. Lozen and her people realized what they were up against in the Battle of Apache Pass when they were forced to retreat, carrying a wounded Mangas Coloradas.

Although there's no written record, it's likely Lozen treated her chief's wound. Kaywaykla remembers Victorio extolling Lozen's ability as a healer, saying, she was "skillful in treating wounds; when I got a bullet in my shoulder she burned the thorns from a leaf of *nopal* [prickly pear], split it and bound the fleshy side to the wound. The next day I rode."

Six months later Mangas Coloradas realized the People could not endure much longer and resolved to meet with the white men to talk peace. Too trusting once again, he went alone to the soldiers' camp under a flag of truce. The soldiers captured him, held red-hot bayonets to his feet, shot him, cut off his head, boiled it, and sent it to Washington.

Lozen, Victorio, Nana, and the rest of the band were devastated. They hid in their home mountains, only emerging for the occasional raid or supply trip. Since the soldiers were less inclined to shoot women, sometimes Lozen was the one sent to Pinos Altos or Mesilla (now Las Cruces) to gather news.

The Apaches spent the next couple of years attending abortive peace conferences and waiting to see where the government would allow them to live. In 1870 the Chihenne moved reluctantly to Tularosa, an area they found too high, too cold, and too rocky for crops. In 1874 they were at last inexplicably allowed back to their ancestral land near Ojo Caliente, and all seemed calm for a year. But soon their allocations of stringy beef and moldy flour ran out, and the children were hungry.

In 1876 the Chiricahua were moved from their designated area in southeastern Arizona to the San Carlos reservation farther north. When Geronimo was captured, he and his band were taken to San Carlos in chains, and the following year the Chihenne were marched there. Consolidating the reservations saved the US government $25,000 for each closed reservation—but the price was in human lives. The camp was near Camp Goodwin in the marshes of the Gila River, and disease, which had already driven away the soldiers, killed many Apaches as well.

By September 1877, Victorio could stand the camp no longer and broke out, leading Lozen and three hundred warriors, women, and children back to Ojo Caliente, where they lived quietly.

Finally, it seemed as if Lozen's skills as enemy locator and warrior wouldn't be needed.

But two years later, once again the government made them move, this time to the Mescalero Reservation. In June rumors flew that Victorio was to be arrested, and, the story goes, he and Lozen chose freedom over confinement.

For the next year they remained on the move all over New Mexico, western Texas, southeastern Arizona, and into Mexico. Geronimo, having escaped from San Carlos, joined them. When ammunition ran low, Lozen and Victorio decided she should return to the Mescalero Reservation and come back with more warriors and supplies. Lozen, who always felt the women and children were her responsibility, also agreed to take a Mescalero woman and her infant back. Traveling was slow, and the two women arrived after many weeks, only to be faced with the worst possible news: Victorio had been killed in an ambush in Mexico.

Lozen was desolate—and angry. She re-joined the band, now led by Nana, in a retaliatory revenge raid throughout the Southwest with the sole goal of killing as many Mexicans as possible. They covered three thousand miles in two months, killed hundreds, won seven battles, stole two hundred head of stock—and, thanks to Lozen's skill in locating the enemy, never lost a warrior.

By 1881 many in the band were homesick for their families, and the group slipped quietly back to San Carlos. Once again, it seemed as if they'd be allowed to live in peace. But fighting broke out, this time at Cibecue. Although the Chihenne weren't blamed, Lozen and Nana feared repercussions and broke out from the reservation again, hoping to join Geronimo in his Mexican hideaway in the Sierra Madre.

Many other Apaches had the same idea, and six hundred gathered in the mountain refuge, Chiricahua, Chihenne, Mescalero, and others. They all hid in Mexico uneventfully for a year, but the war leaders grew restless, and both the need for ammunition for their American-made rifles and the desire to reunite their families grew strong. Geronimo, Nana, and Lozen decided to lead a group into Arizona and free their people from San Carlos. The raid was successful—until the US soldiers followed them across the border and killed a third of those rescued.

By May 1883, morale among the survivors had sunk, and most decided to surrender, including Geronimo, who told the white men he needed a month to round up the families.

By February 1884, the band was settled back at San Carlos, but the agent in charge was unable to maintain peace between the different factions. In July 1885 Geronimo heard a rumor he was to be hanged, so he bolted—accompanied by Lozen, thirty-five warriors, and one hundred women and children. Ironically, they stopped to rest in the Chiricahua Mountains at the now-abandoned Fort Bowie, site of the Battle of Apache Pass where Mangas Coloradas was first wounded.

Again they headed for Mexico, where they hid in mountains accessible by only one narrow but easily defended trail.

By now, the Americans had hired Apache scouts, who knew the ways, trails, and hideaways of Lozen's group, and the casualties began to mount. Discouragement grew. The group had met before with General George Crook, known as Grey Fox, and trusted him to make fair decisions. They sent Lozen and another woman, Dahteste, to talk to the commander to see if a surrender was still possible. Crook agreed to meet with the leaders in March of 1886, in the Canyon de Los Embudos, eighty-six miles south of Fort Bowie.

Writer Peter Aleshire described Lozen's role in the historic meeting:

> *Lozen remained in the back of the group, not talking but*
> *keeping her rifle ready. The White Eyes had never paid much*
> *attention to her and she did not want them to pay attention*
> *to her now. The leaders hid her importance when talking to*
> *the White Eyes, partly to protect her and partly so she could*
> *continue to be their messenger and go into the soldiers' camps,*
> *counting their guns. So Lozen did not speak and Grey Fox*
> *did not bother with her because the White Eyes did not think*
> *women important.*

General Crook said the Apaches would have to be imprisoned for two years before being returned to their reservations. After many hours of talking, all the leaders, including Geronimo, decided to surrender.

During the night, Geronimo changed his mind. With him went the last of the free Chihenne: Lozen, nineteen warriors, fourteen women, and six children.

They rode hard, rarely slept, relied heavily on Lozen's ceremony, and raided from Mexico north to Tucson and back. They stole horses, rode them into the ground, cut meals from the meat, and stole more. Geronimo himself wrote in his autobiography:

> *We were reckless of our lives, because we felt every man's hand*
> *was against us. If we returned to the reservation we would be*
> *put in prison and killed; if we stayed in Mexico they would*
> *continue to send soldiers to fight us; so we gave no quarter to*
> *anyone and asked no favors.*

But the soldiers kept coming. President Grover Cleveland wanted Geronimo dead and was furious with what he saw as Crook's lenient surrender terms for the Chiricahua Apaches. The general, realizing he couldn't keep his promise to the Apaches, resigned. He was replaced by General Nelson Miles, who sent five thousand men—about a quarter of the US Army—in search of the renegades.

Miles was clever, if unethical. In July 1886, he sent Lieutenant Charles Gatewood into Mexico with two of Geronimo's former colleagues to convince him to surrender. According to Gatewood's own account, he told Geronimo, "Surrender, and you will be sent to join the rest of your People in Florida, there to await the decision of the President as your final disposition. Accept these terms, or fight it out to the bitter end."

The talk went on for hours—until Gatewood broke the news that the Apaches' friends and families were already imprisoned in Florida. With that information, the will to fight went out of the warriors, and all agreed to talk to General Miles.

It was a long, sad ride from Mexico's Sierra Madre to southern Arizona's Skeleton Canyon. On September 8, 1886, the last of the renegade Apaches, including, according to some historians, the warrior Lozen, met with General Miles. He and Geronimo placed a stone on the blanket that lay between them and swore to do one another no harm.

Geronimo said, "Our treaty is made by this stone, and it will last until the stone should crumble to dust."

With those words, the free Apaches were free no more. And with those words, Lozen disappears from the record until her death. For years, historians believed one photograph of her survived: It shows her with Geronimo and the other warriors when the train, carrying the prisoners eastward, paused in Texas.

Yet her name never appeared in the roster.

The train took the last Apaches to Fort Marion, Florida. There they joined all the other bands who'd been rounded up from the reservations, even though they'd been living peacefully.

James Kaywaykla wrote:

> *Ours were a mountain people, and moreover, a dry land*
> *people. We were accustomed to dry heat, but in Florida the*
> *dampness and the mosquitoes took toll of us until it seemed*
> *that none would be left. Perhaps we were taken to Florida for*
> *that purpose; from our point of view, shooting would have been*
> *much less cruel.*

After less than a year, the Apaches were shipped from Fort Marion to Mount Vernon Barracks, north of Mobile, Alabama. Eugene Chihuahua, son of the Chiricahua Chief Chihuahua, recalled:

*We thought anything would be better than Fort Marion with its rain, mosquitoes, and malaria, but we were to find out that it was good in comparison with Mt. Vernon Barracks. We didn't know what misery was till they dumped us in those swamps. There was no place to climb or pray. If we wanted to see the sky, we had to climb a tall pine.*

Half the prisoners were wiped out by hunger, disease, and heartbreak.

The woman whose power determined the course of the Apaches never again saw her beloved mountains, wide desert expanses, and vivid Southwestern skies.

Lozen caught the "coughing sickness," as tuberculosis was called, and died June 17, 1889, in Mt. Vernon, Alabama.

She lies buried in an unmarked grave.

# SISTER MARY FIDELIA MCMAHON

(1850–1923)

Builder of Souls, Surgical Suites, and Steam Plants

Spring, along with one-hundred-degree days, came early to Tucson in 1920.

By mid-afternoon on May 25, the room was hot by anyone's definition—and especially for a seventy-year-old woman in a heavy serge habit.

Mother Fidelia was a small, stout woman, quiet but quick to smile. She watched the happy faces of those celebrating around her and resisted the unseemly urge to be proud. Fifty-three nuns crowded the huge banquet table, which was so loaded with roses that the whole room was fragrant. Other home-grown flowers perched on all available surfaces, and festoons of dark green ivy and wreaths of sweet peas hung from every possible knob and railing on both floors of the building.

A deep rumble of male voices, a surprising sound in the convent, came from the adjoining room where visiting clergy were seated for the gala meal.

Fifty years ago, the first Sisters of St. Joseph had arrived in Tucson, and today was the jubilee commemoration. All afternoon and into the evening, hundreds of Tucson residents filled the grounds to overflowing as they came to pay their respects to the nuns. As part of the celebration, the Southern Pacific Railroad band played far into the night.

Mother Fidelia had been here nearly thirty years, and in her time as superior of the hospital, St. Mary's had grown from a twelve-bed frontier clinic to a thriving health-care and teaching facility.

She smiled quietly to herself. God was good. Her time in Tucson and in this world would soon be over, but the hospital was in good hands.

Research is always a treasure hunt, but tracing the life of a nun can be particularly challenging. Keeping letters and journals was often seen as a sign of pride or arrogance. Even at the 1920 jubilee celebration at St. Mary's Hospital, the bishop of Arizona thanked the city on behalf of the sisters because the rules of the order prohibited them from speaking of their own accomplishments.

Consequently, little is known of Bridget McMahon's childhood, except that she was born in 1850 in West Troy, New York, to Michael and Mary Combaugh McMahon. Nor is it known why Bridget chose to become a nun, but the next existing record for her is April 24, 1872, when she entered the Sisters of St. Joseph in St. Louis, Missouri, from St. Bernard Parish in Cohoes, New York. She was twenty-two.

It's clear from her accomplishments that Bridget was an independent, strong-minded young woman, and it makes sense that the Congregation of St. Joseph would have appealed to her. The organization was founded in 1690 in LePuy, France, when Father Jean Pierre Medaille, SJ, called six women together. Their mission was to live communally with God and minister to those who suffered in the community. The congregation grew until the French Revolution when five sisters were beheaded and the group was forced to disband.

The order reorganized after the revolution, and in 1836 six sisters were sent to the American frontier, to St. Louis, Missouri. There they established Carondelet, a school for the deaf, and then began to branch out around the United States. (A century and a half later, a member of the order, Sister Helen Prejean, would become known throughout the world when her book describing her experiences ministering to prisoners on death row became the movie *Dead Man Walking*.)

In a history of Tucson's St. Mary's Hospital and Health Center, Leo Byrne and Sister Alberta Cammack, the now-deceased archivist, described the Congregation of St. Joseph as "a religious society that emphasized individual conviction and inner strength dedicated to the service of God and of the neighbor. . . . Mediocrity was unwelcome, and each candidate was measured by whether or not she had the quality that would enable her to be chosen as Superior of the entire Congregation."

At twenty-two Bridget McMahon surely knew that she was far from mediocre, and she must have been aware of her own quick mind and copious energy. Novices were allowed to pick four names and could hope they'd be assigned one of them. Soon to be known as Sister Mary Fidelia McMahon, Bridget would serve God and her Tucson neighbors well.

In August 1872 Sister Fidelia attended the reception ceremony in St. Louis at the St. Joseph's Motherhouse. She received the habit worn by the order and made her preliminary vows. Two years later, still in St. Louis, she professed her vows to give her life to God's work.

According to the St. Louis Congregation of St. Joseph archives, she taught from 1874 to 1880. By 1880 she was teaching at St. Teresa Academy in Kansas City, Missouri, where she became assistant superior. During the next three years, she served first as superior and then directress.

In 1884 her life changed dramatically when she moved from teaching in Kansas City to St. Joseph's Academy in Tucson, never again to leave the West.

The Arizona Territory was evolving dramatically as well. The population more than doubled in the decade of the 1880s, thanks in part to the thousands of unhealthy people who poured into the area, attracted by advertising, official reports, and newspaper articles that promised vigorous living and good "health in every breeze." Indigent care became a burning issue, because military hospitals were inadequate to care for a civilian population. Early hospitals were no more than rooms rented out to patients for $1.50 per day—unless the illness was small-pox, in which case the patient was carted off to the County Pest House.

The Sisters of St. Joseph played an active role in the new territory. The first seven traveled from St. Louis to San Francisco by train, then to San Diego by boat. Next, they survived a harrowing wagon trip through the deserts and mountains of Baja California, Yuma, and Casa Grande, arriving at last to a triumphant welcome in Tucson on May 26, 1870.

They opened four schools: St. Joseph's in Tucson (1870), San Xavier del Bac (1873), Sacred Heart in Yuma (1875), and St. Theresa's in Florence (1877), in addition to establishing St. Joseph's Hospital in Prescott (1878), which in 1885 became St. Joseph's Academy.

On May 1, 1880, as Sister Fidelia was starting her first teaching job in Kansas City, the Sisters of St. Joseph opened the twelve-bed St. Mary's Hospital in Tucson and received the first eleven patients. According to Sister Aloysia Ames, author of *The St. Mary's I Knew,* medical complaints in the first ledger included sore feet, sore eyes, consumption, vertigo, general debility, wounds, softening of the brain, and tomahawk wounds.

At the time, Catholic sisters seemed to be the only group capable of operating hospitals without losing money, no doubt because the nuns worked so devotedly—and without a salary. They sometimes paid with their lives, and several died of tuberculosis or erysipelas, a form of streptococcus infection.

Another factor that kept Arizona's new hospital solvent was the railway: At eleven o'clock on the morning of March 20, 1880, the first train pulled into Tucson, and not long afterward, St. Mary's and the Southern Pacific Railroad reached an agreement. The sisters did what they could to provide health care, and the railway supplied an average of twenty patients a month. In an early form of employer's health insurance, each employee was docked 50 cents a month to support the hospital fund.

Some things don't change: By 1883 one newspaper writer was already complaining that the sisters' charge of one dollar per day was too high.

Although the hospital was run by Catholic sisters, no records were kept of the patients' religions. Sister Aloysia wrote:

> *This is not surprising, when we consider that in the 1881*
> *Tucson City Directory preserved at the Arizona Pioneers'*
> *Historical Society, there is a statement by George W. Barter: "As*
> *an indication of the tolerant spirit and wholesome deficiency of*
> *prejudice in this city, we will mention that twenty-nine children*

*of Jewish parents constantly attend the Catholic school." The
Protestant population of Tucson was still small. If there were
no religious prejudices there was also no room for nationality
prejudices. Patients admitted to the hospital claimed nearly
every nation under heaven as their homeland or nationality.*

The nuns worked long hours, caring for patients and for the orphans who
lived on the grounds as well, heating water for laundry, cooking, scrubbing the
floor, washing and ironing the linens by hand, growing vegetables for the table,
and raising pigs as a regular source of income.

Tucson is a desert city, and one August day in 1886 a writer in the *Arizona
Citizen* described the town's water as "a little too thick for easy navigation, and
rather too thin for real estate, and totally unfit for use." Not long afterward, the
city council began charging St. Mary's ten dollars a month for water to irrigate
the farm and surrounding trees and gardens.

In 1893 Sister Fidelia McMahon took on the title of "Mother" when she was
appointed superior of St. Mary's Hospital. Because none of her personal papers
or letters have survived, it's only possible to guess about her transition from the
world of teaching to the head of a busy frontier hospital. One secondhand picture of this energetic woman describes her as being kindly and "quiet, friendly,
and methodical."

Until now, the sisters had lived across the road from the hospital in the
orphanage, a multiuse building that also served as the novitiate and provincial
house. Electricity had arrived in Tucson a few months earlier, but it wouldn't
reach the hospital for another ten years. Once the sisters left the hospital for the
day, they were out of contact—consequently, many chose not to leave the hospital at all, in case of a nighttime patient emergency.

Mother Fidelia found that arrangement unacceptable. Her first project was
to commission a two-story convent, with a compact dormitory upstairs and a
parlor, chapel, and two small rooms downstairs. An outdoor staircase provided
access to the upper floor. The walls, made of adobe, were more than twenty
inches thick—truly a blessing during Tucson's summer days.

The following year she arranged for a new two-story addition and maternity
ward that doubled the size of the hospital. By now modern conveniences had
worked their way westward through town. The hospital was able to rent a post
office box for 50 cents a month, and in 1897 telephone service was available for
three dollars a month.

By 1900 the flood of sick newcomers, especially "lungers," had intensified, and
St. Mary's answered the call with Arizona's first sanatorium for tubercular patients.

According to Sister Aloysia: "It is interesting to note that as late as 1915
the building contract states that the construction was 'made according to the

specifications of the Mother Superior,' with no mention of an architect." The sanatorium was a two-story circular structure that surrounded a partially covered courtyard; wide doorways from each of the twenty-six rooms allowed patients to be wheeled outside for sunshine. Mother Fidelia departed from the adobe tradition and hired a talented and experienced stonecutter and builder. Seventy years later, when the building was demolished, the redwood beams were still in perfect condition.

Next she turned her attention to a facility where patients with communicable diseases could be quarantined. Epidemics of typhoid, malaria, scarlet fever, and smallpox were common in Pima County, and Mother Fidelia saw to the building of an adobe isolation cottage. It was a small, rectangular structure heated with a single fireplace, with four rooms that opened onto a wide veranda.

Her next project was to design a surgical suite that included a sterilization room, an operating theater, an emergency room—and space to tie the horses that pulled the ambulance.

Although surgeons need light, large windows are problematic in desert summers. Sister Aloysia wrote: "By noon during the summer the room was like an oven. I am reasonably certain that many an operation performed after regular hours was not a clinical emergency. The appendix was not about to rupture or the hernia about to strangulate. The room was just too hot. By waiting a couple of hours after sunset the patient and surgery team suffered less dehydration from profuse perspiration."

One can't help wondering how the nuns remained hydrated at any time of day. Their habits were heavy full-length black dense twill with skirts that were four yards wide. Over that they wore a starched coverall, and the sisters in surgery added a sterile gown as yet another layer.

Perhaps that's why Mother Fidelia, never one to rest for long, next designed a simple but ingenious ice storage facility. She arranged to have a cavern excavated that was large enough to store one hundred dollars' worth of ice each month. Pipes from the well were laid in the floor under the ice, which chilled the water passing through. From then on, cold well water could be drawn anytime from a faucet to the refreshment and relief of patients, visitors, and staff alike.

One of the ironies of life in the desert is that winter nights can be as extremely cold as summer days are hot. Within a short time Mother Fidelia arranged to make the first payment of one thousand dollars toward the construction of a steam plant.

By 1904 Tucson's population had grown to twelve thousand, and Pima County's population was the same size as those of New Jersey and Rhode Island combined. That year, the sisters cared for 460 patients, some of whom would stay for two to three years.

According to the *Arizona Daily Citizen,* by 1905 Tucson's auto population numbered twenty-five, and gasoline was 14 cents a gallon. Electricity finally arrived at the hospital, which meant a new category had to be added to the ledger: In September the light bill was $19.40.

On May 31, 1911, sorrow came into Mother Fidelia's life. Her niece, Sister Agatha McMahon, had been born in New York, and, like her aunt, joined the order. She'd made her novitiate in Los Angeles, but because her health was frail, she was sent to St. Mary's. In spite of all the best care that could be provided, she died in Tucson at the age of twenty-nine.

Six months later, Mother Fidelia took an administrative step that would propel St. Mary's from being just a hospital to becoming a full-fledged teaching institution. Because of the backbreaking amount of work, and despite the efforts of visiting sisters on loan from other schools and hospitals, it became clear to all that St. Mary's just didn't have enough trained nurses. Mother Fidelia decided to follow the example of hospitals in the East and Midwest and open a nursing school.

Part of her careful planning and preparation included a step necessary to protect the congregation from lawsuits: The Sisters of St. Joseph in Arizona formed a corporation. Interestingly, after some debate it was decided that the sisters would not be allowed to retain their titles on the document that recorded the event. The erasures are still obvious—how odd it must have been for those devout women to see their names without the word *Sister.*

Now in her early sixties, Mother Fidelia contracted a builder to construct a stone-and-brick nursing school according to her specifications. The facility combined bedrooms and a sleeping porch upstairs with a lecture hall and recreation lounge downstairs, all with windows that provided ample light and caught whatever breeze was available. Years later, students and patients alike said it was the coolest building on the property.

In December 1914 the School of Nursing, the only one at the time in southern Arizona, opened to the first class of four young ladies. According to the *Arizona Daily Star,* the sisters hosted an elaborate five-course turkey dinner to mark the occasion. The room was beautifully decorated with violets, roses, and potted plants, and the meal was followed by a musical program, and "a delightful time was enjoyed by everyone present."

The following month marked the beginning of Prohibition, and Arizona went "dry." Ironically, the absence of alcohol counted as a medical emergency because wine and whiskey were used as respiratory, circulatory, and cardiac stimulants. California wasn't yet affected by the law, so the only way St. Mary's Hospital could procure alcohol was from a deluxe Los Angeles grocer—and only then if the shipment was labeled "For the Personal Use of Mother Fidelia," which must have elicited some gentle teasing within the convent walls.

In 1920 church law changed, and for the first time, the tenure of religious superiors was limited to six years. By now Mother Fidelia was seventy and had served St. Mary's as superior for twenty-seven years.

Her life had not been an easy or pampered one. She still lived in the convent she'd had built her first year in Tucson, but since then, the staff of sisters had grown considerably, and more than twenty nuns lived in the dormitory. In 1925 a fire drew the city's attention to the sacrifices the sisters had made over the years and to their need for newer housing. Judge John H. Campbell described his visit to the convent:

> *"Please forgive me, I do not mean to be rude," I said to my guide, "but do you mean to say that your Sisters have to sleep always on those hard little cots?" A nod for a reply. "And that ancient bowl and pitcher belong to 1880, but with modern baths and running water, why is it here?" "Oh, the bath is down the hall." "One bath for twenty-five Sisters and you carry your water to the dormitory in the pitchers?"*

What horrified the good judge the most was that not one of the women had her own closet. "Every woman should have at least that much privacy—every woman NEEDS the privacy of her own clothes closet," he wrote.

In September 1920, due to her increasing age, Mother Fidelia was transferred to the Provincial House in Los Angeles, where she was assigned to St. Mary's Academy as assistant superior. One of the other sisters remembers her as "a good planner and organizer; friendly, easy to talk to, alert, active and interested in all that concerned the Sisters. She was always with the group and delighted in telling stories of Arizona."

On February 2, 1923, the self-effacing but remarkably effective Sister Mary Fidelia McMahon died after a short illness. Her obituary in the *Arizona Daily Star* remembers "her quiet generosity, dignity, and sympathy."

She is buried in Calvary Cemetery in Los Angeles.

# MARY-RUSSELL FERRELL COLTON

꒰ᦗ꒱

(1889–1971)

## Painter of Southwestern Light

*As I walked up the lane in the last golden glow a coyote called
from Switzer's Mesa & presently a whole chorus joined in from
somewhere up back of Dry Lake Mountain. I stood and listened
to the voices of the wild and thrilled beneath those wondrous
peaks, and presently as I looked, they changed to rose, glowing
like dream mountains in the land that never was, then slowly
they grew cold and so very, very awesome and I hurried home to
the warmth of our little shack.*

Mary-Russell Colton, who wrote those stirring words, and her young son, Ferrell,
would be alone in the shack for another month.

It was the summer of 1916, and polio had hit Philadelphia, where
Mary-Russell, her husband, Harold, and their son, Ferrell, lived during the school
year. The Coltons loved the Southwest and spent every summer exploring and
camping, usually in the pine-covered mountains around Flagstaff. Trained as a
painter, Mary-Russell especially savored the clear light and saturated colors of the
northern Arizona landscape.

After reading newspaper accounts of the epidemic back East, the couple
decided Harold would return alone to resume teaching, leaving Mary-Russell
and Ferrell safely in Arizona until late fall.

In one sense the separation was difficult because Mary-Russell had not been
apart from Harold since the start of their marriage. But the transplanted Easterner
also relished the chance to work and explore on her own. Her letters to Harold
described her painting "fever" and how the surrounding peaks inspired her.

The extended stay also gave her more opportunity to search for Indian ruins.
The day before she was scheduled to return to Pennsylvania, Mary-Russell rode
out alone.

*[R]ode up past the Greenlaw mill and struck indirectly toward
Elden. . . . Crossing the lumber railroad I soon came out upon*

*a very high mound, and suddenly realized that I had found the largest Pueblo we have yet come upon. I should say it had been quite equal in size to Walpi, the buildings at the northern end having been at least 2 story, & I believe 3 story, the entire mound is over 15 feet high. . . . Tomorrow I return to make measurements & a sketch & collect pottery for you. I was quite thrilled over my find.*

Mary-Russell had every reason to be thrilled. Even today, Elden Pueblo is still studied by archaeologists and plays "a groundbreaking role in making archaeology and the history of Arizona's earliest residents more accessible to the public."

Mary-Russell Ferrell didn't come from a family of painters or archaeologists. Her father, Joseph, was an engineer, descended from a long line of Pennsylvania farmers. Her mother, Elise Houston, was from the noted Polk family of Tennessee.

Mary-Russell was born at her grandparents' Louisville, Kentucky, home on March 25, 1889, and was named for her aunt, Mary-Russell Buchanan. Her sister, Griselda, was four years older, but she died from diphtheria when Mary-Russell was two.

Her early childhood was a happy one. Joseph Ferrell developed Broadwater Island, a resort for well-to-do Philadelphians. The family spent summers there in what Mary-Russell later called "my childhood paradise," and she fished, hiked, and roamed the island, trailing a retinue of dogs, lambs, geese, chickens, and a Chincoteague pony. She was a quiet child who preferred solitude, reading, and sketching.

She attended Pelham Academy. Much later, she wrote that her "formal" education was "most casual by today's standards" because she learned mathematics from her father, history from her mother, and composition from her aunt. She left Pelham before graduation.

By 1904 Mary-Russell knew she wanted to be an artist and to travel. She was ready to start academic art training, but in July her father died, leaving the family in uncertain financial condition. Elise Ferrell was forced to sell the Broadwater cottage, and mother and daughter moved to a local boardinghouse.

In November, Mary-Russell was accepted at the prestigious Philadelphia School of Design for Women, and, fortunately, a family friend paid her tuition.

There she learned to clean and restore old paintings, and she made friends who were to remain a part of her life for the next forty years. Although she was described as strikingly beautiful, she lived a chaste and diligent life—no dating, no makeup, and at five feet two inches, she even refused to wear high heels.

In 1908 her mother married Theodore Presser, owner of Presser Music Publishing House. The marriage eased Elise's monetary worries, but Mary-Russell, who still lived at home, clashed with her new stepfather. The following summer, Elise suggested Mary-Russell travel to the Selkirk Mountains of British Columbia with Dr. Charles Shaw, a botanist who often took students on his expeditions.

Mary-Russell reveled in the experience. She sketched, camped, rode horses, and hiked in—gasp!—bloomers. She broke a rib in a sledding accident but reassured her mother she was having a wonderful time and was "a new woman living a new life."

The following summer Dr. Shaw asked her to return, and he also invited Harold S. Colton, a young zoology instructor at the University of Pennsylvania. This second trip was grueling and perhaps overly ambitious. Tragically, Shaw was killed in a river accident. The subdued students returned east slowly, passing through Arizona and New Mexico.

The physical and emotional challenges of the trip forced Mary-Russell to examine herself and the life she'd led. In a letter to her stepfather, she asked for his friendship and added:

> *The wilderness of which you have such a horror holds no terrors*
> *for me, no, not even now. It beckons, beckons and claims its*
> *own, that is all, and if it is God's will, I will go back again,*
> ⟨illegible line⟩
> *old with man shall never hold me. I must breathe.*

That summer of 1910 witnessed the flowering of Mary-Russell's love for the American Southwest—as well as for young Harold. They were engaged the following spring, which marked the end of her own financial concerns. Harold had several trust funds and was able to teach without being paid to do so.

The couple was married May 23, 1912, and spent their honeymoon in Pecos, New Mexico. Mary-Russell wrote her mother from there:

> *[We] get along real well, considering we've been married almost*
> *two weeks. We ride and hike over the mesas and along the*
> *roaring Pecos, and paint and read and sleep and eat and are*
> *both perfectly fine. I have 6 sketches already, it is a great country*
> *to paint in.*

On that same trip they visited Flagstaff, little knowing it would later become home, and spent the whole summer camping throughout the West. They also bought two old Hopi blankets, a small start of what would become the Museum of Northern Arizona collection.

The following summer, they again migrated to the Southwest, where they hiked in the Sangre de Cristo Mountains, with two pack burros and a wagon, then visited the Taos, San Juan, and Santa Clara Pueblos, among others.

Mary-Russell loved it all and wrote her mother:

> *Riding for a month caused me to lose flesh, & when I return you will be surprised to find you have a hipless daughter. . . . But don't think that I am fading away from ill health for I am solid muscle from head to toe & have been enjoying good health all summer. I can be in the saddle from dawn to dark, ride forty-five miles a day, without feeling tired, so you see dear, I am not an ill woman, in spite of the hipless condition.*

She must have been healthy indeed, for on August 30, 1914, she gave birth to a sturdy baby boy, Joseph Ferrell Colton.

In 1916 the young family rented a ranch in Flagstaff for the summer. Little Ferrell set his parents on a new course when he showed them a potsherd he'd found. Mary-Russell and Harold were so intrigued they traveled to the Museum of the Southwest in Los Angeles to learn more about prehistory. From then on they resolved to map, record, and protect the ruins around Flagstaff, and they were the first to conduct an archaeological study in the area. It was later that summer that Mary-Russell discovered the Elden Pueblo.

In spite of marriage, motherhood, and her new fascination with archaeology, Mary-Russell had not stopped painting. Early in 1917 she and some classmates formed "The Ten Philadelphia Women Painters," later called "The Philadelphia Ten" when sculptors were admitted. The group continued to hold annual exhibits and traveling shows until 1945.

On September 4, 1917, Mary-Russell gave birth to Sabin Woolworth Colton IV. The delivery was difficult, and, according to one biographer, "This birth seems to have disturbed her equilibrium, and for the rest of her life, she suffered one complaint after another as well as a persistent nervous disorder."

By now America was several months into World War I, and Harold was working for the US Army in Washington, DC Mary-Russell was ill with the flu, the baby with "milk sickness," and Ferrell with pneumonia. Gradually, her mother nursed everyone back to health, and by June the family was able to return to Flagstaff.

During the summer of 1921, some of Mary-Russell's energy returned, thanks to a partial hysterectomy that treated the infected wounds remaining from Sabin's birth four years earlier. She worked hard at her easel and exhibited five new paintings. But most significantly that year, Mary-Russell and Harold met Jesse C. Clarke, a local postal worker and self-educated archaeologist. During the many hours and meals shared by the threesome, the idea of a Flagstaff museum was born.

The following year, Mary-Russell's mother, Elise, left her husband, Ted Presser, and came to live with the Coltons. She died on November 7, 1922, from complications from a bleeding gastric ulcer. Mary-Russell was so devastated that Harold took a sabbatical so the family could flee the East to spend the winter in Tucson.

With spring came temperatures near the century mark, and the family escaped to northern Arizona. They collected more Hopi crafts—all the while wondering why six-year-old Sabin was so pale and lethargic. He was diagnosed with valley fever, and in spite of all medical help, he died May 4, 1924. Mary-Russell was never the same after his death.

Thanks to Harold's financial portfolio and Mary-Russell's inheritance, the Coltons were wealthy. They sold their Pennsylvania home, with all its sad memories, and in 1926 settled in a house they built on the Flagstaff land where they'd camped so many summers.

In spite of her grief, Mary-Russell sent four new paintings to the annual Philadelphia Ten show. One won first prize and the following review: "In the work of Mrs. Colton, one feels an underlying sense of the grandeur of nature and the inconsequence of man."

During the next few years, the couple continued to buy land and develop their collection of relics and archaeological studies.

In May 1928 the first board of trustees of the Northern Arizona Society of Science and Art appointed Harold as president and Mary-Russell as both curator of art and organizer of the arts and crafts section. The Coltons donated their extensive collection of artifacts, and Mary-Russell, seeing a decline in Hopi arts and crafts, initiated a new exhibition to revive their style.

In 1929 the family gave $2,500—more than $20,000 in today's currency—to what had become the Museum of Northern Arizona.

A year later Mary-Russell inaugurated the Exhibition of Arizona Artists, which included three of her own works, and also sponsored a show of art by Native American children of Tuba City schools. In addition she sent eleven paintings to traveling Ten shows.

January 1930 marked the beginning of the decade that was to be the peak of Mary-Russell's life. She found new energy and completed thirty-four paintings. In addition she decided her next mission would be to revive Hopi arts and crafts, particularly textiles, pottery, and silversmithing.

That spring, somewhat nervously, she set the wheels in motion for the first Hopi Craftsman Exhibition. The Coltons visited all twelve Hopi pueblos and gathered two truckloads of entries.

A thousand people attended, and on July 2, 1930, Harold described the inaugural event:

> *Indians swarmed in from the Reservation. The Assistant*
> *Commissioner of Indian Affairs dropped in from Washington.*
> *Then the dry season broke with a gentle rain, which was*
> *interpreted to mean that the benevolent Kachinas that dwell*
> *in the towering Peaks above the town, were pleased. It was,*
> *therefore, a huge success.*

Making a technical improvement in her own work, Mary-Russell discovered that an underlay of gesso gave a brilliance to her paintings that was much more representative of the Southwestern light. She also began studying Hopi dyes and set up a minilab in her studio, performing such experiments as boiling various weeds in sheep urine.

For someone plagued with both physical and emotional difficulties, Mary-Russell had phenomenal drive and energy. In May 1931 she added a Junior Art Show to the other exhibitions she sponsored. It was her belief that

> *Art education must begin with children. We must grow our*
> *own artists. The material is here awaiting encouragement and*
> *cultivation. All about us is great beauty, grandeur of form,*
> *glory of color, sweep of opalescent desert, dark forests and snow*
> *capped peaks. Nowhere in the world has man a more beautiful*
> *setting. Children are sensitive to color and beauty. Young*
> *Arizona is growing up with a remarkable background and a*
> *great opportunity.*

By 1932 Mary-Russell was knowledgeable enough about Hopi folklore that the Bureau of Indian Affairs often consulted her, and in 1933 the museum board appointed her curator of ethnology, as well as curator of art.

The 1930s saw more donations to the museum from the Coltons, including twenty-nine acres in memory of Sabin. But probably Mary-Russell's most significant contribution was the influence of her artist's eye. At the time Hopi silver work was an imitation of Navajo design. Mary-Russell's idea was to transfer the tribe's own symbols from their pottery and basketry to their silver, and Virgil Hubert, the assistant art director of the museum, suggested an overlay technique. Mary-Russell then contacted all the Hopi silversmiths, saying she'd buy anything that incorporated the new design. After a slow start, the Hopi Silver Project took off and made the tribe's style what it is today.

In 1940 Mary-Russell turned fifty, and both her health and energy dwindled.

The December 7, 1941, attack on Pearl Harbor was a tremendous blow and one that she took personally. She lost interest in painting and, for the first time in her life, had her waist-length hair cut short. She devoted all her time to her victory garden and her work as chair of the Red Cross's Nurse's Aide program.

Although the museum flourished after the war, Mary-Russell did not. By 1950 her vacillating emotions and personality changes dominated the family's life. Although her physicians blamed "atherosclerosis of the brain," modern doctors would have diagnosed Alzheimer's disease.

In 1951 she painted for the last time, although she still enjoyed doing pencil drawings and charcoal portraits.

By 1958 Mary-Russell's irascibility had driven off the servants, and Harold resigned his position as museum director to take care of her and attempt to finish his own projects. A year later, she'd grown increasingly paranoid and, feeling slighted one day, even withdrew her museum membership.

Fortunately, she was able to enjoy one last bright spot of recognition. In 1959 the Indian Arts and Crafts Board of the US Department of the Interior awarded her a Citation of Merit, which read, in part, as follows:

> You came from the East into a land which was new and strange to you. Soon you found a new life into which you fit yourself so naturally that you have become as one. Quietly you approached the Indian artist with the warmth of a friend and the humility of a learner, and he responded by giving generously of his culture. To this you added a depth of perception and artistic sensitivity which enabled you to measure his strengths and limitations.
>
> Realizing that this was expressive of a great tradition and part of our national heritage, you exercised every effort to perpetuate this tradition so that generations yet to come might also enjoy it. . . .
>
> Rarely does a non-Indian have the opportunity to establish an Indian tradition. Yet, in 1938, you proposed a development in Hopi silversmithing which had a long, slow genesis. Today that style of silverwork has become familiar, and is popularly regarded as representing a traditional craft expression of these people. But you were careful not to dictate; yours was the role of counselor—in truth, a pupil turned teacher.

By 1962 Mary-Russell was no longer the person she had been, nor even a reasonable adult. Harold, now in his early eighties and already ill with the strain of caring for her, was felled by a stroke. The poor man had difficulty recuperating because Mary-Russell tried to punch any nurse who dared enter his bedroom.

Finally on August 12, 1962, Mary-Russell attacked Harold with a paper-weight. Her distraught husband had her sedated and taken to Camelback Hospital in Phoenix in the only vehicle available on a Sunday afternoon: the mortician's ambulance.

She never returned home. Three days later, Harold had another stroke.

Christmas 1962 was the first Christmas in fifty years that Harold and Mary-Russell spent apart. By now she had forgotten every detail of her life except for a few childhood memories of the Broadwater cottage. The family arranged to move her to a nursing home, where she spent her remaining nine years.

On December 29, 1970, at the age of eighty-nine, Harold Colton died. Ferrell, now living in Flagstaff with his wife and children, took his father's ashes to the family plot in Philadelphia.

Seven months later, on July 16, 1971, Mary-Russell Ferrell Colton died at age eighty-two.

Much earlier, she had asked that the ashes "of my husband may be mingled with mine, when they both shall be committed to the winds of heaven. It is desired that the ashes be released from a plane over the cedar country, on the Painted Desert, east of the Peaks."

For whatever reason, Harold and Mary-Russell's ashes remain buried side by side in the Colton family plot just outside Philadelphia.

# CARMEN LEE BAN

⚜

(1891–1940)

Cultural Pioneer

The six girls—five Lee sisters and their friend Rita—had all been chattering so happily that the winter afternoon had turned into evening without anyone noticing.

"Please," said their hostess, "Won't you stay for dinner? We have plenty." Aurelia, Concepción, Maria Louisa, and Mariana all exchanged quick glances. They looked to Carmen, the oldest.

She smiled. "We'd love to," she said.

A little while later, they all gathered around the table, where a large bowl of soup, rich with meat and vegetables, awaited them. Each person had a flat ceramic spoon, and in the place of forks and knives, the sisters found chopsticks.

Muffled giggles moved around the table as pieces of meat and chunks of bok choy found new life, escaping back into bowls and skidding across plates.

"It was really embarrassing!" Mariana told her mother indignantly when they all returned home to Nogales that night. "The people kept saying, 'You're Chinese, and you don't know how to use chopsticks? You might as well not be Chinese!' They had to give us forks to eat with."

"It's true," Carmen said quietly. "I was ashamed to be Chinese and not do things Chinese people do."

Lai Ngan looked at her dispirited daughters. She said, "Hereafter you are going to learn to eat with chopsticks. Tomorrow, we buy what we need—and I'll give you lessons in Chinese eating."

The story of the Chinese experience in Arizona is one of long hours, hard work, and frugal living. Surprisingly, perhaps, it's also a tale of three nations, not two. Few families illustrate this aspect of Arizona history as well as that of Carmen Lee Ban.

Discouraged by the political and economic turmoil in the wake of the Opium Wars, the Taiping Rebellion, the Sino-Japanese war, and the Boxer Rebellion, 2.5 million people left China between 1840 and 1900. Those who came to America arrived in California, many lured by the hope of gold, others by work on the railroads. Some, like Carmen's grandparents, remained in San

Francisco only a short time. They were actors in a Chinese opera company that toured in the 1870s, and when they returned to China with the opera, they left Carmen's mother, Lai Ngan, in the care of relatives.

Others stayed in the country and kept heading east; the first officially documented Chinese in Arizona were twenty men working in the Vulture Mine near Wickenburg in 1868. The first Chinese woman was recorded in Prescott in 1871; her name is lost, and all that's known is that she came with her husband. We also know that the first Chinese laundry opened in Phoenix in 1872. But it was the Southern Pacific Railroad that eventually drew huge numbers of Asians to Arizona.

By 1882 more than three hundred thousand Chinese had come to work in America, and even as early as 1877, nearly six hundred were in Yuma alone. In 1880 the first train pulled into Tucson, and the census listed 1,630 Chinese in Arizona—not until 1950 would the state see that many Chinese residents again.

And they certainly did work: Chinese laborers laid nearly a mile of track a day from Yuma to Casa Grande, much of it in blistering heat. They were paid one dollar a day (fifty cents less than their white counterparts), from which they were expected to pay their own board.

Ironically, it was that hard work of the Chinese that made them a target of resentment. From the very beginning the new arrivals ran into prejudice and racism. In 1852 California levied a tax on foreign miners, and during the economic slump of the 1870s, the first shouts of "yellow peril!" began to be heard across the country. By 1883 one out of every four miners in Clifton was Chinese, until anti-Asian prejudice drove them out of the mines and into the jobs that no one else wanted and the service industries. Then, they found opportunities in almost every town, according to the Arizona State Historic Preservation Office:

> [I]t was a rare Arizona settlement that did not have a Chinese launderer, cook, or produce farmer, or all three, in the late nineteenth century. The energetic sojourners set up laundries, restaurants, and groceries in mining camps, construction camps, farming communities, Indian reservations, and towns. Anywhere there were customers for their services. In telling the story of Chinese in Arizona, the question is not "Where were they?" but "Where weren't they?"

Although Arizona didn't see the violence and race riots that occurred elsewhere in the West, being on the receiving end of rampant xenophobia was still a part of Chinese life in America. In Bisbee a rule that stood until the early 1930s prohibited Chinese from spending a night in town. In 1879 the *Arizona Daily*

*Miner* announced that "Prescott has about 75 or 80 Chinamen, which is 75 or 80 too many. Now is a good time to get rid of them."

Similar attitudes throughout the nation culminated in the Chinese Exclusion Act of 1882, which prohibited immigration of Chinese workers for ten years. Only educated individuals and their families, or those born in this country, were allowed to immigrate. Anyone leaving the country had to register, and the new law forced all Chinese to carry a certificate of residence with a photograph—a requirement that would later provide employment for young Carmen Lee.

A decade later, in 1893, the act was renewed with even more stringent restrictions.

It wasn't long before the Chinese perceived Mexico as much friendlier territory than the United States. Even as early as 1873, two Chinese shoe and clothing factories prospered in Guaymas. From 1890 on, the Chinese in the northernmost state of Sonora had the biggest immigrant population. One way around the exclusion acts, especially for the Arizona Chinese, was to come in through Mexico, either illegally or as Mexican residents.

These were the times into which Carmen Lee was born on September 3, 1891, at her parents' house on Stockton Street in San Francisco. At age fifteen, Carmen's mother Lai Ngan had wed Lee Kwong, a gambling man and one whose family, like hers, had been part of the opera world. It was an arranged marriage.

Lee Kwong and Lai Ngan's first child was Percy Yeung Lee, born around 1889. Carmen arrived two years later, and her younger sister Amelia was born around 1893.

Somewhat confusingly, Carmen was also known as Lee Cun, Le Cum (according to her mother), and, later, as Mrs. Ng Ban Sing, although she eventually dropped the "Ng."

Perhaps one reason the Chinese experience in Arizona hasn't been well documented is the difficulty English-speaking writers have with the Chinese language and naming conventions. Often, the Chinese characters have several pronunciations depending on dialect, and they're translated into English in various ways. For example, many of the nineteenth-century immigrants came from the southeastern Chinese province near Hong Kong known in English as "Kwangtung," "Guangdong," or "Canton."

To confuse the issue still more, many of the Chinese immigrants who entered illegally abandoned their given names to take on those of already established citizens. Ban Sing wasn't the real name of the man who would become Carmen's husband; his name was actually Lim Yuen Cong.

When the child known as Carmen was around two years old, Lee Kwong received a letter from friends in Mexico, asking for his help to look for gold.

So, he packed his belongings and those of little four-year-old Percy and left Lai Ngan with the two girls.

Nearly a century later, Ngan is still remembered by her grandson as a fiercely determined and enterprising woman. ("She rolled her own cigarettes," Edward Ban said, chuckling. "None of us kids could do that!") She grew tired of waiting to hear from her husband, packed the family belongings, gathered up Carmen and Aurelia, and traveled to Mexico by steamer to find her husband.

The trip must have been grueling for the young mother: Anti-Asian sentiment was running strong, and, according to Mike Tom, Carmen's cousin and Ngan's grandchild by her second marriage, US Customs officials on the steamer confiscated the family's registration certificates. More than twenty years later, Lai Ngan, Carmen, and Percy would all have to testify to the inspector in charge at the Immigration Service in Nogales to apply for citizenship in the very country where the children had been born.

Amazingly, Carmen's mother was able to find Lee Kwong, who was working a gold mine at La Colorada, southeast of Hermosillo.

Mexico was still a more comfortable place for the Chinese than the United States. Prejudice in America was growing, and in fact a 1901 Arizona law made marriage between the Chinese and Anglos a crime, stating "the marriage of a person of Caucasian blood with a Negro or Mongolian is null and void." The 1900 census only shows thirty-two Chinese women in Arizona, while the 1903 census shows three thousand Chinese living in Sonora. Hermosillo and Guaymas were both commercially important for Arizona, and at least ten of the thirty-seven Sonoran shoe factories were owned by Chinese.

One of those factories was where Lai Ngan found her first job. Lee Kwong continued mining. One photograph shows him with eight other men outside La Colorada Mine, all holding rifles, ready for the all-too-frequent Indian raids. Incongruously, his other hand is holding that of his young son, Percy, who in turn is holding firmly onto Carmen, then just a toddler.

Later, Lai Ngan opened a boardinghouse and ran her own small grocery store near the La Colorada Mine. She worked hard enough that she was able to save enough money to buy a small house, but at some point her husband lost it gambling. In a 1979 interview, Carmen's younger sister, Mariana, remembered:

> One day a man came over and said to her, "You owe me some rent." She said, "What do you mean I owe you some rent? I bought this house myself." My mother got so mad. She got a stick and told him, "You get out of here and don't you ever come back looking for rent because I'm not going to give it to you. This is my house and I don't care how many times he sold it, it's mine." So the man never came back. When we left La Colorada,

*my mother just left the house and never got any money for it;*
*maybe my father did.*

During this time Carmen attended public elementary school in Guaymas, and Lai Ngan had five more children: Concepción, Maria Louisa, Mariana, Teresa, and Frank.

By 1905, when Carmen was fourteen, Lai Ngan moved the family north to the border town of Nogales, still in the Mexican state of Sonora.

Two months later, they moved again, this time to the Arizona side of Nogales, where they were the first Chinese family to settle. There, they lived behind the Morley Street grocery store, run by Lai Ngan. Lee Kwong followed a little later and worked selling lottery tickets. Eventually, they moved to an adobe brick house on the hill behind the city hall.

Carmen spent her school years in the Santa Cruz County school system and her out-of-school hours helping her mother in the store. By now she was fluent in both Spanish and English, but spoke only a few words of Chinese. Her son Edward remembers that although the immediate family always spoke English at home, his mother and aunts all spoke Spanish among themselves.

The massive destruction of the San Francisco earthquake in April of 1906 brought one benefit to the Chinese community, including the Lee family. Most of the records of those already in this country were destroyed; there was no longer evidence of where Lai Ngan or Lee Kwong had been born.

The 1910 census shows ten Chinese women in Phoenix, all of whom were married with children. In that same year the Mexican Revolution began, and the thirty-five thousand Chinese who lived there suddenly found themselves unwelcome.

In 1911 Sun Yat-Sen established a republic and overthrew the imperial Manchurian government. Even the Chinese who'd settled far away were affected. Women stopped binding their feet, and men stopped wearing their hair in the long braid down their backs that had shown their loyalty to the old regime.

By 1914 Percy had moved back to San Francisco, where he worked for an import-export company. Lee Kwong, who still missed the city of his early immigration years, went to visit his son and unfortunately had a stroke and died during the trip.

By the First World War, American attitudes toward the Chinese, though not "enlightened," were beginning to soften. One 1918 writer pointed out that the seventy thousand "Chinese in America are more than good laundry men and unsurpassed cooks," and that they were

*honest, hard-working people. They have all the attributes that*
*citizens of a democracy should have. As the prejudice which*

*Americans formerly felt against their yellowskinned neighbors
wears off, Americans are appreciating the absolute integrity and
faithfulness of these people. Young mothers feel safe in trusting
the baby to the family Chinaman; families will leave jewelry
or money about, if the servants in the house are Chinese. They
have the most extraordinary reputation of honesty of any race.*

Perhaps this grudging recognition was part of what convinced Carmen and her family to apply for what was known as a "return certificate" as a native. In 1917, she, Percy, and Lai Ngan were all interviewed by the US Immigration Service, and each testified on behalf of the others that they had indeed moved from San Francisco to Mexico and then to Nogales, Arizona.

It was also at about this time that Carmen needed an extra job to help support the family. She chose photography and began to work behind the camera as well as doing the developing, printing, and retouching at Newman Photographer's in Nogales. When the business was sold in 1918 and became Albert W. Lohn, Photographer, Carmen continued to work there.

In 1919 Carmen and her younger sister Louise moved to Miami, Arizona, just east of Phoenix, where they were able to use their photographic experience working for Kelley Studios. A young man named Ban Sing had become acquainted with Carmen in Nogales and must have been quite enamored, for he made the hundred-mile trip to Miami several times to visit her.

On October 18, 1919, Carmen and Ban Sing were married, and Carmen moved to Tucson, where she would spend the rest of her life. Lai Ngan must have been pleased with her daughter's choice, for Ban Sing was a hard worker. On the rare occasions when he relaxed, he read the Chinese newspaper he subscribed to and enjoyed hunting and fishing.

Picnics and outings were a frequent family event. On July 4, 1920, everyone went to Nogales to spend the day, except Carmen, who was pregnant. What's now an hour's trip down the interstate was then a half-day endeavor. The cars' narrow tires had so much trouble negotiating the deep sandy wash at Canoa Ranch that a windlass was installed on each side and all the cars were winched across.

That afternoon, Carmen Lee Ban's first child, Edward, was born, with the help of a local midwife.

Soon afterward, those years of working in her mother's stores paid off, for she and her husband opened the first of what would be a series of four grocery stores. "They worked very long hours," Edward recalled. "My father would get up around four a.m. and go to the market to pick out the vegetables and meat. He was also the butcher, so he'd trim all the meat and all the produce and arrange the display. My mother was the mastermind, and she did all the accounting."

The last family grocery, like the others, was in midtown Tucson. Unlike the others, it was next door to a large and prosperous Safeway food store, but Edward said the two coexisted peacefully. They catered to different markets, and competition wasn't a problem.

Throughout the early 1920s, in addition to working in the grocery stores, Carmen kept her interest in photography and was employed as a retoucher at the Elite Studio. She also worked for Buehman & Co. Photographers.

There's certainly no doubt that Carmen and Ban Sing worked hard and long, but their photo albums document good times as well. The extended family remained close, and the photographs from the next ten years show gatherings of thirty or forty relatives at picnics, reunions, and get-togethers. Many weekends found the family loading baskets and boxes of food into the Packard to head to somewhere cooler and shadier than the city. Pets were an important part of the family, and Blackie, a black-and-white cocker spaniel, along with a series of cats, appears in many of the pictures. Rarely, it seems, was Carmen without her camera, a folding Kodak.

The reunion tradition continues today, and a 1990s photograph hangs on Edward Ban's wall, showing more than one hundred relatives all gathered at a Tucson park.

Tragically, Carmen died at her Tucson home November 14, 1940, at the young age of forty-nine, not from uterine cancer, but as a result of the radiation burns from its treatment.

All the Chinese exclusion laws were still in effect at the time of her death and weren't repealed until 1943. Officially, no more than 105 Chinese per year were allowed to immigrate to the country until that law was abolished by the 1965 Immigration Act.

# CALIFORNIA WOMEN

# MARY ELLEN PLEASANT

(1814–1904)

## A Whole Theatre to Herself

On May 7, 1899, Mrs. Teresa Bell quietly sat and wrote in her diary as her mind raced with possibilities. Deliberately and carefully, she made a strange and cryptic note about a night seven years previous at her spacious mansion on Octavia Street in San Francisco. Her husband, Thomas Bell, a successful San Francisco businessman, had died mysteriously in the house that night. Only his son Fred, the servants, and Mary Ellen Pleasant, a woman variously described as the housekeeper and Thomas Bell's business partner—when she wasn't being referred to with veiled innuendoes as his mistress or in cruder terms—were present. Teresa Bell had been at her ranch house in Sonoma County at the time of the accident, but her carefully crafted diary entry said that Fred Bell had given her new information about her husband's death—naming Mary Ellen Pleasant as the culprit in what Teresa Bell claimed had only appeared to be accidental.

Nearly everyone in San Francisco assumed that Thomas Bell had died on October 15, 1892, following a fall from the stairway in his mansion when, after an illness, he had arisen in the night and stumbled about. Most people believed that the servants had discovered his crumpled body on the cold, hard basement floor twenty feet below after hearing his cries and that Fred and Mary Ellen Pleasant had been summoned to his side immediately. Seven years later, Bell's widow, Teresa, laid the groundwork for a strange tale about her husband's violent death in her diary, and after Mary Ellen Pleasant's death in 1904, she tried to be sure that everyone knew the gruesome details of that October night.

In 1904, Teresa Bell expanded the note in her diary with a bizarre and frightening tale about the events that surrounded her husband's death. She claimed that on the night he died, he had fallen from the stairs but did not expire until twenty minutes later when he was in Mary Ellen Pleasant's presence. Teresa Bell elaborated her tale, saying that Mary Ellen Pleasant had "put her fingers in the hole in the top of his head and pulled out the protruding brains. . . ." It was a strange and macabre story, which, when Mrs. Bell published it, forever solidified the legend of Mary Ellen Pleasant.

Mary Ellen Pleasant was a strange woman for her time, because it was unheard of for a woman to stand up to authority or to challenge society's norms. Her strangeness made her legendary, and when someone is legendary, the facts are often hard to discern from the myths that surround their lives. In fact, she was a phenomenally successful businesswoman with interests all over San Francisco and throughout California, and her rise to these heights through her own work was a remarkable story. Her story was especially strange, however, because she wasn't a white woman of privilege, but a black woman who devised her own means to power.

Mary Ellen Pleasant claimed that she was born to free parents in the segregated city of Philadelphia, Pennsylvania, on August 19, 1814. The mysteries about her early life are nearly as clouded as those from her infamous years in San Francisco, as she herself was close-mouthed and aloof. According to legend, her father may or may not have been white, and some even suggested he was a Southern slaveholder. Others claimed that he was a Cherokee Indian or a Kanaka—a native from Polynesia.

Who her father was is unknown, but it is likely that he was a freedman living in the North when his daughter was born. Her mother was most likely a black woman—presumably a former slave—from Louisiana. As a young girl, Mary Ellen Pleasant went to Nantucket, Massachusetts, to live with a Quaker family to be educated. Perhaps her family believed that the Quakers' belief in equality of the races would mean a better life for their daughter than they could offer her in their segregated city. Unfortunately, the family she was sent to kept the money that was to be used for her education and, instead, sent her to work. Mary Ellen Pleasant left Nantucket and returned to Philadelphia when she was about fourteen or fifteen, and she always regretted her lack of formal education.

Though she was poor and without formal training, an important first step toward the life she was to lead did begin in Philadelphia. There, she met and married a wealthy black man named James Henry Smith. The couple became deeply involved in the fight to abolish slavery that was fomenting throughout the nation in the years prior to the Civil War, and they were fervent supporters of the Underground Railroad, the route by which escaped slaves from the South made their way to safety in Canada. After they had been married a few years, James Smith died, leaving Mary Ellen Pleasant a substantial fortune, and she continued with the work the couple had started.

In 1848, she married a former slave named John James Pleasant, and not much more is known about her second husband than about the first. Perhaps even in her thirties, before she gained much of her wealth and power, Mary Ellen Pleasant's life had already evolved into a one woman show. She said of herself in later years, "I am a whole theatre to myself." By the time she met her second husband, she was already a woman capable of taking on any role and of taking on anyone who stood in her way.

Sometime between 1848 and 1852, the Pleasants emigrated to the West, following the paths of many black and white abolitionists from Philadelphia. They settled in San Francisco in the new state of California, and Mary Ellen Pleasant made a living working as a housekeeper in the homes of several of the city's wealthiest and most powerful men. She made several very wise investments with her first husband's fortune during these years, gleaning information about the best way to increase her wealth through careful listening during the lavish dinner parties she oversaw. By 1855, she had amassed quite a sum and was the owner of several San Francisco laundries. She was also the holder of enough secrets—gleaned from years of careful watching and listening to make her a powerful force to be reckoned with, and perhaps even a woman to fear.

This shrewd businesswoman could have been one of the wealthiest people in California if she had been interested in making money; for her, though, money was but a means to an end. She gave it away almost as soon as she got it, for the most part using it to bring freedmen and fugitive slaves to California and to help them get on their feet once there. Her philanthropy was extensive, and she exercised considerable political clout as well. It was probably due to Mary Ellen Pleasant's support that a California law forbidding black testimony in a court of law was repealed.

People who tried to stand in the way of what Mary Ellen Pleasant might have termed "progress" certainly knew it after the fact. In October 1866, she tried to take a seat on a San Francisco streetcar, and the driver ordered her to leave his vehicle. Clearly the driver did not know who he was dealing with, for if he had he would have saved himself and the bus company a great deal of trouble. To him, the tall, stately black woman looked like just another former slave, one of many who had fled to California seeking opportunity after the Civil War, and he ordered her off the steps just as he would have done to any other black who approached his car. Perhaps he didn't notice that she was as finely dressed as any of the white women he picked up on his regular route. He probably didn't notice the anger that flashed in the woman's eyes, either. On October 18, 1866, the front page of the *Alta California* carried the story of Mrs. Pleasant's failed ride. The paper reported:

> *Mrs. Mary E. Pleasants, a woman of color, having complained of the driver of car No. 6 of the Omnibus Railroad Company's line, for putting her off the car, appeared yesterday in the Police Court and withdrew the charge, stating as a reason for doing so that she had been informed by the agents of the Company that negroes would hearafter be allowed to ride on the car, let the effect on the Company's business be what it might.*

Shortly after the incident on the streetcar, Mrs. Pleasant, a widow again after the death of her second husband, formed an alliance with multimillionaire Thomas Bell, a cofounder of the Bank of California. No one knows what the true nature of their relationship was beyond business, but business partners they were, and a great deal of mutual respect existed between them. In 1879, Mary Ellen Pleasant introduced Thomas Bell to Teresa Percy. Thomas and Teresa were married and in a few months all three had moved into a fabulous mansion on the corner of Octavia and Bush Streets built to Mrs. Pleasant's specifications.

Perhaps most people preferred to think that Mary Ellen Pleasant—sometimes disrespectfully called Mammy Pleasant, much to her dismay—was, in fact, the housekeeper. No doubt, she did act as an executive in that role, hiring and firing servants, and buying groceries, but she was much more. Mary Ellen Pleasant handled all of Teresa's financial needs, acting as mediator between husband and wife. She also chose Teresa's clothes, friends, and activities.

People all over town wondered at their odd relationship, but Mrs. Pleasant was unlikely to satisfy them. Once she told a judge, "Mr. Bell knew what I was there for, and I knew what I was there for." No more would she say. The strangeness of the relationship seemed to overshadow the good that Mrs. Pleasant was doing around the city, and all kinds of rumors pervaded the general atmosphere of mystery that shrouded the mansion. Stories that Mary Ellen Pleasant trafficked in prostitutes, engaged in the practice of voodoo, and bought and sold babies ran rampant all over town, even before Thomas Bell's death. By the late 1890s, after Thomas Bell's death and even after she and Teresa had stopped sharing the Octavia Street residence, the legend that was Mary Ellen Pleasant's life had found its way into the common history of San Francisco.

In fact, it was the break with Teresa Bell, widow of the man who had been her business partner, that precipitated the growth of the legend of Mary Ellen Pleasant's life. After her husband's death, Teresa Bell turned with anger against the woman who had been her sole support for almost ten years. She threw Mary Ellen Pleasant out of the mansion and conspired with a newspaper reporter to spread the stories of voodoo and prostitution, which were all too eagerly read by a public who wanted a reason for Mrs. Pleasant's success. Teresa also bought interest in a popular magazine that had planned to publish Mary Ellen Pleasant's memoirs, ruling out any chance that Mrs. Pleasant's side of the story could be heard, and managed to steal many of Mrs. Pleasant's other important documents. All the while, she wrote quietly in her diary of the terrible things that Mary Ellen Pleasant had done, and then gave her volumes to a San Francisco newspaperman after Mrs. Pleasant's death in 1904.

Perhaps Teresa Bell was worried about what Mary Ellen Pleasant might do to her if the story was revealed before Mrs. Pleasant was beyond her power to injure her. Still, there is strong evidence that suggests that Teresa Bell went completely mad before she began her campaign to ruin Mary Ellen Pleasant. Teresa's own children had her declared incompetent because, among other things, she claimed she could float through the air, and that she had, in fact, floated over New York City. Teresa also claimed that she could light the gaslights without a match, just by waving her hand. These same children staunchly supported Mary Ellen Pleasant's claim that the Octavia Street house, and many of its furnishings and the jewels claimed by Teresa Bell, were actually hers.

Some historians say that the diaries that were concocted to ruin Mary Ellen Pleasant were much more injurious to Teresa Bell, in that they show what a demented state of mind the woman was in when she made her accusations against a woman who had really done more good for the city of San Francisco and for its less fortunate inhabitants than almost anyone else. As for the murder of Thomas Bell, the *San Francisco Chronicle* reported the story much differently in the days after the incident than Teresa Bell would in her diary.

According to the *Chronicle*, it was about half-past ten on the night of October 15, 1892, when the servants at the mansion on Octavia Street heard the cries of Thomas Bell, and a dull thud after his body had fallen the twenty feet from stair railing to basement floor. They immediately ran to awaken his son and Mary Ellen Pleasant. The story reported that when Mrs. Pleasant and Thomas Bell's son Fred reached the body, she:

> . . . *detected signs of life, however, and busied herself with procuring pillows and blankets, while Fred Bell ran for Dr. Murphy, the nearest physician. Dr. Kearney of 513 Folsom Street, who has been attending Mr. Bell was telephoned for also, and he arrived a few minutes after Dr. Murphy had the unconscious man carried back to his bedroom. The two physicians first directed their attention to rousing Mr. Bell from his deep stupor, but all the resources at hand failed and they devoted themselves to a diagnosis of his injuries. Concussion of the brain was apparent but no fracture of the skull could be discovered.*

The *San Francisco Examiner* told a similar tale with Mary Ellen Pleasant's testimony. It recounted Mrs. Pleasant's words:

> *Mr. Bell had been ailing for about two months now, and has been in bed since last Monday. He was badly run down, the doctor said, and besides he had a trouble of the skin that just kept him in torture. Twenty minutes before 10 o'clock last night he got up without calling anyone and went to the bathroom*

*which is close to his chamber on the upper floor. . . . From there*
*he must have started to go downstairs. There are two winding*
*flights leading from the upper story to the kitchen, and at the*
*bottom of the top flight we found the blanket which I always left*
*on the foot of the bed for him to throw over his shoulders when*
*he arose in the night.*

She went on to say that he must have become disoriented when he arose and taken a spill over the railing. Fred Bell confirmed her story, and the coroner agreed that it had been an accidental death. Still, the rumors that Teresa Bell started about Mary Ellen Pleasant would be accepted readily and over the years became solidified in the public mind as fact. In truth, there was a great deal about Mrs. Pleasant that was unknown, and perhaps because of her successes in a time when being a woman, and what was more, being black, should have kept her from any role above that of housewife or domestic servant, it might have been easier for people to believe that it was voodoo or illegal practice that made her a success.

Many people who knew her described Mary Ellen Pleasant as a formidable, terrifying woman. Others have said after reviewing her story and meeting her, "[If she] had been white and a man, she would have been president," and "Even as a woman she might have commanded an army successfully." She certainly proved that regardless of your sex or race you could be a success, and she used her success to better the situation of others. Whether the public record of her good deeds or the private, then public, musings of Teresa Bell are correct, Mary Ellen Pleasant was one of the most amazing and remarkable people in California. Her life was of the stuff that makes for good fiction, and it will probably never be reconciled with fact.

# TOBY RIDDLE

(1836–1920)

## A Strong-Hearted Woman

The blustering Irishman, Pat McManus, charged angrily toward Toby Riddle carrying his usual weapons, a Colt revolver and a Henry rifle, demanding to know where his horse was. Toby angrily replied, "I turned that horse loose, for the sake of your wife."

McManus was a sutler, a man who followed army camps to peddle goods, but since the beginning of the struggle between the US Army and the Modoc Indians in January 1873, he had been volunteering frequently to go into battle. Toby Riddle was a Modoc, but she was also the wife of one of the white settlers in the area. In the days before April 26, 1873, she told McManus and the other soldiers that she had had a premonition that the Modoc would attack fiercely and that the casualties would be great if they marched that day. Thinking of McManus's wife in Yreka, she frightened his horse away to keep him in the camp when her warnings seemed to fail. It wasn't the first time her warnings had gone unheeded, but this time she'd do something about it.

When Toby was born in 1836 in the part of northern California that her people called home, the Modoc occupied about two to three thousand square miles of land near the California-Oregon border. They held beautiful Tule Lake and its eastern shore sacred. They had views of the Cascades and of the striking peak of Mount Shasta. In the southern part of their territory were forty square miles of lava beds—a maze of caverns and fissures—formed by a volcanic explosion seven thousand years ago. It was a sacred and abundant land for the Modoc, who relied on it and revered it.

At about the time that Toby was born, the US government began a policy of forcing tribes such as the Modoc to leave their homelands and move onto reservations, which were usually on barren pieces of land that white settlers weren't interested in. The Modoc lands were remote enough that, at first, the policy didn't affect them, but in the 1840s that all began to change. The land that the Modoc loved was also prime real estate for the white settlers who had begun to hear of the beauty and fertile lands in the Oregon Territory and realized that more bounty was to be had just to the south. Starting in the 1840s, more and more of these white settlers began moving into the Modoc homeland and claiming pieces of it for themselves.

The Modoc retaliated against this encroachment by attacking wagon trains and killing some of the newcomers, but the diseases brought by the white settlers did far more damage to the native population than the warring ways of the Modoc did to the whites. By 1848 there were only about nine hundred members of the once thriving tribe of two thousand left in their homeland. The year 1848 was significant for another important reason that would also mark the start of even more difficulty for the Modoc. Gold was discovered in a river near the California-Oregon border, and, as a result, miners and settlers flooded into the area, founding towns and trying to get the government to force the Modoc onto reservations. These settlers made frequent complaints about the Modoc, claiming they stole cattle and raided wagon trains. In part the complaints were true, but another tribe to the north, the Klamath, were frequently responsible for depredations blamed on the Modoc. The Modoc and the Klamath were being forced into these means of survival because their native land was being overtaken by their accusers.

Into this world of change and turmoil was born a remarkable little girl who would come to be known as Toby. From early on, Toby was notorious among the Modoc people for her bravery. As a small child she was called "The Strange Child" and "The Little Woman Chief." She was unafraid of the sacred places that most Modoc avoided and exhibited extraordinary courage as a little girl and young woman. When she was fourteen, she even helped her tribe ward off attack from a neighboring tribe alongside the boys her age who were in training as warriors. She was intelligent and, combined with her other traits, not terribly feminine by Modoc standards, though the men of her tribe thought her very attractive.

Frank Riddle, a white miner and hunter who lived in the area around the traditional Modoc territory, must also have seen how attractive the young woman was. When she was still in her teens, the two were married in spite of her family's plans for her to be married to a Modoc man. Naturally, her family was very upset that she had chosen to marry one of the people that were threatening their very existence in the land that they loved. Still, the two remained close to the Modocs, who grew to trust Frank. Toby became utterly and completely devoted to her husband. In spite of the hardships that started in the 1840s, the Modoc managed to remain strong and independent as a tribe, if diminished in size, until the difficult winter of 1861–1862. Toby and Frank Riddle spent time with her family and knew of the Modocs' hardships, and they frequently tried to act on the Modocs' behalf with the whites in the area. Still, the cold, harsh weather killed many of the plants that the Modoc and the game animals they depended on needed for survival. Some of the tribe's elders began to suggest that they sign a treaty with the US government in order to get aid for their people. It would mean moving onto a reservation and leaving their traditional homeland, but it seemed to some that they had no choice.

One of the young men, Kientpoos, who was nicknamed Captain Jack because he resembled a Yreka man named Jack, voiced his opposition to the plan, and he was joined by many others who didn't want to be moved to reservations and forced to become farmers. Still, on February 14, 1864, Chief Schonchin, representing all of the Modoc, went to see a man named Elisha Steele, who Schonchin thought was still the Indian Agent for the area. Though Steele had been removed from that post, he was still interested in brokering a peace with the Modoc, so he proceeded to negotiate. He never told Chief Schonchin that he had no authority, and the two of them agreed that the Modoc would live on their own reservation on the west side of their beloved Tule Lake. In exchange, the Modoc would allow non-Indians to pass through their territory, and they would only visit towns of whites after receiving a pass from the soldiers at Fort Klamath.

This arrangement was opposed by the white settlers who wanted the land for themselves, and no sooner had Schonchin and Steele agreed to it than it was changed by a treaty called the Council Grove Treaty that Schonchin felt compelled to sign because of the Modocs' hardship. The treaty would put Paiutes, Klamaths, and Modocs together on the same reservation in an area that had traditionally been Klamath land, and the effect would be disastrous.

Though the Klamath and the Modoc were related tribes, they always held separate territories, and the difficulties with white settlers since the beginning of the influx into their traditional homelands had created a deeper rift between the two groups. While the Modocs lived in the Klamath territory, the Klamath never hesitated to goad them about the fact that they no longer had land of their own. In addition, when the Klamath discovered that the soldiers who were present on the reservation were willing to let them go their own way without interfering, the Klamath stole lumber and fish from the Modoc and attacked Modoc women who were gathering seeds and grasses.

Captain Jack went to the Indian Agent who oversaw the reservation to ask for help, but was told never to return with a complaint again. Instead of allowing the torment to continue, Jack led a group of Modoc south, back to their homeland around Tule Lake in California. Toby and Frank, who had remained in northern California, must have been pleased to see her people return, but also must have known that more trouble was yet to come.

In the time since Captain Jack and his Modoc followers had been absent from the area, more white settlers had started ranches and farms, but there was still relative peace between the whites and the Modoc after their return. General Edward Canby, who was the commander in charge of army operations in the Northwest, seemed inclined to let the status quo continue and even reported to Washington that, though there were difficulties between whites and Modocs, most accounts were exaggerated. Indian Superintendent Alfred Meacham tended to agree, and urged Canby to let the Indians settle the difficulties between themselves and to turn away from minor infractions of the Modoc against the whites.

Still, as emigration by whites into Modoc territory continued, many of Jack's followers began to urge that war be brought against the whites to regain traditional Modoc territory. Jack was reluctant because Alfred Meacham was trying to work with Jack to set up a separate Modoc reservation on the east side of Tule Lake around Lost River, in order to keep peace. The conditions Meacham set were simple: just don't bother the white settlers. Jack was willing to agree, but land-hungry whites wouldn't allow the land to be set aside for Indian use. Finally, in 1872, the Bureau of Indian Affairs insisted that Captain Jack and his followers be removed from the area and returned to the Klamath Reservation in Oregon. Canby and Meacham were both dismayed at the decision, but had no choice but to follow the order. For months they tried to persuade Captain Jack to leave peacefully, but Jack, supported by an even more determined group of Modoc men, refused to cooperate.

Although Jack also had no desire to go to war against the whites, many of the men under him were urging the start of a war. Jack was able to prevent his warriors from killing the whites who were coming to talk peacefully with them, but he wasn't able to keep them from making their threats. Finally, on November 29, 1872, Captain James Jackson and thirty-six men left Fort Klamath in freezing rain to find Jack and arrest him, thinking that if they were carrying enough firepower, they could get the rest of the Modoc to move peacefully to the reservation. Early in the morning on November 29, the shooting started at the village when the Modoc men refused to surrender their weapons. War was now imminent. After the altercation at the Lost River village, Captain Jack led the warriors, women, and children who had been there to the southwest, where they would fortress themselves in the crevasses and caves of the lava beds. There they were able to barricade themselves in a deep cave that the army couldn't find. General Canby hadn't known about the plans to force the Modoc from Lost River and would have opposed them if he did, but since blood had been shed on both sides, he had no choice but to take troops to the lava beds in order to capture Jack and end the struggle.

When Canby's troops arrived at the lava beds, Jack was still inclined to surrender, but the warriors who wanted to fight back outnumbered him. Early in the morning of January 17, 1873, the soldiers marched on the lava beds, which were shrouded by a thick fog. They were no match for the Modoc warriors who knew the secrets of the maze under their feet and were heavily armed. Thirty-seven white soldiers and volunteers were killed or wounded by the end of the day, but the Modoc were unharmed. The lava beds were a natural fortification unlike any other ever built, and Canby knew that his men were virtually powerless against it. He turned to the gentle and intelligent Toby, trusted by the Modoc and by the whites, to help him find a way out of the maze of politics and warfare he suddenly found himself in.

Toby and Frank and their son, Jeff, were allowed to come and go from the hideout in the lava beds and frequently acted as interpreters during the meetings with Canby and a group of men, including Alfred Meacham, to help work out a solution. The negotiations went on for months with the Riddles' help, though Jack was unwilling to give up anything on his side, and Canby was unable to because of his orders to remove the Modoc from their homeland. Though Canby was sympathetic to the Modoc plight and wanted to avoid further bloodshed without forcing surrender, he was powerless to do so and could barely get Jack to agree to talks.

On April 2, Toby and Frank joined the peace commissioners—as Canby, Meacham, and other men from the army and surrounding area were termed—as interpreters in a face-to-face meeting with Captain Jack. Jack demanded a reservation on the Lost River, removal of the soldiers, and no trials for the Modocs who had killed soldiers and civilians in the battle at the lava beds. Because of his orders from the government, Canby couldn't agree, so the meeting was a failure. Still, both sides agreed to erect a tent halfway between the soldiers' camp and the fortification at the lava beds, where they could continue to negotiate a settlement.

On April 5, during a meeting at the tent, Toby passed Jack's final offer on to Canby. Jack said he was willing to accept the lava beds, where they had held off the army for so long, as a substitute reservation. Without the authority from Washington, DC, Canby could not promise anything, and it seemed to him that Jack's offer was not truly a serious one. Still, the commissioners accepted an offer to meet with the Modoc at the tent on April 10 to talk over a possible peace agreement that involved the lava beds as a settlement.

Toby was becoming increasingly worried that the standoff would not end without serious bloodshed, and during a visit to the lava beds on April 9, a man named Weium followed her and her son out of the rocks and confirmed her fears. He said, "Toby, tell Old Man Meacham and all them men not to come to the council tent again. They all get killed."

As Toby and Jeff returned to the camp, she was very afraid for the whites and also for herself, because she would have to go along to the tent with the commissioners as an interpreter. She said to Jeff, who was just a small boy, "My son, in case I and your father get killed, stay with Mr. Fairchild. . . . But if I can help it, the Peace Commissioners shall not meet Captain Jack and his men in council any more."

Jeff later remembered that his mother sobbed as if her heart would break, as she tried to think of what to do. He was unable to control himself when Alfred Meacham greeted them at the camp with a jovial question about their dealings with Captain Jack. The small boy blurted out the whole story of the meeting with Weium.

Meacham was alarmed enough that he called together the other commissioners to hear Toby out. She addressed them: "I must ask you, before I tell you, not to tell any of the Modocs where you was told what I am going to tell you men, and by whom. My life and man's life and little boy's life will be in great danger. . . ."

All of the men swore that they would not reveal her secret, and she poured out to them the tale of Weium's warning. "The next time you meet Jack and his men in council, you will all be shot to death. What I tell you is the truth. Take my warning. Do not meet the people in council any more. If you do, you will be carried to this camp, dead." In spite of Toby's warning and her obvious fear, Canby dismissed her words because he was sure the Modoc would not attack with such a large force of soldiers nearby. Meacham and two of the other commissioners wanted to at least delay the meeting, and they told Toby that they would postpone it if at all possible. Another of the commissioners, a man named Thomas, agreed with Canby, and when two of the Modocs, Bogus and Boston, rode into the army camp the next day, April 10, he asked them, "Why do you Indians want to kill us?"

Bogus and Boston assured Thomas over and over that was not the case, and asked who told him that. Without thinking of his promise to protect her, Thomas immediately revealed that Toby was the informant. Both Bogus and Boston doubled their reassurances, and Boston ran to Jack to tell him of the leak, while Bogus remained in camp to meet with Meacham and give further promises that the commissioners were not to be harmed.

Soon a runner came into the army camp from the lava beds to say that the meeting was postponed until the next day, April 11, and that Captain Jack wished to see Toby at once. As she bravely mounted her horse, Meacham tried to stop her from returning to the lava beds, but she said, "I am not afraid to go, Meacham." Still, she accepted his gun to carry with her.

Meacham later recalled:

> She parted with her little boy, ten years old, several times before
> she succeeded in mounting her horse. Clasping him to her
> breast, she would set him down and start, and then run to him
> and catch him up again, each time seeming more affected to the
> last, until, at last, her courage was high enough and, saying a
> few words in a low voice to her husband, she rode off.

Once at the stronghold in the lava beds, Toby stood in front of Captain Jack, who demanded to know where she had gotten her information. At first, Toby wove a fanciful tale of the spirits coming to her in a dream to warn her of the danger. Jack wouldn't accept the lie, and finally Toby blurted out the truth about her informer. She said, "I didn't dream it. The spirits did not tell me. One of your men told me. I won't tell you who it was. Shoot me, if you dare. But there are soldiers there. You touch me and they will fire on you and not a Modoc will escape."

After her speech, she drew Meacham's gun against the rifles of most of the Modoc men, while they demanded her death. Jack and eight men went to protect her, and knocked the rifles aside. He insisted to Toby that her informer had been wrong, that he meant to kill no one the next day, and sent her back to camp with an escort.

When Toby returned with the protection of the eight men who had come to her aid in the stronghold, her husband and son rejoiced, as did the rest of the camp. She reported the events of the meeting, but would not shake her belief that the commissioners were in danger if they went to the meeting the next day, nor would she stop her warnings.

On the night of April 10, Canby wrote to his wife, "Don't be discouraged or gloomy, darling. I will take good care of myself and come home as soon as possible." The next morning, Toby urged him again not to go to the tent, and he laughed and said to some of his men, "Well, brother officers, I bid you all a last farewell. From what Riddle says, this is my last day."

Canby and the commissioners, along with Toby and Frank, headed off to the tent in the mid-morning. When they arrived they could see clearly that the Modoc men were not unarmed as had been agreed, but at first, the meeting seemed to go as planned. Then, with neither side willing to budge, at one o'clock in the afternoon, Jack shouted, "Ot-we kantux-e" ("all ready") and he, along with the other warriors who were with them, opened fire at the group of commissioners. The mostly unarmed group was helpless, and except for the Riddles, who were under Jack's protection, only two were able to escape, one by running toward the soldiers' camp, and the other, Alfred Meacham, when Toby shouted "The soldiers are coming!" and frightened away the Modoc warrior who was trying to scalp him.

The killing of the peace commissioners was the end for Captain Jack and his men, as the army redoubled its efforts to force them out of the lava beds and into surrender. Several other battles would ensue, including the one on April 26, when Toby frightened away Pat McManus's horse knowing the Modoc were leading the soldiers into a trap; she was thinking of his wife, and perhaps of Canby's wife as well, since she had been unable to prevent his death.

Eventually, the Modoc were forced to surrender, and Captain Jack was put on trial, along with a number of other Modoc. Toby served as an interpreter along with Frank, and both were devastated when Jack refused to testify and was eventually found guilty and sentenced to hang. Jack was furious because the men who had forced him to attack that day at the tent were going free, because they had agreed to capture him and testify against him.

Up until the night before the fateful meeting with the commissioners at the tent, Jack had remained opposed to any killing, though he was fairly certain that he would no longer be able to restrain the men under him. He had been outvoted by the other Modoc and forced to attack that April day.

In 1874, Toby, Frank, and Jeff went on a lecture tour in the East with Alfred Meacham, who had recovered from his near scalping. Meacham's motive was the money he could make from lectures about the highly publicized Modoc Indian war. Perhaps Toby was motivated by the thought that she could somehow vindicate her people by sharing the truth about their plight. She continued that desire when, in 1914, she helped Jeff write *The History of the Modoc War*.

It was possible, even probable, that Toby—or Winema, as Meacham had called her on the lecture circuit—knew more about the Modoc Indian War than anyone living and had more reason to be distressed by the events than anyone else. During the time that Captain Jack and his band were holed up in the lava beds, she, Frank, and Jeff were the only people allowed to come and go, and the only ones who knew their way in and out.

Mere premonitions had not caused Toby to warn Canby before he headed to the tent on that fateful day, nor had they fueled her need to drive McManus's horse away. While she had been in the caves and clefts underground, Weium had followed her out of the lava beds because he knew with certainty what was going to happen on April 11. It is likely that before the battle on April 26, where the army was ambushed and suffered severe casualties, someone else had come to her to warn her of the danger and she had claimed to learn of it in a dream.

Whether or not Captain Jack, who had been so opposed to the escalation of violence and protected her when she came to the lava beds that night, had given permission to Weium to tell Toby of the planned surprise attack, no one will ever know. It is a secret that died with Toby in 1920 at the Klamath Reservation.

During the Modoc war, the Denver, Colorado, *Tribune* reported that little boys in the city, hearing of the battles from their parents, were playing Modoc Indians in their backyards. Presumably, little girls weren't invited to participate, since to the outside world it appeared that no women were involved in the war—no one had ever heard of Toby Riddle. Still, with the lecture tour that followed, and in the years to come when the story of the Modoc war was recorded, she would not be forgotten. In Oregon, the Winema National Forest is named for the brave woman who was trusted by all and tried to keep the peace. Roughly translated, Winema means strong-hearted woman, and Toby Riddle was certainly that.

# MARY AUSTIN

❧

## (1868–1934)

### A Woman of Genius

Nine days had passed since the agonizing hours that led up to baby Ruth's birth, so Mary's mother insisted that she get out of bed. Mary did as she was told, but within a day she was flat on her back at the doctor's orders. Even the thought of the grueling labor she had been through was painful, so she could scarcely bear to think of it. She had felt so utterly alone during the labor, even in her mother's house, especially when the doctor was called away for four hours in the middle of it to amputate a man's leg. Still, the baby was beautiful, and Mary's brothers Jim and George doted on their little niece. Mary herself looked forward to a much closer relationship with her daughter than she had ever had with Susanna Hunter, her own mother. Still, it would have been nice if Wallace, her husband, had been able to come for the birth of their child. They hadn't seen each other for months, since September when Mary had left Wallace in Inyo, California, to stay with her mother and brothers in Bakersfield until the birth of her baby.

While Mary was still confined to her bed, completely debilitated from the difficulties of her labor, she received news that she and her husband were deeply in debt, and that their creditors were demanding immediate payment. Mary had known that business had not gone well for Wallace since their marriage, but she had no idea how much they owed until she received notice that she was being held liable for the debts he had incurred. Wallace had not earned more than a few dollars since the irrigation company he had been working for failed, and they were ruined. The blow to Mary, especially coming so soon after her terrifying labor, was terrible. Mary's mother and brothers urged Mary to divorce him, as their belief in staying out of debt far surpassed their abhorrence of divorce. Still, that would have made Mary totally dependent on her family, and she was too independent for the sort of life that would mean for her and for her tiny daughter, Ruth.

Mary would later write about her feelings after Ruth's birth when life was at its worst in her autobiography, *Earth Horizon*. She chose to write of herself in the third person, as if making herself into a character from one of her novels.

*She still believed in the solution of the personal problem by the application of intelligence. The surprises of the last two years had been disconcerting, and the obligations of her condition had prevented their being forcefully met. But she thought if she could only talk things over with her husband. . . . This was difficult to understand, but Mary felt confident that there was an explanation. She would go to her husband and they would talk things out and come to an understanding and begin all over again. There was nothing two intelligent people couldn't do together if they set about it.*

In fact, Mary had already made headway toward just the solution that was called for when the news came of their financial ruin—long before she spoke to Wallace about it.

It had been a long road for Mary Hunter Austin from her childhood home in Carlinville, Illinois, where she was born at midnight on September 9, 1868, to her mother's house in Bakersfield, California, where her own daughter was born. Her mother was Susanna Savilla Graham Hunter, the daughter of a staunchly Methodist Carlinville family and the latest in a long line of sturdy and intelligent pioneer women. Susanna was extremely well read and intelligent, and had dreamed of a career in teaching (she did teach for one year) or in writing, but when she was nineteen she did as her family expected and married Carlinville attorney Captain George Hunter. George had immigrated to the United States from England in the late 1850s, and he had taken up the practice of law in Carlinville, where he opened an office over Susanna's father's pharmacy.

In 1861 when the Civil War broke out, George enlisted in the Union army, and shortly thereafter he and Susanna were married. From the day of their marriage, George's life became Susanna's life. She traveled south with him during the Civil War and lived in army camps during the first few years of their marriage, returning to Carlinville only to bear two children who died in infancy. During the war, George was constantly ill with malaria, which kept him at a desk for most of his service and kept Susanna by his side nursing him. The symptoms of the fever would plague him for the rest of his life.

After George's term of service was up in 1864, the young couple settled in Carlinville, and he resumed his law practice. In 1866 their first son, James Milo Hunter, was born. Susanna was always fearful for the family's financial situation because it was difficult for George to make a living, sick as he always was. She grew more anxious when she learned another child was on the way, and she was unable to welcome the new baby with great joy. Their first son, James, was born with a malformed leg, and she constantly fussed over him. With a sick husband and a lame child, she was weary already.

When Mary was born, she was an unlovely child, scrawny with a perpetually downturned mouth, and, though it would be unfair to say she was unloved, she may not have been her mother's first priority. Her husband's needs and those of her son nearly always came first with her, and, as Mary grew older, her relationship with her mother did not improve. Susanna disapproved of Mary's habit of "storying," telling the stories of events as though she had been there, when it was clear she had not. She would also become exasperated when Mary, who was a very perceptive child, would blurt out embarrassing things in company that everyone was thinking, but no one would ever have said out loud. With a red face, Susanna would exclaim, "I think the child is possessed." No punishment Susanna could conceive would cure Mary of her habits, and their encounters could be very disagreeable indeed.

Mary was very close to her father, however, and she spent many happy hours with him looking at books in his study or walking with him in all seasons through the area surrounding the small farm where they lived. George spent many hours in the outdoors, as it seemed to help relieve his bouts of illness. Mary's time with her father was precious to her and helped her develop her love of nature. Walking at his side, she learned to appreciate moist spring days in the sun as much as the crisp winter tromps through snow.

The only other person Mary was very close to as a child was her younger sister, Jennie. Born when Mary was barely two, Jennie was a beautiful, sweet baby, not intractable and frown-faced like Mary. Jennie was everyone's favorite, including her older sister's. The two little girls would spend many hours together as they grew older, and, indeed, it seemed to Mary as though Jennie was one of her only friends.

There was, however, another "person" in Mary's life more important than any other. Mary had learned to read at the young age of four by studying along with her brother, Jim, who had just started school. She discovered something very important when he was learning his vowels one day, and her mother explained the letter "I" to Mary by saying when Mary pointed to her own eye, "No. I, myself, I want a drink, I-Mary." Suddenly, Mary realized that inside her was a person who didn't have to be the little girl that everyone ignored or complained about. She came to associate the printed word with a strong inner self that she called I-Mary. When she was I-Mary, she knew everything or could learn anything, and she had a secret power.

When Mary went to school at the young age of five, I-Mary spoke up when the teacher chided her for looking at a book when she should have been studying her letters. I-Mary told the teacher that she had been reading, not just looking at the book. When the teacher disputed her story, the principal intervened, and when Mary proved that she could read, she was moved two grades ahead of her age level.

Mary's reading skills were excellent. She read everything that she could get her hands on. Her math and social skills were sorely lacking, and her lack of graces, compounded with the fact that she was unattractive by the standards of the day and considered strange because of her imaginative tale-spinning and her extraordinary intelligence, kept her lonely. Jennie and her father were the only people with whom she was close, and she found solace in them, in I-Mary, and in nature.

In 1877, however, events that would change Mary's life forever began. Her father's health grew worse and worse, and after his fourth child, a son, named George, was born in that year, George Hunter Sr. died on October 29, 1878. Mary was devastated by the loss of her father, and her mother, the one person who could have endeavored to make the loss less keenly felt, was preoccupied with the baby and worries about how she was to feed her small brood of children. Jim was twelve years old, and his mother depended on him to support her. The two of them were very close indeed. Jennie and Mary clung to each other. That winter, Mary grew ill with a sore throat, and no one realized for a time how sick the little girl really was. By the time Mary was better, Jennie was ill, and, in 1879, Jennie died. Both of the girls had been suffering from diphtheria.

Mary would learn to rely ever more on herself from that moment on. She had already determined that she wanted to have a career as a writer, and her mother—who was interested in forwarding the cause of women and worked extensively with organizations such as the Women's Christian Temperance Union—agreed to put Mary through Blackburn College, located in Carlinville, so that she could have a career.

Jim was already a student there when Mary started at age sixteen, and she appeared determined to outshine her older brother. Her classmates praised her compositions and poetry, and she grew ever more sure of herself while alienating others because of what she perceived as her superior intellect. However, during her first winter at Blackburn, she grew ill and was forced to return home. The following fall with her mother's approval, she enrolled at the state Normal College in Bloomington, but the curriculum for the study of becoming a teacher stifled Mary's creative impulses, and she was unhappy there. She suffered a nervous breakdown and returned home, where she reentered Blackburn and finished her education in two years. She chose to major in science, rather than English, but she was still determined to be a writer. Her mother failed to see the connection between science and writing, but Mary acted with considerable foresight in choosing her degree, as time would tell, for her first book was a study of natural history.

In the summer of 1887, a year before Mary's graduation from Blackburn, Jim heeded the call of the tales of wealth and prosperity to be had in California, and emigrated there, asking his family to join him when Mary finished school. Mary would have preferred that she and Susanna stay in Carlinville, or that she herself could go east to pursue her writing career, but Susanna insisted that the family move west to join Jim.

The two women and George took the train west to San Francisco, and along the way Mary gathered her impressions in a notebook. San Francisco and what it had to offer entranced her. Her cousin, George Lane, showed her around the city, taking her to restaurants and introducing her to the places where artists and writers were known to gather. Maybe she could have a writing career in the West! Too soon, however, she left San Francisco with her mother and brother on a boat that sailed to Los Angeles, then began the overland journey to the San Joaquin Valley. No place could be more different from the green hills of Illinois, but her imagination stirred at the barren landscape around her. She gained even more material for her writing during the overland journey by horse and wagon to meet Jim at his homestead. Mary had quickly appreciated the eerie beauty in all that was around her in the California desert.

Jim had filed claims in the name of himself, his mother, and his sister on 480 acres that he was sure would make their fortunes, but the reasons for the eerie beauty of the landscape were the same reasons that it was hell for the homesteader who expected to live off the land. At first, Mary and Susanna earned their living by cooking for a local rancher, and Jim and George worked with livestock. Mary was a talented cook, but with her college education and ideas of herself as an intellectual, she was drawn to the idea of teaching. While she was studying for the teacher's examination, she also stirred up much gossip about herself among the other settlers with her interest in learning as much as she could about the land around her from local Native Americans and from General Beale, a longtime settler in the area with a great deal of knowledge about the desert and its people.

Her intellectual pursuits weren't enough to sustain her through that first year, however, and she grew ill from malnutrition. When she was finally well, having treated herself by eating wild grapes that grew in the area, she took a job teaching at a school run by a man who owned a dairy, despite the fact that she failed the teachers' examination twice. In 1890, she met Stafford Wallace Austin while teaching at the dairy. He was an educated man from a prominent family that had made its fortune, then lost it in Hawaii. He had taught school for a few years as well, but finding that the career didn't suit him, he was trying to start a fruit farming operation with his brother Frank in Inyo. Mary was thrilled that such an educated man had taken an interest in her, and the two were married in 1891.

The farming life didn't really suit either Mary or Wallace, as he was called. Her constitution wasn't fit for a rough frontier life as the bout with malnutrition had shown, and her temperament was not suited to housekeeping. Writing was her first love, and she thought Wallace understood that. His wedding gift to her had been a gold pen with a pearl handle. Still, their marriage seemed happy. Then their financial trouble started, with the failure of the fruit farm due to the lack of water. Mary urged Wallace to try teaching again, but he refused. Instead, undaunted by the failure, he went to San Francisco to meet with his brother about an irrigation operation in the Owens Valley while Mary remained in Inyo to write two stories, "The Mother of Felipe" and "The Conversion of Ah Lew Sing."

When Mary joined Wallace in San Francisco in 1892, she promptly carried her two stories to Ina Coolbrith in Oakland, a poetess of some repute who had associations with a San Francisco–based literary magazine called the *Overland Monthly*. With Ina's help and encouragement, she submitted the stories to the magazine before she and Wallace turned south once again to Inyo.

Mary was still in love with the desert landscape and with the characters of the people who settled there. They provided plenty of fodder for her imagination. She drew her inspiration from the Mexican and Indian residents of the area and the miners lured by tales of gold in the desert. She kept busy writing and planning for the birth of their first child while Wallace worked on the irrigation system. One day, however, she returned from a walk to find that their landlord had evicted them—her belongings were on the sidewalk. Mary had known that things weren't going well with the irrigation company, but she didn't know how bad it was, and Wallace wasn't even there to tell her himself. She picked up their belongings and walked until she found another situation for them where she could work for their board. There she was furious to learn from their new landlord that Wallace had turned down the chance to be the principal of the Inyo school, spurring the eviction from their home.

In September 1892, Mary went to her mother and brother's house in Bakersfield to await the birth of her child and to give herself some distance from her husband. While she was still recuperating from her difficult labor, the two stories she had carried with her to San Francisco were published.

Perhaps frightened by the news of the bankruptcy and bolstered by the double good news of his wife's publications and his new daughter, Wallace took a teaching job in the Owens Valley, and Mary, thinking that this was a fresh start, joined him there with Ruth. More difficulty was yet to come, though. Mary knew from the start that the beautiful Ruth was not like other babies, but when she was three a doctor confirmed that the girl was mentally retarded.

Wallace refused to discuss their daughter's condition, and Mary didn't know what to do with a child with such a severe disability. Her frustration grew, and Mary and Wallace separated shortly after the diagnosis. Mary took a teaching job in another Owens Valley town to support herself and Ruth. Their lodgings were squalid, and Mary, never a good housekeeper, couldn't or wouldn't find the time to improve them. Her writing suffered tremendously, but she knew that Ruth was suffering more from a mother who didn't know how to deal with her.

Neighbors were afraid that the baby was being neglected when they saw the conditions the two lived in, and they tried to help. Mary found it difficult to ask for assistance, or even to appear grateful for it when it was offered, so the neighbors found it hard to give. Eventually, and against Wallace's wishes, Mary boarded Ruth with a neighbor family who seemed able to control the little girl's tantrums and take better care of her than she could.

In 1898, Wallace and Mary reconciled and moved together to Independence, California, where Wallace had another teaching position, and Ruth, now six years old, went with them. Once there, they learned that Mary's mother, Susanna, had died in Los Angeles, where Mary's younger brother George was studying medicine. Mary had been ready to set out for a last visit when she heard the news of Susanna's death, but she stayed in Independence after hearing the news.

Mary loved the little town in the Owens Valley with its harsh desert landscape set off by towering mountains in the west, but in 1899, she did set out for Los Angeles with Ruth in tow. There she received the emotional support and intellectual stimulus she needed for her writing, meeting some of the most important literary figures in the United States at that time. When she returned home to Independence in 1900, she had found the inspiration and the knowledge she needed to write her most famous book, a collection of essays called *The Land of Little Rain*, all about her adopted desert home. Wallace built Mary and Ruth a home in Independence that Mary loved dearly and from there she was satisfied, at last, with the views out her window of the Sierra Nevada and Mount Whitney rising above the desert plain, and the knowledge that she was a writer. Mary's time in Independence was very productive, but still she was often ill, overworked, and exhausted with the care of Ruth. She wrote, traveled to stimulate her brain and creativity, and continued to meet and get influence from great literary minds, but she knew that something would have to change for her to live her literary dreams.

In January 1904, she finally placed Ruth in the care of a Santa Clara physician on a trial basis to see if prolonged influence of a professional would help the little girl, and in January 1905, Mary had Ruth committed permanently to an institution and would never see her again. It was a sad decision, and perhaps Mary felt some of the pain of the lack of closeness between her mother and herself when it was made, but it was time for her to move on. In late 1905, she got that chance when her first book was published. In *The Land of Little Rain*, her love for the desert shone like one of the stars in its deep black sky. She wrote:

*Out West, the west of the mesas and unpatented hills, there is more sky than any place in the world. It does not sit flatly on the rim of earth, but begins somewhere out in the space in which the earth is poised, hollows more, and is full of clean winey winds. There are some odors, too, that get into the blood. There is the spring smell of sage that is the warning that sap is beginning to work in a soil that looks to have none of the juices of life in it; it is the sort of smell that sets one thinking what a long furrow the plough would turn up here, the sort of smell that is the beginning of new leafage, is best at the plant's best, and leaves a pungent trail where wild cattle crop. There is the smell of sage at sundown, burning sage from campoodies and sheep camps, that travels on the thin blue wraiths of smoke; the kind of smell that gets into the hair and garments, is not much liked except upon long acquaintance, and every Paiute and shepherd smells of it indubitably. There is the palpable smell of the bitter dust that comes up from the alkali flats at the end of the dry seasons, and the smell of rain from the wide-mouthed cañons. And last the smell of the salt grass country, which is the beginning of other things that are the end of the mesa trail.*

With the publication of the book, Mary was considered an important American writer. She left Wallace and the Owens Valley to join an artist colony at Carmel, and her career took off to new heights. She and Wallace would never divorce, and she would never lose her love for the California desert, but she would become a world traveler; publish more than thirty books including her autobiography, *Earth Horizon*, and an autobiographical novel, *A Woman of Genius*; crusade for women's rights; and finally have the intellectual life she had always wanted.

In *The Land of Little Rain* she said of her beloved desert, "One hopes the land may breed like qualities in her human offspring not tritely to 'try,' but to do." Mary was living proof that, in spite of, or perhaps because of, the landscape that shaped your existence, you could do anything you wanted.

# TYE LEUNG SCHULZE

(1887–1972)

## Unbound Feet, Unfettered Heart

At thirteen, Tye Leung had made up her mind, and it would change her life forever. She wouldn't marry the man her parents had chosen for her—a complete stranger who wanted her to go with him to Butte, Montana. It would be terrible to leave Chinatown, her friends, and even her family, who had tried to make her go with the old man. But her next decision would have to be to leave her family behind, at least temporarily. She would go to the Presbyterian Mission Home and ask the matron there, Donaldina Cameron, to hide her from her parents, just as so many other young Chinese girls had done in San Francisco near the turn of the century.

Tye's decision to leave home and go to the mission wasn't an unusual one; in fact, it was a choice that too many young girls in turn-of- the-century San Francisco had to make. Tye was unusual, however, and her choice would help many other girls in her position and in worse circumstances change their lives as well.

In 1901 when she left home, Tye had been living in a two-room apartment in Chinatown with her mother, father, six brothers, and one sister. Tye and her brothers and sister had been born in the United States after her parents immigrated from China, so they were all US citizens. Not very many Chinese families lived in this country at the time because of a law that prohibited Chinese immigrants from entering. Tye's parents had arrived before the Chinese Exclusion Act of 1882 effectively ceased what had been a growing population entering this country looking for a better life, particularly in a city they called Old Gold Mountain, San Francisco.

Before the Chinese Exclusion Act passed, most of the Chinese immigrants had been men who came to work for the railroad or in the gold mines of California. Very few families traveled together to the United States from China because it was very expensive. Sons and husbands hoped to make enough money to earn passage for their families in China to join them. It was very unusual for any Chinese women to make the trip on their own, as they were bound by the taboos of a male-dominated society that kept them from venturing out on their own. In fact, most of the Chinese women of that time who could have paid for the trip were literally bound, having had their feet painfully tied from the time they were babies to keep their feet tiny, which was intended to emphasize their beauty and gentility, but also impeded their ability to walk. Such women were unable to walk far without pain, and were seldom even seen outside of their homes without the escort of a male relative.

Tye Leung's parents were unusual, because not only had they made the trip to the United States as a couple, they had allowed their children to learn American customs, and even the girls attended school. By the time she ran away to the mission, Tye had spent six years in an American school and she was one of the few people in the United States who spoke both English and Chinese.

Tye must have known the kinds of things that other girls were escaping from when they ran away to the Presbyterian Mission Home. In addition to leaving their families to avoid marriage to strangers, some girls were trying to run away from a situation in which they were enslaved. Times were hard in China and families sometimes sold their daughters to get money for food. Many times these girls were sent to the United States to work as slaves for more wealthy Chinese families, or they were forced to work as prostitutes in Chinatown. Frequently, when these girls found out about the mission home, they would send messages to Donaldina Cameron telling her that they were in desperate need of help. On the days that they were to escape from their owners, the girls would wear yellow ribbons and the mission home's rescue team would whisk them out of a crowd during their daily errands. They also conducted raids on the brothels where they were held.

Tye Leung's skills were in great demand at the mission home because she could understand the girls and help comfort them when they arrived, frightened and unable to communicate with their rescuers. In time, Tye Leung went along with the rescue teams on their crusades, working as an interpreter. It was a dangerous job, but she was proud of her work. She was helping girls who were worse off get their freedom, just as she had gotten hers.

In 1910, Tye's skills were noticed by the matron at the new immigration station in San Francisco Bay at Angel Island. Like Ellis Island in New York Harbor, Angel Island served as a checkpoint for immigrants. Many of the people who tried to pass through Angel Island made it through without difficulty, but because of the Chinese Exclusion Act, the Chinese were detained there for weeks, months, and even years while trying to gain entry into the country. They were housed in uncomfortable barracks surrounded by barbed wire and were forced to go through intense interrogations. All the while, just across the bay, their families waited for them, but no relatives were allowed on the island. Many of the missionaries who worked there tried to provide comfort and solace for the immigrants, but the language barrier was a major obstacle. Clearly, someone with Tye Leung's skills was needed at the station.

Tye worked as an assistant to the missionaries who ran the station and as an interpreter. She was able to help and reassure hundreds of Chinese women and children who were alone in the country without money or help of any kind, and were trapped on the island. In this job, Tye became the first Chinese-American woman to work as a civil servant for the US government.

In 1912, Tye made history again when she became the first Chinese-American woman in the United States to vote in an election. Although the law allowing women the right to vote throughout the country was not passed until 1920, California women were allowed the right in 1911. Along with two other Chinese-American women, Clara Lee and Emma Tom Leong, Tye Leung exercised that right in the face of tremendous publicity. People interested in the rights of women, and of the Chinese, wanted to draw attention to the smart, pretty young women who were trying to make a difference by casting their vote. A picture of Tye behind the wheel of a Studebaker-Flanders 20 car ran in the newspaper to show that Tye was a progressive believer in the vote and in modern conveniences. In fact, she never owned a car, but the picture would do a lot to further the thinking of the modern Chinese woman toward voting and independence.

After the historic election and while she was still working as an assistant and interpreter at Angel Island, Tye met an American man named Charles Frederick Schulze. He was an immigration inspector, and the two fell deeply in love. Their parents were strongly opposed to the two marrying, and there was also a law in California from 1840 to 1948 that prohibited people of different races from marrying. The two decided that nothing would stop them, and they headed north to Vancouver, Washington, for the ceremony. Tye would later remember, "His mother and my folks disapprove very much, but when two people are in love, they don't think of the future or what [might] happen."

When they returned to San Francisco, which was, after all, their home, both Tye and Charles were forced to resign from their jobs because of their cowork-ers' strong feelings against the marriage. They also found that neither the white community nor the Chinese community was ready to accept them as a couple, and they were socially outcast.

Charles went to work as a mechanic for the Southern Pacific railroad, while Tye got a night job as a telephone operator at the Chinese telephone company. The couple lived near Chinatown and had four children, who later remembered that their parents were one of only a few interracial couples in the area. Indeed, sometimes their children were called *fan gwai jai* by their Chinese neighbors, which meant "foreign devil child." Still, Tye made a place for them in the commu-nity. Her unceasing volunteer work as an interpreter in hospitals and wherever else she was needed was enough to gain them acceptance in the Chinese community.

Charles and Tye lived a very happy life together in spite of the troubles they faced as a couple. Both of them were very independent and they each kept up their own interests, while sharing them with each other. Tye remained active in the Chinese Presbyterian Church, while Charles attended Grace Cathedral. Both loved music, and Tye spent hours playing the piano and an instrument called the Chinese butterfly harp, while Charles played French horn with a military band. The children would accompany Tye to weddings, birthday celebrations, and the Chinese opera, where they learned about their mother's culture, and they were sent to school where they learned American customs. On Sundays, the Schulzes had family time, and they made it clear that both sides of the family were to be respected and experienced with fun and joy.

Tye and Charles's marriage was unusual for many reasons, but the most important for Tye was that she was able to keep up her own interests because Charles didn't expect her to take on the traditional role of a Chinese wife. Had Tye married the Chinese man her parents had chosen for her in Butte, Montana, she would undoubtedly have been expected to stay home and care for the house and the children, and not to have a life of her own, and certainly not to have any help from her husband. Although Tye did most of the cooking and cleaning in the Schulze home, Charles stayed home with the children and cooked and cleaned for them when she was at work. He also cared for his aging mother, who lived with them.

When Tye died at the age of eighty-four in Chinatown, she was a beloved figure, who had done much to help her neighbors and to forward the rights of the Chinese people. She may never have been aware of how much she did, starting with the day she ran away to Donaldina Cameron and refused to succumb to the tradition that just a few years before would have bound her feet and her heart.

# COLORADO WOMEN

# "AUNT CLARA" BROWN

(ca. 1803–1885)

### Angel of the Rockies

Clara Brown, an African-American slave, watched in despair as her youngest daughter, Eliza Jane, climbed trembling onto the auction block. Clara wanted to comfort the frightened child, but she knew that disrupting the auction could prove calamitous for herself and her daughter. Besides, she was in no position to help. Her own turn on the block was only minutes away.

The sun burned as hot as a blister on that summer day in 1835, as the bidding began in the public square in Russellville, Kentucky. When it finally subsided, the auctioneer shouted his familiar refrain, "Going once, going twice, sold!"

Clara could hardly bear to watch as Eliza Jane, her face twisted with terror, was led away by her new owner. Clara didn't recognize the buyer, and she knew her daughter might be taken off to some distant place, never to be seen again. The same was likely to happen to her husband, Richard, and their two older children, Margaret and Richard Junior, who stood numbly nearby.

By day's end Clara's worst fears had been realized. Her husband and two older children had been sold and had disappeared from her life forever. But she never abandoned hope of finding them or her dear Eliza Jane.

Remarkably, Clara didn't become bitter over the breakup of her family or other indignities she suffered as a slave and a black woman.

"My little sufferings was nothing, honey," she told a reporter in 1885, "and the Lord He give me strength to bear up under them. I ain't complaining."

Instead, after winning her freedom in the late 1850s, she made her mark as Colorado's first black settler and a prosperous entrepreneur. She also devoted much of her time to helping the needy. Her fellow Coloradans called her their "angel of the Rockies"—high praise for someone who had so many hardships to overcome.

Clara was born in the slave quarters of a Tennessee plantation at the dawn of the nineteenth century. Sources variously claim her birth year as 1800 or 1803, and she herself couldn't remember the exact date during an 1885 interview. In that same interview, she told a reporter from the *Denver Tribune Republican* that her grandparents were American Indians.

"Thus her peculiar cast of face is accounted for," the reporter wrote. "It is wholly unlike the usual African type, and must impress all who study it with its singular strength."

When Clara was barely more than a toddler, she and her mother were sold to tobacco farmer Ambrose Smith. When Smith moved to Kentucky, strapping Clara went along to toil in the fields and clean and cook in the Smith home. Her days were dominated by drudgery and hard work, but religious revivals offered her some respite. One preacher in particular made an impression that changed Clara's life. According to biographer Kathleen Bruyn:

> *So vividly did the young evangelist describe Jesus' agony that she then and there concluded that no sacrifice any human being could be called upon to make could compare with the voluntary suffering of the Son of God. Never in her life did Clara subscribe to the "hellfire and damnation" syndrome which ordinarily drove sinners to the mourners' bench. Compassion, not fear, motivated her all her life.*

Clara married another slave named Richard, and together they had four children. One of them, Eliza Jane's twin sister, Paulina, drowned at a young age. The family faced a second calamity in 1835, when Ambrose Smith died and his heirs decided to sell his slaves to settle his debts. The decision ripped apart Clara's family like a hurricane leveling cotton.

If there was a bright spot in the devastating event, it was that Clara was purchased by George Brown, a merchant and friend of Ambrose Smith, who had a reputation for treating his slaves decently. Clara adopted his surname. When Brown died in 1857, he left a will that freed, or manumitted, her. By law, she had to leave Kentucky within a year if she were to retain her freedom, so she moved to St. Louis and then on to Leavenworth, Kansas.

Clara was content working as a domestic in Kansas, but she was unsettled by the debate raging there over whether slavery should be banned. Though free, she still feared slavery. Rumor had it that slave traders were kidnapping free blacks in Kansas and ferrying them to states where they could be sold as slaves.

Clara was intrigued by reports that blacks enjoyed more freedom on the western frontier. She also wondered whether members of her family might have taken refuge there.

In April 1859 Clara learned of a wagon train that was leaving shortly for Colorado. She asked if she could join the train as its cook in exchange for her fare. The organizers agreed.

Two months later, the sixty-wagon expedition arrived in Auraria, a scattering of cabins at the confluence of Cherry Creek and the South Platte River.

Unlike most of the people swarming to Colorado, Clara did not suffer from gold fever, but she figured she could profit from those who did. She took a job at Auraria's City Bakery, where she cooked for prospectors and miners.

As she had hoped, Clara found greater acceptance in the West. Most of her customers and neighbors were friendly; they called her Aunt Clara or Aunty. When she befriended the Reverend Jacob Adriance, a Methodist minister to the homeless, she knew that he had barely enough food for himself, much less others. So she cooked extra helpings at dinnertime and delivered the food to the minister, claiming that she accidentally had cooked too much. It would be a sin to waste food, she told him, as she forced him to take it.

Clara also opened her own one-room cabin for prayer meetings, but most of the new settlers were more interested in gold than in God. As Clara listened to their tales of new ore discoveries in the mountains, she saw another opportunity. She moved to Central City to open a laundry, reported to be the state's first. She charged fifty cents to wash and press a bundle of clothes.

Clara's business was immediately popular. She wisely reinvested her earnings in mining claims and property and began to grubstake prospectors who were down on their luck. Some of her investments paid off handsomely. By the end of the Civil War, she had accumulated ten thousand dollars' worth of property, according to historian Jeanne Varnell.

"It was said that eventually she owned seven houses in Central City, sixteen lots in Denver, plus mines and properties in Georgetown, Boulder, and Idaho Springs," Varnell wrote.

What Clara didn't invest, she donated. She prepared meals for penniless miners and their families and cared for them when they were ill or injured.

"She was always the first to nurse a sick miner or the wife of one, and her deeds of charity were numerous," reported the *Denver Republican* in 1890.

Clara also loved to donate to church construction funds. She didn't care what the denomination was; she believed that God worked through many. The only time Clara pinched pennies was when it came to her own needs. She shunned fancy clothes and living quarters.

Clara did dip into her savings so she could visit Kentucky a decade or so after her departure. She went in hope of finding her husband and children, but after several weeks of searching, she failed to find any clues as to their whereabouts. She began to think that perhaps God wouldn't lead her to her family because He had other plans for her. Perhaps He wanted her to help some of the impoverished ex-slaves, including a nephew she had met on her visit to Kentucky.

The former slaves hadn't fought in the Civil War, but they were still among its victims. They could not get jobs because the war had devastated the nation's economy. Clara invited a number of former slaves to return with her to Colorado. She agreed to pay their way and house them temporarily, but they would be responsible for finding themselves jobs and permanent housing. When Clara returned, Colorado newspapers applauded her generosity.

But Clara refused to rest on such laurels. She knew she must work harder than ever to ensure the success of those she had sponsored. Doing so was getting more difficult; she was now in her late sixties, and she tired quickly. Her finances ailed as well. Her trip to Kentucky had eaten up her savings, and her investments had faltered. Floods had destroyed buildings she owned in Denver and washed away the records that proved her ownership of lots in the city. In 1873 a fire destroyed three buildings she owned in Central City. Then she was conned by crooks who realized that this trusting, illiterate black woman was an easy target.

Still, Clara's compassion did not die. She raised money to help former slaves known as Exodusters, who had fled to Kansas from the South in the late 1870s. These former slaves, who moved west following Reconstruction, called themselves Exodusters because they felt they were on an "exodus" or journey to freedom. Their plan was to form their own independent communities. The Exodusters had been freed by passage of the Thirteenth Amendment, but they continued to be exploited by white landowners. Thousands of Exodusters flocked to Kansas when they heard rumors that they could find free homestead land, farm equipment, and rations there. But for most, the stories were as illusory as a prairie mirage. They found no homes and little food in the so-called Promised Land.

Clara rushed to Kansas to distribute relief money that she had raised in Colorado. When she returned home in the fall of 1879, the *Central City Register* reported.

> *Aunt Clara Brown, whom everybody in Central knows, returned from a visit to Kansas some few days since, whither she went to look into the condition of the colored refugees and in the interest of the sufferers generally. There were about 5,000 all told, and they are getting on as fast as could be expected. The greater portion have found employment, and the balance will, doubtless, in the course of time. Aunt Clara says they are an industrious and sober class of people who only ask an opportunity to make an honest living. Their cry is work, work, and that is being given them as fast as possible. She was kindly received by [Kansas] Governor St. John and the people generally. She thinks that in another year these people will be well-to-do and self-supporting.*

Clara now tired even more quickly in the high mountain air, and she was troubled by edema. She had to rest in bed frequently. Alarmed friends urged her to move to Denver, where the lower altitude might help her to recuperate. An old friend, Denver Mayor Lee Sopris, arranged for her to live in a cottage rent free. Other friends delivered meals, and a doctor agreed to treat her at no charge.

By this time, Clara doubted she would ever see any of her family again. For years she had tried to locate someone who might know anything about her husband and children, but to no avail. Her efforts finally paid off in the spring of 1882 when an old friend wrote that a woman matching Eliza Jane's description was living in the Midwest. Though Clara was close to eighty and in poor health, she was determined to investigate. Friends offered to pay for the trip.

According to one account, Clara took a train to Council Bluffs, Iowa, and was traveling through town by streetcar when she saw a familiar figure walking along the muddy street. She stepped off the streetcar and joyfully reunited with her daughter. She learned that Eliza Jane had married another slave, but he had disappeared during the war. Eliza Jane had raised five children on her own.

Clara returned to Denver accompanied by her daughter and a granddaughter. She felt at peace with the world, having fulfilled her lifelong dream of finding Eliza Jane. But while her spirit soared, her health worsened. On October 26, 1885, she died from congenital heart disease.

Clara's funeral drew mourners of all races who wanted to pay tribute to her spirit and good works. She died destitute, so the Colorado Pioneer Association paid for a burial plot at Riverside Cemetery in Denver. Later, a permanent chair was dedicated to her at the Central City Opera House. She was inducted into the Colorado Women's Hall of Fame and was memorialized with a stained-glass window at the Colorado Capitol.

These honors acknowledged Clara's role as one of the state's founders, as well as her devotion to helping others despite the many barriers she faced herself. As the Colorado Pioneer Association said, Clara was a "kind old friend whose heart always responded to the cry of distress, and who, rising from the humble position of slave to the angelic type of a noble woman, won our sympathy and commanded our respect."

# FLORENCE SABIN

❦

(1871–1953)

## Distinguished Scientist

Five-year-old Florence Sabin was touring a Denver school with her mother when she noticed a group of students drinking from a wooden pail. As each child finished sipping water from the ladle, he or she handed it to the next person waiting in line. Florence, thirsty from walking, tugged at her mother.

"I want a drink, too," she said.

"No," her mother firmly replied. "All your life I want you to remember not to drink out of anyone else's cup, no matter how clean it looks."

Florence was puzzled by her mother's warning, but for the rest of her life she remembered what she later described as that "first lesson in good public health practices." It was the first of many lessons she learned on the way to becoming one of the nation's leading health researchers and teachers.

Florence reached the top of her profession despite many barriers that stood in the way of women interested in science and medicine. She became the first woman elected to the National Academy of Sciences, the first female full professor at one of the nation's top medical schools, and the first female president of the American Association of Anatomists.

Yet, despite her groundbreaking accomplishments, Florence remained a modest woman who preferred the anonymity of her laboratory and classroom to the public stage. She sought neither fame nor fortune but toiled to find a way to improve the human condition.

"A time will come when men and women will live their allotted span quietly, peacefully, without illness, free from pain, until they pass gently, as a tired child closes sleepy eyes, from this world to the next," she once said, voicing the goal to which she devoted her life.

Even after her retirement from teaching and research in 1938, Florence couldn't resist getting involved in efforts to improve Colorado's public health system. She lobbied for some of the nation's strongest public health laws, thereby enabling many Coloradans to lead longer and healthier lives.

Dr. Alfred Cohn of the Rockefeller Institute once said of Florence:

> *How came you to possess these many skills and virtues? . . . It*
> *has been, I think, because of your great humanity. You have*
> *cared deeply for your kind. And men have come to recognize in*
> *you that rare total person—of wisdom and of sentiment—heart*
> *and mind in just and balanced union.*

Florence became that "rare total person" in spite of—or perhaps because of—a sorrowful childhood. She was born in Central City, Colorado, on November 9, 1871, one of two daughters of George and Serena Sabin. Two younger brothers died in infancy, and her mother died on Florence's seventh birthday.

Her father, a mine superintendent, felt incapable of caring for his two young girls, so he enrolled them in a Denver boarding school. Eventually, they were hustled off to live with relatives in Chicago and then Vermont. It was while attending the Vermont Academy, a fine girls' school, that Florence first developed her love of science.

In 1889 Florence joined her older sister, Mary, at Smith College—one of the few institutions of higher learning in the nation that accepted women. Always painfully shy, Florence buried herself in her books and avoided socializing. When she looked in the mirror, she saw a homely girl with frizzy hair and squinty eyes. She doubted any man would ever want to marry her, so she committed herself to building a career.

Science, especially medicine, was the subject that intrigued her most. She had relatives who were doctors, and her father had dreamed of becoming one, too. But she knew society had trouble accepting female physicians. There was a practical problem, too: Few medical schools admitted women students.

Still, Florence was inspired by the idea of becoming a doctor. Sitting at her dormitory desk, she absently scribbled on a piece of paper: "Florence Sabin, M.D. . . . Dr. Florence Sabin . . . Dr. Florence . . ." She liked the ring of it.

But soon another barrier threw itself in her path. Her father's health failed and his mining ventures faltered. He could no longer afford to pay Florence's tuition, so she took a job teaching at a Denver boarding school for two years and then returned to Smith College as an assistant instructor. She scrimped and saved every penny she could.

During Florence's junior year at Smith, she learned that Johns Hopkins University in Baltimore was opening a new medical school. Three wealthy women had pledged money toward its construction, but only on the condition that women be admitted on the same basis as men. In 1896 Florence was among the first sixteen women to take advantage of this opportunity. She excelled despite a daunting schedule that included embryology, physiology, and physiological chemistry. She particularly liked histology and anatomy, which were taught by a brilliant professor, Franklin P. Mall. According to Mary Kay Phelan, author of *Probing the Unknown: The Story of Florence Sabin:*

> *Early in her Hopkins career she heard [Mall] quoted as having said that from among ten thousand students, there might be one thousand who were highly intelligent. Out of this thousand perhaps five would start in research. All five could prepare specimens but only one would become a trained investigator. Already Florence's interest in research was stimulated. If only she could be that one in ten thousand.*

Florence soon demonstrated that she had the aptitude. In her second year she published a research paper titled "On the Anatomical Relations of the Nuclei of Reception of the Cochlear and Vestibular Nerves." Doing so was a rare honor for such a young student. Clearly, here was a budding scientist of abundant promise.

By her third year Florence was caring for patients. During her fourth year she delivered nine babies, some of them in shacks with no indoor plumbing. She preferred the quiet of a laboratory to the chaos of doctoring under such primitive conditions. So when Dr. Mall asked her to build a model of a newborn's brain stem, she jumped at the chance. No one had ever built such a model, and she was flattered to be given a task of much great significance.

Florence devoted every spare moment to the project. First she carefully dissected a brain stem. Then she used her observations to produce a three-dimensional model. When doctors studied the finished product, they were stunned to find that Florence had uncovered new information about the structure of the human brain.

In 1900 Florence graduated from Johns Hopkins and began her medical internship. At the same time, she continued her research and wrote about her findings. Her book, *Atlas of the Medulla and Mid-brain,* was for years considered the most authoritative text on brain stems.

Florence's friends encouraged her to become a practicing physician, but she was happier conducting research.

"All good laboratory workers are good cooks," she told them. "And I like to cook."

Eventually, Florence shifted her inquiries to the lymphatic system, which plays a critical role in the immune system by circulating body fluids that nourish and cleanse cells. She read all that she could on the topic—much of it in German—and then outlined the experiments she needed to reach her goals. Her research showed that lymphatic vessels develop from layers of cells in special fetal veins. This finding proved earlier theories wrong—and earned her a $1,000 award for the best scientific thesis written by a woman.

More important, Florence's breakthroughs were shattering the widespread belief that women lacked the drive, patience, and intellectual capacity to be good researchers.

"When the results of Florence's work became known, she was acknowledged as one of the first pioneers in proving that women can do work of the same caliber as men," according to biographer Phelan.

Florence's accuracy and originality contributed to her growing reputation as a top-notch researcher. As she squinted into a microscope, she kept her eyes open to new ideas. She would not be bound by conventional wisdom. She also wasn't afraid of being wrong and once wrote:

> *The investigator who holds back his conclusions until he is absolutely sure, never progresses far. When I reach certain conclusions, I do not hesitate to publish them, even though after further study, I may find I was wrong; then I do not hesitate to say that I have changed my mind.*

As Florence's star rose, Johns Hopkins officials decided to break with tradition. They allowed Dr. Mall to add a woman—Florence—to the staff of his anatomy department. Florence was thrilled. She could now support herself doing something she really loved.

Of course, mankind benefited, too. Florence was destined to make more valuable discoveries, including the role of white blood cells called monocytes in defending the body against infection. She also developed a method that allowed her to study living cells through a microscope. Researchers everywhere eventually adopted her technique.

In 1905 Florence was promoted to associate professor of anatomy, the university's first full-time female faculty member. Other academic honors and speaking engagements from around the world soon followed. When Mall died in 1917, Florence had all the credentials necessary to replace him as head of the department. But university officials balked at giving the job to a woman, even one as accomplished as she. They played it safe and hired a man.

Florence's feminist friends and pupils were outraged, but she ignored their entreaties to resign in protest.

"I'll stay, of course," she told them. "I have research in progress."

Johns Hopkins did offer her something of a consolation prize—she was promoted to full professor, another first for a woman at the medical school.

As a teacher, Florence influenced a new generation of researchers and doctors. From 1902 to 1925 all the freshman medical students at Johns Hopkins were required to take her anatomy course. They found her to be a tough taskmaster. She insisted that her students check and recheck all observations and discover answers independently. When one young man kept pestering her in class with questions about obscure topics, Florence soon realized that he was trying to fritter away time to prevent her from giving the next day's assignment. The next time he asked a question, Florence assigned him to find the answer in a two-volume textbook written in German. He was to report to the class on his findings the next day.

Despite her no-nonsense approach, Florence developed lifelong friendships with students and colleagues, shedding her shyness as her confidence grew. She loved to host dinner parties, and invitations to them were prized because she was such a good cook and conversationalist. She enjoyed inviting a mélange of guests—lawyers, writers, artists, musicians, students, and professors—and assigning them sides in debates on world affairs, art, literature, and politics. One of her guests was Gertrude Stein, who flunked out of medical school but made quite a name for herself as a writer.

Florence's parties gave people a chance to see a more intimate side of her.

"She developed a rare kind of affection, which was never imprisoning or demanding, but always left people free," said Dr. Lawrence Kubie, a student who became an internationally famous psychiatrist. "Everyone who touched her life felt this. . . . To them all she brought affection, simplicity and a spirit of unassuming and irrepressible youthfulness."

Some of Florence's best friends were suffragettes. She did her bit for women's rights by marching in parades, writing for feminist publications, and eventually becoming chairwoman of the National Women's Party. She also actively urged young women to consider careers in science.

"It matters little whether men or women have the more brains; all we women need to do to exert our proper influence is just to use all the brains we have," she once said.

Despite her long association with Johns Hopkins, Florence couldn't pass up an offer in 1925 to create a new department of cellular studies at New York City's Rockefeller Institute, the world's preeminent research facility. Over the next thirteen years, she supervised eleven research projects, some of which led to key discoveries about the causes and characteristics of tuberculosis, one of the world's leading killers.

Florence also championed the Gotham Hospital Plan, an endowment designed to help impoverished women pay their hospital bills. She didn't succeed in implementing the plan, but it did serve as a model for subsequent hospital insurance programs.

Florence continued to win accolades for her path-breaking work. In 1929 *Pictorial Review* magazine awarded her five thousand dollars for the "most distinctive contribution made by an American woman to American life in the fields of art, science and letters." President Herbert Hoover invited her to the White House. *Good Housekeeping* named her one of the twelve greatest living American women, choosing her over Jane Addams and Helen Keller. Fifteen colleges awarded her honorary degrees. In 1951 her home state named a building on the University of Colorado campus after her, and eight years later it made her the subject of one of two statues representing Colorado in the US Capitol Statuary Hall.

Dr. Simon Flexner, director of the Rockefeller Institute, once described her as "the greatest living woman scientist and one of the foremost scientists of all time."

Florence had certainly earned the right to retire in 1938. At the age of sixty-seven, she returned to Colorado to live quietly with her sister. But when residents discovered the famous doctor in their midst, they asked her to help fix the state's ailing public health system. It was a huge task. Colorado had one of the worst public health records in the nation. The state spent less than most on public health despite having abysmal death rates due to disease and infant mortality.

"We think of our state as a health resort, but we're dying faster than people in most states," Florence contended.

At the age of seventy-three, Florence crisscrossed the state, investigating its public health problems and campaigning for more funding and new health laws to replace those enacted six decades earlier. She forcefully lobbied the state's movers and shakers. One senator later remembered being accosted in a drugstore by "this little bump of a woman with a twinkly sort of smile that made her eyeglasses seem to light up."

Florence's health agenda dominated the 1946 election in Colorado. When the newly elected governor was asked how he planned to get the program through the legislature, he replied, "I'll have the little old lady on my side. There isn't a man in the legislature who wants to tangle with her. She's an atom bomb. She's a dynamo."

In fact Florence succeeded in getting most of her legislative agenda passed. The "Sabin Health Laws" became national models.

Next, Florence turned her attention to health issues in Denver. She became the city manager of health and charities and pressed for better sewage disposal, garbage collection, rat reduction, restaurant sanitation, and tuberculosis treatment. Within two years Denver's death rate plunged to half of what it had been before her tenure. Florence donated her salary to medical research.

Florence finally retired from public service—this time for good—in 1951, so she could stay home and care for her ailing sister, Mary. Florence herself was seventy-nine.

"She had by then accomplished more for health in Denver than had been accomplished in all the city's previous history," said Colorado historian Hope Stoddard.

At the age of eighty-one, Florence's own health began to fail. She entered the hospital with pneumonia and, while watching her beloved Brooklyn Dodgers play in the World Series on October 3, 1953, she suffered a fatal heart attack during the seventh-inning stretch.

More than half a century later, Florence is still revered in Colorado. She reached the pinnacle of the science, teaching, and public health professions, and her work improved the lives of countless people. All of this she accomplished in the face of personal adversity and professional barriers. As writer Genevieve Parkhurst said in *Pictorial Review:*

> *Only by a complete devotion to her work has Dr. Sabin come to her large place in the world of science. Although she puts aside with a smile any hint that her way was not always easy, those who have followed her career closely, as associates and friends, declare that being a woman set many obstacles in her path. Wherever she triumphed it was by harder work and under greater difficulties then men would have encountered in the same circumstances. But she, herself, was never concerned with gaining credit. Her one desire was to make the best contribution she could toward easing humanity's pain.*

# JOSEPHINE ROCHE

(1886–1976)

Labor Advocate

Hundreds of embittered strikers picketed the Columbine Mine near Lafayette on a brisk fall day in 1927, demanding safer working conditions and higher wages. Suddenly, their shouts were interrupted by the burp of a machine gun that opened fire from atop a water tower. When the racket stopped, six coal miners lay dead and dozens more were wounded.

At her office in Denver, Josephine Roche shuddered when she heard news of the shootings—an echo of the infamous Ludlow Massacre of 1914. As one of the Columbine Mine's biggest shareholders, she knew she had to do something. She rushed to the mine and ordered the guards there to bury their rifles and the machine gun in an abandoned shaft. Then she met with the miners and promised them justice.

As soon as she returned to Denver, Josephine called an emergency meeting of the board of directors of the Rocky Mountain Fuel Company, which owned the mine. Some of the directors berated her for disarming the mine's guards. They worried that the angry workers might seek revenge.

But Josephine refused to back down. A self-professed believer in "humanity over profit," she realized that her best hope of improving conditions at the mine was to become the majority stockholder. So she bought out another owner and hired a company manager who was willing to cooperate with the workers. Promising to "substitute reason for violence, confidence for misunderstanding, integrity and good faith for dishonesty," she invited the United Mine Workers of America into the state, negotiated a union contract, established collective bargaining, and boosted wages to seven dollars a day—the highest in the industry.

Josephine wasn't simply being kindhearted. She was an astute business executive who believed that the workers would respond to her gestures of good faith. She was right. Productivity skyrocketed. The company was soon able to bill itself as Colorado's second-biggest producer of coal.

This was neither the first nor the last time that Josephine defied convention. A lifelong social activist who once described her only hobby as "humanity," she battled ignorance and injustice on many fronts. She fought gambling and prostitution as Denver's first policewoman. She campaigned to reform federal child labor laws. She worked to get the downtrodden out of soup lines and into jobs. She became one of the first women to serve in a presidential cabinet and the first to run for governor of Colorado.

"In 1936, Eleanor Roosevelt referred to her as one of America's greatest women," according to Rocky Mountain Fuel executive Gerald Armstrong. "She is a person with spirit, with love, and dedication [who] courageously faced many adversities."

Josephine's background offered little hint of the reformer she would become. She was born into a wealthy family in Neligh, Nebraska, on December 2, 1886. Her father, John Roche, was a prosperous banker and investor who could afford to send his daughter first to Vassar, where she earned a degree in sociology in 1908, and then to Columbia University, where she earned a master's degree in social work in 1910. In her master's thesis, "Economic Conditions in Relation to the Delinquency of Girls," she argued that low wages for women could force them into prostitution.

The Roches moved to Denver in 1906, when John Roche took the helm of Rocky Mountain Fuel. The company had mines in Louisville and west of Denver, as well as in Lafayette.

Even as a youngster, Josephine questioned conditions at the mines. "I was about twelve, and I wanted to go down in a coal mine," she told a reporter for the *Rocky Mountain News* in 1975. "My father said it was too dangerous. I can remember saying, 'If it is too dangerous for me, why isn't it just as dangerous for the men?'"

Josephine first turned her humanitarian instincts into action as a college student, when she did volunteer work with the poor in New York City. She also spent two summers working as an assistant for a juvenile court judge named Benjamin Lindsey. After graduation she got an intriguing offer from Denver Police Commissioner George Creel. He asked her to become the capital city's first female cop.

Josephine jumped at the chance, although it meant patrolling the theaters, saloons, gambling dens, and brothels of Denver's seediest district. As the city's new "inspector of amusements," her charge was to stop the exploitation of vulnerable young women. By all accounts, she did her job well—perhaps too well. She pushed so hard to close Denver's brothels that the Fire and Police Board was bombarded with complaints. The board fired her, alleging that she was hurting the business community.

"My activities on behalf of social betterment were obnoxious to the administration," she later wrote. Josephine appealed to the Civil Service Commission and won back her job, but she had only wanted to make her point. She quit the next day to become a probation officer for Judge Lindsey, who was gaining an international reputation for his juvenile justice reforms. The new position was a good fit. Josephine was an eager convert to the Progressive movement that was sweeping the country in the early 1900s, and in 1914 she became secretary of the Colorado Progressive Party.

That same year, a violent strike at a coal mine in southern Colorado convinced her to expand her crusade for social justice. On the morning of April 20, 1914, National Guard troops opened fire on a tent colony of some 1,200 coal miners and their families at Ludlow. The miners had been protesting their shabby treatment by Colorado Fuel and Iron, a company controlled by the Rockefellers. The soldiers and miners exchanged gunfire into the evening, when the guardsmen torched the colony and burned it to the ground. As many as twenty inhabitants died, including two women and eleven children. The Ludlow Massacre, one of the darkest chapters in American mining history, spawned a national outcry for mining industry reforms.

Josephine rushed to Ludlow to comfort the grief-stricken families. Then she escorted miners' wives to New York City to testify before the US Industrial Relations Commission.

During World War I, Josephine focused her attention and energy on helping the war effort. She served in England as a special agent for the Belgian Relief Committee and then returned to New England to organize the Belgian relief effort. Later, she directed the Foreign Language Information Service, which explained US war policies to the nation's foreign language newspapers. She also served as an editor at the US Children's Bureau and campaigned against child labor in the sugar beet industry. She once attacked industry for its apparent belief that "children are cheaper than machines."

When Josephine's father fell ill in 1925, she returned to Denver. As president of the Rocky Mountain Fuel Company, John Roche had a reputation as a "union-hating" man. When he died in 1927, Josephine inherited his stock and his board seat. She became vice president of the company in 1928 and president in 1929.

This was foreign territory for the social crusader. She was now one of those corporate officials whom she had held in such low regard. But she also recognized that she now had the power to directly benefit her workers. She quickly set out to implement her own progressive policies.

"Labor and management have been misjudged, even persecuted," she said. "Both are right. Big business needs big labor, and both can benefit if each will hear the other."

Josephine's employees responded to her efforts to improve their salaries and working conditions by becoming Colorado's most productive coal miners from 1929 to 1944. Later, when Colorado Fuel and Iron slashed prices and wages in an effort to sink Rocky Mountain Fuel, her workers persuaded their union to loan Roche's firm $80,000 to help keep it afloat. Her company struggled again the following year, and she was forced to cut wages from $7 a day to $5.25, but she offered her miners land to farm and credit at the company store to help them get by.

Although Josephine devoted much of her energy to the company, it wasn't her sole undertaking. In 1934 she challenged Colorado's incumbent governor, Ed Johnson, in the Democratic primary. In a report on the contest, *Literary Digest* noted that Josephine wasn't married—a two-year marriage had ended in divorce in 1920—but she was "distinctly feminine." The article continued:

> *There are none of the usual semimasculine trappings about her, such as flat-heeled shoes, and severely cut clothes. Her movements are quick, almost nervous, but they also are feminine. Her face is framed in soft waves of unbobbed hair: a smile comes readily to her firm lips. Many of her statements are punctuated by a pleasant, slightly nervous laugh. One might apply to her personality such adjectives as forceful, vital, direct.*

In her direct way Josephine campaigned to liberalize Colorado's outdated constitution, reform the tax system, build more highways, and bolster New Deal programs and humanitarian efforts. Her campaign slogan was "Roosevelt, Roche, and Recovery." By contrast, Johnson, her adversary, despised the idea of expanding the federal government in an effort to rescue the country from its economic woes.

Josephine's supporters included the progressive *Rocky Mountain News.* "As a private individual Miss Roche has already accomplished more than most Coloradoans in government," the newspaper said.

But Josephine's lengthy résumé and boundless enthusiasm weren't enough to overcome Johnson's advantage as an incumbent. She narrowly lost the race. Three days later, President Franklin Roosevelt appointed her assistant secretary to the treasury to oversee the US Public Health Service, making her only the second woman ever to hold a subcabinet post. Roosevelt considered Josephine "the very embodiment of the New Deal in Colorado." In her new job she directed fifty-six thousand federal workers in an effort to pull Americans out of poverty.

Josephine resigned in 1937, after her successor as president of Rocky Mountain Fuel died. She returned to Denver hoping to revive the now-ailing company, but it was beyond rescue. Growing numbers of consumers were switching from coal to natural gas, as the latter became more available and less expensive. The company was forced to file for bankruptcy in 1944. When it was resurrected, it ceased mining and focused on owning and managing land, water, and mineral rights. In 2006 it was sold to a private investor.

Bankruptcy trustee Wilbur Newton was quick to point out that Josephine was not to blame for the company's demise. He noted that Rocky Mountain Fuel had accumulated too much debt before she took charge. "She faced an impossible situation for seventeen years," he added. "She did not take the salary from the company she was entitled to, but turned it back. . . . [She] was tireless and unselfish in her efforts to preserve the company as a going business."

Because of her close ties to the United Mine Workers, the union hired Josephine to manage its welfare fund in 1947. The job took her away from Colorado, but she returned periodically for visits. She died in Bethesda, Maryland, on July 29, 1976, at the age of eighty-nine.

Once described by a reporter as a "tiny wisp of a woman whose eyes snap behind tinted glasses," Josephine made an indelible mark not only on the history of Colorado, but also on that of the nation. Most notably, perhaps, she demonstrated that mine managers could cooperate with labor to achieve mutual goals. In their book *Colorado Profiles*, John H. Monnett and Michael McCarthy summed up her contributions this way:

> *Josephine Roche was a woman for all seasons, and her seasons spanned almost the entire social and political life of twentieth-century Colorado. Progressive, New Dealer, laborite—her politics ran like a long, bright thread through the sometimes dark years, and so did her sense of social justice. Josephine Roche was one of Colorado's most brilliant businesswomen and one of its most potent social activists, and she fused the two entities into one of the state's most remarkable personalities. She was, simply, a woman of great grace who believed in the most fundamental of human tenets: That the sanctity of the human spirit was the most important thing in life.*

# IDAHO WOMEN

# LOUISE SIUWHEEM

## (1800–1853)

### Angel of the Coeur d'Alenes

War cries echoed through the hills, warning of the approach of an enemy tribe. The peaceful Coeur d'Alene encampment was suddenly under attack by avenging warriors from the Spokane tribe. The Spokanes charged the Coeur d'Alenes, encircling them with vastly superior numbers well prepared for battle.

Seeing her tribe outnumbered and realizing her people had no chance to survive such a surprise attack, Louise ran to her tepee and grabbed the large wooden cross she kept there. Holding the cross above her head, the pious woman marched through the encampment, imploring her people to follow her. The parade of chanting Coeur d'Alenes, led by Louise, marched straight at their menacing enemies.

The Spokane warriors could not believe their eyes. The sight of this woman, bearing a cross, dumbfounded them and filled them with fear and awe. The men lay down their weapons and retreated in great haste, vowing never again to challenge the Coeur d'Alenes.

Legend has it that this pious, nineteenth-century Joan of Arc saved her tribe from certain death with her bravery and unwavering Christian faith on more than one occasion.

When a Nez Perce war chief sent an envoy by canoe across Lake Coeur d'Alene to challenge her tribe into battle, the people turned to Louise, a respected tribal leader, for their response. She sent word back to the Nez Perce chief that her people were Christians, not warriors; and, if the Nez Perce stayed on their side of the lake, the Coeur d'Alenes would not fight them, but if they approached, they would all be killed. Thus dissuaded, the Nez Perce chief took his war party and departed.

Although there is no way to verify them, these legends have been passed along throughout the years. Stories state that Coeur d'Alene chiefs respected Louise Siuwheem for her wisdom and bravery and sought her counsel ever after and that Louise's intervention prevented much bloodshed between the Coeur d'Alenes and neighboring tribes. Louise held a position of great respect as the sister of the head chief, Stelaam, an iron-willed ruler whom many, including early priests, found difficult. Louise often acted as an intermediary on her brother's behalf, which may be the root of such stories.

Born around 1800, Louise was the daughter of a chief of the Coeur d'Alene tribe. They called themselves Schitzu'Umsh, but early French fur trappers, who found the people to be shrewd traders, sharp or hard-hearted like needles, dubbed the tribe Coeur d'Alene, meaning "heart of the needle, or awl." The chief's daughter was given the name Siuwheem,[1] or "Tranquil Waters," in the language of her people.

Siuwheem was married when she was a teenager to a member of the Spokane tribe called Polotkin. The couple raised three sons. When her husband became crippled, Louise took on the role of provider for the family as well as nurse to her invalid husband.

Siuwheem's grandfather, the great Chief Circling Raven, had dreamed of a visit by two black-robed angels who descended from heaven to teach his people of a great spirit. This vision was passed on by Chief Circling Raven to his children and grandchildren. In April 1842 Jesuit priest Father Pierre-Jean De Smet, "the Saint Paul of the West," arrived among the Coeur d'Alene tribe. Father De Smet was the superior of the Rocky Mountain Missions when he met three Coeur d'Alene families who had traveled east on a buffalo hunt. The families had their children baptized by the priest and urged him to visit their tribe. Father De Smet was welcomed by the Coeur d'Alenes, but none received him so joyously as Siuwheem, who saw in him the fulfillment of her grandfather's prophecy.

Father De Smet described his initial impressions of Siuwheem: "Before her baptism, even, she was remarkable for her rare modesty and reserve, great gentleness, and a solid judgment. Her words were everywhere listened to with admiration and pleasure, and her company sought in all families."

Siuwheem and Polotkin were among the first of their people to be baptized. At his baptism Polotkin took the name Adolph, and Siuwheem took the name Louise, meaning "defender of the people." The priest sanctified the union of Adolph and Louise in the eyes of the church by performing an official marriage ceremony.

"Enlightened by a special grace," Father De Smet said of how Louise used her influence to induce many Indian families to follow her to the banks of Lake Coeur d'Alene to hear the priest preach the law of God. After her baptism Louise renounced all material wealth and pledged devotion to the priests, "I will follow the Black Gowns to the end of the world. . . I wish to profit by their presence and their instructions to learn to know the Great Spirit well, to serve him faithfully, and to love him with all my heart."

---

1. "Sighouin" is the spelling used by Father De Smet and later writers. Father Connolly of the current Sacred Heart Mission spells and pronounces the name "Siuwheem," as it appears on her headstone.

In 1843 the Jesuits built a mission on the banks of the St. Joe River near the southern end of Lake Coeur d'Alene. During construction of the St. Joseph's Mission, Louise moved her family onto the grounds to be near the missionaries and "The Lodge of the Lord." Father Point became the mission's superior, succeeded by Father Joset in 1845. The Coeur d'Alene Mission was Father Joseph Joset's favorite mission; and, even after being appointed superior of the Missions of the Northwest, Father Joset chose to remain with the Coeur d'Alene people, making his headquarters on their land.

While still caring for the needs of her invalid husband and children, this frail woman, who was often in delicate health herself, spent all available time receiving instruction from the priests and sharing her knowledge and enthusiasm with other members of her tribe. The priests struggled with the Coeur d'Alene language. Father De Smet described his difficulty comprehending and speaking it even after many years working among the tribe. Louise offered the missionaries invaluable help in translating and teaching her people. She was given the position of tribal catechist, head teacher of the catechism, and devoted herself to religious instruction. Thus Louise became known as a great teacher.

In addition to teaching Louise took the position of defender of her religion. She was often at odds with the medicine men of her tribe who, fearing the loss of their own power, tried to disrupt the work of the missionaries. Frequently putting her own safety in jeopardy, Louise tirelessly worked to oppose the powerful medicine men. She boldly intruded upon them, entering their lodges uninvited, in order to lecture them.

One of the leaders of the medicine men was Natatken, a relative of Louise's who staunchly resisted Louise's teaching. Louise persevered, however, until she finally led Natatken and his wife and children directly to the priest to receive the sacrament of regeneration. Natatken took the Christian name of Isidore and became one of the most zealous members of the church, responsible for converting many of his followers to Christianity.

Louise also sought to ensure that once converted, her tribesmen did not revert to unsanctioned practices such as gambling. Chief Emotestsulem, who had been baptized as Peter Ignatius, became consumed by a prior addiction to gambling after his conversion. Upon learning of this Louise walked for two days to find the chief and return him to his duties as a tribal leader. Though it was contrary to tradition for an Indian man to publicly accept criticism and advice from a woman, this woman commanded such respect, even among men and chiefs, that she was able to convince Emotestsulem to renounce his habit and repent. Louise met each challenge with patience, courage, and perseverance.

This gentle woman harbored a special love for the children of the tribe, especially the young girls. Father De Smet wrote of her work among the children:

*By her motherly vigilance over the behavior of her children,*
*by the simple and persuasive gentleness with which she treated*
*them on all occasions, Louise had inspired them with the most*
*profound respect and entire confidence . . . that . . . a single word*
*from the lips of their good mother, was an absolute order, a law*
*for them, which they accomplished . . . with eagerness and joy.*

It was not uncommon for Louise to take in children whose parents could not care for them. Louise adopted two children who were unwanted because of their severe disabilities. One such orphan was Ignatius, a crippled, blind child who was stubborn, unruly, and a most disruptive member of the family. Though both children she adopted died at early ages, they received the same love and attention that Louise provided her own children, no matter how difficult their needs.

Louise Siuwheem's lodge became a shelter for young girls in need of counsel. She eagerly took them under her wing, offering guidance and instruction. In recognition of her endless work with children, she became known among her tribesmen as the "Good Grandmother."

This Good Samaritan was also an accomplished healer. Father Gazzoli (successor of Father Joset) said that he never arrived to administer to a sick or injured person that Louise was not already there ahead of him. She devoted herself to nursing the sick and dying no matter what time of the day or night she was called.

Although Father De Smet had intended for the St. Joseph Mission to be a permanent settlement, the yearly spring flooding of the St. Joe River raised havoc with the mission's crops. Father Joset decided to build another mission, which was started in 1848, on the banks of the Coeur d'Alene River about 12 miles east of the lake. The new mission was designed by Father Ravalli, who had visions of an elegant Doric-style church and grand mission. Using crude tools and makeshift supplies, the Jesuits and the Coeur d'Alene people set out to build the magnificent mission, a labor that was to take them five years.

Louise's leadership again proved invaluable to the priests when she convinced the tribal members to devote their labor to the construction of the new mission. Building of lodges was not seen as traditional work for Indian men, who scorned it as women's work. Louise offered high praise to those people who labored on the project and public criticism to those who refused to work. In the end more than 300 tribal members participated in the mission's construction.

The natural leader showed great managerial skills in organizing the labor of her people. Women and children were placed on teams and assigned such duties as cutting straw, mixing mortar, carrying water, and weaving grass mats. Built without nails, the church had a framework formed from giant timbers connected by willow bars and woven grass plastered with adobe, which formed walls a foot thick. The facade was later sided with wooden planks. Through the devotion and labor of Louise and her Coeur d'Alene people, the Mission of the Sacred Heart of Jesus was finished in 1853, where it still stands near Cataldo, Idaho.

In 1853 Louise became bedridden by illness, said to be consumption (tuberculosis). That summer she called upon Father Gazzoli to administer last rites. On her deathbed she implored her husband, Adolph, not to return to the home of his people, where there were no priests. Her dying wish was for her children to live good, spiritually rich lives and for those around her to join in one last hymn. Before the singing of the hymn was finished, Louise had passed away.

One of those kneeling beside the bed ran out crying. "'Siuwheem, good Siuwheem is dead.' The cry was taken up and echoed in the valley and the foot of the high mountains which encircle the Residence of the Sacred Heart," described Father De Smet in his writings on the life of Louise Siuwheem. A sudden desolation and grief went through the tribe as they mourned for a beloved mother and grandmother, a faithful friend, teacher, translator, nurse, and social worker who led her people through peaceful times and war times and had lived in great poverty without ever showing her own needs or suffering.

Louise was buried in a plain coffin built by her youngest son and placed into a grave dug by her children. With a prayer and a personal farewell, each person in attendance at her funeral threw a handful of dirt onto the coffin. Her service was performed by Father Gazzoli, who believed Siuwheem to be "the spiritual directress, the guardian angel of her whole tribe."

On August 15 of each year, Coeur d'Alene tribal members make a pilgrimage to the old mission in memory of the good grandmother and the coming of the "Black Robes." Today no one is exactly sure where on the mission grounds Louise's grave lies. In 1985 Louise's great-granddaughter, Blanche La Sarte, and Father Tom Connolly had a monument placed at the old mission to honor Louise.

The Sacred Heart Mission, now more commonly called the Cataldo Mission or Old Mission, has the distinction of being the oldest standing building in Idaho. In 1975 the mission became an Idaho state park, officially titled Old Mission State Park. It stands today as a lasting monument to Louise Siuwheem and her people.

# KITTY C. WILKINS

(1857–1936)

## Queen of Diamonds

Nothing could have prepared the two young cowboys for their encounter with the approaching rider. A golden palomino galloped up the dusty ranch-house road that late summer day. The horse's flowing yellow mane and tail were a perfect match for the rider's own flaxen mane. The startled cowboys stared in disbelief at the stunningly beautiful blue-eyed blonde coming toward them. After riding for several days along the border between Idaho and Nevada in search of work with a cattle outfit, the gorgeous woman before them seemed like an apparition.

Regaining his composure, the younger of the two asked, "Can you tell us where we can find the boss?"

"I am the boss," replied the woman firmly.

The two youthful cowboys had just met the legendary "Horse Queen of Idaho," Kitty Wilkins. Through her talent for raising and trading horses and penchant for garnering publicity, Kitty also earned titles such as "The Golden Queen" and "The Queen of Diamonds." The latter was a reference to her ownership of the Diamond Ranch.

The daughter of two western pioneers, J. R. and Laura K. Wilkins, Kitty was born in Jacksonville, Oregon, in 1857. Twenty-one-year-old J. R. Wilkins and seventeen-year-old Laura were married in 1853 in Fort Madison, Iowa, where he had moved from Indiana and she from Maine. Shortly after their marriage, the Wilkins couple joined a wagon train to follow the Oregon Trail west. They resided in Oregon City and then in the Rogue River Valley at Jacksonville, where Kitty was born, before moving to California. A gold rush brought the family to Florence, Idaho, in 1862. Kitty took great pride in the fact that her mother was the first woman to arrive at the gold camp. She said, "I feel that my brother and I can justly claim that our parents came to Idaho before any others."

After making several more moves in and out of Idaho, J. R. Wilkins settled his wife and children on a large spread in southern Idaho's Bruneau Valley. The Wilkins Island Ranch was located on land at the fork of the Bruneau River near Jarbidge Mountain, rather than on an actual island. The Wilkinses' holdings spread to other outposts along the Snake River, at Mountain Home and into Nevada. Their range was 75 miles away from the main ranch, stretching into the Owyhee Mountains.

Although her father had several thousand head of cattle and horses, Kitty always preferred raising horses to cattle. In addition to loving horses, the shrewd Miss Wilkins saw them as much more profitable, stating, "A 3 or 4 year-old steer ... worth but $20, while a horse of the same age is worth $85–$100... horses are much more easily raised and do not require half the care."

Considering it romantic, Kitty loved to tell reporters about her start in the business. Neighbors bidding the Wilkins family goodbye upon one of their departures from Oregon gave two-year-old Kitty two twenty-dollar gold pieces. Her father bought the toddler a filly, and, as Kitty put it, "from the increase all of my bands have come."

Kitty was a gifted rider whose brothers taught her to shoot both pistols and rifles proficiently, "that being a necessary part of a woman's education out there [in the West] in those days." Kitty was sent to a private school for girls in San Jose, California, for her formal education and social refinement. She also traveled throughout the United States to all the major cities as part of her cultural enlightenment.

Upon returning to Idaho she was at first lonely, until she developed a taste for the family horse business. Kitty later expressed her feelings about Idaho and her business to an Eastern reporter, "Do I like living away out in Idaho? Oh, so much! I go out to roundups in the spring and fall and enjoy myself ever so much. It is a fascinating business and grows upon you."

When her father took young Kitty on one of his trips east to a horse market, she became hooked on the business of selling horses. From that time on she constantly accompanied her father to market his horses. Within a few years of that first trip, Kitty had developed her own distinct marketing plan and could sell horses better than her father. She was a shrewd businesswoman and an excellent judge of horseflesh. She prided herself on selling only high-quality stock. To one Midwestern reporter she boasted, "I bring the best stock to market that comes from the West. I never ship a blemished animal from the ranch. They are all sound when they leave there."

Kitty and her younger brothers eventually took over their father's ranch. While her brothers concentrated on cattle ranching, Kitty took over the horse outfit. No one ever questioned Kitty's authority or business sense. She was the undisputed boss of the Diamond Ranch.

Wild horses abounded on the range between Nevada's Humboldt River and Idaho's Snake River. These mustangs became the property of anyone who could catch and put a brand on them. Kitty saw a way to expand her own small herd, started with the purchase of the forty-dollar filly when she was just two. She hired the best riders and set out to claim every unbranded mustang from the Nevada/Idaho line to the Owyhee River in Oregon. Kitty registered the Diamond Brand, a brand that was to become synonymous with fine horse stock, and set to work branding every wild horse she could bring in.

In addition to registering her own brand, hiring the finest cowboys available, and raising sound stock, Kitty marketed her horses in the most lucrative fashion. She bought stallions from around the world to develop her stock. Her lines included Clydesdales, Percherons, Morgans, Normans, and Hambletonians. After this she claimed to have "no native Oregon or Spanish horses" on her ranch.

Rumors put the Diamond Ranch holdings at 20,000 head of horses. In reality that number may have been closer to 5,000 head on the ranch at any one time. It took up to forty men during fall roundup to cut out and brand stock on the Diamond Ranch.

Kitty's marketing skills got her contracts with lucrative horse markets in the East and as far away as Dawson City in the Yukon Territory. One of her best customers was the US Cavalry. At one point she was supplying six train cars of broke horses every two weeks to Eastern markets. Since each stock car held twenty-six horses, Kitty's hands had to break 156 horses for each shipment. Because the Diamond Ranch cowboys were breaking broncs continuously, they became known throughout the West as some of the West's most skilled riders.

Kitty Wilkins ran the "hardest riding outfit west of the Mississippi River," according to Harvey St. John, Kitty's youngest bronc rider and personal friend. Cowboys who rode with the Diamond Ranch were among the finest in the world. Buffalo Bill's Wild West Show hired some of the Wilkinses' horsemen; others became top rodeo champions. The young cowboy described riding for Kitty: "If a man weren't a good rider when he went to work for her, he was a good rider when he left or he wasn't riding at all—unless in a hearse."

The Queen of Diamonds ruled her cowboys with an iron hand. Although they were hard-edged, rough-hewn characters, some of whom became notorious outlaws, they respected Kitty, and her word was law on the Diamond Range. Any hand that disobeyed her was run off the range immediately.

The lovely horse queen caused an instant sensation when she arrived in the East to market her animals. As her obituary characterized it: "The sight of a beautiful, slender, young blonde, dressed in modish fashion, personally selling her stock, and knowing a complete knowledge of each horse's good points, created a furore [sic]." Citizens of the Eastern cities were awed by Kitty Wilkins's beauty and grace. She was interviewed wherever her travels took her. A reporter in St. Louis was stunned by Kitty's looks and so described their meeting:

> *The reporter was hardly prepared to meet the tall young*
> *woman, dressed in a swell, tailor-made costume, her blonde*
> *curls surmounted by a dainty Parisian creation, who greeted*

*him with perfect self-possession. One might be excused for imagining that Western ranch life would coarsen any woman, no matter what her natural tendencies might be, but one glimpse of Miss Wilkins is enough to completely dissipate the idea. She is a strikingly attractive woman.*

Meanwhile, a Sioux City reporter described Kitty as a

*. . . tall stately blonde, with fluffy, golden hair, large blue eyes that have quite a knack of looking clear through one, regular features and pearly teeth which glisten and sparkle when she smiles, and she has a habit of smiling very frequently. Her lips are red and full, and her mouth and chin denote a certain firmness of manner, no doubt acquired in her peculiar calling.*

San Francisco awarded Kitty their "Palm" for beauty when she visited that city. This was an honor bestowed by the local newspapers and reported in the society pages.

Being the most notable, if not only, woman horse dealer in the country, Kitty attracted a great deal of attention from the press. She was adept at public relations, promoting her fame wherever she went.

The beautiful Kitty never married. It is said that she loved only one man in her life—the Diamond Ranch's top foreman. He and Kitty were engaged to be married when the engagement ended violently. Kitty's fiancé was shot in a typical range dispute over a watering hole. Reportedly Kitty never showed a romantic interest in another man.

The end of World War I also signaled the end to prosperity in the horse market. Automobiles and machinery were taking the place of horses. Irrigation projects took over the once-expansive horse ranges.

Kitty saw the changes occurring and, already a wealthy woman, decided to retire from the business. She chose to spend her remaining years in a grand home in Glenns Ferry. People who knew Kitty claimed that her beauty never really faded. Even in retirement she kept abreast of current issues and progress across America.

A respected Idaho pioneer, Kitty was a guest of honor at the Boise Centennial Celebration. She headed the pioneer parade in a horse-drawn carriage. The horse queen's ornate saddle was put on display at the Idaho State Historical Museum, along with her portrait.

Kitty C. Wilkins died of a heart attack at the age of seventy-nine on October 8, 1936, at her home in Glenns Ferry, and was buried in Mountain Home.

Perhaps the passing of this notable pioneer horsewoman can best be described in Kitty's own words. When her brother and business partner, John, passed away just three weeks prior to her own death, Kitty reflected:

*The years are taking their toll of these early pioneers and few remain to tell us of the romantic beginning of the wonderful west we know. It is difficult for us, in our ease and comfort of present day surroundings, to conceive of the hardships, the privations and the suffering endured by these men and women that they might establish and build up a country for their families and those who would follow.*

# EMMA RUSSELL YEARIAN

(1866–1951)

## The Sheep Queen of Idaho

When the train suddenly stopped in the middle of the vast prairie, the petite girl from Illinois stepped out and saw her first western sky. For the first time this young woman, who had dreamed of going west from the time she was a small child, smelled the musty-sweet aroma of sagebrush, heard the sound of a nighthawk dive, and witnessed millions of stars blanketing the night sky. It was as if she were a part of it all—part of this magnificent western prairie night that fall of 1887.

Emma Russell was born in Leavenworth, Kansas, on February 21, 1866. Her parents, William W. Russell and Della (Burbridge) Russell, moved to Illinois when Emma was a small child. William Russell, a Civil War veteran and son of a Revolutionary War veteran, was captain of the guards at Maynard Penitentiary in Illinois. At a time when most women were educated in and for the home, Emma graduated from high school in Chester, Illinois, and then from Southern Illinois Normal College at Carbondale in 1883.

In the fall of the year 1887, she said goodbye to her widowed father and set out to follow her dreams west to the Rockies. Emma arrived in the Salmon River country and found work, first as a governess and then as a teacher, following jobs from town to town until she landed at a one-room, sod-roofed schoolhouse in the Lemhi Valley. The young schoolteacher boarded with a prominent local family from whom she bought a stocky gelding, which she rode sidesaddle to and from her teaching job.

For weekend entertainment Emma traveled to dances held in various ranch houses. She played the popular tunes of the day on the piano for local partygoers. On many cold nights it was necessary to place heated rocks in the bottom of the buggy to keep the musicians' feet warm as they traveled through the cold night air. At these ranch-house dances, a fiddle player named Thomas Yearian caught the young schoolteacher's eye.

Thomas was a cattle rancher in the valley. His father had discovered gold and wisely invested the money in land rather than squandering his windfall as many miners had. Thomas Hodge Yearian and Emma Russell were married on

April 15, 1889. The couple settled on the Yearians' ranch in Lemhi Canyon, on land Thomas's parents had homesteaded. While living on the homestead in a log cabin covered with a sod roof, Emma and Thomas had six children, one of whom died in childhood.

The education of her children was a top priority for Emma, and the pursuit of this goal made Emma Yearian into one of Idaho's top businesswomen, and the only woman in Idaho to run a large sheep ranch. Emma knew education cost money, and the sheep ranchers seemed to have more money than the cattle ranchers in the area. Besides, she saw much of the grassy rangeland going to waste around her. She tried to talk Thomas into giving up cattle ranching for sheep. This he refused to do, but he did agree with her plan to add sheep to the ranch. In 1908 Emma traveled to Dillon, Montana, where she introduced herself to the bank president, who also served as Montana's governor, and asked for a loan to buy her first yearlings. Although he had his doubts about a woman running this business, her determination impressed the bank officer, and Emma was given her first loan. With the aid of a hired hand, her husband, and her ten-year-old son, Russell, the newly purchased 1,200 ewes were herded over the mountains and into Idaho.

Rancor left over from Idaho's Range Wars of the 1890s still festered between cattle and sheep ranchers. The Yearians' Lemhi River Valley neighbors were not pleased with Emma's new endeavor. Cattlemen hated sheep, claiming they ruined the range for cows by grazing clear to the roots, killing off all the grass. Although nobody pointed a gun at her, the neighbors did continually cause summons to be served on Emma, ordering her to appear in court and defend her violations of the Two-Mile Limit Law. Idaho's Two-Mile Limit Law was enacted so that no sheep could be legally grazed within 2 miles of another ranch property. The narrow channel of the Lemhi Valley made it impossible to herd the sheep without crossing into the 2-mile barrier. Though she was frequently summoned to court, she was never convicted, a fact she attributed to good lawyers.

The Two-Mile Limit Law and a need for more winter grazing land prompted Emma to buy up land from neighboring ranches. By 1933 Emma Yearian's 2,500-acre ranch consisted of 5,000 head of sheep. She installed a shearing plant on the home ranch at Lemhi and a lambing camp up the canyon. Emma personally ran the operation, from hiring camp tenders and herders to dealing with the wool buyers.

People thought of the ranch as Emma's, though she ran the sheep and Thomas ran the cattle. The sheep proved more profitable. On one trip to see her out-of-state bankers, when Emma arrived by train, sitting on a coffin in the baggage car for want of available seats in the passenger car, a reporter took her picture and dubbed her "the Sheep Queen of Idaho."

In 1910 Emma built a grand, six-bedroom house of limestone block. One of its kind in the valley, the home had a generator, sixteen-volt electric lights, and indoor plumbing. To Emma's thinking this new manor was a much superior abode in which to raise her family than the sod-roofed, log cabin had been.

The Sheep Queen was an astute monitor of world affairs. Her grandson, Thomas Savage, wrote in his semibiographical novel, "Nobody touched the newspapers until she had read them; each evening after supper she retired with them to the bedroom upstairs where she had her roll top desk. . . ." She studied world events, believing they set a pattern for future trends that could well affect her business. Closely following the events unfolding in Europe in 1911, Emma believed there would soon be a war there. So, predicting the start of World War I, and knowing the soldiers would need wool uniforms, Emma asked her bankers for a loan of $35,000 to increase her wool production in anticipation of this need. Of course her predictions were dead on, and her sheep ranch prospered through the war years.

Starting with a relatively small herd of inexpensive ewes, Emma developed one of Idaho's finest flocks of Rambouillets. She then bred Rambouillet rams with Cotswold ewes, producing fat lambs covered with abundantly thick, heavy wool—as she described them: "the best dual purpose sheep in this country."

Then came the winter of 1918. The previous summer had been unusually hot and dry, with the drought lasting well into fall. When snow hit, it hit with a vengeance. Blinding blizzards, howling winds, and below-freezing temperatures took their toll on the livestock in the valley. Hay was shipped in by train at a cost of four times the normal price. People whispered that this would be the end of the Sheep Queen. When the exorbitantly priced hay ran out, Emma got back on the train and went to see her banker, asking for a loan of $100,000. According to her grandson the banker wondered aloud why he should lend such a considerable sum of money to Emma at such a difficult time. "Because I believe in myself," was the Sheep Queen's reply. Emma Yearian returned to Lemhi with the money, which pulled the ranch through this difficult period.

Her considerable business acumen also brought the ranch through the Great Depression. During the Depression many previously successful ranchers lost everything. In her biography on Emma, Madge Yearian writes that during these years, "you could see cattle lying down dead of starvation." Emma came through, as she herself said, with "her head bloody but unbowed."

Mrs. Yearian also had her hand in many local organizations. Emma had been affiliated with the Order of the Eastern Star since 1890, and she was a member of the Episcopal Church of the Redeemer at Salmon. She was the first woman to serve on the Lemhi County Agricultural Agency Committee; she served on the Predatory Animal Board and held both the offices of president and vice-president of the Lemhi County Wool Growers' Association. Reportedly, she presided over the Wool Growers' Association while simultaneously heading the Cattle and Horse Growers' Association. A charter member of the County

Business and Professional Women's Club, she represented the group on a 1929 goodwill tour of Europe. During the tour Emma was introduced in Switzerland as a representative of the 52,000-member National Business and Professional Women's Club—and as the Sheep Queen of Idaho. A Swiss newspaper then reported that Emma was "the queen of 52,000 sheep."

In 1930 Emma ran for the Idaho State House of Representatives on the Republican ticket; Thomas was a Democrat. She became the first woman from Lemhi County to serve in the state legislature. The salary for legislators was five dollars per day during Emma's Depression-era tenure of 1931–1932. While serving in the House, Emma was chairman of the State Library Committee and sat on the Highways, Livestock, and Mining Committees. She is credited with the passage of Idaho's brand-inspection law, which substantially curbed the practice of rustling by imposing harsh penalties for altering brands on livestock. In honor of an earlier Lemhi Valley heroine, Emma sponsored the bill that created Sacajawea Park and another bill to install a monument to the Shoshone woman on top of the Continental Divide near Salmon, Idaho. Emma's bid for reelection met with defeat, as "Hoover Democrats" came into vogue across the nation. While Thomas, the Democrat, attended the town's election-night gala, Emma quietly sat by the radio at her son's home.

Emma had a knack for storytelling and enthralled locals with her tales of early Lemhi County. She was a definitive authority on agricultural laws and property and water rights, and people sought her advice on such matters. A generous benefactor for her favorite projects and charities, Emma never turned her back on a friend or employee. The sight of Emma Yearian touring her sheep ranch on foot with the aid of a walking stick became commonplace in her later years.

The end came for eighty-five-year-old Emma on Christmas Day, 1951. A week earlier she had suffered a massive heart attack while she sat at her dining room table writing Christmas cards. The entire town of Salmon closed down for the funeral of the Sheep Queen of Idaho. In 1977 the Idaho Commission on Women's Programs elected Emma Russell Yearian to the Idaho Women's Hall of Fame in recognition of her many accomplishments.

# KANSAS WOMEN

# LILLA DAY MONROE

(1858–1929)

Suffragist and Journalist, Counting Women's Votes and Stories

When she crept up to her grandmother's attic, Joanna Stratton didn't expect to find anything unusual. It was winter of 1975, and she was visiting her grandmother in Kansas while on break from Harvard. In all probability, she was bored.

Time moves slowly in the Midwest, especially when it's bitterly cold outside. When the air outside gets so cold it practically burns the skin to the touch, the whole world—for comfort's sake—shrinks down to the size of your home, where you can sit by the fire or burrow under a blanket with a cup of hot cocoa. So, with her world shrunk down to the size of an old Victorian home, Joanna went exploring upstairs.

It was something she always did when visiting her grandmother, this snooping around among tattered old ball gowns and once-fashionable hats, scanning titles of tattered books and magazines on dusty shelves, thumbing through boxes of family letters and silvery black-and-white photographs, opening trunks and drawers and cabinets to see what awaited her there. This was a day like any other day that Joanna had spent with relatives in Kansas.

Surely she must have known that her great-grandmother, the one who built this house in 1887, was a person of note in Kansas history. No doubt the family was proud that Lilla Day Monroe had been the first woman to practice law before the Kansas Supreme Court, that she had been a real spitfire and lobbied to have a statue dedicated to the memory of hardy pioneer women on the grounds of the Kansas State Capitol. The statue, still standing to this day, depicts a cloaked woman kneeling with an infant in one arm, the other arm wrapped around a studying boy, and a rifle slung across her knee. Her clothing drapes over her in a way that almost deifies her. This statue, Joanna must have known, was her grandmother's idea.

But she didn't go snooping through the attic looking for history with a capital *H*. She was just exploring, as we all do in grandparents' attics and basements, searching for clues about who our grandparents were before they were grandparents, who our parents were before they were parents, and, if we're lucky and our families have stayed in one place for long enough as Joanna's had, maybe even who our great-grandparents were before they were anything at all.

While indulging in this habitual time travel on that particular winter day, however, the dark-haired scholar stumbled upon the kind of thing scholars always dream of stumbling upon. She opened an old filing cabinet that had been pushed into a corner. Ducking her head to squeeze into the tight space, she began skimming the yellowing papers inside. She had just found the personal stories of eight hundred Kansas pioneer women, written in their own words. In her introductory remarks for *Pioneer Women: Voices from the Kansas Frontier,* Stratton wrote:

> *It was an exhilarating moment of discovery for me. As I sat poring over the carefully penned writings, a human pageantry came alive for me. . . . I shivered with Emma Brown in her rain-soaked soddy. I watched Hannah Hoisington defend a neighbor's cabin against a pack of wolves and marveled as Jenny Marcy confronted a stampede of Texas longhorns. I celebrated Christmas day with little Harriet Adams and joined in a polka with lighthearted Catherine Cavender. I saw Anna Morgan held hostage by the Cheyenne. I witnessed Mrs. Lecleve endure childbirth alone in her cabin. I sang hymns with Lydia Murphy Toothaker and campaigned for woman suffrage with the Reverend Olympia Brown.*

Lilla Day Monroe had believed, correctly, that one day, people would care to know how these hardy women lived and endured in the state's earliest days. The cowboy and the railroad worker and the bootlegger and the soldier had all been hallowed and mythologized. Nobody had asked, just yet, what women had been up to all that time. But she knew, or maybe just hoped, that one day surely someone would. She suspected, however, that it might be too late to get answers, so she took it upon herself to ask the questions and to preserve the answers so that when people got around to asking, these eight hundred answers would exist.

She placed her original call for Kansas pioneer women's personal memoirs in a magazine she edited. Her intent was simply to run the responses in that very magazine's pages. She did publish a few of the stories that way, but quickly realized that the flood of responses merited more than a series of magazine stories, which ran the risk of being printed today and forgotten tomorrow. She decided to continue compiling stories and then to dedicate herself to organizing the material for an eventual book. She quit her substantial work outside the home to focus her efforts on this project full-time. Her mail was never boring.

It contained heartache and triumph, suffering and redemption, once-ordinary details of a kind of daily life nearly forgotten by the early twentieth century. But Lilla got sick, and in 1929, she died before this grand opus ever saw print. Her great-granddaughter, Joanna Stratton, would complete and publish that book sixty-one years later, inspired by that fateful day spent rummaging in Lilla's attic.

Lilla Day Monroe was born in Indiana in 1858 and came to Kansas in 1884—at the tail end of what is now known as the "frontier era." She settled in Wakeeney, a western Kansas settlement created by pioneers traveling westward in search of better lives for themselves and their families. Many of them stopped about where Lilla stopped, at the midpoint between Kansas City and Denver, Colorado.

In short order, she met, fell in love, and married Lee Monroe, an attorney. Not only did she keep home and raise four children; she also clerked in her husband's law office. At home, she spent many grueling years stealing moments for her own study of the law. Eventually, she passed the bar exam. In 1895, Lilla Day Monroe became the first woman to practice before the Kansas Supreme Court. Knowing the law and the Constitution was important to her as she tirelessly championed what she believed to be the great causes of women—in particular, the cause of suffrage.

Her interest in the rights of women was sparked by a fairly ordinary scene that left a strong impression on her when she was just a little girl. On a visit to the general store, she happened to witness a disturbing scene.

A couple stood near the counter, and the woman asked the man if she could have a dollar. "To buy what?" the man asked. The woman explained that she needed a few things: some gingham, an apron. The other shoppers, like Lilla, could not help but eavesdrop. They became curious as to whether the woman would be given the dollar. Apparently, they did not do a very good job of pretending not to listen. The man realized he had an audience and played to it. Holding out the dollar, he quickly yanked it away as soon as his wife reached for it. When she realized she was being held up for ridicule, the woman began to cry—and so did Lilla. She would remember this story for the rest of her life.

In September 1906, she gave a talk on the history of the woman suffrage movement. In Kansas, at this time, women had the right to vote in municipal elections. This right had been granted decades earlier. And yet Kansas had not yet given its women the right to vote above and beyond the municipal level, and the United States had not yet granted universal suffrage.

Lilla began her speech frankly. "Before entering upon this history, I think it is my right to establish some sort of comradeship between myself and the gentlemen present by telling them just how it happens that I was chosen to make them miserable."

She went on. "No woman wants to talk on woman suffrage to a man. It is inevitable that the man should feel aggrieved. . . . You will go away feeling that I have said unpleasant things, and my committee that handed me the topic will not be able to help me bear the burden of your displeasure."

Lilla proceeded to relieve the men in her audience of any guilt the subject of woman suffrage might have caused them to feel, explaining that it was she and her sisters in arms whose responsibility it was to demand change. "[These] conditions are, have been, and will continue so long as women do not object."

And object Lilla did. She claimed that the vote was like the dollar that the woman in the general store had requested. She believed that women were being ridiculed for asking for something to which they had a basic, absolute right, and that for unfair reasons, only men could grant it. She argued that economic power and the right to vote were intertwined—that so long as women couldn't vote, politicians did not have much motivation to defend them. And she argued that the right to vote in municipal elections was only a few cents of the full dollar requested.

She fought for women's causes, not only as a lawyer and a speaker, but also as a journalist. She started and edited two magazines: *The Club Women* and *The Kansas Women's Journal*. And it was for these magazines that she began her project of recording and saving the stories of other pioneer women.

Teachers described the conditions trying to educate youth in a territory where school districts and formal public education systems had not yet been established, and where for a time schoolhouses had not been built. Textbooks could not be easily or cheaply shipped to rural areas, and teachers relied on whatever books the children were able to gather from their homes—often just tattered Bibles. Some taught in dugouts with dirt floors and walls, burlap hanging between the students and the walls so that the children would not go home covered in dirt. The students sat on benches. The teacher had no chalkboard.

Others taught in spare rooms of their own homes, or in students' houses; at the time, it was not unusual for teachers to live with students for a time, teach lessons, and then move on to the next home in the village. The funds did not exist to pay them well enough to secure their own lodgings, so this approach solved two problems at once. Teachers seemed to start working at around age sixteen or seventeen, and most were women simply because so few other opportunities were open to them. One teacher who submitted her memoirs boldly asserted that one-third of the women in Kansas at some point taught school. If the women included in this book are in any way representative, she was lowballing her estimate.

Lilla collected stories from farm wives confessing loneliness and isolation, and women who as young girls had helped their fathers out in the fields as well as their mothers inside the homes. She heard from a woman who had grown up in Abilene, where cattle stampeded as the guard dog lay snoring and her mother fainted from terror, leaving the girl to her own devices as she did her very best to wrangle the thousand or so bovines alone. There were women who hid from border ruffians during the Civil War years, and one whose mother went about town with a gun demanding that the pro-slavery man who wanted to kill her husband show himself so she could give him a piece of her mind, and maybe more.

Lilla's greatest accomplishment, perhaps, was to know how brave and strong the other women were in her midst, and to think their bravery and strength mattered enough that history might want to take note.

All eight hundred manuscripts she collected and organized were later typed by her daughter. After her great-granddaughter Joanna finished writing the book Lilla had been preparing to write herself, the complete collection of stories was donated to the Kansas State Historical Society, where students of history can still enjoy reading them today.

# ELLA DELORIA

❧

(1888–1971)

## Sioux Anthropologist, Teacher, and Novelist

In the Sioux Indian territory of South Dakota, a huge gray rock mysteriously shoots up out of the ground. You cannot miss it. The towering basalt structure with deep, vertical grooves etched into its surface is a well-known landmark in the area.

The white men call it Devil's Tower, but that isn't what the Indians call it, because the Indian religions have no such thing as a devil. The Indians call it Bear Rock. According to a Sioux folktale, the vertical lines are the furious scratch marks of a hungry bear.

The story begins something like this: Two little boys were playing with a ball, and when the ball flew out into the sagebrush, they followed it out of the village. They heard the rustlings of an animal, and followed the animal to a stream. Then they saw a herd of antelope, and followed the antelope even further from the village. When they got hungry and it was time to go home, the two boys looked around and were startled to discover that they did not know where they were. They began walking in the direction that they believed "home" was, all the while walking further and further away. . . .

This is, in some way, how Ella Deloria's story begins as well. Though her story eventually takes her to Lawrence, Kansas, Ella Deloria was born to the Sioux tribe of South Dakota—to whom the story of Bear Rock belongs. The two boys who started walking away from the village, in Ella's story, were her father and her grandfather.

Ella's grandfather Sawse was a medicine man who had a vision that four generations of his family's men first adapted to the white settlers' ways for survival but then came back to once again find themselves grounded in Indian traditions once all danger had passed. Part of this vision was that he would pass along stories of his people to his son, who would pass them to his grandson, who would pass them to his great-grandson and so on. That way, no matter how far the Deloria family wandered from the old ways, they would know them, preserve them, and eventually, when it was safe, return to them.

Sawse anticipated the permanent occupation of Sioux lands and advised his son Philip to embrace the new ways. He set the example by resigning from his post as chief of his band of the Sioux tribe—the Yankton—and taking up farming. He also chopped down trees and sold wood to the settlers traveling along the Missouri River by steamboat.

Having spent his earliest years visiting the sick with his medicine man father, these memories forever etched in his mind, the young Philip attended boarding schools and returned to the Yankton Indian Reservation as a Christian missionary. He married and had a son, but his wife and son both died—first his wife, of influenza, and then his son, of tuberculosis. The grief-stricken but resilient Philip eventually remarried. His second wife gave birth to two daughters and a son. But the wife and son, unbelievably, died like those who came before them. This time Philip grew despondent. He also despaired because his father's vision was increasingly imperiled by the absence of a third generation of sons who could do their part to fulfill it. Philip almost did not recover from his anxiety and grief. He was completely overwhelmed by doubts about his faith, his future, his legacy, and his decision to follow the white settlers' religion and way of life. But finally, he pulled himself together. And again, he married.

His third wife, Mary, already had two daughters when she and Philip met. But Philip and Mary had a child of their own as well. Born during a frightful blizzard in 1889, her English name was Ella Deloria. Her Sioux name, Anpetu Waste Win, meant Beautiful Day Woman. And it surely wasn't the weather that made the day beautiful.

On the occasion of Ella's birth, Philip decided he was done waiting for a son to whom he could pass along the stories of his father and his tribe. He treated Ella as though she were that son, entrusting his legacy to her with utmost confidence. Perhaps this was why that treacherously snowy day was so beautiful to him.

Ella was treated like a son in every sense, even though Philip and Mary did eventually have sons, as well as another daughter. It was Ella who inherited the stories, who met the elders firsthand, and who drove teams of horses with her father, one time resulting in an accident that caused the horses to go wild, the wagon to tumble, and Ella to lose her thumb. As the family heir, she was trusted to do everything and spared nothing.

Although she was a missionary's daughter, she was raised with one foot planted firmly in each world: the white settler's world, and the native, indigenous world. Her upbringing on the Standing Rock Indian Reservation gave her a special perspective and an ability to understand both cultures equally.

Ella spoke all three dialects of the Sioux language, which gave her an advantage over most white anthropologists and ethnographers, whose ranks she joined when her formal studies took her to Columbia University in New

York City. Although she was officially studying to become a teacher, it was at Columbia that she met famed anthropologist Franz Boas. Although the white scholar's openness to the possibility that the American Indian was just as intelligent as the European settler who displaced him might strike today's reader as both obvious and tame, it was something of a mind-blowing assertion at the time—and one that resonated, with particular emotional force, in the heart and mind of one Ella Deloria.

At the turn of the century, it was generally believed that if the Indians had been capable of it, they would have developed the very machinery and other trappings of "civilization" that the white man had developed in Europe; the fact that they had not was routinely trotted out as proof of their inherent inferiority. Franz Boas was revolutionary in his suggestion that there might be other explanations for the differences in the paths that these separate civilizations had followed.

In her own book, *Speaking of Indians*, Ella Deloria quotes Franz Boas enthusiastically. In particular, she draws her readers' attention to the following notion:

> *We must bear in mind that none of these [ancient civilizations] was the product of the genius of a single people. Ideas and inventions were carried from one to the other. . . . As all races have worked together in the development of civilization, we must bow to the genius of all, whatever group of mankind they may represent*

Returning to her own argument, she comes back from this quote with an unusually eager affirmation of Boas's words. "How true!" Ella writes. She adds that, having developed in isolation from other cultures for so long, with needs that differed greatly from the needs of the European, the Native American tribes had invented the things *they* needed—as opposed to all kinds of things that may have seemed crucial to Europeans, but which they themselves did *not* need.

"Imagination and inventiveness are common human potentialities," she argues. "All people invent." She goes on to explain to her readers that it was the Indian who had learned to cultivate corn by the mid-fifteenth century and taught this to the white settler. She also hints that Indian culture did not continue to progress at the same rate after the mid-fifteenth century in large part due to the abrupt disruption of daily life that occurred with the arrival of those very settlers.

"Knowledge of the cultivation of corn, beans, squashes, and other crops had reached most of the tribes," she explains. "Even the most mobile of them had learned to grow corn. Do we realize that these agricultural products were developed by the Indians? From a wild plant with a tiny ear came maize; from a species of the wild cucumber vine came squashes and pumpkins; and so on. . . .

They had their own aims and their own methods for achieving them; and those aims and methods were the direct outgrowth of their peculiar situation and life circumstances. They differed in their habits and outlook simply because they were not exposed to the influences of outside cultures. Otherwise, they were just some more of earth's peoples climbing."

Ella's parents did end up having three more children after Ella, and her bond with her younger sister Susan would dramatically reroute the course of Ella's life. At around the time when Ella was finishing up her studies at Columbia, her mother died, and Susan started having serious health problems stemming—the family would later learn—from several benign brain tumors, which would have to be removed.

At a time when she might otherwise have been furthering her career, Ella found herself instead tending to her sister. She took Susan with her to Lawrence, Kansas, and got a job teaching at Haskell Indian School. She taught physical education and drama—both totally unrelated to her area of specialization—and stood out among teachers there, the majority of whom were white. The Indian students she taught eventually grew up to appreciate her sensitivity to their predicament as they left their tribes and families behind and not only learned but also assimilated.

As Paul Boyer wrote in a special report on Native American colleges prepared for the Carnegie Foundation in 1997, "From the times of the first English settlement, Native Americans have been encouraged to participate in this ritual of Western Civilization. But the goal was almost always assimilation, seldom the enhancement of Indian students or the well-being of their tribes."

Haskell was no exception. Students were not allowed to go home to their families for three full years after arriving, because that would set the school back in its efforts to condition the young people to live in the manner of whites. In the school's records, letters from a mother begging the school to let her children come home to see their dying father one last time appear to have gone unanswered. The cemetery includes heart-wrenching grave plots etched with the names "Somebody's Brother" and "Somebody's Sister."

Ella Deloria's role as a teacher was much more about who she was than the subject she taught. One former student says of Ella Deloria and the other native teacher, Ruth Muskrat Bronson, "They taught their students to have healthy respect for themselves as individuals and a pride in their heritage. They taught us about Indian values and kept them alive in us. . . . They taught us that we could accomplish anything we set our minds to. . . . They taught us how to defend ourselves, as Indian people, without getting angry or defensive."

Ella wrote pageants—that is, educational plays about Indian culture—for her students to perform at white churches and schools. For most of her students, this was a rare opportunity to dispel myths about themselves and to express pride in their heritage in an era when ethnic pride and culturally sensitive approaches to teaching were foreign concepts in mainstream America. Her students would recall the excursions as "expressions of our Indianness that may not otherwise have been possible, given the poverty and discrimination so prevalent on most reservations." At the same time, she was also taking care to familiarize her students with social environments outside their own tight-knit communities, hoping to prepare them to survive wherever their lives might take them.

Throughout her tenure as a teacher in Lawrence, Ella maintained contact with Franz Boas, continuing to work for him doing ethnographic research on Indian tribes on the side as much as her teaching schedule would allow. When physical education facilities at the school were under construction, for example, Ella cranked out reports to Boas, who paid her per report. But she could never earn enough money to support herself and Susan—who required brain surgery—if she allowed herself the time it would take to fully dedicate herself to studying the culture, language, and traditions of the Dakota Sioux.

In a letter she wrote to Dr. Boas in 1926 that accompanied her writing, Ella tried to explain to her mentor—who had evidently asked her whether she might be available to lecture on the Sioux Indians—that the need for money was all that stood in her way.

My sister has had to defer her operation, until I can get the necessary amount of money together. . . . I wish somehow it were possible for me to leave here, and take her with me to do this type of work, but I realize how it is difficult to gain money for such things . . . I know I can do it, but it is the need for a steady income that I can bank on while I am getting myself known, that is holding me back.

Meanwhile, the research Ella was doing whenever she possibly could was truly groundbreaking. Being Indian herself and fluent in Indian languages, Ella had access to information that was far beyond the reach of her colleagues. When Indian women discussed their problems among themselves, Ella was there to listen to and record their conversations. But native women did not consider it proper to air concerns to men, or to outsiders, and so their fears and dissatisfactions could only be learned through another native woman. As such, the Office of Indian Affairs sent her to South Dakota in 1936 to attend a meeting between Washington officials and native women, where the women would learn about the proposed Reorganization Act, which sought to reorganize tribal lands, expand freedom of religion, and allow tribal self-government. The women themselves had requested the meeting out of concern for future generations.

Those who attended were not, as Ella had imagined, young women with European-style educations who would be well versed in national politics, but in fact they were older women with very little, if any, formal education. Because Ella could understand both what the women said during the official proceedings, in

English, and what they said to one another off the record, in Dakota, she was able to shed light on their fears and frustrations. One woman hoped that the land would be reorganized, for example, because presently the land that she had fenced in, plowed, and sown to grain was serving not as fertile farmland, but as a refuge for grasshoppers who hid there from the hooves of white men's cattle, who stampeded the leased Indian lands surrounding her plot. "I am doing very well at pasturing grasshoppers for white ranchers," Ella transcribed in her notes, "instead of raising grain to feed my family!"

While listening to these women, Ella secretly wished that she could stay and continue learning of their lives, their desires, and their fears.

When Franz Boas asked her to teach American Indian dialects to anthropology students at Columbia University, Ella was finally able to quit teaching at Haskell and to travel to reservations for research, interview elders, and publish scholarly works on her findings. She wrote three major works: *Dakota Texts,* documenting myths and stories; *Dakota Grammar,* which is a guide to the Dakota language; and *Speaking of Indians,* which sheds light on the day-to-day life and culture of the Dakota people. In *Speaking of Indians,* Ella explains everything from how quarreling members of a tribe resolve their conflicts to how families merge on the occasion of marriage, to the relationship between how Dakota people address one another and how they address God in prayer.

Her most lyrical work, a tenderly written novel called *Waterlily,* was not published until 1988. It is the story of a family and a tribe, told from the perspective of many generations of women: the grandmotherly Gloku, her daughter-in-law Blue Bird, and Blue Bird's daughter, Waterlily.

But the character who perhaps most resembles Ella Deloria herself in this novel is not any of these women, but a man by the name of Woyaka, the tribe's prized storyteller. Remember that Ella's grandfather had a plan and a vision to be carried out by future generations of sons. Remember, too, that her elders decided to treat Ella as a son to whom they could pass along stories that could bring the old ways back to life long after they had disappeared.

In *Waterlily,* when explaining to a crowd of spellbound children how he became a teller of tales, the fictional Woyaka says to them:

> *Regard me, my grandchildren, and observe that I am very old. I have passed more than eighty winters. Many a man of lesser years finds his eyesight fading, his hearing gone, his memory faulty, while I retain my powers and remember everything I hear. That is because my grandfather had a plan for me, and never rested in carrying it out. The day I was born he looked on me and vowed to make me the best teller of stories that*

*ever lived among the Tetons. And to that end he never gave
up training me. . . . "Now tell me," he would say, "what was
that you heard last night?" And woe to me if I could not give
it step by step without a flaw! Gravely, he would then tell me,
"Grandson, speech is holy; it was not intended to be set free only
to be wasted. It is for hearing and remembering." . . . Did other
boys find life easy? Could they daydream all they liked and
fritter their time away? Then it was because their elders had no
plan for them. My grandfather had a plan for me and that was
why he had to be stern—to carry it out. In truth, I was his very
heart, and he was a kind man by nature. But he wanted me to
be a storyteller, and he spared no means to make me one. "You
owe it to our people," he would say. "If you fail them, there may
be nobody else to remind them of their tribal history."*

Maybe this character was pure fiction. But his story sure sounds an awful lot like Ella's. Only in her case, to tell the story of her own tribe, she had to go very far from home in order to return—to New York, to Kansas, and through periods of extreme poverty, all to bring the world the stories of the people who were her home.

Which brings us back to the boys in the Dakota tale at the beginning of the chapter. In trying to get home, they kept traveling further and further away.

They wished that their elders would find them and take them home. They hoped to see their mother or father, their aunts or their uncles, but none of these comforting, familiar faces appeared. Instead, a big bear found them and chased them, and though they ran as fast as they could, they still could not outrun him. Just as they were about to be eaten for sure, the ground shook and a rock emerged beneath them, raising them up off the ground, carrying them safely out of reach of the growling, slobbering, ferociously hungry bear. The bear clawed at the rock and clawed at the rock and kept clawing at the rock, trying to climb it, but he couldn't. And finally he got tired and wandered off, leaving only the marks of his claws.

According to legend, nobody knows how the boys got down and found their way home. Nobody has proof that they did make it home, but members of the Dakota tribe do have faith in the boys' survival. As the elder who told the story to visiting ethnographers said, "We can be sure that the Great Spirit didn't save those boys only to let them perish of hunger and thirst on top of the rock."

And Ella Deloria didn't suffer for naught; she lived a tough life and died poor and under-recognized, but because of her, the Dakota language survives on the printed page, and her people's stories and customs remain safely preserved for generations to come.

# PEGGY HULL

## (1889–1967)

### Foreign War Correspondent, Soldiering through Adversity

Plenty of reasonable human beings have lived entire lives governed by these prudent words of wisdom: Better safe than sorry. But intrepid World War I reporter Peggy Hull always suspected there was more to life than playing it safe.

It's not just that the young journalist from Kansas reported on the lives of American soldiers from within earshot of gunfire—though she did. It's how she got to the battlefield in the first place that reveals her true grit. The battles she waged and risks she took on her way to the front line required at least as much courage as the job she was expected to do once she got there.

Throughout her career, she followed opportunity from city to city and state to state, letting go of what was certain and secure in favor of what held promise and possibility, unwavering in her confidence that, even when the odds were against her, her talent and determination would pay off. And they did.

Peggy had more in common with the soldiers she covered than with her fellow correspondents. "I did not go to war because I liked the excitement or what my colleagues would sometimes erroneously refer to as the glamour," she would later say. "I went because I was not a man and could not carry a gun and do something for my country." Peggy Hull could turn a phrase to win the hearts and minds of even the most hardened readers. But first and foremost, she was a fighter, and to her, the pen was a weapon.

She had to fight for survival from a young age. Peggy was born Henrietta Eleanor Goodnough on a farm just a few miles outside of Bennington, Kansas, in 1889, and her childhood offered very little in the way of security and stability. When she was five years old, her parents divorced, and the split was fraught with drama. Her father accused her mother of having an affair, neglecting her domestic responsibilities, and being unfit for parenthood. Her mother accused her father of failing to provide sufficient financial support, and of neglect and cruelty. She claimed to have married her husband when she was too young to know what love was, and she refused to uphold wedding vows made when she was too young to understand them. The court granted the couple a divorce, which was uncommon in those days.

But the spectacle did not end there; Henrietta's father demanded custody of his children, pointing to an incident that happened when Henrietta was a baby to support his claim that her mother, Minnie, could not be trusted with the safety and well-being of her own children. While Henrietta, her older brother Edward, and their mother were all traveling together by horse and buggy, they traversed an uneven Kansas field, and Edward fell out of the buggy. Once on the ground, he was then run over by the buggy's rear wheel. He lay unconscious in the field for quite some time, and when he came to, he was all alone. His arrival home was the first signal to his mother that he had been missing in the first place. From that moment on, the shy little Edward stuttered.

The judge devised a compromise regarding the Goodnoughs' custody battle: Edward would stay with his father, and Henrietta would go with her mother. But Henrietta missed her father, and she missed her brother. Furthermore, townspeople shunned her mother, and shunned Henrietta along with her.

The family was happy to pick up and move from Bennington to Marysville and make a new start, the first of many new starts in Henrietta's young life. Her mother and grandmother ran a boardinghouse in Marysville for a while, but when Minnie fell in love and married a housepainter, she and Henrietta moved in with him. Minnie and her husband moved around Kansas and Colorado several times, sometimes taking Henrietta with them and sometimes leaving her with relatives. By the time Henrietta was in high school, her mother and step-father had finally resettled with some success in Bennington, where Henrietta got to know her brother again. She came into her own, playing the mandolin and becoming the star of the town's very first girls' basketball team. But instability had interrupted her education so many times that in spite of being a studious girl who loved to read, Henrietta did not graduate from high school. The town gossips tsk-tsked, agreeing that it was a pity the girl was allowed to run wild. Henrietta grew up eager for an opportunity to prove them all wrong and to show that it was not such a pity after all.

A voracious reader, the budding young writer favored works by a female journalist named Nellie Bly, whose stunts are considered forerunners of modern-day investigative reporting. Bly did things like trying to go around the world faster than the main character of Jules Verne's *Around the World in Eighty Days*, and faking a nervous breakdown to get herself committed to a mental institution, from whence she could report firsthand on the conditions patients endured inside.

Bly's writing inspired the adventurous Henrietta, who, now unhappily studying pharmacology with expectations of working in a drugstore, quickly sent off job inquiries to Kansas newspapers. She heard back from an editor in Junction City, Kansas, who claimed to have all the reporters he needed, but he could use a typist—if she wasn't afraid of messing up her fingernails, of course.

That was all the encouragement Henrietta required. She was determined to work her way up to writing and reporting in addition to typing. With hope as her only cargo, off she went. To supplement her meager newspaper wages, she worked odd shifts at a department store on the side.

Her family, it should be noted, did not approve of her foray into journalism. Working for a newspaper was considered lowly and crass in those days, especially for a woman. But coming as it did from a family whose reputation could hardly get much worse, this disapproval did not register as worthy of serious consideration. Henrietta loved the crazy intensity of newsroom, calling the atmosphere "part monastery, part abattoir." Eventually, as she predicted, she was writing her own stories, not just typing other people's.

Throughout her early career she advanced by moving eagerly from newspaper to newspaper, an approach that took her all over the United States: Colorado, Hawaii, California, Minnesota, and Ohio are among the states where she resided, making a name for herself almost everywhere she went. Although she did have a short-lived, ill-fated marriage along the way, for the most part, she was single. Her need to support herself financially led her to come up with a variety of clever business ideas, such as offering her readers a personal shopping service called "Let Peggy Shop for You."

It was in Ohio that many important pieces finally fell into place for this struggling writer. First, her editor insisted that Henrietta Eleanor Goodnough was much too unwieldy for a newspaper byline; her first assignment was to come up with something punchier. And so she became Peggy Hull, which turned out to be a great career move.

Second, she came up with an idea for a column that gave her name recognition—and paid her bills, which were substantial as she now lived out of a trunk in a hotel. The scheme: She produced semifictional, semifactual advertising stories about her life in Cleveland. The stories were written in the style of one friend confiding in another. In the course of her stories, she would stumble into high-end retail stores in town and always managed to find exactly what she needed. In a storm she might find a great umbrella, for example. The stores were paid advertisers, and Peggy ran a disclaimer alongside the column making sure readers understood that the proprietors of those shops named in her column had paid for the mention.

Her basic strategy, as she put it, was to make things happen to her. And that is how a third all-important piece of the big puzzle fell into place in Cleveland. One of the things that conveniently happened to Peggy in her column began what would turn into an obsession with military life and war reporting. Peggy joined the Women's Auxiliary of the Ohio National Guard's training school.

Cleveland, it just so happened, was the first city in the nation to establish a National Guard training course for citizens. The idea behind it, at least on the surface, was to prepare civilians for any possible emergency. But in retrospect, it is clear that this was a training ground for the troops who would eventually serve overseas in World War I—a war in which America was not yet involved but soon would be.

Although women could not enlist as soldiers in World War I, they were invited to join the Women's Auxiliary of the National Guard. Peggy didn't miss a beat. She signed up almost immediately. Reporting the news to her readers, she was ecstatic. Her words leapt off the page, as though adrenaline could manifest itself in type.

"I'm a soldier now!" she wrote in the *Cleveland Plain Dealer.* "I'm going to learn to shoot a rifle and do Red Cross work. . . . The drills and exercises are splendid from a health standpoint and the military training teaches self-control, a good thing for the majority of us."

When the Ohio National Guard was called to the Mexican border to search for Pancho Villa, the Women's Auxiliary did not participate in the effort, but Peggy wanted desperately to go and pleaded with her editor to send her as a correspondent. But he wouldn't dream of sending a woman to an army camp, even if she did want very badly to go.

This prompted her to make a bold career move, one that set the precedent for her future dealings with skeptical editors who did not take her ambitions seriously. Although she had a good job, a job she very much needed, she announced to her boss that if he wouldn't send her to the border to cover the Ohio National Guard, she would go anyway. She would write articles keeping people abreast of what was happening. If he didn't want them, she would sell them to any paper that would take them—perhaps even a competitor. Her boldness was rewarded: Her editor reluctantly agreed to buy the articles, but Peggy would have to fund her own voyage because he still wasn't going to be responsible for sending a woman to an army camp.

Because of her advertising scheme, the more Cleveland businesses she managed to name in her column, the more money she made. To scrape together the money required to get herself to the border as a free agent, she squeezed in as many advertising shout-outs as she could in the coming weeks. After all, she would need all kinds of things for her expedition: sturdy luggage, for example, and good boots for hiking. Not to mention the perfect restaurant for an extravagant send-off dinner with friends the night before her departure, and the beautiful dresses it would break her heart to leave behind.

When she went to an Ohio training camp to do her reporting in anticipation of the journey, she was the lone woman in a crowd of twelve thousand men. She claimed to have forgotten for brief moments that she would not be fighting alongside the soldiers there. Between training sessions, Peggy furiously wrote her articles; she felt she had discovered her life's purpose in war reporting.

As she left for the border, her farewell words to Cleveland readers sounded very much like a soldier's good-bye: "When I come back, I want to feel that you are all here waiting for me and that you have not forgotten me."

While on the border, Peggy persuaded a commander to let her go along with twenty thousand soldiers on a fifteen-day hike into New Mexico. "When I finally gained his consent," she later told the Marysville, Kansas, *Advocate-Democrat,* "I knew my military career depended on that hike." In other words, if she didn't make it to the end of the hike, or if she embarrassed herself in any way, she could forget ever persuading any commander to let her tag along on future expeditions. But, on the other hand, if she stuck it out, she might prove her hardiness and commitment once and for all.

She woke up at 4:00 a.m., put on her uniform—a wool skirt, a flannel shirt, and an army hat—and marched out the door to the sound of a bugle blowing. She was busy daydreaming about the journalistic acclaim that she would earn as a result of this hike when she tripped over a boulder, landing in a bush on the side of the road.

The next sign of trouble was a pain in her feet. It spread from her feet to her legs, and from her legs to her back. She lagged behind with a few straggling soldiers who struggled to keep up as well. The members of this unfortunate crew offered one another words of encouragement, helping each other make it to camp that night. When she finally made it, she was so tuckered out that she fell asleep on the floor of her tent before dinner.

Day two was not much easier. The hikers encountered a brutal sandstorm. "I felt as though I had never had a bath," Peggy wrote. She seriously questioned her desire for a career as a military correspondent at this point, but she had talked other people into letting her do this, and she knew that giving up was not an option.

On day four, she finally received her first sign of much-needed validation. "Private Hull," a voice said while she was in line for dinner. She turned around. "You have been promoted to the rank of first lieutenant."

When she got to her hotel in the border town where the troops were stationed, she was proud—and exhausted. She saw her silky soft nightgown in a heap on the bed and could not wait to curl up in it and drift comfortably off to sleep.

She did not go with the troops across the border into Mexico, but she waited eagerly to witness their return. Meanwhile she covered life on the border, but because the Ohio boys weren't around and she hadn't been in Cleveland in such a long time that keeping up her advertising column was no longer possible, she went and found a job with a local El Paso paper, letting go of her home base in Cleveland altogether. With that, Peggy became a Texan—but not for long.

When the United States declared war on Germany, Peggy was determined, once again, to march in lockstep with her country's armed forces. Steeling herself with an answer to every objection, she walked into her managing editor's office and asked to be sent to France as a war correspondent. Her editor was shocked at the preposterous suggestion. Not only was she a woman, but this was a small paper with a circulation of twenty-five thousand. Send her to France? Was she out of her mind?

Maybe. But she did not leave his office until she had talked him into it.

Peggy had a lot of things to do before going abroad to report from a war zone beyond getting authorization. She thought these steps would be easier than getting her editor's permission, but she was wrong. She went to New York, where her first order of business was getting a passport from the State Department, and her second order of business was getting the two visas she would need: one to work in England and another to work in France. For these, she would have to appeal to the British and French consulates.

Most of her male colleagues simply completed the paperwork and got their passports issued as a routine process that might involve some minor bureaucratic frustrations, but surely nothing more—assuming their credentials were in place. When Peggy submitted her paperwork, she was flat-out denied. Her only recourse was to appear in person before a judge. Upon hearing this news, her male colleagues placed bets on whether she'd get her passport and head off to Europe, or if she'd have to travel back to Texas with her tail between her legs. The ordeal tested her nerve. She was physically trembling by the time she arrived to discuss her case, which made her question whether she really had the bravery this assignment would demand of her. "What a lot of useless emotion I was going through over a passport," she wrote to her readers back home in the *El Paso Morning Times*. "[If] I felt like this about the verdict how in the world would I feel if a submarine hit my ship?"

The meeting went smoothly. Peggy handed over copies of the *El Paso Morning Times* containing her work, and got her passport without having to put up a fight. Having earned the State Department's approval, she thought she'd sail through deliberations at the British and French consulate.

Wrong again. Peggy was not accredited as an official US war correspondent. The War Department had never granted a woman accreditation. Peggy's editor had reluctantly agreed to send her, and the State Department had reluctantly given its stamp of approval, but aside from that, she was on her own—no government protection, no one to usher her into army camps, no transportation provided. As a result, the British consul who reviewed her case was skeptical. He didn't understand why the paper she worked for would send a woman, especially one who had never been out of the country before. She listed her qualifications, detailing her border experiences with the Ohio National Guard. The consul sent her away empty-handed nonetheless. Refusing to accept this decision, Peggy requested that the State Department send the copies of the *El Paso Morning Times* that she had submitted for her passport. When she returned, the same consul who had given her a hard time on her first visit conceded, "Your paper is all right."

When she finally boarded her ocean liner, she was overcome with doubt. As a little girl, she'd imagined growing sweet peas in a garden, marrying a nice man, and raising children some day. As she embarked for the unknown, she wondered what on earth had prompted her to venture off to war, sleepless in an undulating ship cabin instead of drifting easily off to dreamland in a cozy bungalow back home. But she did her best to cling to her conviction that this was what she had been put on earth to do.

Peggy spent twelve days on the ocean liner, gradually adjusting to seasickness and to her British shipmates' funny way of talking. She was temporarily delayed in London, waiting for permission to continue on to France. While in London, she wrote cheeky articles about the idiosyncrasies of British life, including the way the British greet one another over the phone. Instead of "hello" they would say "who's that?"—which utterly confused a jet-lagged Peggy. Back home, a reader from England who had settled in El Paso wrote to the paper, confessing that she had once believed this Peggy Hull character to be mythical, not real. Reading Peggy's accounts of life in Britain, however, she finally knew for sure that Peggy was not only real, but she was also really in England. Nobody could possibly capture London life so vividly from here in the States, she asserted. Reading Peggy's columns transported her back home.

When Peggy finally arrived in Paris, she checked into her hotel then went straight out to a sidewalk cafe in hopes of absorbing the atmosphere in war-torn Paris. She had barely arrived when she witnessed the American troops marching into the city. Making the scene that much more powerful, it happened to be the Fourth of July. Peggy reported that the arrival of American troops instantly changed the mood on the streets of Paris from dismal and gray to celebratory and hopeful.

Her inability to understand the French language put her in all kinds of humorous situations—as well as a few dangerous ones. She was reading in bed one night when the power suddenly went out, and she heard sirens. It was an air raid. She ran into the hallway of her hotel but could not understand what people were frantically saying to her. Finally, not knowing what to do, she ran back into her bedroom and hid under her blankets, covering her head with all she had: a pillow.

Eventually, Peggy's war coverage got the attention of papers outside of El Paso. She started contributing to the *Army Tribune*—read by soldiers—and to the *Chicago Tribune* and other US papers. She got busier and busier, but her lack of accreditation still resulted in missed opportunities. But in place of opportunities that were simply handed to other correspondents, Peggy went out looking for opportunities of her own—and found them. This is what made her stories unique.

She went on a road trip to small villages dangerously close to the front lines, and she even stayed in an army barracks and in an army hospital, where she heard the shrieks of a wounded soldier in surgery one night. When she walked through the camp in a white fur coat with an American flag pinned to it, American soldiers saluted her as though she were a general.

Once again giddy at her intimacy with the American soldier's experience, she wrote, "I've lived in a tent. I'm living in barracks. . . . There is nothing I don't know about being a soldier in France except how it feels to live like a general."

Admittedly, she also carried a sewing kit with her to the front so that she could assist the troops with repairing the buttons on their uniforms.

Before long, the inside connections Peggy developed and the special access her inside sources granted her caused other correspondents to stop seeing her as a novelty. They started seeing her not as an equal, but as a threat. They complained about her to the authorities and demanded that she be sent home.

Peggy was not sent home, but given the hostile climate, she decided to return home on her own. She wrote a scathing farewell letter, which was printed in the *El Paso Morning Times* on December 13, 1918. Concluding the letter, she assured her jealous colleagues that when the war was over, if they needed jobs, they could always join her in El Paso. And she promised to be gracious should their stories ever push hers off the front page.

Peggy made a true soldier's return home to El Paso. She was invited to speak before groups of businessmen about her experiences, and drew standing ovations from all her crowds. She wasn't done reporting from abroad. She also reported on World War II, by which point she had paved the way for other female war correspondents to go along with her.

Still it would be a long time before women taking dangerous jobs in journalism would be considered anything other than laughable. Peggy Hull did it before it was fashionable and long before there was anything even resembling a movement.

She even did it in uniform.

# MISSOURI WOMEN

# ALICE BERRY GRAHAM

❧

(1850–1913)

# KATHARINE BERRY RICHARDSON

❧

(1858–1933)

## Mothers of Mercy

On the night of June 1, 1897, Doctor Alice Berry Graham answered the phone to hear a voice say, "Come quick, there's a mother down here trying to give away her little girl." It was a saloonkeeper in the West Bottoms area of Kansas City—not a good place for a woman alone at night. The area housed the stockyards and the train depot along with the hotels and saloons where cattlemen and drummers collected and caroused on summer evenings. Despite the danger, Alice ventured out and found the five-year-old child, a cripple, and her mother in a room behind a dance hall. Confronted by the indignant doctor about her lack of care for the girl, the mother complained she was tired of the child's "bawling." Borrowing a shawl to wrap up the dirty, ragged little girl, she took the child from her mother and brought her back to the office building where Alice and her sister, Doctor Katharine Berry Richardson, worked and lived.

Once the two doctors had cleaned up the little girl, they addressed the problem of what to do with her. They ended up taking her to a small maternity hospital where they were able to rent a bed. Doctor Richardson operated on the child's injured hip, and once she'd recovered, placed her in an orphanage.

After helping a second abandoned child, the two sisters realized they had found a shared mission that became a lifelong effort to aid poor, sick children. A dream that began with one child in a rented hospital bed dream grew into one of the nation's top children's hospitals—Children's Mercy Hospital in Kansas City, Missouri.

That's a great story and it may be true. In another account, one that seems to be verified by a 1924 newspaper article, Katharine described their first charity patient differently: She told of Alice finding a crying baby in a trash bin. Lack of verifiable documentation makes it difficult to tell the history of these two remarkable women with accuracy. Chances are, both of these incidents happened at one time or another. The plight of poor children at the turn of the last century was desperate, and the sisters could have related many heartbreaking accounts.

Details of the sisters' early years are sketchy, too. Their parents were Harriet Benson and Stephen Berry. Alice was born on March 3, 1850, in North Warren, Pennsylvania. Shortly afterward, the family moved to Flat Rock, Kentucky, where Stephen owned property and ran a grist mill. A second daughter, Claire or Clara, was born in Kentucky, as was the last child, Katharine, who was born on September 28, 1858.

Stephen was known to be a man of strong opinions and great respect for the responsibilities of citizenship. The girls never forgot his tutelage, and years later Katharine could still recall his words: "The responsibility of an American extends beyond his own family. Wherever you go it is your duty to make good citizens of your neighbors."

During the Civil War, the Berrys were Union sympathizers but lived in a community loyal to the South. Everyone in the community was expected to take an oath pledging allegiance to the Southern cause. Stephen not only refused, he also tacked a notice on the mill door stating that he was a Union supporter. Angry neighbors put a bounty on his life, and he was forced to flee to Ohio, where he joined the Union army, leaving his wife and children in Kentucky.

Harriet, too, held strong convictions and sympathized with the Union. Confederate supporters had taken possession of the mill and were operating it. In the dark of night, Harriet removed parts of the machinery, which she then buried. The mill would grind no grain to support the insurrection!

Following the war, Stephen returned to Kentucky. Harriet had died in his absence, leaving nothing for him there. He took the three girls and returned to Pennsylvania. He had little money then and never managed to make much more, but he insisted that his daughters receive an education.

In keeping with the popular sentiment of the time—that girls were expected to become good wives and mothers only—the middle daughter, Claire, married. Alice and Katharine, however, finished school and prepared for college. Since they had no money for college, the two agreed that Alice would take the teachers' examination and teach school to pay for Katharine's tuition. Katharine earned both bachelor's and master's degrees from Mount Union College in Ohio; she then went on to the Woman's Medical College of Pennsylvania. In addition to her studies, Kate tutored other students to help pay her way. She graduated with her medical degree in 1887.

Now it was Alice's turn. Katharine taught school while Alice completed a dental degree at the Philadelphia Dental College.

Huge pieces to the puzzle of Alice and Katharine's lives before their coming to Kansas City in the mid-1890s are missing. Alice married and became widowed during the time between Katharine leaving for school and both women leaving for Kansas City. Upon Katharine's graduation, the two sisters decided to settle in the west. Katharine would go first and Alice would join her after she finished school. To settle the question of location, they dropped a coin on a map of the United States. It landed on La Crosse, Wisconsin.

In 1893, Katharine married Doctor James Richardson, a dentist who practiced in Eau Claire, about ninety miles north of La Crosse. Why and exactly when the Richardsons and Alice moved to Kansas City is unknown.

Upon their arrival, they rented space in an office building in downtown Kansas City, where they not only hung their shingles but also made their home. Many obstacles stood in the way of their success, not the least of which being the attitude of the medical and dental communities. Women were considered an oddity and definitely not welcomed. With careful planning and frugal habits, Alice and Katharine managed to eke out a living in their chosen professions. For example, they rose early and aired out the rooms so their patients wouldn't smell the breakfast bacon when they arrived.

Through events in 1897, the sisters saw the tremendous need of the poor in the community. Impoverished people couldn't afford health care, and even if they could, few hospital beds for sick children were available. Pediatrics was a relatively new field. Until the Civil War, infant care had been considered part of obstetrics. Children were treated as little adults and simply received scaled-down services.

As Alice and Katharine found more needy children, they realized their meager resources would soon be exhausted. They needed their own hospital. They had been renting beds in a small maternity hospital run by a group of women. The hospital was about to go under financially, but the lease was not up for another year. The doctors knew the licensing board would never grant a license for a general hospital run by women, so they made arrangements to take over the lease and very quietly began to change the focus of the institution. Soon the women had a dozen beds filled with indigent expectant mothers and children.

No other hospital in town would take these poor patients. Although some male physicians did send patients there, the women still remained unrecognized or helped by the medical community. The community in general ignored them—except for a mocking cartoon in a local newspaper. Doctor Richardson, wearing an apron and a towel wrapped around her head, was depicted standing on a stool simultaneously cleaning and directing the activities of others below. The caption read: "Only women. A hospital from which men are to be entirely excluded."

The two doctors did perform housekeeping chores along with the other women staff members—anything to save money. They both devoted themselves to the hospital, taking only a couple of hours a day to see their private, paying patients.

With the lease for the rickety building at Fifteenth and Cleveland about to expire, the doctors needed to find another place for their patients. They were able to rent space in another women's hospital at Eleventh and Troost, but then that lease ended as well. So they farmed out patients to private homes and made house calls until other arrangements could be made.

They were at their funds' end—but not their wits' end. They began speaking to groups throughout the area and soliciting donations from anyone who would listen to them. They finally accumulated enough money to buy a large home, which had once been the residence of former Kansas City mayor R. H Hunt. Their hospital, first known as the Hospital of the Free Bed Association, opened with five beds on January 1, 1904. Over the next two years, the capacity expanded to accommodate twenty-seven patients and the sign in front of the building was changed to read MERCY HOSPITAL. Doctor Richardson paid tribute to her sister in the inscription on the cornerstone: "In 1897, Dr. Alice Berry Graham founded this hospital for sick and crippled children to be forever non-sectarian, non-local, and for those who cannot pay."

Doctor Graham took over many of the business functions of the hospital, while Doctor Richardson served as primary physician and surgeon. Doctor Graham, in a brilliant combination of education and solicitation, produced a monthly mailer, the *Mercy Messenger*. Larger than a postcard and of heavy paper stock so it would hold up to being passed around, the piece usually featured an ill or crippled child—sometimes before and after photographs—and information on the hospital. It also included child-care tips for mothers.

Fund-raising was an ongoing task. Eventually, Mercy Clubs—groups of supporters from across the region—were started, adding to the hospital's financial resources. Doctor Richardson adamantly insisted that the hospital would accept no money that was not a free gift and would not spend money it did not have. When the time came to build a new hospital, the construction was stopped several times and did not restart until funds had been procured.

The year 1908 was a difficult one for the sisters. Doctor James Richardson, Katharine's husband, who had been an invalid for several years, died, and Doctor Graham was diagnosed with cancer. Through her battle with the disease, she continued soliciting funds for the hospital—making public appearances as long as she could, contacting the Mercy Clubs, and writing *Mercy Messenger*.

Doctor Richardson kept her hands firmly on the reins of the hospital as it grew in reputation and size. She stuck to her guns, even when doing so might have seemed counterproductive. At one point, she received a visit from a prominent businessman and his lawyer. The gentleman had what he considered to be an extremely generous offer: He volunteered to take complete financial responsibility for the hospital. There was just one condition—that the name Mercy be dropped and the institution named after him and his wife. Doctor Richardson's "No, thank you," came firmly and bluntly. "I would never change the name of Mercy," she told him. "Many people have contributed to this hospital. I wouldn't name it for myself or even for my sister. The name must remain Mercy—the people's hospital." The businessman and his lawyer left shaking their heads.

Doctor Richardson, dedicated to her children and her hospital, refused to be cowed even by the most intimidating interrogator—not even the politically powerful and wealthy newspaper publisher William Rockhill Nelson. He was the type of man who, when he said "Jump," expected a response of "How high?" One one occasion, he requested that Doctor Kate come to the newspaper office. When she entered the room, he did not rise and instead greeted her with a curt, "Sit down, young lady."

Kate complied, and Nelson began questioning her, pointing out that his newspaper had given her a great deal of free publicity. "I want to find out about you," he told her. He asked what she had been doing with all the money she had been collecting, seemingly calling the legitimacy of her operation into question. Kate still had enough red in her graying hair to quickly stand and tell him off. She gave him a brief summary of her background, education, and early experience in Kansas City. She spoke heatedly about the condition of poor and crippled children in the city and what the hospital was doing for them. She ended by challenging him to send someone to verify what she had said. With that, she stormed out of the office, thinking she had made an enemy.

Nelson did check out everything she had told him. He not only published her story, he also continued to publish stories about the needs of the hospital and its little patients.

One of those needs was a bigger hospital. The hospital on Highland had become so crowded that the staff was putting two, sometimes three, children in each bed. In memory of his daughter, a local businessman, Jemuel Clinton Gates, donated a two-acre plot on the corner of Woodland and Independence Boulevard. By this time, Alice was quite ill, but she and Katharine, along with their supporters, began raising money for a new structure. It was a lengthy process, and Alice did not live long enough to see the start of construction. Doctor Alice Berry Graham died on May 3, 1913. The new Mercy Hospital opened in 1917.

Over the years, Doctor Richardson and Doctor Graham had broken many barriers—among them, opening a training school for nurses. A century ago, nurses were not held in high esteem, and nursing was not considered a proper career for "nice" women. In England, Florence Nightingale had worked hard to change this opinion, becoming famous during the mid-1800s as the "Lady with the Lamp" during the Crimean War. Afterward, she wrote extensively on hospital administration, nurses' training, and reforming the health care system.

Doctor Graham and Doctor Richardson insisted on high standards from their nurses. It took two years for a girl to complete the course. The nurses were expected to be clean and tidy at all times with properly laundered and ironed uniforms. Their long dresses were blue gingham with long, white aprons. Their caps were designed, at Katharine's request, by Florence Nightingale herself.

One of the ongoing concerns of both women was the lack of facilities for black children. This was a time of strict segregation and prejudice, and many staff members balked at treating the black children. Although Doctor Richardson designated one bed in the new hospital on Independence for a critically ill child regardless of race, she knew that was woefully inadequate. Working with a local black doctor who had a small facility, she arranged for several black physicians to come to Mercy to train in pediatrics. She also talked some of her nurses into training black nurses to work specifically with children. While asking for donations for her own hospital, she also asked people for money for what would become the Wheatley-Provident Hospital, the only black-owned facility of its kind in the Midwest.

Until the end of her days, Doctor Richardson refused to take a salary for her work at Mercy. "If I can be hired, I can be fired," she said, "and I plan to work until I die." She also refused to tell her age, saying, "If you tell your age . . . they will want to retire you." She never retired. While preparing her schedule on June 2, 1933, she suddenly doubled over in pain, and she died the following evening.

Two years before her death, she was awarded an honorary Doctor of Law degree from Mount Union College. The president of the school paid her this tribute: "Had Union College done nothing but turned out a Katharine B. Richardson, all the sacrifice and hardships of the past would be repaid." Today, Children's Mercy Hospital, now located at Twenty-fourth Street and Gillham Road, stands as a monument to these two amazing sisters, doctors, and women—Alice Berry Graham and Katharine Berry Richardson.

# ROSE CECIL O'NEILL

(1874–1944)

Illustrious Illustrator

"No thirteen-year-old girl could draw this!" That was the reaction of the editors at the *Omaha World-Herald* who were judging entries in the newspaper's contest for the best drawing by a Nebraska youngster. The entry in question—an elaborate pen-and-ink illustration entitled "Temptation Leading Down into an Abyss"—was certainly not what one would expect of a child's artwork. But then, the editors had never met Rose O'Neill.

Almost nothing about Rose's life was conventional. As unusual as her upbringing was, one big fact made everything work: Rose and her brothers and sisters were surrounded with love and respect.

Rose's father, William Patrick O'Neill, Irish to the bone and larger than life, had big ideas and little practicality. Rose described her Papa as "a romantic with lucid moments." Her mother, Alice Aseneth Cecelia Smith O'Neill, known as Meemie, had been a teacher before her marriage and sang and played the piano beautifully.

Rose was born on June 25, 1874, in Wilkes-Barre, Pennsylvania, where William owned a bookstore and art gallery and Rose enjoyed a fairy-tale childhood. The family—Papa, Meemie, Rose's older brother Hugh, and Rose—lived in a cozy cottage trimmed with Victorian gingerbread. Called Emerald Cottage, the charming little house sported painted cherubs cavorting on the ceiling of the octagonal drawing room and was surrounded by trees and roses and had a two-story birdhouse that looked just like a dollhouse in front.

Meemie played the piano and sang, and Papa recited Shakespeare and spun fantastic tales about Ireland and the "little people." Tall, handsome, and a veteran of the Civil War, William O'Neill had a great love of books and was well-versed in the classics, art, and mythology. He was personable and outgoing, and it didn't seem to bother him that he was hopeless as a businessman. Rose's mother, nine years younger than her father, was both educated and talented.

When Rose was four, the O'Neills moved out of the quaint home William had built for Meemie. His bookstore and gallery had failed to make money, and the bill collectors were hounding him for payment. The Homestead Act, enacted by the US Congress in 1862, offered free land in the West to those who promised to stay on and improve the land for five years. Free land sounded like a good idea to a man who had little money. So the O'Neills loaded their books, furniture, and clothing into a covered wagon and traveled over a thousand miles to Nebraska.

The sod house where they would live must have been a big disappointment to William's gently bred wife. She had never needed to learn to cook or keep house, let alone farm. Now the family was on their own—away from servants and away from civilization.

William's ideas of living on the land seemed not to involve work. He would have preferred sitting in the shade reading poetry. But even a dreamer like William O'Neill had to come to grips with the price of groceries. His solution, he decided, would be to travel and sell great books to other homesteaders. Unfortunately, these hardy farmers who worked from sunrise to sundown saw little need for books, other than their Bibles. Meanwhile, Meemie spread her rugs over the bare dirt floor, learned how to milk a cow, and coped with floods and blizzards while William was gone.

By then, the family had grown to five; Meemie had given birth to Rose's sister Lee on the journey from Pennsylvania. It soon became obvious that other means of supporting the family would have to be found. Meemie got a job teaching at a school some distance away—far enough that she could come home only on weekends. So William became "Mr. Mom," long before it was acceptable. He proved to be an entertaining, babysitter, but Lee was unhealthy, and soon Meemie had to give up her job and come home.

In Rose's autobiography, she skips over these difficulties and does not explain how the family managed to live during the next few years. She wrote, "I (don't) remember how we came to decide we were not successes as agriculturists, but, it seemed, rather suddenly we abandoned the prairie and went to Omaha."

Rose was equally vague about her own formal education. Her father made sure the children were steeped in great literature and their houses were always full of books. Rose loved to draw. She entertained herself by drawing on any piece of paper she could find. William, who was years ahead of his time in discarding inflexible gender roles, fully expected his daughters to have careers and encouraged all their endeavors. Rose would later remember fondly how he meticulously whittled points on pencils so she would have good instruments for drawing and left stacks of paper in convenient places so she could draw whenever the mood struck.

Papa loomed large in the children's life; he was the life of their party. In contrast, Meemie seemed somewhat stodgy. She also seemed to take more control over the family's financial destiny during this period. Someone needed to do it—especially since there was now another O'Neill, Rose's brother Jamie.

Papa saw no reason for formal education for Rose. She was already far beyond her contemporaries in literature, art, music, and dramatic arts. Meemie argued that she still needed a conventional grounding in the more traditional subjects, like arithmetic. Meemie prevailed, and at age nine Rose was enrolled in a local Catholic school. Some of the other children made fun of her shabby clothes and elegant language. Rose was much more likely to spout a Shakespeare sonnet than the simple poems the other students memorized, and knowing *Ivanhoe* by heart certainly marked her as singular among her peers. Her life became easier when her classmates discovered she could draw, and they begged her to decorate their papers and schoolbooks with her illustrations of fat, funny frogs.

Although William still made occasional attempts to sell books and Meemie taught piano, the family, which with the birth of Rose's sister Callista now numbered seven, could never make ends meet. Consequently, the O'Neills had to move frequently, and Rose often had to leave school when the tuition came due.

Papa had decided Rose should become an actress, but she was much more interested in drawing. She pored over every art book in her father's extensive collection—not to copy the paintings and sculptures but to get ideas for different ways to draw the subjects. When she ran out of books at home, she checked out books from the library.

The *Omaha-Herald* contest marked a turning point in Rose's life. She'd worked hard on her entry, drawing a detailed study of a figure descending through rocky terrain. With its shading and shaping of hundreds of tiny pen strokes, her finished illustration was far and away the best piece of artwork the judges saw. Believing Rose must have copied the picture, they searched through art books looking for the source but couldn't find it. The judges then summoned Rose to the newspaper, where they tested her, making her draw while they watched. At last, convinced this little girl was indeed the artist, they presented her with a five-dollar gold coin. It was her first paid illustration and the beginning of her career.

About a year before the art contest, Meemie gave birth to Edward. He was a beautiful, happy baby, and his brothers and sisters doted on him—especially Rose. She cuddled and loved on him, carried him around, played with him, and drew pictures of him. The whole family was distraught when, at about two years of age, Edward got sick and suddenly died. The children planted violets all over his grave. Rose never forgot her darling baby brother, and a bit of Edward lived on later in her drawings of Kewpies.

Papa was still set on a stage career for his eldest daughter. Rose was fourteen, tall, and dressed in her mother's clothes when she auditioned for a comedy that was touring the Midwest in the summer of 1888 or '89 and was given a tiny part. The next year, she got a part with another touring company. In the meantime, her father had helped her land a couple of illustration jobs, and as she got busier with art, she abandoned the theater. During this period, the O'Neills added another member to the family—Clarence, known as Clink, the seventh and last of the O'Neill children.

By the time Rose was nineteen, she was busy drawing for editors in Omaha, Denver, and Chicago. It was time for the big city—New York. For a young woman to travel alone was uncommon then. Upon arriving in the city, however, Rose's reputation was well-protected because she lived in a convent run by French nuns. The sisters would accompany her as she made the rounds visiting editors and publishers and displaying her portfolio. The half-tone process, which made possible the printing of photographs in newspapers and magazines, was still in its infancy. Newspapers and magazines were illustrated with drawings, instead, and good illustrators were in demand. Rose was among the best and soon began selling her work regularly. She would never again live in Omaha.

Rose's family also moved again—this time to the Ozarks in southern Missouri. They were settled in two shabby cabins in the woods when Rose came home for the first time. It was a difficult trip. Springfield, the closest train station, was fifty miles away. Papa, Callista, and Lee came to meet her and helped her load her trunk and drawing materials onto a wagon driven by an old Ozarker. The ride to the O'Neill property was long, and the road got rougher and the countryside wilder. She was exhausted, and the very trees began to assume sinister shapes. Her wonder at the moonlit woods soon overcame her fear, though, and she imagined the tangled vines and trees to be peopled with fairies, elves, and all sorts of wondrous creatures.

After a night's sleep, Rose awoke to the wild beauty of the Ozarks. She wrote, "I called it the 'tangle' and my extravagant heart was tangled in it for good."

Although the cabins were rough, they were surrounded by roses and a little spring-fed stream that provided fresh water. One of the cabins served as the living area and bedrooms; the other was used for cooking and dining. Both buildings were filled with books, which were stacked everywhere. All of the O'Neills read voraciously. The family ignored the inconveniences and delighted in their woodland home, naming it Bonniebrook.

Rose continued to work while she stayed at Bonniebrook. A mailman on horseback came by twice a week, leaving mail in a sack hung on a tree at the mouth of the valley that led to Bonniebrook. Among the letters Rose found in the mail sack were those from a special friend, a young man she had met several years previously. Their courtship in New York had been carried out decorously under the watchful eyes of the nuns. Gray Latham came from a prominent Virginia family. His father was a pioneer in the motion picture industry, and Gray and his brother worked with him.

When Rose returned to New York from Bonniebrook, she brought with her many drawings she had done in Missouri. She sold almost all of them. She was working with increasingly more magazines, and in 1896, she became the first woman illustrator on the staff of *Puck,* a popular humor magazine. The magazine *Truth* published a cartoon strip she had drawn—the first published cartoon strip by a woman.

In the same year, at the age of twenty-two, Rose married Gray Latham. He was handsome and romantic and an entertaining companion. Unfortunately, he enjoyed his social life much more than working, and as the income from Rose's career increased, he seemed to make a career out of spending it.

Rose was supporting not only the two of them but also her family in the Ozarks. Always generous, she gave willingly, but Gray's attitude began to irk her. When she realized he was going to her editors and collecting her paycheck and spending it, she was disappointed and disgusted. After five years of marriage, she'd had enough, and upon returning to Bonniebrook, she and her father rode to the county seat in Forsyth, where Rose got a divorce.

While she was in Missouri, a series of anonymous letters arrived. They were filled with positive comments about her work—both her drawings and the stories she was writing. Rose was intrigued by the mysterious missives and surprised when, after a number of letters, her correspondent signed his name. The author was Harry Leon Wilson, her editor at *Puck.*

Harry was seven years older than Rose and frequently taciturn, whereas she was ebullient. The two shared ambitions to become novelists and, with that common goal, became engaged. They married in 1902.

Harry was a man of unpredictable moods—possibly suffering from what, today, might be diagnosed as bipolar disorder. One minute he could be charming and talkative, and the next, silent and cold. After a strange, three-month camping honeymoon in Colorado, the couple traveled to Bonniebrook.

Thanks to Rose's success, the house had undergone major changes, metamorphosing from caterpillar cabins to a fourteen-room mansion. The couple spent three winters there. Harry worked on his book, *The Spenders,* and Rose illustrated it. She also wrote and illustrated her own book, *The Loves of Edwy.* Both books were successful. The *New York Times* described Rose's book as "mystical and humorous."

In New York, Harry and Rose had many artistic and literary friends. Among the best were the novelist and playwright Booth Tarkington and his wife Laurel Louisa (who went by Louisa). Harry and Booth collaborated on several projects, and in 1905, Booth suggested that Harry and Rose accompany him and Louisa on a trip to Europe.

Again, their social circle included famous figures in contemporary cultural life. Their connections led to Rose being encouraged to send some of her drawings to the Beaux Arts Salon, a most prestigious annual exhibition in Paris. All of her works were purchased, and she was made an Associate of the Société des Beaux Arts, allowing her to exhibit in future salons without having to submit her work to the judges first.

Regardless of Rose's successes, when Harry and Booth were together, they belittled Rose and Louisa. The two women had their own defense: They invented "Wernicks." The name came from a furniture maker who had designed an expandable bookcase with pullout glass fronts to protect the contents. Louisa announced that "when our husbands attacked our characteristics we should have wings to unfold" to escape. The Wernicks had little skinny legs with rubber overshoes, gossamer wings, and a "hiney protector." Thus, when their husbands became too full of themselves and overbearing, the women called on their Wernicky senses of humor to deflect criticism.

Even with her Wernick defense, Wilson's black moods wore on Rose. After a while she realized, while on a visit to Bonniebrook, that she dreaded going back to New York City and Harry. "You don't have to go back," Meemie told her. So her five-year marriage to Harry ended.

Rose never married again, and she never had children. But she had babies—hundreds of naked little babies. Although she had occasionally decorated her illustrations with chubby cherubs, they didn't assume a unique personality until 1909. Rose invented the Kewpie—a little cupid, but spelled with a K "because it seemed funnier." She actually dreamed about the little creatures. "They were all doing acrobatic pranks on the coverlet of my bed."

The Kewpies, who were noted for doing good deeds in funny ways, first appeared in cartoons, but they became so wildly popular that manufacturers clamored for their endorsement. Kewpies sold everything from Jell-O to the Rock Island Railroad. Rose expanded their world, giving them their own village, Kewpieville. She added other characters, including Scootles, a baby tourist who frequently visited Kewpieville, and a pup called Kewpidoodle.

The popularity of the androgynous little elves with their tiny blue wings and wisps of blond hair on their mostly bald heads grew enormously. Children begged for Kewpie dolls to hold. So Rose became a doll merchant. Working with factories in Germany, she oversaw every step of the production process. Kewpies were produced in bisque china and ranged in size from tiny to tall. Rose won the hearts of factory workers when she complained that the smallest dolls didn't meet the standard of the larger models. "He ought to be the very best," she told them, "because he is for the poor children."

Rose had very specific ideas about society's rules and social conditions, and she used her illustrations as well as her Kewpies to make gentle points about justice and equality. Nowhere was this more obvious than in her passion for women's suffrage. While she made several public appearances, marched in suffrage parades, and even went to Washington, DC with a group of women from the New York State Woman Suffrage Party to meet with President Wilson, her greatest contributions to the movement came through her artwork. In addition to creating appealing drawings of Kewpies mimicking the famous painting, "The Spirit of '76," she drew more pointed works. Her drawing of "Sheepwoman" in the *New York Tribune* was accompanied by her opinion, "Man has made and ignorantly kept woman a slave. He has forced upon her certain virtues which have been convenient to him." She went on to say that women had a deeper understanding than men; "What she knows, man must figure laboriously through logic."

She also carried on her own quiet revolt against the strictures of fashion. "I was always rebellious against harness [corsets] and hairpins," she wrote in her autobiography, "and I cut my hair quite a while before the general cropping." She favored loosely flowing gowns and romantic fabrics.

The Kewpies made Rose a wealthy woman—freeing her to travel the world and to explore more "serious" forms of art. She was able to work more on drawings she called her "Sweet Monsters." Steeped in mythology and fascinated with the idea of the origin of man from animals, she created illustrations of robust, gargantuan creatures, which were well received in Paris. She may have been encouraged by the sculptor Auguste Rodin, and she later created several sculptures of her imaginative monsters.

By the early 1920s, Rose, while considering Bonniebrook her true home, owned several other properties. She kept an apartment in New York City, a country home in Connecticut, and a villa on the Isle of Capri. Always generous, she allowed her friends and many struggling artists to make her houses their homes—and some of them stayed for years. She helped finance her siblings' educations, and, of course, she supported her family at Bonniebrook. She also received many requests for help from strangers and often sent money.

Then the Great Depression hit, and people spent less money on magazines, books, and dolls. By the late 1930s, Rose realized she had spent almost all her money. After Meemie died, Rose sold her other homes and moved permanently to Bonniebrook. She began writing her autobiography, working on a new character, and planning a new doll. She wrote, "I don't know what came over me in these unmirthful times. But suddenly I had to make a laugh. I call him Ho-Ho." The new doll was a jolly Buddha-like figure. The timing couldn't have been worse. In December 1941, the Japanese had attacked Pearl Harbor, and no one wanted to produce a doll with Asian features.

Impoverished, Rose died on April 6, 1944. She was buried with simple ceremony at her beloved Bonniebrook. Callista, her sister and closest friend, sang. It was just as Rose had wanted when she told her sister, "I want my feet to face the creek because when it floods, it will wash my feet."

Rose Cecil O'Neill may be best remembered for her Kewpie, but her legacy is so much greater. She was an illustrator, painter, sculptor, poet, and author of short stories and a number of books for both adults and children. An advocate for justice and quality, she was also loved for her kindness and generosity. Fame and fortune didn't spoil her. Perhaps her finest tribute came from one of her Ozark neighbors: "I never seed nobody went so fur, and then looked back."

# NELL DONNELLY REED

꧁ ❧ ꧂

(1889–1991)

Ready-to-Wear Revolutionary

"Dear Paul, These men say they want $75,000. . . . if this is reported to the police you will not see me again." These words were written in a shaky hand by a frightened Nell Donnelly to her husband.

Mrs. Donnelly was one of the wealthiest businesswomen in Kansas City in 1931. Her chauffeur, George Blair, had just pulled the green Lincoln into the driveway of her home when it was blocked by another car. Several men surrounded the Lincoln, forcing George out of the driver's seat. The kidnappers drove George and Mrs. Donnelly into the country near Bonner Springs, Kansas, where she was forced to write the note to her husband.

When Nell failed to return home as expected, Paul, who was ill, had frantically called Nell's office and their acquaintances. He tried to reassure himself that she had simply been called away on business or had sent him a message that had gotten sidetracked.

The next morning he received a call from one of the company's lawyers; ransom notes had arrived there. The kidnappers had demanded seventy-five thousand dollars and threatened to blind Mrs. Donnelly and kill the chauffeur if demands were not met or authorities were notified.

The lawyer, James Taylor, called his law partner, former US Senator James A. Reed, who was not only one of the Donnellys' lawyers but also a friend and neighbor. Reed's abrupt departure mid-trial from a Jefferson City courtroom tipped reporters that something big was happening. Somehow, the word of the kidnapping got out, and reporters were on the phones to Kansas City editors before Reed could reach the city.

Upon learning that the story was already out, Reed issued a statement to the newspapers announcing that the ransom would be paid if Mrs. Donnelly was released unharmed. He added a threat, "If a hair on her head is harmed, I'll spend the rest of my life if necessary, seeing to it that the guilty ones are punished."

Kansas City in the 1920s and 1930s was a rough town with an unholy alliance between mob bosses and political figures. Stories differ as to whether it was Senator Reed or Chief of Police Lewis Siegfried who contacted Mafia leader

Johnny Lazia. Whichever it was, the mob man was quick to deny any connection with the crime. One of Lazia's henchmen later reported that the police chief had threatened to shut down the city—booze, prostitution, gambling, everything—hitting the Mafia in the pocketbook if Mrs. Donnelly was not found.

Lazia marshaled his forces, sending scores of his men to comb the city for leads. After hours of fruitless searching, they finally came up with a clue—a restaurateur who had taken food to the hide-out. Several carloads of mob men descended on the remote farmhouse, brushing past the surprised kidnappers and grabbing Mrs. Donnelly and George. They drove the two shaken victims to a lighted spot in town and called Chief Siegfried, who immediately sent men to pick them up.

After police unraveled the story, three individuals were apprehended and sent to prison. Mrs. Donnelly went back to work at the company she'd founded—one that changed the way American women dressed.

Nell Donnelly, born Ellen Quinlan on March 6, 1889, was the twelfth of John and Catherine Quinlan's thirteen children. John was an immigrant from Ireland; Catherine, the daughter of Irish immigrants. Nell grew up in Parsons, Kansas, and upon graduating from high school, enrolled in the local business college. At sixteen, she moved to Kansas City to find a job, and in the process, she found Paul Donnelly, a twenty-three-year-old employee of Barton Shoe Company in St. Louis. The two were married the next year, 1906.

Sympathetic to Nell's desire for more education, Paul paid her tuition to Lindenwood College in nearby St. Charles. Following her college graduation, the couple moved to Kansas City and settled into the traditional pattern of the time—Paul went off to work and Nell became a stay-at-home housewife.

She had learned to sew as a child, and finding the garments worn at home by most women of the time to be drab, unattractive, and unflattering, she bought some pink-and-white-checked gingham and designed her own frilly, pinafore-style housedress. Neighbors and friends admired her work and begged her to make them copies of her colorful and comfortable dresses and aprons.

As more and more women called her for housedresses, Nell realized she had found a niche market. She was ready to expand. Packing up her courage along with samples of her work, she marched up to the marble and black-tiled building housing the George B. Peck Dry Goods Company in downtown Kansas City. The buyer was impressed and ordered eighteen dozen dresses to be delivered in two months.

Nell had to hire several women to meet the deadline. The dresses sold out immediately, and the store ordered more. Nell bought more fabric, hired more women, found a larger space to work, and within a few years, she had a debt-free, thriving business with eighteen employees and a quarter of a million dollars in sales.

In 1919, the business was incorporated as the Donnelly Garment Company. Paul was listed as president, Nell as the secretary/treasurer. Their titles didn't reflect reality. Paul handled the finances. Nell was the creator and innovator. Without Nell, there would have been no business.

Throughout the Roaring Twenties, the business roared, too. Demand for more styles and choices kept Nell busy with frequent trips to the fashion capitals of Europe to spot trends and to get ideas for new designs. But it was more than her ability to be on the cutting edge of fashion that made the company successful. She also incorporated production principles from other industries, like automobile and aviation, using assembly-line techniques perfected in large manufacturing plants.

While standardizing production techniques, she didn't subscribe to one-size-fits-all. She designed her dresses to fit a variety of sizes and shapes, and individual garments were constructed in such a way as to make simple alterations easy, with deep hems, adjustable waists and shoulder straps, and belts with sliding fasteners.

Her simple housedresses soon got dressed up and went to town. The line expanded from around-the-house styles to clothing for working women, as well as casual and sportswear for women. She didn't abandon the home front, though, and in 1925 she patented a clever apron—the Handy Dandy—which a worker could sew in one step.

Always looking for ways to produce clothing more efficiently without skimping on quality, she applied the textile industry. She worked directly with mills eliminating middleman costs, and used cotton and rayon, sometimes known as "artificial silk," instead of pricier fabrics. Both she and her creations were now known as "Nelly Don," giving both persona and personality to the business.

Even the bursting financial bubble of 1929 didn't disrupt Nelly Don's success. It did, however, highlight Nell's concern for her employees. Since she'd started the business, her employees had been hired seasonally to put out the summer and winter lines. Knowing that many of her employees' husbands were out of work, she kept her factory running year round, concentrating on the Handy Dandy aprons during the off-seasons.

Although the business was successful, making the Donnellys millionaires, things were not going smoothly in the marriage. It would be easy to speculate that she not only designed the pants in the family, she also wore them. In addition, Paul's drinking was a problem, and he was a less-than-faithful husband.

The couple lived in a large, comfortable home next to James A. Reed and his wife, Lura. A former mayor of Kansas City and three-time US Senator, Reed had hoped to be the Democratic candidate for president in 1928. During his campaign for nomination, neighbor Nell Donnelly was one of his largest contributors. When Al Smith received the party's nod, Reed served the rest of his term as senator and retired from Congress, returning to Kansas City to resume his law practice with his partner, James Taylor. Among the firm's clients was the Donnelly Garment Company.

Nell came from a large Catholic family and had always wanted children. Paul was vehemently against it. In the summer of 1931, Nell and her niece Kate made a trip to Europe. Nell was going to adopt a child. She returned home with a baby boy whom she named David Quinlan Donnelly.

That was the story the world knew until 2006, when Kate's grandson, Terence Michael O'Malley, produced a film and book about his illustrious relative. In it, he revealed that the baby was actually Nell's, born at St. Luke's Hospital in Chicago—and David's father was James A. Reed. None of these facts were made public at the time. To the world, David was Paul's and Nell's adopted son.

David was just fourteen weeks old when his mother was kidnapped. This dramatic event was splashed over the newspapers and later stories appeared in popular crime magazines.

Less than a year later, Nell made headlines again, this time for filing for divorce. In her complaint, she stated that her husband had frequently been absent from their home and treated her with neglect. Paul did not contest the divorce. Nell bought Paul's interest in the Donnelly Garment Company, and the business was now truly hers alone.

Reed, whose wife had died a month before Nell's divorce, remained a close friend and neighbor. In December 1933, Nell invited a group of friends to her home for a holiday dinner. After the meal, she and Jim Reed stood before another guest, a judge, and surprised almost everyone by taking their wedding vows. Nell's niece Kate was her maid of honor. The bride was forty-four; the groom, seventy-two. This was the beginning of a very happy period in Nell's life. She and Jim made a splendid couple, and Jim became a doting dad to David, whom he officially adopted. The business was thriving and so was Nell.

Jim enjoyed the outdoors—fishing and hunting—and the couple purchased a ranch in Michigan, where they could get away and enjoy the sports. Deer were plentiful on the nearly seven-thousand-acre property, and the family liked to fish in the lakes on the ranch. Not all of Nell's trips were strictly for relaxation. She sometimes brought employees with her, making it a working trip, but after work, she always took time for play.

Nell was recognized in the garment industry for her business acumen. Her insight didn't stop at financial matters; she was also concerned for the welfare of her workers and was ahead of her time in creating an employee-friendly workplace. Of course, in the beginning, her employees had been friends and neighbors. Her business was like a family, and it just kept getting bigger and bigger.

Nell wanted her employees to do their best, and she worked hard to find the things they did best. If someone was having difficulty in her position (most of the Donnelly employees were women), Nell would move her around until she found an area where she could be most successful. According to a family story, Nell fired only one worker and that was because the employee simply didn't want to work!

The list of accommodations Nell made for her employees was long. While working on concrete was standard in most factories, Nell's factory had hardwood floors. Coffee and doughnuts were available to workers as they arrived at their jobs, and in the afternoon, a lady came around with a cart with lemonade and snacks—the precursor of the coffee break. The company also had a cafeteria, and in 1937, when air conditioning became feasible, it was installed in the plant and offices. There was a dispensary with attending nurses and a doctor who visited once a week. The Donnelly Company was the first in Kansas City to provide hospitalization insurance and life insurance.

Nell paid tuition for any employee who wanted to take night classes, and she set up a scholarship fund for employees' children who wanted to attend local colleges. This was in addition to paying good wages. And she was assiduous about making sure employees were paid on time. One payday, which happened to be a bank holiday, James arranged for a local bank to open so that employees could cash their checks, giving them funds for the upcoming weekend.

Employees could buy remnants of fabrics at bargain-basement prices as well as "irregulars" or "seconds," garments with small flaws that made them unsuitable for retail sale. As if all these amenities weren't enough, Nell also purchased a farm where her workers could fish, hike, or picnic during their time off. Then, in 1937, she bought a three-story, stone home as an employee clubhouse. The house had a reading room, dance floor, and areas for other activities. She had several outdoor ovens built on the five-acre property. The clubhouse sat at the northwest corner of Swope Park, one of the country's largest municipal parks, giving groups access to even more space for activities.

Nell was into team-building activities before anyone knew of such a thing. Employees put on plays and participated in athletic activities. Every year, she held a giant Christmas party for workers and their children.

Meanwhile, Kansas City's garment industry was growing—in its heyday, becoming second only to New York City. It was never a capital of high fashion. Instead, local companies targeted middle America—the ready-to-wear crowd rather than the *haute couture* few.

In 1935, the state of the garment workplace was described as "the worst sweatshop market in the US." The International Ladies' Garment Workers Union had been working to unionize the factories. Employees at companies that manufactured coats and suits were all union members by 1938. The dress manufacturers were the next target. The majority of workers at Donnelly weren't interested; they already had more benefits than the union could promise.

Union president David Dubinsky knew that he needed to break Donnelly, the largest company, in order to make sure the rest of the industry fell in line. Battle lines were drawn, and Nell and James prepared to take on the ILGWU. The union picketed the Donnelly Company. Nell's workers banded together and wrote their own oath of loyalty to her and the company. Of 1,300 employees, only six failed to sign the declaration. The workers voted to reject the union's attempts to represent them.

To Dubinsky, the declaration of support was a declaration of war. He pledged one hundred thousand dollars to bring the company, the largest dress manufacturing business in the country, to heel. Among other tactics, he took out ads in major newspapers declaring that the employees were in violation of the National Labor Relations Act, giving the impression that Nell was resisting the union's standards for the workplace.

The workers took umbrage at Dubinski's accusations, with one commenting that it would take more than one hundred thousand dollars to make them yield. They also formed their own organization, which they called the Donnelly Garment Workers Union. The ILGWU upped the ante to two hundred fifty thousand dollars, and union officials contacted department stores that carried Nelly Don designs trying to persuade them to cancel orders.

In 1939, a federal judge ruled against the ILGWU and ordered that it must cease and desist in its efforts. That was just the beginning of an appeals and review process. The litigation that followed was complicated and involved several different parties, including the National Labor Relations Board. The legal battle ultimately wound up in the US Supreme Court. The company defeated the union efforts with a Supreme Court decision in 1947. As long as Nell owned the company, its own employee organization was in charge.

The company's legal battle had lasted longer than another concurrent conflict—World War II. While the lawyers wrangled, Nell and her company worked harder than ever. Always the innovator, Nell looked at the needs of America's new work force—Rosie the Riveter and Mary the Manufacturer. All the quality she'd always put into her clothing was reflected in the work clothes she produced for women who found themselves filling jobs vacated by servicemen. This work was often physically demanding, even dirty. So she designed the dresses, skirts, blouses, slacks, and overalls for easy wear and care. Her efforts were recognized with two Army/Navy "E for Excellence" achievement awards.

In the midst of the busyness with the war effort, Nell suffered a great loss. Her beloved husband died at their Michigan ranch on September 8, 1944. Nell would describe the eleven years of their marriage as the happiest time of her life.

Nell, at fifty-five, was still in the prime of life. She continued to run her company, building it, by 1947, into the world's largest ladies' ready-to-wear manufacturer. Staying at the forefront of modernization, she began construction on a huge new building to accommodate the continually growing workforce. It incorporated the latest in heating, cooling, and lighting technology and covered two city blocks.

In 1956, after a half-century in the business, Nell sold her interest in Donnelly Garment Company. The company, which new owners renamed "Nelly Don," stayed in business until the 1970s, when the firm declared bankruptcy and ultimately closed.

Nell may have left the business world, but she was anything but retired from life. At sixty-seven, she still had lots of interests and energy. She enjoyed traveling and loved the ranch in Michigan, where she continued to fish and hunt. The interest she'd showed in improving the lives and working conditions of her employees now found broader outlets. A strong supporter of her alma mater, Lindenwood, she established scholarships there, and on the local level, she served on the Kansas City school board. She sat on a number of boards of nonprofit, arts, and cultural organizations. She shared her love for the outdoors by donating over seven hundred acres of land to the Missouri Department of Conservation; the James A. Reed Wildlife Area was named in honor of the Reeds' contributions.

Her achievements were recognized with many awards. She received two honorary degrees: Doctor of Laws from Lindenwood College and Doctor of Humanities from Coe College. The National Federation of Republican Women named her Woman of the Year in 1977, and at the age of 101, she was given the Lifetime Career Achievement Award by the Career Club of Metropolitan Kansas City.

Nell Donnelly Reed died forty-seven years to the day after her husband, Jim. She was 102 years old. A woman of determination, energy, creativity, and intelligence, she shaped and led an industry. She worked hard and gave unselfishly. Her company may be gone and her fashions all but forgotten, but she left a legacy in the lives she touched and the land she loved.

# MONTANA WOMEN

# LUCIA DARLING PARK

1839–1905

Pioneering Teacher

Lucia Darling stood on the crest of Salt Lake Hill and skeptically surveyed the valley below. For the past three months, she and the other members of her wagon train had jolted across mountains and plains, heading for a place they had come to think of as their "Valley of Promise." On September 18, 1863, they had finally reached their destination, and the scene before them, Lucia later wrote, "was not an inspiring one."

Below them on the banks of Grasshopper Creek sprawled the slapdash mining camp known as Bannack City—site of the first significant gold strike in what would one day be Montana. Lucia noted that there were "log houses of varying sizes and descriptions. In the distance, the most conspicuous sight was the gallows, fittingly erected near the graveyard in Hangman's Gulch, just beyond the town."

As Lucia and her companions stood speechless with disappointment at the looks of their new home, a four-year-old boy in their party voiced the thought that might well have crossed all their minds: "Say, Papa," he said, "I fink Bangup [Bannack] is a humbug."

Twenty-three-year-old Lucia had arrived at the barbarous boomtown with her uncle, Sidney Edgerton, and his family. Earlier that year, President Abraham Lincoln had appointed Edgerton chief justice of the newly created Idaho Territory, which then encompassed all of what is now Montana. So Lucia and the Edgertons had packed their belongings and left their home in Tallmadge, Ohio, to head west via train, riverboat, and covered wagon.

When they reached Bannack, the family settled in a five-room cabin that squatted on the bank of Grasshopper Creek, a tributary of the Beaverhead River. Although the log shack with its leaky sod roof and single small window suffered in comparison to the picket-fenced home they had left behind, Lucia considered it "very homelike and comfortable" once they had stretched carpets over the floor and hung pictures on the muslin-covered walls. As she explained with characteristic optimism, "[one] is not inclined to be fastidious as to the style of the house he occupies" after many months of hard travel.

Bannack in 1863 was a turbulent and lawless place, a jumble of saloons, gambling halls, and hurdy-gurdy houses bulging with high-spirited miners. The ready availability of gold—an estimated five million dollars' worth was taken from the gulch in the first year alone—had attracted a notorious band of outlaws led by none other than the charming and handsome local sheriff, Henry Plummer.

An early Bannack resident, Emily Meredith, offered a blunt assessment of the town in a letter she wrote to her father in April 1863:

> *I don't know how many deaths have occurred this winter, but that there have not been twice as many is entirely owing to the fact that drunken men do not shoot well. There are times when it is really unsafe to go through the main street on the other side of the creek, the bullets whizz around so, and no one thinks of punishing a man for shooting another. What do you think of a place where men will openly walk the street with shotguns, waiting to shoot some one against whom they have a grudge, and no one attempts to prevent it?*

Granville Stuart, one of the first successful prospectors and cattlemen in Montana and later one of the state's most prominent citizens, had an equally dim view of the place. In his book *Forty Years on the Frontier,* he wrote:

> *The rich "diggings" of Grasshopper creek attracted many undesirable characters and I believe there were more desperadoes and lawless characters in Bannack in the winter of 1862–3 than ever infested any other mining camp of its size. Murders, robberies, and shooting scrapes were of frequent occurrence. . . . There was no safety for life or property only so far as each individual could, with his trusty rifle, protect his own.*

Still, as Stuart acknowledged, the respectable folk far outnumbered the outlaws, and they were eager to bring a semblance of civilization to this infant settlement. When word got out that Lucia had been a teacher in Ohio, parents in Bannack begged her to open a school for their children. She consented.

Her first task was to find a suitable classroom. With her uncle as escort, she visited one of the town's most prominent landowners to ask if he could provide a place. Forty-one years later, in 1904, she still vividly remembered the encounter.

> *With some difficulty, we found his humble residence and rapped loudly at the door. For some time, no one responded, but finally a man's voice called "Come in." Pushing open the door, we saw*

*in the dim light a man lying on buffalo robes on the floor. He*
*did not rise to meet us, for he had not fully recovered from*
*the results of imbibing too freely from the favorite and profuse*
*beverage then so plentiful, and his voice was still too thick to*
*be easily understood. My Uncle stated to him our errand. "Yes,*
*glad of it," he said, "D——d shame, children running around*
*the streets, ought to be in school. I will do anything I can to help*
*her, she can have this room. . . . I will give it to her for cheap.*
*She shall have it for fifty dollars a month. . . . It is dirt cheap."*

Taking in the rude cabin with its mud-plastered walls, sod roof, and earthen floor, Lucia decided that, yes, the place offered plenty of dirt, but it was by no means cheap.

And so it was that she opened her school, often credited with being the first in Montana, in the front room of the Edgertons' own home—and in the shadow of the gallows that would soon see frequent use.

Lucia Aurora Darling was born October 9, 1839, near Kalamazoo, Michigan. Her mother died when she was ten, so she went to live with her relatives, the Edgertons, in Ohio. Well-educated, she began teaching public school there at the age of fourteen.

Although Lucia's early life was comfortable and sheltered, she had a lively, dauntless nature that stood her in good stead during her westward journey. Her courage and high spirits are evident in the daily record she kept of the slow and arduous trip to Idaho Territory.

The first part of the adventure was pleasant enough. Lucia and her relatives traveled by train to Saint Joseph, Missouri, and then by riverboat to Omaha. There, they spent a week buying covered wagons, oxen, guns, milk cows, ponies for the children to ride, and a dog they hoped would serve as both sentry and hunter. They also stocked up on provisions: bacon, ham, coffee, tea, salt, sugar, dried fruit, and canned peaches. The women bought silk masks designed to protect their complexions from the sun, wind, and rain. Finally, the party of sixteen, which included Lucia's cousin Wilbur Fisk Sanders and his family, squeezed their belongings into their wagons and pointed their oxen west.

Life on the Oregon Trail soon became fairly routine. The emigrants rose early and ate a hearty breakfast of coffee, ham or bacon, biscuits or pancakes, gravy, and milk. They stopped for an hour or two at midday and then halted early enough in the evening to get supper, milk the cows, put up a tent, and gather fuel for a fire before dark. To keep their spirits up, they often indulged in "a jolly time" of singing and telling stories in the moonlight or playing checkers over a meal. Lucia, in "calico dress and cordia sun bonnet," often wandered away from the train to explore the local landmarks. She also passed her time reading, napping, picking and pressing wildflowers, and writing frequent letters home.

Each day, the Edgertons' wagon train crept ten to twenty miles closer to Bannack, sometimes in a torrent of rain. Along the way, it passed hundreds of rotting buffalo carcasses, as well as several graves of unfortunate travelers. On July 3, Lucia described one of the latter.

> *Passed a little grave by the roadside—the board at the head*
> *containing the name of Lora Hough. The sight was a sad one*
> *to us, for we have the long journey before us and nothing worse*
> *could happen to us than to have to leave one of our member in a*
> *lonely grave like this one.*

The trip was always tiring, sometimes frightening, and often uncomfortable. Lucia bathed in muddy rivers and cold mountain streams, slept in a crowded wagon or on the hard ground beneath, and blistered her hands cooking over a small camp stove. She also took her turn at guard duty, watching in the night for Indians, bears, and hungry wolves with a loaded revolver by her side. As it turned out, the party had more trouble with mosquitoes than with native peoples or wild animals.

Lucia and her family seemed to take most hardships of their journey in stride. Once, when one of the men returned empty-handed from a hunting foray, she described the party's reaction in her journal. "As we saw him coming we thought he had game on his shoulder which proved to be his boots," she wrote, "and which we demanded to fry for supper as he had brought nothing else."

Despite their unenthusiastic first impression of Bannack, Lucia and her fellow travelers must have been relieved to reach the end of their trail. But as Lucia soon discovered, life for the thirty or so family women in town was unusually confining. According to her cousin Martha Edgerton Plassman,

> *there was almost no visiting among the women. . . . Women*
> *stayed at home and generally found plenty to keep them*
> *occupied in the absence of conveniences. Marketing could*
> *have been regarded as amusement but marketing was not safe*
> *where pistol play was the chief amusement of some of the male*
> *inhabitants. . . .*
>
> *Shopping, it will be understood from this, partook of the*
> *nature of a foray into the enemy's country, and was not to be*
> *lightly considered. Among the earliest pioneers, men did most of*
> *the marketing and nearly all the gossiping.*

So Lucia entertained herself by sewing, reading, and singing. If she did venture out of the house, it was usually to go riding or to pick berries—and, of course, to teach school.

Lucia's school opened in October 1863. At first, her dozen or so students attended class only in the morning. They had no desks and no standardized textbooks but used whatever they could scrape together. The room was heated by a temperamental wood stove, and classes were dismissed in mid-December because of extreme cold. They would resume again in the spring.

Meanwhile, however, Lucia's students were free to witness one of the most terrible chapters in the history of Montana. Fed up with the more than one hundred murders and robberies attributed to the Plummer gang, several men from the gold camps of Bannack, Virginia, and Nevada Cities—Wilbur Fisk Sanders prominent among them—met in secret two days before Christmas to form a "vigilance committee." Their intention was to take the law into their own hands and hurry the wheels of justice along.

In the next month, the Vigilantes, as they became known, executed twenty-two desperadoes, four of them in Bannack. On January 10, 1864, the bodies of Sheriff Plummer and two of his cohorts dangled from the gallows in Hangman's Gulch, within sight of Lucia's home and classroom. Another man, "Dutch John," joined them at the end of the rope two days later.

Although Lucia's school has commonly been referred to as the first in Montana, it by no means represented the first effort at schooling in the region. Catholic missionaries had taught Native American children as early as the 1840s, and a school was established in the fall of 1861 at Fort Owen in the Bitterroot Valley for children of the traders there. During the summer of 1863, Kate Dunlap taught in Nevada City, and Mrs. Henry Zoller taught primary students for two months in Bannack.

But Lucia may well be described as the first Montanan to teach a full term of school in a building erected solely for that purpose. At the beginning of her second year of classes, when her enrollment had swelled to twenty students and outgrown the Edgerton home, a pair of local men built a log schoolhouse on the opposite side of Grasshopper Creek. It later was used for committee meetings by the first territorial legislature.

As it happened, another member of Lucia's family also played a ground-breaking role in Montana education. Her uncle Sidney Edgerton—first governor of Montana Territory—convinced the legislature to create a public school system.

Lucia and the Edgertons didn't stay long in Montana. In 1865 they returned to Ohio, and shortly after the Civil War ended, Lucia went to Selma, Alabama, to teach emancipated black slaves. For nine years, she served as principal of the women's section of Berea College in Kentucky.

On September 17, 1885, Lucia married Servetus W. Park, a successful banker and businessman who had two children from a previous marriage. They settled in Warren, Ohio, where Lucia was a tireless church and civic worker. She was such an asset to her community that her death on August 18, 1905, was prominently reported on page one of the local newspaper. In it, she was described as "a woman of unusual intelligence combined with rare tact and a heart full of sympathy."

Although her time in Bannack was brief, Lucia Darling Park played an important role in the development of Montana. By bringing with her to the West the influence of education, she helped the territory mold its new citizens and fostered hope for its future.

# MOTHER AMADEUS

(1846–1919)

## Lady Black Robe

On January 18, 1884, a train rattled into the station at Miles City, Montana Territory, and coasted to a stop with a great, steamy sigh. In a billow of black, six travel-weary nuns stepped down to the platform. There to greet them was a crowd made up mostly of crude and crusty cowboys.

In the 1880s, Miles City was a rowdy cow town with about 2,500 residents, two general stores, and sixty-five saloons. To its townspeople, the newly arrived representatives of God were a welcome—and morally uplifting—addition. According to one account, "the motley gathering . . . hailed the nuns with delirious enthusiasm, and those gathered about the saloons doffed their sombreros, removed their pipes, and observed a reverential silence when the nuns, with lowered veils, walked past."

The leader of this little flock of Ursuline nuns was Mother Mary Amadeus, a tireless and selfless woman who, even as a small child, had yearned to be a missionary among the Indians. In 1884 her ambition was about to be realized. Over the next three decades, despite chronic illness and crippling injury, she would open eight mission schools among the Native American tribes of Montana and three among the Eskimos of Alaska. The Cheyennes would call her Maka-ma-he-hona-wihona, or The Great Holy White Chief Woman. The Eskimos would simply call her Anyachak, "Mother," and her name would become synonymous with Catholic missionary efforts in the West.

But on that frosty day in Miles City, Mother Amadeus had more pressing concerns than the salvation of souls. No one had thought to arrange a place for the nuns to stay. At the suggestion of Bishop John Brondel, who had come all the way from Helena, Montana, to welcome them, Mother Amadeus and her companions settled for the night at a boardinghouse owned by a widow named Bridget McCanna.

That first night must have been a true test of the Ursulines' faith. Their room was cold and filthy—so filthy they didn't dare use the single bed. They sat huddled all night on the floor, leaning against the thin wall that separated their quarters from a Chinese laundry. Snow and moonlight filtered through cracks in the walls and roof, and somewhere nearby they could hear a noisy craps game in progress.

The morning proved no more hospitable. According to Mother Amadeus's friend and biographer, Mother Angela Lincoln,

> as soon as the first streaks of dawn peopled the streets, the nuns left the house, and began the first of their many trails through the deep snow to the church. The night had turned it into a very block of ice. They unlocked it, and with hands frozen and unused to such labor, they gathered chips and made a big blazing fire. When the Bishop [Brondel] appeared in the sanctuary at 8 A.M., he was greeted by a genial warmth, the symbol of all his future dealings with Mother Amadeus and the Ursulines.

Later that day, Mother Amadeus set out to find a suitable house for a convent. She rented a small cottage on Palmer Street for about thirty dollars a month, paying for the first two months with money donated by a generous patron back home. She knew she would have to trust in Divine Providence to supply the rent in future months, because the nuns had no regular source of income.

Next, the nuns went shopping for provisions: a sack of flour, a dozen eggs, three pounds of tea, five pounds of coffee, a quart of milk, sixteen pounds of potatoes, three pounds of bologna, and six pounds of other meat. Mother Amadeus also bought a wood stove to heat their new home. That night, they slept on the floor wrapped in buffalo robes, their heads resting on whatever might pass for a pillow—a satchel, a Webster's dictionary, and, in Mother Amadeus's case, a world atlas.

Though they now had a better roof over their heads, the nuns had little else to call their own. The people of Miles City apparently hadn't considered how to provide for their welfare. In *Life of The Reverend Mother Amadeus,* Mother Angela described their meager daily existence and their serene acceptance of it.

> Now began for Mother Amadeus and her nuns the poetry of privation. . . . [L]ack of money made them suffer keenly for want of the simplest necessities. . . . [T]heir beds were . . . hard, and they were undoubtedly very hungry when they sat down to the scantily furnished table, their rations, short rations of corn meal and a half dozen oranges which a dealer brought because "They were rotten. I cannot sell them. . . ." And the nuns only laughed at the table and passed the bread plate about saying: "I'm not hungry."

One day, so the story goes, the chaplain from nearby Fort Keogh met a young girl running breathlessly down the street and stopped her to ask her errand. She was going, she said, to the butcher shop to buy ten cents' worth of liver for the nuns, and she hurried on. Horrified, the pastor devoted his next Sunday sermon to the bitter plight of the Ursulines. The abashed townspeople made sure the missionaries had plenty to eat after that.

Not long after their arrival in Montana, the nuns opened a boarding school in Miles City. Then, on March 30, 1884, Mother Amadeus and three of the Ursuline sisters set out for the Cheyenne Indian reservation to establish their first mission among the native people. With an escort of soldiers from Fort Keogh, they traveled southwest for four days across cactus-covered badlands, fording the Tongue River twice. At about noon on April 2, they reached their new home—an abandoned, three-room log cabin with a floor and roof of mud. It would be called Saint Labre's Mission, the first in a long line of charitable ventures founded by Mother Amadeus.

Mother Amadeus was born Sarah Theresa Dunne on July 2, 1846, in Akron, Ohio. She was the fifth child of Irish immigrants John and Ellen Dunne. When Sarah was small, her father and older brother joined the stampede to California to look for gold. In 1856 the rest of the family followed—except for Sarah and a sister, Mary, who were left at an Ursuline boarding school in Cleveland.

From the beginning, the Ursulines were favorably impressed with little Sarah. In the sentimental view of Mother Angela, she was

> *so tiny, so delicate, she stood in the sunshine of everyone's heart.*
> *. . . laughing, leading, praying, playing. Her brothers write*
> *of her: "She was our youngest, always considered pretty, very*
> *bright and active, good-natured, keen, witty, courageous. Her*
> *eyes were steel blue and very clear; her hair, golden at age*
> *six, changed at nine to light brown; her forehead, rounded*
> *and protruding." The lines of the child's face mirrored her*
> *character—there were no angles—all was winning, sweet,*
> *attractive, sunny.*

Mary Warner, Sarah's friend for sixty years, also recalled her in glowing terms.

> *Never was she rude or rough in look, word, or act. . . . In school,*
> *no one could surpass Sarah in class standing, so bright was*
> *she. Sarah would divest herself of everything to give pleasure to*
> *another. I never knew her to make an unkind remark of any*
> *human being, and this feature alone would mark her as one of*
> *God's darlings. Self-sacrifice was the leaven of her life.*

Sarah showed an interest in the religious life even as a child. According to Mother Angela, she would sometimes tell her playmates, "Someday I shall be a missionary in the Rocky Mountains and in Alaska." When her parents summoned her and her sister to join them in California, Sarah refused, mincing no words. "We have the right to frame our own future," she wrote to them. "But if you insist, we shall both come, and if our lives prove unhappy, the blame will be on you." Needless to say, they relented.

After five years at the Cleveland boarding school, Sarah entered the Ursuline convent in Toledo, Ohio. There, on August 23, 1864, she pronounced her holy vows as Sister Mary Amadeus. Ten years later, when she was only twenty-eight, she was unanimously elected Mother Superior, head of the entire convent.

Meanwhile, Native Americans in Montana Territory were becoming increasingly bitter as white settlers swarmed onto their homelands and hunting grounds. Hostilities reached a climax on a hot summer day in 1876, when several thousand Sioux and Cheyenne warriors annihilated Lieutenant Colonel George Armstrong Custer and his command at the Battle of the Little Bighorn. But their victory was short-lived. US troops soon subdued the tribes and drove them onto reservations, forcing them to accept an uneasy truce.

Catholic authorities in Montana thought the presence of nuns among the vanquished peoples might help keep the peace. So, in 1881 an appeal went out for volunteers. When the news reached the Toledo convent where Mother Amadeus lived, thirty Ursulines offered to go west. Their bishop chose six of them and put Mother Amadeus, whom he considered the "flower of the flock," in charge. They set out for Montana in 1884.

For the next twenty-five years, Mother Amadeus and her nuns—known as "Lady Black Robes" since they were religious sisters to the black-robed Jesuit priests—traveled across Montana, establishing mission schools. Six months after opening Saint Labre's, she was called to Saint Peter's Mission, about thirty-five miles southwest of Great Falls, to found a boarding school for Indian girls. Then, in quick succession, came schools for the Gros Ventres and Assiniboines at Saint Paul's Mission on the Fort Belknap reservation (1887); for the Crows at Saint Francis Xavier on the Little Bighorn River (1887); for the Kalispels, Pend d'Oreilles, Kootenais, and Flatheads at Saint Ignatius in the Flathead Valley (1890); for the Blackfeet at Holy Family near Browning (1890); for Chief Plenty Coups and his Crow followers at Saint Charles in Pryor (1892); and for Chief Charlot and his Flathead people at Saint John Berchman in Arlee (1892). Mother Amadeus also founded two parochial academies in Anaconda.

Life at these missions was often harsh and grueling. In her book *Ursulines of the West,* Mother Clotilde McBride described some of the hardships that Mother Amadeus and her fellow nuns endured.

*Most of the experiences of those days were recorded only by guardian angels—the rigors of the weather and extreme poverty, snow up to the waists of the nuns, winds that blew them flat on the ground, their shoes often frozen to the floor when they tried to put them on in the morning, nights spent sitting up when the scanty supply of bed clothing had to be given to the children, sickness among members of the [Ursuline] community, malignant diseases among the children, time after time provisions running low until there was but a little oil and a handful of meal in the house.*

The annals of the Ursulines are peppered with references to illness and death among the students and nuns and to fires on the prairie and at Saint Peter's Mission. One entry, on January 31, 1893, notes that the temperature one winter day in Helena was fifty-two degrees below zero, and another describes snowdrifts fourteen feet deep.

As if these trials weren't enough, Mother Amadeus often suffered bouts of nausea and vomiting, the results of an accidental poisoning when she was twenty-eight. Her diet consisted of little more than milk and bread. Because she was so frail, she also was a frequent victim of pneumonia. Very soon after her arrival at Saint Peter's, she became so ill that a priest administered the last rites. Remarkably, she recovered.

Mother Amadeus lived primarily at Saint Peter's Mission while in Montana and established a novitiate there, but she traveled extensively to oversee the Ursulines' other mission schools. These journeys through near-empty wilderness, across rugged mountains and bridgeless rivers, sometimes led to near disaster.

One such journey, in December 1894, almost ended in drowning. On her way to Billings from the Pryor school, Mother Amadeus and her companions had to ford Blue Creek, a tributary of the Yellowstone River. Her driver guided his wagon into the swollen stream but mistook the location of the ford. Mother Clotilde described what happened next.

*[The horses] halted abruptly, snorting and trembling. Icy water rose over the wheels and up to the waist of the nuns, while huge cakes of ice knocked against the carriage, threatening to overturn it at any moment. The driver fainted, but an Invisible Power held the horses. Mother Amadeus succeeded in rousing the man and then instructed him to crawl out carefully over the back wheels, get to shore, and go for help to a cowboy camp that they had passed on the way. For three quarters of an hour, the nuns sat motionless in that deathly water until aid came. . . . It*

*was discovered the next day that the fore feet of the horses had
stopped on the brink of a deep hole and that the hind legs of the
poor animals had been floating in the stream.*

On another occasion, while traveling from Saint Labre's to Saint Xavier's,
Mother Amadeus's driver lost control of his horses. Seeing that they were
headed toward a precipice, the nun warned her companions to jump—just
before their buggy sailed over the edge of the cliff and was dashed to pieces
below. As the party continued on foot, a pack of "gray and ghastly" wolves
dogged their tracks. Mother Amadeus knelt and prayed, and the wolves disappeared as silently as they had come.

The famous and beloved nun was not so lucky in October 1902. On the way
to Miles City by train, she was crippled for life when her eastbound locomotive
crashed at full speed into a westbound train. She was thrown violently to the
floor, breaking her hip. For nine weeks, she lay immobilized in a Helena hospital
with heavy weights suspended from her feet. Yet, according to Mother Angela,
she had "a smile, a word of counsel and consolation for every one." The badly set
bones never healed properly, and Mother Amadeus carried a cane for the rest of
her life. But even that couldn't stop her from exploring new frontiers.

Mother Amadeus traveled to Rome several times on business, and during
one trip she got permission to found missions among the Eskimos of Alaska,
fulfilling another lifelong dream. In 1905 she sent three nuns to Akulurak, a little
village about ten miles from the Bering Sea, where they opened a mission known
as Saint Mary's. She followed them to Alaska herself a few years later and spent
the last years of her life shuttling back and forth between Alaska and a convent
she had established in Seattle, Washington.

But Montana had not seen the last of Mother Amadeus. After her death
in Seattle on November 10, 1919, she was brought back to Saint Ignatius and
buried in the shadow of the Mission Mountains. At her graveside, the Flathead
Indians chanted their traditional dirge for a fallen hero.

Mother Amadeus's magnanimous nature and magnetic personality inspired
effusive tributes. Her friend and biographer Mother Angela saw in her something
of a saint, noting that

*she had many bitter trials, she met with many heavy crosses, but
she lifted and carried them. She led a life of incessant activity,
walking painfully with a cane and counting one sleepless night
after another. . . . She was an organizer, a pioneer, and she has
stamped her name upon the soil of Montana and Alaska. . . .
Her unanswering, buoyant trust [in God] was catching and
peculiarly characteristic. Yet she was as active, intelligent, and*

*prudent, as untiring in her work as though its success depended entirely on herself and upon herself alone. . . . She had a mother's heart, and a mother's heart is the most perfect thing God has ever made.*

Mother Amadeus and the Ursuline Sisters were not the only religious women to play a part in the development of Montana. Representatives of other Catholic orders, especially the Sisters of Charity of Leavenworth and the Sisters of Providence, braved primitive conditions and dire poverty to found schools and hospitals in the wilderness. Their influence can still be felt throughout the state in such communities as Helena, Great Falls, Missoula, Billings, and Butte—cities that have thrived in part because of their good works.

# NANCY COOPER RUSSELL

❧

(1878–1948)

## Woman Behind the Man

Nancy Cooper hustled around the steamy kitchen, helping "Ma" Roberts set the table and put the final touches on a special meal. Mr. Roberts was due home any minute, and he had sent word that he was bringing a dinner guest.

A jangle of spur rowels on the back porch signaled the arrival of the hungry pair. Ben Roberts breezed into the kitchen, followed by a sturdy cowboy who stopped short when he saw the pretty seventeen-year-old girl who had joined the Roberts household since his last visit. Mrs. Roberts introduced Nancy to their guest: Charlie Russell, former cowpuncher, fledgling artist, and close friend of the family. Nancy, she explained, had come to live with the Robertses in Cascade, Montana, to help care for their three children and do some of the housework.

Some say it was love at first sight. For the rest of the evening, Charlie was unusually gregarious, regaling his hosts with story after story of life in the good old days, when the West was still wild. Nancy was obviously enchanted. Thirty-four years after their introduction in October 1895, she described her first impression of this dashing maverick who would change her life:

> *The picture that is engraved on my memory of him is of a man*
> *a little above average height and weight, wearing a soft shirt, a*
> *Stetson hat on the back of his blonde head, tight trousers, held*
> *up by a "half-breed sash" that clung just above the hip bones,*
> *high-heeled riding boots on very small, arched feet. His face was*
> *Indian-like, square jaw and chin, large mouth, tightly closed*
> *firm lips, the under protruding slightly beyond the short upper,*
> *straight nose, high cheek bones, gray-blue deep-set eyes that*
> *seemed to see everything, but with an expression of honesty and*
> *understanding. . . . His hands were good-sized, perfectly shaped,*
> *with long, slender fingers. He loved jewelry and always wore*
> *three or four rings. . . . Everyone noticed his hands, but it was not*
> *the rings that attracted, but the artistic, sensitive hands that had*

*great strength and charm. When he talked, he used them a lot to emphasize what he was saying, much as an Indian would do.*

Charlie began spending a lot of time at the Roberts home, courting the sweet-faced, buxom lass whom everyone called Mamie. In the evenings, the pair would stroll along the bank of the Missouri River and out onto the wooden bridge that spanned it, talking and gazing at the fiery colors of the sunset reflected in the muddy current. Charlie proved just how captivated he was when he gave Nancy his beloved pinto, Monte.

Everyone warned the pair not to marry. The local doctor told Charlie that Nancy had frequent fainting spells—the sign, he said, of a bad heart. He predicted she'd be dead within three years. Folks reminded Nancy that Charlie had a drinking problem. On top of that, he was fourteen years older than she and a footloose bachelor who might well be set in his ways. And he'd never managed to make a decent living for himself. How could he ever be expected to provide for a family?

But, as Charlie might have said, love is as blind as a bear in a blizzard. He proposed to Nancy, an event later recounted by his nephew Austin Russell.

> *It took Charlie months to make up his mind, and when he finally asked Nancy she refused. He took her for a walk at sunset, they went down by the river and crossed the echoing, wooden bridge, and on the bridge he proposed, and she said No.*
>
> *Years afterward, he made a little watercolor of it—an autumn evening, the sky darkening to night, a cold wind blowing and they have just left the bridge. Nancy, downcast, is walking in front with her hands in a muff, her coat buttoned up tight and a little black hat on her head. Charlie following close behind with his coat blown open and sash and white shirt showing . . . his arms extended in a pleading, persuading, arguing gesture, his hat on the back of his head. That's all there is to it; not much of a picture, but it tells the story.*
>
> *In the end, of course, she said Yes.*

Charlie and Nancy were married at twilight on September 9, 1896, in the parlor of the Roberts home. Charlie had slicked himself up for the occasion, and Nancy wore a blue wedding gown that Mrs. Roberts had helped her make, along with a matching string of blue beads—her wedding gift from Charlie.

After the ceremony, the handful of guests celebrated with cake and ice cream while the newlyweds went on their "honeymoon." It was a short trip. The couple walked hand in hand about three hundred feet to the one-room shack that the Roberts had loaned Charlie for a studio. Charlie had spent almost all the money he had fixing it up to be their first home. In fact, according to Austin Russell, the pair started their life together with only about seventy-five dollars between them.

Despite everyone's reservations, Mr. and Mrs. Charles M. Russell would stay devoted to each other for the next thirty years. And Nancy would have a profound impact on the course of Charlie's artistic career. Charlie himself later acknowledged in his own quaint fashion, "The lady I trotted in double harness with was the best booster an' pardner a man ever had. . . . If it hadn't been for Mamie I wouldn't have a roof over my head."

Today, some historians go even further. If the pair hadn't married, one of them contends, "it is doubtful that Russell would have created the prodigious body of artwork he did, a life's work that is truly one of our most cherished national treasures."

Nancy Cooper was born on May 4, 1878, in Mannsville, Kentucky, a town named for her great-great-grandfather. Her mother, Texas Annie Mann, had married young, which proved to be a disastrous mistake. Nancy's father, James Al Cooper, abandoned his pregnant wife within months of the wedding, so the mother-to-be moved back to her parents' home and resumed her maiden name.

As soon as Nancy could walk, she joined her mother and grandparents working in the family tobacco fields, plucking worms off the leafy plants. When she was five, she contracted diphtheria, from which she barely recovered. For the rest of her life, her health would be fragile.

In 1884 Nancy's mother was married again, this time to her cousin James Thomas Allen, who had just come back to Kentucky after trying his hand at prospecting in Montana. Allen wanted no part of another man's child, so Nancy continued to live with her grandparents until her grandfather died and her step-grandmother went home to her family.

Nancy rejoined her mother in 1888, the same year her half-sister, Ella, was born. Two years later, Allen bundled his family onto a train and headed west to Helena, Montana, in search of a fortune in gold. When he had no luck finding a mining claim, he left his family behind and moved on to Idaho, dreaming of silver. He would send for them, he said, when he got established.

Life was hard for Texas Annie and her daughters with no one to provide for them. Mrs. Allen tried to earn a living with her sewing, while Nancy got a job doing domestic chores for fifty cents a day. One winter evening, she came home from work to find her mother in bed, burning with fever and coughing in fits. For the next nine months, she watched Texas Annie waste away until finally, when Nancy was sixteen, her once-lovely mother died of tuberculosis. Friends sent word to Allen, who returned to Helena just long enough to fetch Ella and take her back to Idaho. Nancy was left to fend for herself.

With the help of sympathetic friends, Nancy got a job with the Roberts family in Cascade, twenty-five miles southwest of Great Falls. They treated her so much like family that she called them Ma and Pa Roberts. Through them she met the most important man in her life.

About a year after their wedding, Nancy convinced Charlie to move to Great Falls, where there would be a bigger market for his paintings and sculptures. Charlie had quit the cowboy life and started trying to make a living as an artist only about three years earlier, and so far business was not exactly booming. A big part of the problem was Charlie's sociable nature. His buddies were always dropping in for a chat, or he was wandering over to the Mint or Silver Dollar Saloon for a friendly drink with the boys. He was too modest to ask people to buy his work—anyone who did was a "sucker." Instead, he gave many of his paintings away as gifts or used them as currency to pay his bills at the bars and grocery stores. Money was scarce, but Charlie was used to living on slim rations.

Nancy was more ambitious. She believed in her husband's talent and saw in it a ticket to prosperity. According to Russell biographer Harold McCracken,

> *from the beginning she rode herd on him in an effort to keep him from spending too much time in the local saloon. . . . The bitter memories of her own parents' wrecked marriage had unquestionably left their mark—and a deep desire to find happiness and security for herself. . . .*
>
> *When [Charlie] was working on a picture and some of his former cronies dropped in for a visit or to invite him downtown for one-or-two [drinks], she refused to let them into the house or Charlie out. For this determined behavior, Nancy Russell was soon heartily disliked among some of the characters around Great Falls.*

Though Charlie no doubt missed these gabfests with his friends, he conceded that Nancy had his best interests at heart. "If she hadn't prodded me," he said, "I wouldn't have done the work I did."

One day, Charles Schatzlein, a Butte storekeeper who had sold some of Charlie's pictures, stopped by the modest Russell home with a notion that would prove profitable for both Montana and American art. In *Good Medicine*, a collection of Charlie's letters that she edited after his death, Nancy recalled the man's advice:

> *"Do you know, Russell," he said, "you don't ask enough for your pictures. That last bunch you sent me, I sold one for enough to pay for six. I am paying you your price, but it's not enough. I think your wife should take hold of that end of the game and help you out."*

From that time, the prices of Charlie's work began to advance until it was possible to live a little more comfortably.

Oddly enough, Nancy found that the higher she priced Charlie's paintings, the more people seemed to want them. Instead of the twenty-five dollars or so that Charlie had gotten for his oils, Nancy began asking—and getting—hundreds of dollars. Charlie admitted to his friends that he was embarrassed by Nancy's boldness and shocked when people paid the prices she asked. But he also had to admit that his reputation was growing. Schatzlein had judged correctly. Charlie had the soft heart, but Nancy had the head for business.

Eventually, Nancy realized that Montana was no place to make one's name and fortune as an artist. There simply weren't enough people there who could afford to invest in art. So she began to wrangle exhibitions in some of the nation's major cities: first in Saint Louis, Charlie's hometown, then in Chicago and Denver, and finally in New York.

Though Charlie hated this place he called "the big camp" with "too many tepees," New Yorkers loved his realistic renderings of life among the cowboys and Indians of what was fast becoming the Old West. In 1911 Charlie exhibited at the prestigious Folsom Galleries in New York and in 1914 at the Dore Gallery in London. To Nancy's awe and delight, the Russells were soon dining with European nobility. They would never have to worry about money again.

By now the Russells had moved into a spacious two-story home in one of Great Falls' most respectable neighborhoods. Today, the white clapboard house on Fourth Avenue North is the nucleus of the C. M. Russell Museum complex. The Russells also built a lodge on spectacular Lake McDonald in Glacier National Park. They would spend almost every summer at this place, which they called Bull's Head Lodge for the symbol with which Charlie signed his art.

There was still one thing missing from the Russells' life, and Charlie especially felt the void. In 1916, when he was fifty-two and Nancy thirty-eight, they adopted an infant they named Jack. Nancy was not an attentive mother. She often was out of town on business, and when she was home she seemed to have little patience with childish wants and needs. Much of the time, she left Jack in the care of friend and neighbor Josephine Trigg, though she tried to compensate by giving him all the material things she thought a boy could want. Charlie, on the other hand, doted on his son and, in Nancy's opinion, hopelessly spoiled him.

The Russells were now more prosperous than even Nancy had ever dreamed. But, according to author McCracken,

> *success carried Charlie and his wife further and further apart*
> *in their respective conceptions of what were the most important*
> *things in life. . . . [T]he fruits of good fortune were much more*
> *appetizing to her than to him. Although Charlie's paintings*

*were bringing prices running into five figures, she still rode herd
on him with as unrelenting persistence as she had in the hungry
days when they had first come to Great Falls.*

By now, Charlie had spent close to sixty years in the saddle, and he was nearing the end of the trail. Yet, even when he began to complain of feeling poorly, Nancy kept him at his easel. Soon Charlie was diagnosed with goiter, an enlargement of the thyroid gland, but he refused to undergo surgery. He wasn't about to let anyone "slit his throat," as he put it. When he finally consented to an operation at the Mayo Clinic in Rochester, Minnesota, it was too late. The goiter had already damaged his heart, and his doctor predicted he had three months to live. Charlie made the man promise not to tell Nancy, but she already knew  she had instructed the doctor to keep the bad news from Charlie. They went home pretending for each other's sake that all would be well.

On October 24, 1926, Charlie Russell died of a heart attack while checking on his sleeping ten-year-old son. Nancy devoted the rest of her life to promoting his work, even refusing two marriage proposals so that she could remain Mrs. Charles M. Russell. She moved to Pasadena, California, where she died on May 23, 1940, after suffering a stroke and developing bronchial pneumonia. She was buried by Charlie's side in Great Falls.

Cowboy actor William S. Hart, a longtime friend of the Russells, once offered a touching tribute to the couple's devotion: "One could never say Charlie without saying Nancy, too, for they were always together—a real man and a real woman."

# FANNIE SPERRY STEELE

⚜

(1887–1983)

Champion Bronc Rider

On September 1, 1912, the most ambitious rodeo of its time got off to a sour start. A steady drizzle soaked the corrals and exhibition grounds at Victoria Park in Calgary, Alberta, where the first Calgary Stampede was about to get under way. Cowboys in rain slickers hustled to and fro on the backs of dripping mounts. Supply wagons and milling livestock churned through the mud.

As twenty-five-year-old Fannie Sperry and her mother, Rachel, gamely inspected the displays—including exact replicas of Old Fort Whoop-Up and the original Hudson's Bay Company trading post—a man burst out of one of the horse barns, shouting for a doctor. But it was too late. Cowboy Joe Lamar had just been thrown and trampled to death by a bronc with the deceptively innocuous name of Red Wing. Though she didn't know it, Fannie would soon have her own confrontation with the murderous beast.

Fannie Sperry had not come to Calgary to sit demurely on the sidelines and applaud the action. She had been invited to compete for the title of "Lady Bucking Horse Champion of the World." And she had every intention of winning.

The final day of the Stampede dawned clear and sunny. More than sixty thousand people crowded into the stands and watched as the Duke of Connaught—Governor General of Canada and uncle of the King of England—rode into the arena in an open coach pulled by two white horses. Wearing a uniform smothered in medals and a naval officer's hat crowned with a plume, he climbed into the royal box with his wife and daughter and settled down to watch the performance.

The male bronc riders went first, followed by exhibitions of stagecoach driving and rope tricks. Then came the finals of the women's bronc-riding competition. Each participant drew a slip of paper from a hat to determine which animal she would ride. Fannie drew the killer horse, Red Wing.

A more timid soul would have cringed at the prospect of climbing onto the back of one of the most dangerous horses in the bucking string, but Fannie was delighted. If she could stick to Red Wing, surely she would deserve the championship!

Fannie waited nervously as her competitors burst from the chutes atop a series of seething mounts. Finally it was her turn. The best, one of the judges announced, had been saved for last. Fannie Sperry of Mitchell, Montana, would attempt to ride the deadly bronc. Writer Dee Marvine described what happened next:

> *The glistening sorrel stood taut, and a shudder rippled across his flanks as Fannie eased into the saddle. Positioning the toes of her boots in the stirrups, she adjusted her grip on the buck rein. The familiar feel of her own saddle provided small comfort, as she poised her body against the cantle, her legs gripping the horse's girth. She signaled, and the gate opened.*
>
> *The ride that followed is recorded in rodeo annals as one of the best ever made by a woman—or a man. Fannie rode the murderous horse, never losing control, never sacrificing balance and style. When the hazer pulled her free in front of the royal box, a thundering ovation measured her triumph. She saluted the audience with a bow and a wide sweep of her hat.*

The judges' decision was quick in coming. The first Lady Bucking Horse Champion of the World was none other than Fannie Sperry! Along with the title went a check for one thousand dollars, a gold buckle, a saddle hand-tooled with roses—and a reputation that would change her life.

Fannie Sperry was born March 27, 1887, in the shadow of the Bear Tooth, a mountain north of Helena, Montana Territory, which has since become known as the Sleeping Giant. Along with two brothers and two sisters, she grew up on the family ranch and was infected early on by her mother's love of horses. Even as a toddler, she later said, it was obvious which way her "twig was bent." Her mother often liked to tell the story of the day little Fannie waited by a spring, hoping one of the wild horses that roamed the hills behind the homestead would come to drink. When a maverick pinto approached, the toddler wielded a long scarf for a lasso and vowed to "tetch me a white-face horthie!" By the age of six, Fannie had a pony of her own.

Rachel Sperry had a no-nonsense way of teaching her children to ride. She simply plopped them onto the back of a gentle horse and told them not to fall off. If they disregarded the command, she gave them a smart smack on the behind and lifted them back into the saddle. By the time the Sperry children were teenagers, they were all expert riders capable of breaking and shoeing their own horses.

Fannie first rode for a paying audience in the summer of 1903, when she was only sixteen. She thrilled residents of Mitchell, a tiny settlement not far from the Sperry ranch, by sticking like a cocklebur to the back of a writhing, white stallion. Her black braids and free right hand swung like horsewhips as the animal tried to buck her off. Onlookers were so impressed that they passed a hat and gave her all the money that was collected.

A year later, Fannie began her professional riding career—not as a bronc rider, but as a relay racer. Patterned after the Pony Express race that Buffalo Bill Cody incorporated into his Wild West show, the relays thrilled audiences in Helena, Butte, Anaconda, and Missoula. The racers changed horses several times, riding each animal an equal distance. Sometimes they had to change their own saddles. Because the riders mounted and dismounted at high speed, the threat of spills and accidents kept tension—and interest—high.

In the summer of 1905, a Butte, Montana, show promoter contracted with Fannie and three other girls to ride relay races throughout the Midwest. Billed as the "Montana Girls," they were scheduled to perform in Butte before heading east. The day before the relay races, the manager of the Butte show talked Fannie into riding an "outlaw" bronc known as Tracy. Unfortunately, the local newspaper later reported, "she had about as much chance to ride Tracy as [boxer] Jim Jeffries would have of earning a decision in a bout with a circular saw." The horse bolted out of the chute, ran about 150 yards, and stopped dead, catapulting Fannie over his head. According to the *Butte Miner,*

> she made several revolutions in the air, and then struck the
> ground with a dull thud. Women screamed, for it seemed that
> the frail equestrienne had been dashed to death. But Miss Sperry
> arose gamely, and approached the black demon, who had become
> entangled with the bridle reins, and was savagely pawing up the
> dirt in an effort to extricate himself. It was a rare exhibition of
> grit, and two thousand voices howled their approval.

Fannie had every intention of remounting the wild-eyed bronc, but men in the arena wouldn't allow it. Instead, they put a cowboy on the horse, and the show continued.

Fannie was one of only about a dozen women daring enough to ride bucking horses professionally just after the turn of the century. And she was one of only a tiny handful who rode "slick and clean," without hobbling the stirrups. Women bronc riders often tied their stirrups together with a cinch strap under the horse's belly, making it far more difficult to be thrown out of the saddle. Some considered it a less competitive way to ride. As Fannie put it, "it isn't giving the horse a fifty-fifty chance—fifty per cent in favor of him that he'll buck you off, fifty per cent in favor of you that you'll ride him." She also considered it too dangerous. With the stirrups hobbled, a rider couldn't kick free in time if a horse began to rear over backward, increasing the chances that she would be crushed beneath it.

Fannie went on to win many accolades in her riding career. In 1912, the same year as her triumph at the Calgary Stampede, she teamed up with a partner—a thirty-four-year-old cowpuncher and part-time rodeo clown named Bill Steele. She met Bill while performing at a county fair in Deer Lodge, Montana, and she married him only a few months later, on April 30, 1912. They spent their honeymoon on the rodeo circuit.

It was in Sioux City, Iowa, during the second rodeo that the Steeles entered together, that Fannie received the most serious injuries of her career. Her steed stumbled, pinning her beneath it. "She arose from the ground immediately and stood uncertainly on her feet for a moment," the *Sioux City Journal* reported, "then fainted in the arms of her husband." A badly sprained back and hip kept her out of competition for several weeks. Yet, at her first show after her convalescence—a Frontier Days celebration in Winnipeg, Manitoba—she won her second women's world bucking horse championship.

What motivated Fannie to devote herself to so dangerous a sport? After all, she stood only five feet, seven inches tall, weighed about 120 pounds, and was described as "lithe, supple, and graceful." She once justified her obsession this way:

> *How can I explain to dainty, delicate women what it is like*
> *to climb down into a rodeo chute onto the back of a wild*
> *horse? How can I tell them it is a challenge that lies deep in*
> *the bones—a challenge that may go back to prehistoric man*
> *and his desire to conquer the wilderness . . . ? I have loved it*
> *[bronc riding] every single, wonderful, suffering, exhilarating,*
> *damned, blessed moment of it. . . . Pain is not too great a price*
> *to pay for the freedom of the saddle and a horse between the legs.*

In 1914 Bill and Fannie launched their own small Wild West show, touring towns and cities across Montana. During these performances, Fannie got a chance to show off her skills as a sharpshooter. With a rifle, she shattered china eggs that Bill held between his fingers and knocked the ash off cigars he clenched between his teeth. Once, when trying out a new rifle, she winged Bill in the finger. He simply used another to hold the egg, so the audience wouldn't notice the miss. When Fannie nicked that finger, too, blood gushed from Bill's hand, and they cut the act short. Bill must have been relieved to skip the cigar trick.

On another occasion, Bill was thrown from a horse, knocked unconscious, and presumed dead. The show promoter frantically cast about for someone to take his place for the rest of the program and found a willing substitute in Fannie. She later explained:

*There wasn't even time for me to go to him, for I had to get ready to make his ride for him. That may seem callous, but we were show people in our own right, and "the show had to go on." I could lament for Bill later, but the horse had to be ridden right then.*

Fannie retired from professional riding in 1925. She and Bill—who had survived the fall—settled on a ranch near Helmville, Montana, where they worked as outfitters, guiding hunters into the backcountry. When Bill died in 1940, Fannie continued the small business alone for another twenty-five years. She died in Helena, Montana, on February 11, 1983, at the age of ninety-five, after having been inducted into both the national cowboy and cowgirl halls of fame.

"If there are not horses in heaven, I do not want to go there," she once said. "But I believe there will be horses in heaven as surely as God will be there, for God loved them or He would not have created them with such majesty."

# NEVADA WOMEN

# SARAH WINNEMUCCA HOPKINS

## (1844–1891)

### A Sparrow Among Eagles

In 1864 twenty-year-old Sarah Winnemucca, a Paiute Indian, stood on the stage of Henry Sutliffe's Music Hall in Virginia City as the audience rose, their applause thundering in an avalanche of praise. She nervously brushed her hands against her buckskin skirt, the swaying fringe revealing ornately beaded boots. Long, coal-black hair fell across delicate features as she turned to smile at her father, Chief Winnemucca, who stood stoically behind her.

Sarah and her father hoped their presentation would mend escalating tensions between white Nevada settlers and the Northern Paiute Indians, as well as garnering enough food and clothing to keep the Paiutes from starving or freezing that winter. It was the beginning of a journey that would leave Sarah heartbroken, destitute, and ill as she attempted time and again to bring understanding and cooperation between two very different cultures. Not until long after her death would she be heralded as a peacemaker between the two races.

Sarah Winnemucca's birth the summer of 1844 near the Humboldt River occurred just prior to the great influx of gold seekers crossing the desert plains to California. Captain Truckee, the Paiute chief and Sarah's grandfather, served as guide for parties heading west and considered the white man his friend and peer.

Her parents, Winnemucca and Tuboitony, named Sarah *Thocmetony*, meaning "shell flower." She spent her childhood beside her mother and other Paiute women and children traveling miles each day gathering roots, herbs, and wild seeds to flavor the fish, ground squirrels, and larger game caught by the men. Crunchy delicacies of roasted crickets and grasshoppers were favorite treats. Although they considered the Pyramid Lake region their homeland, the Paiutes were hunters and gatherers, not settling to farm but preferring to rely on the land for sustenance.

The Paiutes kept their past alive by relating ancient tales. The story of Cannibal Owl, who snatched naughty children, pounded them into pulp, and ate them, is a typical legend. When her father described the first white men he saw as owl-like with scraggly gray beards and colorless, ghostly eyes, Sarah steadfastly believed she would be eaten if caught by one of these white apparitions.

Sometimes nightmares become reality. As white miners and settlers penetrated farther into their territory, Sarah's people learned to avoid the newcomers—encounters usually ended in tragedy for the unsophisticated Paiutes. One terrifying incident cemented Sarah's fear of the white intruders.

Sara's mother, Tuboitony, and the other women were gathering seeds when a band of white men approached. As Tuboitony ran, little Sarah and her cousin lagged behind, unable to keep up with the fleeing adults. Rather than endanger the entire band, Tuboitony dug a trench in the sandy soil and ordered the two little girls into the ditch. She pushed dirt atop them and spread sagebrush over their heads to protect them from the sun. She then fled, leaving the girls to their fate. The sun rose higher and hotter before starting its westward descent toward a darkness filled with unknown terrors. Would the white men find them, smacking their lips as they stoked a roaring fire before pounding them to death? Or would marauding coyotes discover them first? Suddenly the girls heard rustling in the bushes and knew their fate was but a few feet away. In her book *Life Among the Paiutes: Their Wrongs and Claims*, Sarah described what happened next:

> *At last we heard some whispering. We did not dare to whisper to each other, so we lay still. I could hear their footsteps coming nearer and nearer. I thought my heart was coming out of my mouth. Then I heard my mother say, "Tis right here!" Oh, can any one in this world ever imagine what were my feelings when I was dug up by my poor mother and father?*

Captain Truckee ruled the Northern Paiutes wisely and compassionately. Having guided the whites into California, he understood they would soon wield more power than his people could ever muster. In 1851 he took a contingent of Paiutes to California to learn the white man's ways. Six-year-old Sarah, convinced she would be eaten by the dreaded white owls, cowered under a blanket as they crossed the Nevada plains.

After returning to their homeland, Winnemucca and Tuboitony sent Sarah and her younger sister Elma to live with Major William Ormsby, who ran a stage depot in Genoa, then part of Utah Territory. The Ormsbys taught the girls to speak and write English. In return, Sarah and Elma worked in the depot store, helped with household chores, and were companions for little Lizzie Anne Ormsby. The Ormsbys' kindness toward the two girls during the year they lived with them alleviated some of Sarah's doubts about white savages. It may have been during this time that Thocmetony acquired her English name of Sarah and her sister became known as Elma.

By the winter of 1858, the influx of white settlers had devastated the vast herds of wild game, fish, plants, and seeds that the Paiutes relied upon for sustenance. As bitter winds howled and snow drifted to towering heights, the Paiutes were forced to ask for assistance from Virginia City citizens—warm clothing and enough food to make it through the winter. But their pleas were ignored, and many froze or starved to death. The following winter brought little relief and even colder temperatures.

Old Captain Truckee, perhaps sensing his pending death, requested that Winnemucca and Tuboitony send Sarah and Elma to school in California to learn about the new world emerging around them. The San Jose school seemed amicable to the girls, but after only a few weeks white parents objected to their children sitting next to the Indians and insisted they leave.

White settlers, prospectors, and businesses now dominated the West. Virginia City boasted a white population of almost 15,000, and they wanted the Paiutes off the lush, productive land surrounding Pyramid Lake. The Natives were already restricted in where they could hunt and fish. Now the white populace wanted to determine where the Indians could live, pledging to provide food, clothing, and farming equipment if the Indians would stay within proscribed reservation boundaries. None of these promises materialized.

Winnemucca, now tribal leader after Captain Truckee's death, took the plight of his people to the citizens of Nevada. He walked onto the stage of Sutliffe's Music Hall that day in 1864 with Sarah, Elma, son Natches, and a handful of other Paiutes seeking assistance from the people of Virginia City. Sarah interpreted her father's words for the audience.

The Paiute group continued on to San Francisco and made their plea before an audience at the Metropolitan Theater. Sarah donned the expected attire—buckskin skirt trimmed with fringe and ornately beaded boots. She had quickly assessed the delight of white audiences when she romanticized her appearance, dressing as writers depicted Indians in western dime novels rather than in more traditional attire. Though the troupe was well received in San Francisco, their appeals were largely ignored.

In 1865, when Chief Winnemucca and his men were on a hunting expedition, a cavalry troop rode into the Paiute camp and accused the Indians of stealing cattle and slaying two white men. Refusing to believe the Indians' denial, the cavalry slaughtered thirty women, children, and old men. Sarah's sister Mary fled to the mountains to warn Chief Winnemucca and his men not to return. By the time the Mud Lake Massacre was over, Mary and Sarah's mother, Tuboitony, lay dead.

Conditions on Pyramid Lake Reservation became unbearable. The Paiutes were desperate for food and clothing. Tempers flared between the two races.

The summer of 1868 brought no relief for the destitute Paiutes. Sarah and Natches went to Camp McDermit near the Oregon border seeking assistance from the army. Recognizing her ability to speak several languages—English, Spanish, and various Indian dialects—the army hired Sarah as an interpreter. Natches, with the promise of protection and provisions for his people, was sent to bring in Chief Winnemucca. That July, around 500 Paiutes chose to relocate to Camp McDermit rather than starve to death.

Sarah believed her people could become productive farmers if taught how to plow and sow, skills they had not needed as hunters and gatherers. In a letter to Ely Samuel Parker, commissioner of Indian affairs, she offered her solution to the problem of feeding her people and respecting their needs:

> *So far as their knowledge of agriculture extends they are quite ignorant as they never had an opportunity of learning but I think if proper pains were taken that they would willingly make the effort to maintain themselves by their own labor if they could be made to believe that the products were to be their own and for their own use and comfort.*

Nothing came of her request for assistance, so in 1870 Sarah returned to San Francisco, where newspapers touted her as "Princess Sarah." But once again, false promises and undelivered goods were all the Paiutes received.

While she was still at Camp McDermit, First Lieutenant Edward D. Bartlett caught Sarah's eye with his dashing uniform, expert horsemanship, and happy-go-lucky lifestyle. Marriages between Native Americans and whites were forbidden in Nevada, so the couple traveled to Salt Lake City and wed on January 29, 1871. Unbeknown to Sarah, Bartlett had deserted his company. His fun-loving nature seemed to need the nourishment of copious amounts of liquor, purchased with money acquired by pawning Sarah's jewelry without her knowledge. The marriage was over within the year, although not legally dissolved until 1876.

In 1872 the Paiutes were relocated to the Malheur Reservation about 80 miles north of Camp McDermit. Resident Indian agent Sam Parrish and his wife were well liked, never demeaning the Paiutes' customs or needs; they also paid fair wages for work. When Mrs. Parrish opened a school, she and Sarah taught side by side. Under the supervision of Agent Parrish, the Paiutes accepted the confines of reservation living.

Unfortunately, life does not continue along straight and serene courses. Sam Parrish, never much of a religious man, was soon relieved of his duties, because the law insisted reservations be under Christian leadership. His replacement, former army officer W. V. Rinehart, bore ill will toward the Paiutes and soon ran afoul of the determined Sarah.

Rinehart blamed all the problems he encountered at Malheur on Sarah's insistent requests for fair treatment of the Paiutes. He refused to pay them for work they performed and withheld much-needed food and clothing. He closed Mrs. Parrish's school. Rinehart claimed Sarah was disloyal and purposely stirred up trouble. He threatened to put her in prison but, instead, banished her from the reservation.

In June 1878 a contingent of neighboring Paiutes begged Sarah to help their starving families. "You are our only voice," they pleaded. Realizing that assistance had to come from the highest power of the land, she decided to go to Washington, DC.

Sarah made it as far as the Oregon–Idaho border, where the Bannock tribe, as destitute as the Paiutes, rallied against their oppressive Indian agent. With war pending, Sarah returned to her people.

Chief Winnemucca refused to join the Bannock uprising. In retaliation, the Bannocks held him and a contingent of his band hostage. When Sarah learned that her father was behind enemy lines, she vowed to bring her people to safety, offering her services as interpreter and scout to General O. O. Howard, commander during the Bannock War. Along with her brother Lee and his wife, Mattie, she set out across miles of treacherous, rocky terrain to rescue the Paiute prisoners, stopping only for fresh horses before heading out again. Nearing the Bannock stronghold, they quit their horses and, on hands and knees, crawled up the side of the mountain.

Peering into the enemy camp, they found the Bannocks butchering cattle for an evening feast. The shadowy figures stealthily maneuvered their way through enemy lines to the imprisoned Paiutes, then led seventy-five of their people to safety. Over a three-day period, the triad rode more than 200 rough miles to bring the Paiutes home.

Sarah continued to serve under General Howard as interpreter and scout during the Bannock War, slipping in and out of enemy camps, stealing plans, intercepting Bannock war signals, and aiding in the capture of Bannock warriors.

After one particularly bloody fight, soldiers found a Bannock baby on the ground covered in dirt. The little girl was turned over to Sarah and Mattie, but knowing they could not care for the baby and continue to scout for the army, they entrusted her to two Bannock women prisoners. After the war, Sarah found the child's parents and reunited the family. The grateful couple named their daughter Sarah for her rescuer.

Sarah and Mattie were often called upon to hunt down fleeing Bannock prisoners. During one escapade across rock-hard ground, Mattie's horse slipped and tossed her brutally to the earth. Her injuries were severe, and Sarah feared for her sister-in-law's life. By August 1878 the Bannock War was over. Because the Paiutes had not joined the hostile Bannocks, they assumed they would be allowed to stay at Malheur Reservation. The army, however, considered all Indians prisoners of war regardless of tribe. The Paiutes were ordered to Yakima Reservation in Washington Territory, a distance of more than 350 miles over treacherous mountain ranges. They would travel in the middle of winter clad in threadbare blankets and worn-out boots.

On January 6, 1879, fifty wagons started out across the mountains of Oregon and Washington. Elderly Paiutes froze to death and were left beside the road; children died in their parents' arms. Sarah watched a mother and her new baby die. Mattie struggled against unconsciousness in the back of a roughshod wagon.

The Paiutes were promised warm clothing, an abundance of food, and comfortable lodgings at the end of their journey. What greeted them after almost a month on the hard, bitter road was a hastily built, unheated 150-foot shed that let in cold winter winds and drifting snow. Firewood was nonexistent, and scant food was provided to the already emaciated group. The Paiutes were assured that wagonloads of warm clothing were on the way. With spring came the promised goods: twenty-eight shawls and a handful of fabrics. Everything else had been sold to the highest bidder before reaching the Indians. Mattie died at the end of May.

Sarah taught school at Yakima, but as soon as she received her pay from the army for her scouting and interpreting duties, she set out again for Washington, DC. She was determined to secure aid for her people and to return them to Pyramid Lake. Her route was circuitous.

In November 1879 she went to see General Howard, who had not forgotten her invaluable help during the Bannock War. He gave her a letter of introduction to Washington officials. Stopping next in San Francisco, where her heroic deeds during the war had made her a celebrity, she took the opportunity to speak at Platte's Hall. She told of her people's history, how Captain Truckee had welcomed white settlers and led them across the Nevada desert to the gold fields of California. She recounted the treatment received at the hands of Indian agents such as W. V. Rinehart, and then she detailed the horrible march to Yakima.

An 1879 article in the *San Francisco Chronicle* recognized Sarah's stamina and poise:

> *Sarah has undergone hardships and dared dangers that few men would be willing to face, but she never lost her womanly qualities. . . . She speaks with force and decision, and talks eloquently of her people. Her mission, undertaken at the request of Chief Winnemucca, is to have her tribe gathered together again at their old home in Nevada, where they can follow peaceable pursuits and improve themselves.*

Chief Winnemucca, Natches, and a cousin joined her on her trek to Washington, DC. There they met Carl Schurz, secretary of the interior, who promised to send supplies and suggested they return home to await the glut of provisions that would be forthcoming. Before leaving the capital of freedom, they toured the White House, where they met President Rutherford B. Hayes.

Yet Sarah's nemesis, Agent Rinehart, had already laid the foundation for her defeat in Washington by sending a barrage of letters to E. A. Hayt, commissioner of Indian affairs, disparaging her character, calling her a woman of low means, and accusing her of prostitution. Schurz may have become aware of Rinehart's accusations, for he reneged on his promises to send provisions to the destitute Indians.

Failing once again to obtain aid, Sarah's loyalty came under question by her own people. She had traveled between two diverse worlds for so long, experiencing the harsh existence of reservation life along with the comforts enjoyed in white settlements. Some of her people felt she had sold out for a more lucrative lifestyle.

Once again Sarah tried to find companionship and love in the arms of a white man. Fair-haired Virginian Lewis H. Hopkins, like Edward Bartlett, liked the action of gambling halls and saloons. Although he was five years younger than Sarah, the couple married in San Francisco on December 5, 1881.

The newlyweds enjoyed little wedded bliss. When Chief Winnemucca died in 1882, Sarah's brother Natches became Paiute chief, and she was once again asked to intercede on the tribe's behalf. She and Hopkins traveled east in 1883. On this trip Sarah met two sisters, Elizabeth Palmer Peabody and Mary Mann.

Elizabeth Peabody, considered the first woman book publisher in the United States, also owned a bookstore frequented by the literary elite of Boston. She arranged a series of lectures for Sarah, encouraging her to detail the history and culture of the Paiute people, to explain to America that the Indians had no land, no citizenship, and no government representation.

Elizabeth then urged Sarah to write down the history of the Paiutes. Sarah considered herself a poor writer but Mary Mann, widow of educator Horace Mann, offered to edit her work. The commingling of three compassionate hearts and minds resulted in Sarah's book *Life Among the Paiutes: Their Wrongs and Claims*, published in 1883 and thought to be the first book written by a Native American woman.

On April 22, 1884, Sarah spoke before Congress, petitioning for an allotment of land for her people at Pyramid Lake. Although Interior Secretary Schurz opposed the action, a bill was passed on July 6, 1884, giving each family 160 acres of Nevada land. It was not good land—that had been gobbled up by white settlers—but at least they would be back on home soil.

While Sarah counted on the money she received from her lectures and the sale of her book to provide funds for her people, Lewis Hopkins preferred to gamble away a good portion of her earnings. Very little was left by the time they returned to Nevada. With her scant savings, plus the financial help of Elizabeth Peabody and Mary Mann, Sarah opened the Peabody Institute—a school in Lovelock, Nevada. She had always believed that education would bridge the disparities between the races, and said so in an article in the *Winnemucca Silver State* newspaper in 1886:

> *It seems strange to me that the Government has not found out years ago that education is the key to the Indian problem. Much money and many precious lives would have been saved if the American people had fought my people with Books instead of Power and lead. Education civilized your race and there is no reason why it cannot civilize mine.*

When Mary Mann died, she bequeathed her small estate to Sarah to help run the Peabody Institute. Sarah managed to keep the school open for a while but was soon inundated with financial woes. With her physical and emotional strength weakening, she was finally forced to close the establishment in 1888.

Ill, tired, and discouraged, Sarah went to live with her sister Elma at Henry's Lake on the Montana–Idaho border.

Sarah died in October 1891. She was only forty-seven years old. Although exhausted from years of fighting for her people, she had never quit. Her own words expressed her determination to return the Paiutes to the land of their ancestors: "When I think of my past life, and the bitter trials I have endured, I can scarcely believe I live, and yet I do; and, with the help of Him who notes the sparrow's fall, I mean to fight for my down-trodden race while life lasts."

# ELIZA COOK

## (1856–1947)

### Pills and Politics

The dark, foreboding horse and buggy tore down the road, gritty dust devils ascending skyward attempting to avoid the careening carriage. Each passing house seemed to sigh in relief as the buggy lunged forward into the night. The driver, a woman who could barely reach the reins, held no fear of the rough terrain that lay before her.

Clad in black from head to toe, the woman walked into the house that was her destination and surveyed the surroundings. A figure lay motionless on a cot in the far corner. The other occupants of the house watched in silence as the woman leaned over the inert body and reached into her cavernous bag. She smiled at the bedridden soul, and then turned to the anxious family waiting in fearful expectation. Suddenly the shadow of death that had hovered so near the house for days seemed to evaporate into the dusty corners of the room. The doctor had arrived.

Eliza Cook traveled a road few women before her had dared. As one of the first physicians on the Nevada frontier, man or woman, she ministered to the sick and injured, the elderly and the newly born, those who sought her out and those who declared they would never have a "doctress" come near them. Growing up during an era when most men who called themselves doctor had not attended medical school, when the healing art was more a guessing game than a scientific, lifesaving profession, Eliza discovered her calling for medicine at an early age.

One of five children born to John and Margaretta Gratrix Cook, Eliza made her appearance on February 5, 1856, in Salt Lake City, Utah. She later called her birth "an unappropriate blessing." Her father's belief in polygamy, plus his stinginess with money (he refused to buy shoes for his two daughters), encouraged Margaretta to leave her husband, taking Eliza and her sister, Rebecca, to Soda Springs, Idaho, then to White Pine County, Nevada. By 1870 the trio finally settled in Sheridan, Nevada, just south of present-day Carson City.

The threesome lived frugally. Margaretta took in laundry and sewed for the local townsfolk. Eliza once told a reporter the first Christmas gifts she remembered receiving were a cracker filled with raisins and a handmade wooden doll.

Few schools existed in Carson Valley when the abbreviated family arrived, and the two girls relied on their mother and a handful of borrowed books for their education. One of the books Eliza came across detailed home medical cures and remedies. This might have been a copy of William Buchan's book *Domestic Medicine*, which was first published in Scotland in 1769 and became popular in America about a hundred years later. Or she could have studied John C. Gunn's medical tome of the 1800s, *Domestic Medicine, or Poor Man's Friend*, in which he listed potions and poultices aimed particularly toward the western and southern states. Whatever she read, the book piqued her interest in medicine and she decided to pursue "doctoring" further.

Medicine of the 1800s offered scant cures for the sick and injured. Dirty conditions, poor nutrition, and backbreaking work often made health a precious commodity. There were few proven remedies for the ill and injured. Folks usually found something that worked for one condition and used the same remedy repeatedly for whatever other ailments they encountered.

Women were expected to find solutions for their family's ills, often scouring their gardens and kitchens for cures. Eliza was fascinated with common household items that many believed resolved certain medical situations. She probably helped her mother with a common activity among frontier women—collecting raspberry, spearmint, and peppermint leaves, along with roots and bark, to alleviate ailments and illnesses. Mothers wrapped strips of raw bacon around their children's necks to soothe sore throats. Wood ashes applied to cuts helped curtail bleeding. Rhubarb bitters, catnip tea, carrot scrapings, and fresh snow were all thought to contain curative powers. In a pinch cactus fiber could be used to sew up a wound.

Religious and mystic beliefs also played roles in healing. Some sects refused to call a physician no matter how dire the situation. Others relied upon spirits of the dead to save a wretched soul. According to historian Ronald M. James, early Nevada pioneer Mary McNair Mathews claimed that "[w]hen one of her son's fingers was accidentally cut off, she placed it in a brandy jar, calling on a background in sympathetic magic, so that it would not hurt him in the future."

Shortly after reading the medical book she'd found, Eliza had the chance to use some of her elementary knowledge on her first patient. Dr. H. W. Smith hired her to nurse his ailing wife back to health. Mrs. Smith was suffering from puerperal fever, a condition usually originating in childbirth due to unsanitary conditions. The doctor had little in his black bag to ease his wife's suffering and became increasingly impressed with Eliza's care and concern for her patient. He offered her a job as his assistant and nurse even though she had no medical training.

Encouraged by Dr. Smith, Eliza read everything in his limited medical library. After about six months under his tutelage, Dr. Smith felt she was ready to enter one of the few medical schools that admitted women.

Over the years, women had repeatedly tried to enter all-male medical institutions, and the road had been rough and often unfriendly. The first woman to seek admission to a medical school was Elizabeth Blackwell in 1847. When she applied, she was informed the only way she could attend was if she dressed like a man. She refused. On her second attempt, she applied to Geneva Medical College in New York. School officials decided to let the all-male student body decide if she should be allowed to attend. After hearing her application, the men thought it was a joke and decided to go along with the prank by voting to admit her. To their great surprise, she readily accepted and completed her studies as a physician in 1849. The first women's medical school opened the following year.

Some male physicians felt the entrance of women into the medical community would threaten their practices economically. They argued that women were too frail and delicate to view the intimacies of the human body; they were too emotional to handle the horrors of surgery, the scourge of disease and human misery, the shame in examining a naked torso. Their hysterical nature and inferior intellect would prevent them from performing the more difficult tasks and would "harden women's hearts and leave them bereft of softness and empathy." These same practitioners, however, praised a woman's ability to take on strenuous nursing chores. Of the seventy-five medical schools operating in the United States in the early 1880s, only a handful allowed women students. One of them, Cooper Medical College in San Francisco (now Stanford University), had been admitting women for about five years when Eliza applied in 1882. She was accepted into its two-year program, considered all the education a doctor needed.

Eliza joined only a handful of women who were admitted into the prestigious medical community even though more than thirty years had passed since Elizabeth Blackwell had first walked into a classroom. Little had changed in the study of medicine during that time, but a few new procedures were now taught. Doctors had learned how to measure temperature, pulse, and blood pressure, even if they did not always know for what reason. Thermometers, tongue depressors, and stethoscopes appeared in medical bags alongside lances and probes. If the doctor appreciated the need for sterilization to ward off infection, she also toted along a copper pan in which to boil her instruments.

After graduating in 1884, Eliza set up practice in Sheridan at the home of her sister and brother-in-law, Rebecca and Hugh Park. She followed the routine of many women doctors, who returned to their hometowns where they had family and social connections, eliminating the burden of establishing businesses in locations where they were virtually unknown. Opening an office in her sister's home also gave Eliza, a single woman, a cloak of propriety when seeing patients.

The winter of 1889–1890 roared into Carson Valley like a stampede of Saturday-night cowboys headed for the closest saloon. With snowdrifts piled high across the plains, only the bravest dared to venture out. On a clear but bone-chilling day, a young boy skated as fast as he could across the frozen Carson River. Mr. Hickey had sent him on a mission—Mrs. Hickey was ready to have her baby and needed the doctor quick.

Hugh Park hitched up the horses and sleigh to take Eliza on the treacherous 3-mile ride. But the snow was too deep; the horses would never make it to the Hickey place. Ingenuity being an absolute necessity in the early West, Park and three of his neighbors crafted a sleigh from old snowshoes, settled Eliza and her black bag in the back, strapped themselves to the front of the makeshift sleigh, and set off across the valley.

When Mr. Hickey, who was probably pacing outside the house waiting for the doctor to arrive, saw the human-drawn sleigh plowing through the heavy snow, he greeted the men with a wee bit of Irish whiskey. Eliza, a temperance advocate since early childhood, chastised the men before disappearing into the house to attend to Mrs. Hickey. Little James Hickey arrived several hours later. Eliza and her four-man team strapped themselves into their makeshift sled and headed out across the drifting snow for the long ride home.

Aware she must continue her studies if she was to compete with the medical men of Nevada, Eliza attended classes at the Women's Medical College of Philadelphia in 1890, one of a handful of female medical schools that had cropped up as more women sought careers in medicine. The following summer she pursued graduate work at the Post Graduate Medical College in New York.

Returning to Nevada in 1891, she at first opened an office in the Golden Eagle Hotel in Reno, but stayed only six months before returning to her roots in Sheridan. There Eliza tended to a community of Nevada women and men who brought her their broken bones, illnesses without names or cures, scalded hands from open fires and boiling water, bites from snakes, scorpions, and spiders. She made her own splints and created some of her own concoctions for treatment of these ills as well as ordering other remedies through the mail. Each dose of medicine was carefully wrapped in a sterilized piece of tissue paper.

Many of her patients were pregnant women, who welcomed the compassionate caring of another female during childbirth. Eliza understood that a homestead in early Nevada relied on a mother's hand to keep food on the table, livestock fed, and children clothed and educated while the man of the house left each day to work in the mines or plow the fields. If a new mother was unable to leave the birthing bed and tend her household, everyone suffered. As Dr. Cook's reputation grew, women knew a call to her meant the family would receive care beyond the birthing of a newborn. Eliza arrived to bring a new life into the world and care for the mother, but for days afterward she'd return to the remote farmhouse or ranch to care for the family—washing clothes, cleaning dishes, cooking, and performing general housework.

By the end of the nineteenth century, more than 7,000 women were practicing medicine in the United States, although the American Medical Association did not acknowledge them until 1915. Women doctors were still a rarity in Nevada as late as 1918 when a census listed only eight licensed female doctors, two of them retired and only one who had been practicing longer than Eliza.

For many years Eliza, along with many others, believed she was the first woman to practice medicine in Nevada, but a good many doctresses had in fact preceded her. Since physicians were not licensed in the state until 1899, and Eliza was the first woman to receive a state-issued medical license, the assumption remained unquestioned for some time.

There was another side to Eliza: She abhorred the evils of alcohol. Even as a child, she was repelled by the use of liquor, joining a youth temperance group, the Band of Hope, when she was fourteen years old. When the women of Carson Valley formed a local chapter of the Women's Christian Temperance Union, she became actively involved and served as president from 1896 until 1901. She often lectured on the evils of drink and admitted she "made myself very objectionable at times, I've no doubt." No wonder she was appalled when Mr. Hickey brought out the whiskey before she delivered his son.

At the same time she was involved with the Band of Hope, young Eliza read a passage in the Bible that disturbed her. Genesis 3 says in part, ". . . thy desire shall be to thy husband and he shall rule over thee." In an interview with the *Nevada State Journal* in 1941, Eliza remembered the words she had read many years before. "That man should rule over woman was to my mind most unjust," she said. "I protested to my mother and she told me the husband's rule was right only when it was a righteous rule." Margaretta had already experienced the unrighteous rule of her own husband. "That silenced my tongue for a time, but not my mental protest." Equality for women was another cause Eliza embraced.

As she did with everything she challenged, Eliza took on the women's suffrage movement with a vengeance. A letter she wrote to the *Reno Evening Gazette* in 1894 outlined her views on a woman's right to vote, succinctly laying out her platform. She argued she would never feel "a citizen of these United States, . . . until I have the rights and privileges of the masculine citizen."

She did not mince words in her tirade against the world's assumption that man was a more intelligent and worldly person than his female counterpart:

> . . . *man cannot fill woman's place in the economy of nature nor in social economy. How then can he fill her place in the political economy of the nation?*
> . . . *I believe in the fullest development of every human being, and believe that this can never come except through*

*activity of all the faculties. I believe the responsibility of citizenship*
*will arouse the dormant powers of some of our women.*
*. . . I believe a woman fully as capable of assisting in the*
*government of the nation as the government of the home, and I*
*have observed that the greater portion of the latter is left to her.*
*. . . [I]f to vote is the evidence of a man's freedom and*
*citizenship, the absence of that right shows that woman is*
*neither free nor a citizen.*

In October 1895 women from across Nevada gathered at McKissick's Opera House in Reno to establish the Nevada Women's Equal Suffrage League. Eliza was elected one of the first vice presidents and later became president of the Douglas County Equal Suffrage League. Diligent in her quest for a woman's right to vote, she often lectured to groups in the evenings after long days tending to the physical needs of the community.

In 1896 Eliza published a missal on the rights of women. Titled *The Woman Yet to Come*, it outlined the duties of a woman who has equal status. While she would be far from perfect, tomorrow's woman had the duty to "do more and better work than we do because [she will be] better prepared. . . . Surely, she who cleans is as worthy as they who make unclean!"

The text continued, "As a citizen, our coming woman will be as active as such a woman should be, and will aid by voice and vote in establishing the right. She will not be a political cipher, and consequently will take an active, intelligent part in all governmental affairs." Unlike many of her suffrage counterparts, Eliza lived long enough to see the women's rights bill pass in the state of Nevada in 1914. In 1920 it became the Nineteenth Amendment to the US Constitution.

By 1901 Eliza needed a break from the rigors of running a medical practice, as well as working for women's suffrage and fighting a losing battle for temperance. She talked a friend into spending a year traveling with her to the Holy Land, Greece, Egypt, the British Isles, and Europe. When she returned, she lectured on her travels, much to the delight of her Carson Valley neighbors, some of whom had never ventured more than a few miles beyond their own front doors.

In 1911 Eliza built a home in Mottsville, Nevada, that became her sanctuary from the trials of a medical practice and her work with the suffrage movement. She relished the time she spent working in her garden and abundant apple orchard. On a three-foot woodstove, she filled her house with the aroma of freshly baked apple pies, one of which usually accompanied her when she set out to deliver a new baby. She dispensed dozens of homemade cookies to her younger patients, and continued to treat the ills of the community until 1921 when, at the age of sixty-five, she decided she had practiced long enough.

Although she no longer tended to the physical needs of her patients, for the next twenty years she continued to treat their hearts by crocheting small outfits for almost every newborn in Carson Valley. Their stomachs she soothed by making sure every child she encountered received a cookie hot from her tiny oven, or a crisp, shiny apple from her orchard.

Dr. Eliza Cook died in her sleep at her home in Mottsville on October 2, 1947. Beside her lay a handwritten document, "Outline of My Life," in which she briefly told of her early childhood, her medical practice, and her work with the suffrage and temperance movements. She lived ninety-one years and witnessed a vast number of changes both in the medical field and in women's rights. She was representative of the emerging woman of the twentieth century, capable of performing any task she set out to do.

# MAUDE FRAZIER

∘᪶᪶᪶∘

(1881–1963)

Education Reformer

Coming from a family of teachers," said Maude Frazier, "I was expected to follow the tradition. Yet I was cast in the wrong mold to fit comfortably as a teacher of that period." Rather than adhering to a prim and proper lifestyle and following the rules and regulations imposed on teachers in the early 1900s, Maude preferred a brisk bicycle ride across town or a speedy gallop out over the Nevada desert. Maude Frazier bent and broke the rules of feminine comportment, but her visionary insights into the educational needs of rural Nevada schoolchildren made her a pioneer in Nevada education.

Maude was born on April 4, 1881, in rural Sauk County, Wisconsin. Like many children, she loved playing in the attic amid discarded family relics, probably imagining great adventures and undiscovered lands. When she happened upon a cache of her grandfather's papers hidden under years of dust and debris, detailing his adventures as he migrated into the Northwest Territory, she realized her wanderlust longings were inherited and not strange ideas that only she harbored. In later years she remembered her many hours spent rummaging through attic antiques and lamented that today's children would never know the secrets and untold stories languishing in corners of ancient dormers. "As the years pass, I keep thinking that our greatest lack today is *attics*. Modern homes never have them, with the result that young people live only in their own generation, feeling no intimate connection with the past. Their roots will go deeper if their homes have attics!"

Reluctantly obeying her parents' wishes that she become a teacher, Maude attended Wisconsin Normal School in Stevens Point, Wisconsin. After passing the teaching examination, she taught in small Wisconsin timber towns and iron-mining communities. In these economically depressed districts, she first encountered children eager to learn but lacking the tools and teachers to do so, something she never forgot as she made her way beyond rural Wisconsin fields.

To supplement her meager teacher's salary, Maude worked a variety of jobs. In her autobiography, she remembered clerking in country stores and taking in sewing. The day she spilled ink on the only skirt she owned forced her to develop a more creative bent. She dyed the rest of the skirt to match the inkblot and proudly considered herself lucky to now own a brand-new black skirt.

Unfortunately, Maude's yearning for great adventures did not fit the demeanor expected of a proper schoolmarm in the early 1900s. She preferred to play ball rather than watch. She enjoyed ice-skating and swimming, activities frowned upon by staid school board members, almost always men. Even upswept hairdos and bright-colored dresses adorned with too many ruffles could lead to a distressed look or disciplinary action. Although Maude looked every bit the schoolteacher in her neatly coiffed hairdo and rimmed eyeglasses, she chafed under the scrutiny and demands placed upon women in general and teachers specifically. "It is quite possible that it was never intended by the good Lord that I should be a schoolteacher. At least not so soon after the turn of the Twentieth Century, when they were definitely a distinct species." For the rest of her life, she bristled under the scrutiny of male supervisors, whether it be regarding her dress, her demeanor, or her recommendations for education reform.

Maude often remembered her grandfather's words, and she yearned to explore new worlds and experience great adventures. Because she was already chafing under the latest Wisconsin rules imposed upon teachers—restrictions against dancing and playing cards at any time—she pored over newspaper articles describing the rush for gold in the West. Newly formed mining communities begged teachers to come and educate their children. Female teachers who first went west were often dismissed if they married, and with so few marriageable women in the barren outback of America, it wasn't long after their arrival that they met and married a love-starved rancher, cowboy, or prospector. A 1901 article in the *Tonopah Bonanza* newspaper claimed that twenty applicants had applied for a teaching position but the school board was looking for an "old maid," hoping she would stay longer than some of the previous women who had taken the job, only to be swept away to a preacher within months of their arrival.

Maude applied for teaching positions in several far-off territories, turning down an opportunity in Alaska before accepting a job in Genoa, Nevada, in 1906. With trepidation, her parents put her on the train, probably expecting she would be scalped before reaching her destination. She arrived safely, however, and began a career that would fulfill her desire to provide learning-starved, impoverished children with a meaningful education.

Maude was the first to admit she made mistakes while learning her trade, but she was surprised when school board members criticized her for riding her bicycle around town, "... something," she said, "which no nice girl would think of doing. Their objection to such a means of getting about always appeared incongruous to me, since the board members expect this same dignified teacher to perform all the undignified tasks of janitor work" for the grand sum of $22 a month.

*In those early years of my teaching career, I did discover that
there was nothing to compare with this janitor work to let off
steam which had arisen from anger. Taking out one's ire on
broom or mop really makes the dirt fly! I had plenty of reasons
to need this physical exertion.*

Along with the majority of schoolteachers in the early 1900s, Maude was
expected to handle situations far beyond her teaching duties. She had to locate
books, paper, pencils, and slates for her pupils; cut and carry wood for the stove;
tote the drinking water from sometimes far-off streams; and sweep and scrub
the schoolhouse floor, if the schoolhouse was fortunate enough to have a floor.

Teachers in Nevada dealt with floods and fires, stampeding cattle and
runaway horses, raiding Indians, drunken cowboys, outlaws, and down-and-
out prospectors. Snakes, scorpions, coyotes, and other strange desert creatures
greeted Maude upon her arrival. She was a novice in the desert, unsure whom to
trust or how far to wander.

When she entered the Genoa schoolhouse, there was not a book to be
found. Children brought materials from home, and Maude utilized this assort-
ment of teaching tools as best she could. Her charges ranged in age from five to
fifteen, and their educational background was just as diverse. She taught children
who eagerly wanted to learn and those who would rather be riding the range or
searching for ore in the mining fields.

Maude traveled to some of the most remote areas of Nevada, teaching
whoever showed up at whatever school facility available. In Dinero Gorge, she
held classes in a tent with no supplies. Lovelock and Goldfield, both prosperous
districts, provided ample school materials, including a piano. In Seven Troughs,
about 30 miles from Lovelock, a tent school sufficed until a brothel was moved
to make way for a roughly constructed schoolhouse. Even then, floorboards
were spaced so far apart that dropped pencils had to be retrieved from under the
building. In winter Maude and the children wore layers of clothing and huddled
under blankets brought from home to keep warm. She taught in temperatures
from below zero to more than a hundred degrees and found that most of her students seldom complained and rarely missed school—so great was their desire to
learn. The lack of materials was a nuisance, but Maude soon realized that a "good
school is a thing of the mind and spirit and not a thing of gadgets."

During summer breaks, she learned to ride and could often been seen tearing
on horseback across the range amid a herd of cowboys, her six-foot frame sitting
tall in the saddle.

For sixteen years Maude tended to the educational needs of western Nevada children. During the summers of 1918 through 1920, she attended school at the Uni-

versity of Nevada in Reno. In 1920 her exemplary work at the university afforded her the opportunity to become principal in Sparks, Nevada. When she tried to rent a room in Sparks, however, the landlady told her, "Do you think I have sunk so low that I would rent a room to a woman? Especially a woman teacher?"

The following year, she applied for a job in Las Vegas as deputy superintendent with the Nevada Department of Education. Maude at first viewed the sparsely populated community with skepticism, claiming it "was the most unprepossessing place I had ever seen, and nobody at that time could have convinced me that I would ever come to love it as I eventually did. It became dearer to me than any other spot on earth."

The four men who had previously held the position of deputy superintendent declared no one could traipse across such a vast desolate terrain and live to tell about it. The area consisted of more than 40,000 square miles, all of which Maude had to travel alone. The first thing she did was buy an old Dodge car she dubbed Teddy, for Teddy Roosevelt "because it was such a rough rider." After a few lessons in auto mechanics, she and Teddy headed out to visit the schools within her immense jurisdiction.

> *Teddy and I became a team as we covered the trails. Garage men were our friends. They drew crude maps on any scrap of paper available, listed landmarks along the way, made lists of supplies and equipment I must carry. I would need a shovel, an axe, tow ropes, two jacks, good tire pump, canteens of water, gas and oil. Neither must I ever be without an abundance of canned goods, which in turn necessitated a can opener. A bundle of wiping rags and a blanket completed the requirements.*

To her supplies she added canned tomatoes, two flashlights, magazines, and a deck of cards.

Teddy cooperated as much as possible, but occasionally even the old workhorse could not get out of the sifting sand that sometimes rose above its hubcaps. Maude would let the air out of Teddy's rear tires, making it easier to ride atop the sand. After the Dodge gained its footing again, she would pump the tires back up before continuing her journey. Sometimes she and Teddy languished for hours surrounded by a storm of dust before she could see well enough to drive.

Although warned about the dangers lurking in the desert—absolutely no road signs to guide her (in fact, few roads), wild animals, snakes, and even more perilous and unfriendly human predators—she encountered none. Strangers stopped to help if Teddy struggled and sank in the sand. They offered her water, food, even a place to stay if darkness fell before she reached her destination. She never felt afraid and actually enjoyed the solitude, relishing "the ever-changing lights and shadows on the far mountains, the gorgeous desert flora—cacti, Joshua trees, Spanish dagger—an occasional friendly coyote, the vivid sunsets, the clean smells of the desert, and of course Teddy, ready to do his best."

As she traveled unmarked trails, she remembered the four superintendents who preceded her. "Every time I would stop to wipe my brow and rest my back, I would think of those men and how they would laugh if they could see me now, and thus I derived energy to attack my job again."

The time Maude had spent teaching in rural schools, and now as deputy superintendent, reinforced her conviction that the most talented teachers should be sent to the most remote regions. These areas, she claimed, needed teachers who could handle unexpected situations without relying on superiors for guidance. They must know something about a wide range of subjects from math to history to foreign affairs, and be able to provide social as well as educational stimuli so their charges would grow both academically and communicatively. She lauded one such teacher who impressed her by using what was on hand—jars filled with scorpions and spiders to teach biology, plus a resident snake that was allowed to roam freely about the classroom to keep the mouse population at bay. "To me," said Maude, "she was a perfect example of making teaching fit the community."

Although she tried to implement improvements in schools under her jurisdiction, her position carried little weight with local school board constituents, who preferred making their own decisions and were not impressed with the lady agitator. When she attended staff meetings with the state superintendent and his all-male staff, they let her know they resented the presence of a woman within their domain. "I was well aware," she said, "that when a woman takes over work done by a man, she has to do it better, has more of it to do, and usually for less pay."

When a new superintendent was elected in 1926, Maude lost her position as deputy. In 1927 she ran for and won the position of Clark County school superintendent, which included the Las Vegas school district. At the time, Las Vegas had two elementary schools and one very dilapidated high school. Also taking on the task of high school principal, Maude urged the people of Las Vegas to build a new high school before the old one collapsed. With a city population of less than 3,000, she had her work cut out for her in pushing through a bond issue to provide funds for a new school, but two events helped win her cause: Las Vegas experienced a population explosion when construction began on the Hoover Dam 30 miles south of the city, and the ancient school building finally met its demise in a devastating fire.

Las Vegas schools thrived under Maude's direction, so much so that by 1946 she proposed a statewide reorganization of the school system. She had never forgotten the children she first taught in the isolated rural communities of Wisconsin and Nevada, and she still hoped to provide them with better teachers and a decent education.

To accomplish her lofty educational goals, Maude, at the age of sixty-seven, ran for an assembly seat in the Nevada State Legislature. Losing in her first attempt, she ran again in 1950 and succeeded to the assembly, where she served for the next twelve years. Once gaining leadership of the Education Committee, Maude set about redesigning the state school system, a task that took her ten years. As one legislator recalled, Maude did her homework. "She knew to the penny how much money was available, knew by heart how many students would be affected by a bill."

During her legislative terms, Maude saw many of the suggestions she had first proposed in the 1920s to improve Nevada schools come to fruition. More than 200 school districts were consolidated into seventeen county districts, teachers' salaries and facilities were standardized, tax bills were passed to fund schools. Along with her drive for better school standards, she found time to work on and helped pass the first civil rights bill in 1959.

Once she had straightened out the Nevada school system, Maude set her hat toward developing a southern division of the University of Nevada.

Established in Elko in 1874, the University of Nevada was relocated to Reno in 1886. Maude urged the legislature to institute a southern campus to serve the educational needs of Las Vegas and surrounding communities. Concerned about diminishing the student base in Reno, the legislature grudgingly agreed to fund $200,000 for a Las Vegas branch of the university, but residents would have to foot the additional $100,000 needed for its construction.

Maude knew where to find the money. By 1955 gambling and star-studded shows permeated the Las Vegas Strip, even though the town had yet to reach its height of celebrity. Maude and a handful of enthusiastic citizens took their cause to the people who had the money and the power. They enlisted the aid of club owners, singers, and dancers, along with educators and civic leaders. Together they organized a telecast to help raise the necessary funds. Her hard work paid off in April 1956 when she was handed a shovel to dig the first spadeful of earth establishing Nevada Southern University, the southern campus of the University of Nevada.

The first university building was named Maude Frazier Hall. No one was prouder of that school than the lady who had maneuvered her way across the open desert in old Teddy to provide an education for the rural children of southern Nevada.

In 1962, Maude broke her hip, but nothing as insignificant as a broken bone could stop an eighty-one-year-old tomboy like Maude Frazier. Maneuvering her crutches through legislative halls, she accepted the position of lieutenant governor when Governor Grant Sawyer asked her to fulfill the term of Rex Bell, who had died suddenly. For six months she reigned as the first woman to hold one of the most prestigious positions in Nevada government. Her crippled old hip never healed properly, and Maude was soon relegated to a wheelchair. But even that did not stop her from doing whatever she wanted. Brent Adams, a Washoe County district judge, loved to tell the story of how he watched her cook chicken by setting a bowl of flour on the floor next to her wheelchair, dropping the chicken into the flour, and then tossing it across the room to a waiting frying pan.

The one thing Maude could not control was time, and time finally ran out for the lady educator and legislator on June 20, 1963, at the age of eighty-two. No one had made more of an impact on the education of children in Nevada than Maude Frazier. Her relentless pursuit of better schools and better education made her a figurehead among Nevada educators. She considered herself a "desert rat" but wanted more than dust-filled classrooms for the students she found in run-down schools. Because her ideas differed from those expected of female schoolteachers of her day, because she chose to ride bicycles and roam the desert alone and unafraid, and because she tackled jobs considered "man's work," she wanted more than anything to impress upon children that

> . . . they must not be afraid to be different. We turn out people who know the same things, do the same things, think the same way. Yet it has been the non-conformists, the people who dared to be different, who dared to experiment with new ideas, who have contributed most to the world—the Edisons, the Wrights, the Marconis.

And even though early in her career she questioned her decision to teach, she also promised, "If I was going to be a teacher I was going to be a good one." That she definitely accomplished.

# NEW MEXICO

# MARY COLTER

(1869–1958)

## Architect of the Earth

The city of St. Paul, Minnesota, grew up on the banks of the Mississippi River, right in the heart of Sioux Indian territory. Because of the prevalence of Indian culture in the region, many homes, including eleven-year-old Mary Jane Colter's, were decorated with Indian art and artifacts. Mary's favorite possession was a collection of Sioux drawings that a friend had given her. Mary was fascinated with the way these simple paintings reflected the land and the culture that had inspired them. They spoke to her of America in a way that the European-inspired landscapes hanging on her parents' walls did not, and she cherished them as her most precious treasure.

In the 1880s a smallpox epidemic swept the Indian community, and Mary's mother burned all of the Indian articles in the house to prevent the spread of disease, except, that is, for Mary's drawings, which Mary hid, preferring to risk smallpox rather than part with them.

Rescuing Indian art and culture from the flame of extinction and putting it on display so that others could appreciate its beauty was an exercise that Mary would repeat again and again, on a much larger scale, for the rest of her life.

Mary Colter's love of ancient cultures and her desire to communicate the beauty she saw guided her long career as an architect and designer for the Fred Harvey Company. Mary succeeded in a "man's job" in a "man's world," opening up a gateway to the West and giving birth to a uniquely American, southwestern style.

Mary Colter was born in Pittsburgh, Pennsylvania, on April 4, 1869. She was the daughter of William and Rebecca Colter, who owned and ran the Hats, Caps, and Clothing Store on Butler Street in Pittsburgh. Mary's father grew tired of life in Pittsburgh, however, and moved his family west, hopscotching back and forth from Texas to Colorado and finally to St. Paul in 1880, when Mary was eleven years old.

From the time she was a little girl, Mary Colter was drawn to art. The public schools in St. Paul offered classes in music, drawing, and sculpting to all students. Mary pursued her studies enthusiastically, graduating from high school when she was only fourteen years old. Because of her youth, and perhaps because she was a girl at the turn of the twentieth century, Mary was not accepted to any art schools, which relieved her parents who, regardless of how mature and self-directed their daughter was, didn't want her going far away from home at such a tender age.

Mary wasn't able to realize her dream of going to art school until 1886, but her success was marred by a series of unhappy circumstances. Mary's father died of a sudden blood clot in his brain, leaving his wife alone with three unmarried daughters and no visible means of support. Mary convinced her mother to send her to art school so that she could earn money to support the family through teaching, and her mother at last agreed.

With money left by her father, Mary attended the California School of Design in San Francisco, studying art and design. She also worked as an apprentice in an architect's office, which gave her the skills that would serve her later in ways that she probably couldn't have even dreamed of at the time.

Mary graduated in 1890 and returned to St. Paul to find a teaching job to support her mother and sister as she had promised. At the age of twenty-three, Mary settled into a job teaching freehand and mechanical drawing at Mechanic Arts High School in St. Paul. She remained in that position for fifteen years, wondering when her thirst for adventure would finally be satisfied.

Then one day, quite unexpectedly, everything changed for Mary Colter. While vacationing in San Francisco, she visited a school friend who worked in a Fred Harvey gift shop. Mary told the manager of the shop that she was a designer and was interested in working for the Fred Harvey Company. Although she didn't realize it at the time, Mary's casual comment would change the course of her life.

The Fred Harvey Company worked in tandem with the Santa Fe Railroad, opening luxurious restaurants and hotels along the railway west. The Santa Fe Railroad owned the structures, and within them, Fred Harvey created a relaxed and comfortable dining and lodging experience that drew an increasing number of travelers to New Mexico, the Grand Canyon, and eventually on to California. Mary's flair for distinctly American architecture and design and her understanding and appreciation of Native American and Spanish cultures made the Fred Harvey Company the perfect arena for Mary to express her vision.

In the summer of 1902, Mary got her chance to prove herself. The Fred Harvey Company wired Mary, offering her a job as the designer and display arranger for the Indian building adjoining their newest property, the Alvarado Hotel in Albuquerque, New Mexico.

Native American arts and crafts had become very popular among tourists. Fred Harvey capitalized on the new public palate for all things Indian by deciding to incorporate a salesroom featuring Indian handicrafts into his new hotel.

Mary accepted the job and began what was to become a forty-year relationship with the Fred Harvey Company. In Mary Colter, Fred Harvey had found exactly what he needed to make his new southwestern style a success—an architect with a purely American vision.

Mary went to work with her usual vitality, arranging pots here, piling Navajo blankets there, creating not just a retail display but an entire world that mirrored the ancient culture of the region and plunged patrons into what was for most of them a new and exotic lifestyle.

When the Indian building opened in 1902, Mary returned to her teaching job in St. Paul, but a deep and abiding passion had been ignited in her. She longed for the next opportunity to head west. Finally, in 1904, the Fred Harvey Company called once more and asked Mary to design an Indian building for the El Tovar, a grand hotel they were building on the western rim of the Grand Canyon. This time Mary would be designing not only the interiors but the very walls themselves. Everything from the ground up would reflect Mary's vision.

Mary Colter's Indian building, called Hopi House, opened on January 1, 1905. Mary's design was guided by a Native American preference for structures that lived in harmony with their natural surroundings and reflected Native American activities and religious beliefs.

One of the Indian rooms in Hopi House housed a Hopi altar, a sand painting, and two religious articles from the deeply spiritual Hopi culture that had never been shared with Anglos before. In addition to the Indian rooms, there was a Spanish-Mexican room and a Totem room, which featured carved masks and bowls fashioned by the northwestern tribes.

With Hopi House Mary Colter created the perfect atmosphere for tourists to rest, relax, and reflect on the beauty of the environment. And then, of course, there was a salesroom so that tourists could take home a souvenir pot or blanket to remind them of their trip. The Hopi House was very popular, and the Fred Harvey Company was becoming increasingly impressed with Mary Colter's style.

After Hopi House was completed, Mary returned to her teaching job in St. Paul, and one can only speculate how eager she was for the next Fred Harvey project to carry her back to the land and the work that she loved.

In 1908, when an offer from Fred Harvey wasn't yet forthcoming, Mary, hungry for a change, took a job as a display designer and decorator with the Frederick and Nelson Department Store in Seattle, Washington. She moved her entire family from St. Paul to the Pacific Northwest. Sadly, a year later Mary's mother, Rebecca, developed a dangerous anemia and died on December 17, 1909.

At last, in 1910, fortune smiled, and Mary was offered a permanent position with the Fred Harvey Company. Tourism in the Southwest was booming. Mary was hired to decorate and design all of the new Fred Harvey hotels, restaurants, and facilities. In 1910 it was very unusual for a woman to have such an important and powerful position in a large company. But in addition to competence and vision, Mary also had enough moxie to hold her own managing railroad engineers, contractors, and crews of workmen who weren't used to taking orders from women.

Mary did have a very pronounced personality and a driving work ethic. But she also had an infectious sense of fun, and she knew how to be diplomatic, especially with the Fred Harvey architects who were drawing the working plans for her buildings and with the Fred Harvey Company itself, which was footing the bill.

Yet, as it is with most dynamic and passionate visionaries, Mary created strong feelings in people. Folks either liked her a lot or not at all, and the reviews from the workmen were varied. Many remembered her as an irritable and difficult taskmaster who scrutinized every detail of construction and rarely compromised. And thanks to an unfortunate tendency to refer to the workmen as her "boys," her crews often referred to Mary as "the old lady." But whether fan or detractor, nobody could argue that Mary had taste and charm. Mary really knew how to make a room look good. Stewart Harvey, Fred Harvey's grandson, said of her, "The charm of the hotels was what she did. She knew how to make something look better than it was."

In 1910 Mary began work on the Fred Harvey Company's new Kansas City headquarters and the interiors for the new Santa Fe Railway station at Lamy, New Mexico. Lamy was a transfer point just fifteen miles south of Santa Fe. The new hotel there, El Ortiz, had been designed by Louis Curtiss in the Mexican adobe style. It was a hacienda-style structure, with the rooms arranged on one level around a courtyard. Mary lavished the interior with expensive, heavy Mexican furniture, Indian pots, and *retablos* (Spanish religious figures).

When patrons entered the lobby of El Ortiz, Mary wanted them to feel as if they were coming into someone's home as honored guests. After a visit to El Ortiz, Owen Wister, author of *The Virginian,* said, "This little oasis among the desert hills is a wonder taste to be looked back upon by the traveler who has stopped there and forward to by the traveler who is going to stop there. The temptation was to give up all plans and stay a week for the pleasure of living and resting in such a place."

Fred Harvey and Mary Colter turned their gaze back toward the Grand Canyon in 1914. With the arrival of the railroad, tourism had exploded in the region, and the Fred Harvey Company was struggling to keep up with the demand for facilities to accommodate tourists coming to take in the splendor of this natural wonder.

While the Fred Harvey Company considered opting to continue in the Swiss-chalet style that had taken root in the region, they ultimately decided to go with Mary Colter's neoprimitive, southwestern style.

In 1914 Mary worked on Hermit's Rest, an observatory and gift shop built on Hermit Rim Road along the Grand Canyon's edge. The road wound along for eight breathtaking miles, offering sweeping, epic vistas around every bend, and the drive culminated at the road's end with a stop at Mary's triumph of organic architecture.

Visitors enter Hermit's Rest through an arch of seemingly randomly piled rocks, crowned with a broken mission bell. The actual building looks like a pile of haphazardly arranged stone and timber, with a chimney rising like a primitive steeple from the low crouch of the hideaway. It is a remarkable structure, seemingly springing out of the earth. Seen from a distance, the building virtually becomes one with the canyon's face. Upon the building's completion, visitors from far and wide agreed it was the most imaginative rest stop they had ever seen.

Hermit's Rest contained a fireplace alcove and a salesroom where postcards, photographs, and paintings were sold. But the most valuable thing that Hermit's Rest offered was free for the taking: a spectacular view of the Grand Canyon, stunningly framed by Mary Colter's sensitive and imaginative eye.

In 1921 a 420-foot-long swinging suspension bridge stretching across the Colorado River was completed, making the inner canyon accessible to travelers. Mary Colter then began work on the Fred Harvey Company's newest venture, Phantom Ranch, a community of cabins and a large hall, arranged in a cluster at the end of the mule trail at the very bottom of the canyon. When the ranch opened, Mary Colter, at the age of fifty-three, and her sister Harriet, fifty-nine, took the mule trip to the bottom of the canyon for the opening celebration.

Next, Mary and the Fred Harvey Company turned their attention to New Mexico once more, with the renovation of the Alvarado Hotel in Albuquerque. The Alvarado had developed a reputation for some of the region's best celebrity sightings. And as had become characteristic of the Fred Harvey Company, they noticed a popular trend and capitalized on it. They began renovations on the hotel, doubling its capacity and making it the largest Fred Harvey hotel in the world. The Alvarado Hotel, with its aura of glamour and celebrity, was designed to play to the growing California mystique. It invited travelers westward, toward the land of movie stars and orange groves.

From 1923 to 1946 Mary Colter created many new buildings and interiors for the Fred Harvey Company including El Navajo in Gallup, New Mexico; La Fonda in Santa Fe; and the Bright Angel Lodge at the Grand Canyon. Mary Colter retired in 1946 and moved into her new home on the Plaza Chamisal in Santa Fe. She lived to see her work celebrated as some of the most unique and creative American design visions, but she also lived long enough to see many of her beloved buildings go on the auction block.

For Mary Colter it was a tragedy watching her buildings be dismantled and sold. She observed, "There's such a thing as living too long."

Mary Colter worked as an architect and a designer for forty years, creating environments that revealed the beauty of the American West for generations of tourists the world over. Her structures and interiors introduced a new and truly American spirit to architecture and design, turning away from European-inspired stylization toward a uniquely American simplicity and an organic harmony with the land.

When American tourists turned away from rail travel, many of Mary Colter's buildings were torn down, but many, such as Hermit's Rest and the Bright Angel Lodge, remain. They are a testament to Mary's comfortable and sensitive appreciation for the beauty of American cultural diversity, which is at the heart of New Mexican and American life.

# NINA OTERO-WARREN

(1881–1965)

### The Spirit of Old Spain in the New Southwest

Nina Otero-Warren, who was in her lifetime a suffragette, an outspoken activist, an esteemed author, an influential educator, an eminent politician, and a full-fledged, larger-than-life character, could trace her Spanish ancestry all the way back to the conquistadores. Despite her often progressive and controversial ideas about so many things and the new trails she blazed for women in government, Nina always remained fiercely faithful to and proud of her traditional Spanish heritage. It was this grounding in the elegance and integrity of her Spanish colonial past that gave her the insight, the compassion, and the sheer gumption she needed to put her personal stamp on New Mexico's emerging future, and to build bridge of peace between Spanish colonial, Native American, and Anglo cultures, so that all could coexist in harmony in the Enchanted Circle.

Maria Adelina Isabel Emilia (Nina) Otera was born in La Costancia on October 23, 1881. Her mother, Eloisa Luna, was a descendant of Don Tristan de Luna y Arellano de Castillo, who came from Spain to seek his fortune in the New World in 1530, just thirty-eight years after Christopher Columbus made his infamous landing in the Americas. Since that time, generations of Lunas had been colonizing the land, and by the time Eloisa was born, the Luna family controlled one of the largest and most powerful *hacendados* in the region.

The family's fortunes had waxed and waned over history. The Apaches killed Nina's great-grandfather, Antonio de Luna, in 1779. It was reported that all he left his widow was his land, a small amount of livestock, two small houses, and a pair of scarlet trousers. His son, Antonio Jose Luna, proved more prosperous than his father, but only by way of a well-conceived marriage into the wealthy, socially prominent neighboring Baca family. The two families' lands combined, creating a powerful alliance between the two most powerful families in the region.

Nina's mother, Eloisa, the youngest child of Don Antonio Jose and Isabella Baca Luna, was petite, beautiful, bright, socially vivacious, and very, very rich. In her youth she had enjoyed all the advantages of being the child of a wealthy and powerful family. She and her brothers and sisters always had nannies, servants, maids, and private tutors well into adolescence. Eloisa was also well educated, and fluent in both Spanish and English. Eloisa was, in any sense of the word, quite a catch.

Nina's father, Manuel Otera, led a similarly privileged life steeped in aristocratic Spanish colonial tradition. His ancestors purchased a huge tract of land from the Mexican government before the United States occupied New Mexico, and their grant totaled more than one million acres. Albert attended Georgetown University in Washington, DC, and spoke four languages fluently.

Manuel was as handsome as Eloisa was beautiful, with the fair skin, reddish blond hair, and azure-blue eyes of his Valencian heritage—unusual and exotic coloring that Nina would later inherit. When the couple met, they were uniting the Chaveses and the Oteros of the Estancia Valley with the Bacas and the Lunas of Valencia County. Needless to say, this was big news at the time, the match of the century, and their wedding was said to be the most splendid and fantastical occasion ever to occur in New Mexico. Eloisa was only fifteen years old on her wedding day. Her new husband was only nineteen. Manuel bought Eloisa a beautiful blue gown, which was the customary color for wedding dresses prior to Queen Victoria, trimmed with Duchesse lace imported all the way from Brussels, Belgium. The wedding feast itself is said to have lasted for two solid weeks, and guests wondered how they ever had to time to conceive their first child so quickly, because they were never alone for all of the revelers coming and going for months.

The couple moved into the family hacienda in La Constancia. Their first child, Eduardo, was born on August 24, 1880. Nina, their second child, was born just a year later. The Oteros settled down to enjoy the same affluent, privileged life their parents had, and planned to offer their children the bucolic upbringing they had enjoyed as the offspring of prosperous ranchers in old New Mexico. Unfortunately, life was filled with unpleasant surprises right from the very beginning. For Nina and her family, there was always an unexpected bend in the road up ahead.

In 1881 Eloisa's father died, leaving the grand antebellum mansion to his son Tranquilito. A year later, Tranquilito also died, leaving the family land to Eloisa's younger brother, Manuel. Then things took an even more tragic turn when Eloisa, now pregnant with her third child, lost her young husband in a gun battle over a land dispute in 1883 when he was just twenty-three years old, after only four years of marriage.

The Whitneys of Massachusetts, who owned the Pacific Railroad Enterprise in the territory at the time, had disputed the ancient Spanish claims of the Oteros to secure passage for their railroad. Two weeks before the shooting they supposedly had won a territorial supreme court decision, overturning the Spanish land grant and handing over the land to Whitney. Although the case was on appeal, the Whitneys had gone ahead with their plans to run the Oteros off the land. When Manuel and his men showed up to reclaim what they believed was rightfully their land, James Whitney shot Manuel at point-blank range, severing his carotid artery. The funeral was in Belen and was, much like his wedding just a few short years earlier, the largest ever witnessed in New Mexico history. Less than a month later, Eloise and Manuel's third child, Manuel Jr., was born.

Although Whitney was apprehended for the killing, a judge released him on his own recognizance, allowing Whitney to escape to California. Although this ruling caused a huge public outcry, Whitney wasn't tried until many years later, and eventually was acquitted on the grounds of self-defense. This was the first time but certainly not the last that Nina was affected by Anglo injustice against the old Spanish order. And it is clear that she never forgot.

Eloisa returned to her family home in Los Lunas, named for the Lunas, Eloisa's family name. She began the obligatory period of mourning, which generally meant dressing in black, never going out, never laughing, listening to music, or having fun, and definitely not dating for three years. To Eloisa, however, who was only nineteen years old at the time of her husband's death, this must have seemed like an eternity of gloom. So, when her mother and brothers suggested that she take a trip east to find a suitable nanny for her children, Eloisa did not object. She went to Pittsburgh, Pennsylvania, and returned with a firm Irish nanny, Elizabeth Doyle, whom the family called Teta, who would be with the Otero family for the next sixty-three years until her death in 1947. Teta turned out to be the start of a whole new chapter for Eloisa and her children.

In 1884 Eloisa met Alfred Maurice Bergere, who came to Los Lunas, for a baptism and wound up finding a wife. Alfred instantly fell in love with Eloisa and stayed in love with her for the rest of his life. As a businessman who traveled throughout the Southwest for the Spielbergs, a family that ran a successful department store in Albuquerque, Alfred could easily pop in and visit Eloisa whenever he was in town, which seemed to be more and more often from the moment he met her.

Alfred was articulate, polished, well educated, and cultured, much like her former husband had been, although Alfred was as thoroughly Anglo as Manuel had been thoroughly Spanish. Eloisa returned Alfred's affections and although they tried to respect the three-year mourning rule, it proved impossible for the young lovers to stand on ceremony. With Eloisa's family's permission, they began a courtship in the traditional Spanish style, and when they weren't able to be together, they exchanged love letters. Teta had to help Eloisa with her letters, as Eloisa could not write fluently in English. Finally in 1885 they were married. It was a simple ceremony compared with the lavish celebration of her first wedding, but somehow happier and more reassuring. Eloisa was no longer a fifteen-year-old girl, and her groom was a full-grown and capable businessman who could take control of the family's cattle and sheep business and secure the Oteros' place in New Mexico's political future.

Alfred devoted himself to running Eloisa's ranch and tending to the sheep and cattle, although as a sales and marketing man, he never proved very talented at ranching. He also took over the care and education of the children. Alfred offered the children the benefit of his own experiences in the Anglo tradition but never interfered with the Old Spanish and fiercely Catholic traditions that Eloisa insisted upon following.

Nina attended St. Vincent Academy in Albuquerque, but when it became clear to her parents that she had an active and quick intelligence that required more formal schooling, Alfred sent her to St. Louis to Maryville College of the Sacred Heart. When she was thirteen, Nina returned from what was perhaps some of the best schooling available to young girls at the time and took up her life with the family on the ranch.

In the Bergere-Otero household, as in many Spanish households at the time, the education of girls was not given over strictly to women, but the men got involved as well. Growing up, Nina spent long hours with her uncles and cousins, and the *peones,* or cowboys, riding and roping and herding sheep and cattle. She was smoking, drinking, and playing cards with the men by the time she was fifteen—the legal drinking age in Spanish households at the time. It was even a rite of passage in many Spanish colonial families to invite their child in for the first drink of whiskey and first cigarette on the child's fifteenth birthday. Apparently Nina was no exception and during one of the family's many rail trips even ran afoul of the law for trying to smuggle two boxes of cigars over the Mexican border. Additionally, thanks to her friends the *peones,* Nina knew how to handle a gun and in later years would be the one to teach her nephews how to shoot as well as she did.

When young Nina wasn't out roping and riding in the fields, she was expected to be in the home, helping with the care and rearing of her younger siblings, of which there were an ever growing number. One of her favorite responsibilities was to pass on to her brothers and sisters the fine education she had received at Maryville, and she did so with zeal, although many of her siblings saw her as less enthusiastic than bossy.

As Nina grew into a young woman, she began to get a little bored with life at the hacienda and started spending increasing amounts of time in the city, making new friends and looking for excitement in the swirl of people and things to be found there. Fortunately and unfortunately for Nina, in 1898 the very same land dispute that had taken her young father from his family came back to roost, and forced the family to leave the ranch that Nina had begun to take for granted.

Unable to resolve the conflict over the claim of Manuel Otero and James Whitney, the US Supreme Court declared the Otero land to be public domain, and the Oteros, including Eloisa, lost more than one million acres of their family's claim. It was just one more example of what happened at the time to many Old Spanish claims. An increasingly powerful Anglo government suddenly did not recognize grazing land, depriving many Old Spanish families of their ancestors' land. It was an injustice that Nina would never forget.

Fortunately for the Otero-Bergere family, Eloisa's brother Miguel Otero was named territory governor and moved his good friend Alfred and his family to Santa Fe, the territorial capital, so they could all live close together. Now invited to all the best parties, and enjoying the favor they were receiving from Miguel Otero's good relationship with Republican President William McKinley, the Oteros became the apple of Santa Fe society and Nina found the thrill and excitement she had been searching for. The house the family initially rented on Lincoln Street quickly became too small, so Governor Otero made it possible for the family to move into larger quarters at La Casa Grande, or the Big House on Grant Avenue. The property had once been officers' quarters where Ulysses S. Grant himself is said to have lived at one time.

Eloisa, although pregnant with her tenth child, was still beautiful and charming, and thoroughly enjoyed socializing with the elite social and political circles that composed Miguel Otero's world. Nina had inherited her mother's social enthusiasm and grace, and threw herself into the whirlwind of Santa Fe social life. Nina was a familiar figure at all the finest parties, poised at the center of a group of important men, a cocktail in her hand, a long cigarette holder poised just before her lips, exchanging bawdy jokes with the best of them.

The years slipped by easily in this fashion, as they generally do when party hopping with politicians, and before she knew it, Nina was twenty-six years old and, unlike most of her girlfriends, still unmarried. People, including Nina, began to worry that she would be left on the shelf. After all, twenty-six was quite old in a culture that allowed girls to marry at fifteen. Finally, in 1907 Nina, who always understood and knew how to deliver what was expected of her in some fashion so long as it suited her, met Rawson D. Warren, the commanding officer of the Fifth US Cavalry stationed at Fort Wingate in New Mexico, and got married at last.

Rawson was an intelligent and educated man who had grown up in Pennsylvania, New York, and California. He had graduated from Leland Stanford Jr. University, and even had an advanced degree from New York University. He was nine years older than Nina and something of an iconoclast himself, so in the beginning the two seemed perfectly paired. Nina and Rawson were married in St. Francis Church right on the plaza in Santa Fe and like her parents' marriage before her, marked a high point in the social history of the territory. The papers enthused that the wedding was the most magnificent, most elegant, and finest ever to have occurred in Santa Fe.

As is often the case, the marriage wasn't as stellar as her over-the-top wedding. When Nina arrived at Rawson's home at Fort Wingate, she found the regimented, mundane routine of the wife of an officer to be completely at odds with her sense of things. She was bored out of her mind and longed for the social whirlwind of Santa Fe and the company of her friends and family back at home. Even worse, she soon discovered that she and Rawson had nothing whatsoever in common. They really were not compatible in any discernible way, which was a shift for Nina, whose parents had always been in love.

The final straw came when she discovered that Rawson had a common-law wife and two children in the Philippines he had never told her about. To a good Catholic girl like Nina, this sounded a lot like bigamy. Nina had had enough.

And so just two years later, Nina, who was now Nina Otero-Warren, left her husband but kept his name, declared herself a widow, and began the most productive and fulfilling chapters of her life, as an independent woman who could control her own destiny.

Happily back with her family and friends in Santa Fe, Nina once again took over the care and education of her siblings, and began casting about for a productive way to spend her life as an unmarried and independent woman. It was at this point that her uncle Solomon Luna introduced her to the women's suffrage movement. Solomon supported women's right to vote and was using what influence he had as a state official to make sure that women's suffrage was ratified in New Mexico.

Although women's suffrage had been voted down consistently for over a decade, there was new hope for the movement at the time Nina became involved. Many believed that statehood would result in the passage of women's suffrage. This turned out to be incorrect. New Mexico became a state, and rather than gaining the right to vote, women actually lost the right to community property under the new state laws. Then Solomon died, depriving the suffrage movement of one of its greatest champions. With her characteristic steely determination, Nina picked up the gauntlet and resolved to use all of the talent and influence at her disposal to make sure that women in New Mexico could vote.

But then life once again intervened. On September 3, 1914, Eloisa died at the young age of fifty, leaving her husband, Alfred, stunned and broken. Nina, who was in New York at the time working with the suffrage movement, was called home to care for her nine brothers and sisters, and to preside over the Otero-Bergere household. Her sister Anita, who had been living in a convent and was about to take her vows as a nun, was also called home. From the beginning, Nina put Anita in charge of the house, and she went out to build a career to carry the family forward.

Nina also continued to campaign tirelessly for women's suffrage, using her uncanny ability to speak to women and men, Anglo and Spanish, as equals, and to bring about conciliation rather than confrontation. It soon became apparent to many in prominent political circles that Nina Otero-Warren had what it took to be a capable and effective political force, and in 1917 she was appointed to the office of superintendent of public schools in Santa Fe County. In 1918 she later ran for and won that same position when it became an elected office, becoming at thirty-seven the youngest and one of the very first women to be elected to government in New Mexico.

The battle for suffrage was put on hold when the United States entered World War I. Nina worked tirelessly alongside her friends Erna Fergusson and Alice Corbin Henderson to encourage civilian cooperation with the war effort. Together these women literally went farm to farm in rural areas encouraging national patriotism and soliciting cooperation and donations even from those who felt disenfranchised completely from the national or even the state government, let alone the war effort.

In 1918 Nina became chair of the Red Cross Membership Committee for Santa Fe County and was just about to leave for overseas service with the Rocky Mountain Division of the Red Cross in Europe when the war ended. Nina was happy about the war ending but always said she was sorry to have missed out on her trip abroad.

When the war ended, Nina picked up right where she had left off, determined to convince her fellow New Mexicans, not through force but through gentle persuasion, that suffrage was the right thing to do. And under the guidance of Alice Paul, Nina worked her ameliorating magic and women finally won the right to vote in New Mexico on February 19, 1920. In the last days before the final vote, Nina gained admission to the Republican caucus, becoming the first woman in the state to participate in this boys-only club.

Nina instantly became a celebrity and a new role model for a more empowered generation of women, who could have a voice in their government and determine their own fate. As she had so many times in her life, Nina found a way to use the best of the Anglo and Spanish influences that had molded her to join opposing forces and arrive at a peace.

Riding on a wave of popular support, just one year later, thanks to a new piece of legislation that allowed women to run for office, Nina Otero-Warren became the very first woman to be nominated as the Republican candidate for the US Congress. She lost to the Democratic candidate, John Morrow, by just ten thousand votes, less than 9 percent of the voting electorate.

Her political life over for the moment, Nina returned to her job as an educator and superintendent of schools. During Nina's administration she raised the salaries of teachers from the meager $546.03 annually that they had been paid in the past, and lobbied for the renovation of dilapidated school buildings. She increased the school year to nine months and regularly traveled to schools throughout her region to see and hear the needs of her teachers and students firsthand. Under her tenure, Santa Fe schools went from being the worst in the state to the best, and restored profitability to the system as well.

In her downtime, which was not very plentiful, to say the least, she socialized with the notable writers and artists of her day who had come to Santa Fe in search of inspiration and enlightenment. Nina met Mary Austin, Ruth Laughlin, Frieda and D. H. Lawrence, and of course, Mable Dodge and Tony Luhan. But for the most part, Nina spent her life working hard in the field, ensuring that every child, regardless of his or her background, got a good education that would allow him or her to compete in a new and increasingly industrial, less agrarian world.

It was at this point that Mamie Meadors entered Nina's world, a woman who would change her life forever, and bring her the companionship, and tireless devotion she had failed to find in her marriage. When the demands of job and home became too much for Nina, she resolved to hire an assistant, and she immediately thought of the woman who had been by her side through her run for office, helping in the wings, and proving herself to be a devoted confidant, friend, and clerical assistant. She immediately thought of Mamie Meadors.

Mamie had come to Santa Fe from her home in Wichita Falls, Texas, in search of "the cure" after a bout of tuberculosis. Her doctor had given her less than six months to live, a prediction she long outlived. She also outlived her doctor by twenty-five years. Mamie lived with her friend Salome, also a friend of Nina's, and worked as a librarian in the public library on Washington Street. From the moment they met, Mamie and Nina were instantly compatible and through their work together on Nina's campaign had learned that they could rely on each other.

Like many things in Nina's life, her relationship with Mamie was a perfect marriage of opposites. Where Nina was outgoing, Mamie was shy; where Nina was outspoken, Mamie soft-spoken. Nina was social; Mamie was intensely private. Nina liked her whiskey; Mamie liked her tea. Yet together they made a perfect pair. Eventually they purchased together and homesteaded a 1,200-acre parcel of land, upon which they built two adobe houses that to this day sit side by side on the top of a ridge twelve miles outside of Santa Fe.

Together in the years that followed, Nina and Mamie fought many good fights on behalf of the less fortunate, the Spanish and Mexican people of the region, and the Indians. When Nina was appointed inspector of Indian schools in 1922, a time when Anglo law was taking more and more land away from the Indians and ravaging their culture, Nina and Mamie fought back. When the government proposed adoption of the Bursum Bill, which sought to rob even more land and water rights from the Indians, Nina and Mamie made sure the public outcry was heard all the way in Washington.

During their inspections of Indian schools, Nina and Mamie discovered appalling conditions and worked tirelessly to improve the quality of life for

Indian children. Nina spoke frequently on the deplorable conditions for Indians in the Southwest and worked hard to help an ignorant Anglo community understand that Native Americans were not savages, but intelligent and valuable human beings who deserved to be in control of their own children, their own destiny, and their own day-to-day lives. She spoke out loudly against an educational system that removed Indian children from their homes to anglicize them, making them unrecognizable to their parents, and they to them, upon their return. Eventually Nina's outspoken criticism of the boarding school education model cut short her career as inspector of Indian schools, and she was replaced after only two years at her post. She remained, however, a passionate advocate for Native Americans for the rest of her life.

Ready to be inspired by the next great campaign of her life, Nina turned to her good friend Mary Austin, who told Nina that she had to write a book about her memories of her early life to preserve the precious heritage of the Spanish colonials in New Mexico.

Nina did take her friend's advice to heart, although it took her ten years to pick up the pen. Finally, after Mary's death in 1934, Nina turned to her stepfather, Alfred Bergere, and told him she was looking for a land grant to start her own homestead with Mamie. Alfred, who was a registrar, had access to all the available land grants in the state, and Nina and Mamie chose a parcel just twelve miles outside of Santa Fe.

To secure their grant, Mamie and Nina had to agree to spend an average of five months a year on the desolate land grant, construct two houses, install a fence, provide for irrigation, and plant crops to prevent erosion. They agreed to all of these conditions and in June 1931, Mamie and Nina signed a contract with builders to begin constructing their two single-room adobe houses on a hill overlooking the Sangre de Cristo and Jemez mountain ranges. They moved into their new homes in the spring of 1932 and named their new hacienda Los Dos, "the two of us." Then Nina sat down and started work on what was to be her first and only book, *Old Spain in Our Southwest*. This passage, which begins her book, not only captures the spirit of her richly textured Spanish colonial heritage mixed with her Anglo upbringing, but also speaks volumes about the opposing forces that shaped Nina and the new Southwest, which struggled to find a way to peacefully coexist at a time of great transition.

> *A storm was coming over the country around Santa Fe,*
> *the ancient City of Holy Faith. This southwestern country,*
> *explored and settled nearly four hundred years ago by a people*
> *who loved nature, worshiped God and feared no evil, is still a*
> *region of struggles.*

    *I spent this night on my homestead in a small adobe house in the midst of cedars on the top of a hill. We face the great Sangre de Cristo range as we look to the rising sun: a beauty too great for human beings to have had a hand in creating. Cedars, Pinones, twisted, knotted, dwarfed by the wind, were all around me. Arroyos were cut in the ground, innocent looking in dry weather, but terrible in storms, for the water rushing through them can fell trees and roll bowlders as easily as children roll marbles.*

    *I watched the sun sink gloomily behind a yellow light. The hills looked gray and solemn. At a distance we heard a dog bark, a coyote howl. A shepherd was calling to his dog. The shepherd and his dog, taking warning of the coming storm, were herding sheep to protect them better. Here and there the shepherd picked up a stray lamb and carried it in his arms. He made a fire quickly and soon the fragrance of coffee and burning cedar filled the air. Smoke rose above the trees, a signal in olden times of hospitality, perhaps, or hostility, for the Indians have not always been friendly. Soon the herder laid a sheep pelt, thick with "wool in the grease" and gray with sand, on the most level stretch. He threw his only blanket over his shoulders and lay down on the extemporized bed. A look at the fire, a glance at the sky, the exclamation, "God help us!" and he dropped asleep to the sound of his sheep bleating.*

    *In the only room of my house, a melancholy candle was flickering as if gasping for breath. As the darkness came down like a curtain, I lit the fire to try to make the room more cheerful. I had a feeling of vastness, of solitude, but never of loneliness. Crickets and myriads of other insects were incessantly buzzing. This night was alive with sounds of creatures less fearful than humans, speaking a language I couldn't understand, but could feel with every sense.*

    *In the night the storm broke, wild and dismal. The wind hissed like a rattler, and as it struck the branches of the trees, it made a weird sound like a musical instrument out of tune. Trees were bowing as if in obeisance to their Master. An unmuffled candle alone illuminated the small room. It kept vigil through the stormy night.*

    *At dawn, the clouds parted as if a curtain were raised, revealing the outline of the mountains. The hush following the*

*storm was tremendous. Again I heard a voice in the canyon.*
*The shepherd was kindling his fire and rolling up his sheep pelt.*

*"Ah me," he said to himself, "we must get out of this wild*
*canyon. Here we must leave four of our little lambs dead. Bad*
*luck! But . . . then . . . ere comes the light, the sun, and, after*
*all, this is another day."*

*As the shepherd was extinguishing the campfire, there*
*appeared on the top of the hill a form with arms stretched to*
*heaven as though offering himself to the sun. The shepherd from*
*his camp and I from my window watched this half-clad figure*
*that seemed to have come from the earth to greet the light. A*
*chant, a hymn—the Indian was offering his prayer to the rising*
*sun. The shepherd, accustomed to his Indian neighbors, went*
*his way slowly, guiding his sheep out of the canyon. The Indian*
*finished his offering of prayer. I, alone, seemed not in complete*
*tune with the instruments of God. I felt a sense of loss that they*
*were closer to nature than I, more understanding of the storm. I*
*had shuddered at the wind as it came through the cracks of my*
*little house; now I had to cover my eyes from the bright rays of*
*the sun, while my neighbors, fearing nothing, welcome with joy*
*"another day."*

Nina and Mamie lived happily and peacefully during their summers at Los Dos. Nina would write while Mamie tended to the garden. A bottle of whiskey, a bottle of bourbon, and a bucket of ice would appear every afternoon at sundown along with a regular assembly of nephews and grandnieces, as well as artists, writers, painters, sculptors, and poets. The conversation was so lively that they were always late for the dinner bell, which the teetotaling Mamie always rang promptly at six.

In 1937 Nina was offered the position of supervisor of literary education. She accepted the job and hired Mamie as her assistant. Together once again on the trail of a great campaign, they went farm to farm, teaching adult literacy so that the children who had no access to school could still learn from their parents how to read and write. Eventually Nina was even invited to take her literacy program to Puerto Rico, and at last got her chance to travel abroad. Ever the entrepreneur, and in the spirit of her enterprising ancestors, in 1947, and at an age when most people would be thinking about retiring, Nina and Mamie opened the Las Dos Real Estate and Insurance Agency. Nina said she liked to sell big houses, and she sold a lot of them.

On August 10, 1951, Mamie died while being rushed to the hospital with Addison's disease. Nina was devastated by the loss. For a while, all activity at Las

Dos Real Estate came to an abrupt halt. Nina seemed to have lost her taste for the business she had built literally brick by brick with her partner. But as was typical of Nina, and like her mother before her, Nina's period of mourning was cut short by the life force inside of her. After six months, Nina hired an assistant, and just like she had always done, went back to work.

Nina died in 1965, leaving generations of a perfectly blended Spanish/ Anglo family behind her, who to this day gather, together with the neighbors who now live on Nina and Mamie's original homestead, to raise a glass to Nina, and to the New Southwest she helped to shape with her courage, her compassion, and her indomitable spirit.

Nina as an activist, as an educator, as a community leader, and as a person was an interesting marriage of the opposing yet somehow complimentary forces that shaped her. Fiercely independent yet gentle and conservative; outspoken yet subtle; enterprising and ambitious yet down-to-earth and patient; unyielding but able to bend, Nina taught a culture how to grow and change for the better, just by being who she was.

# LAURA GILPIN

## (1891–1979)

### Cowgirl at Heart

Eighty-eight-year-old Laura Gilpin gripped her camera with aging but still steady hands, leaning as far as she could out of the small plane that carried her over the 250,000 acres of Navajo land that had become her adopted homeland. The tiny craft's wings dipped in the desert wind, seeming to almost lightly kiss the top branches of the piñon and cedar trees that dotted the landscape she had loved and photographed for nearly sixty years.

Laura had spent her life trying to capture and communicate the emotion of the deeply carved chasms of the Canyon De Chelly, the awesome limitlessness of the northern New Mexico desert, and the conquered but enduring nobility of the vanishing Rio Grande snaking its way tentatively southward, to "surrender its surplus to the sea." Laura Gilpin's photographs of the great Southwest helped others see through her eyes and understand what she considered the beating heart of the natural world, the timelessness of the terrain, and humanity's fleeting but inextricable connection to nature.

"In this great southwest," as Laura herself explains in her book, *The Pueblos: A Camera Chronicle,* "the vast landscape plays an all-important part in the lives of its people. Their architecture resembles the giant erosions of nature's carving. It is a land of contrasts, of gentleness and warmth, and fierce and raging storms; of timbered mountains and verdant valleys, and wide, arid desert; of gayety and song, and cruel strife."

Laura Gilpin got her first camera, a Kodak Brownie, as a present for her twelfth birthday. By age seventeen she was experimenting with autochrome and beginning to establish the very first cornerstones of her unique niche in the history of photography and of New Mexico. Laura was interested in the region as a maternal force that guided and defined the lives of the people who lived there. To her a photograph should not only document the land but also reflect its inner beauty. This idea was already a departure from the reality-based, male-dominated tradition of photography at that time.

Laura's male counterparts, such as Ansel Adams or such nineteenth-century photographer explorers as William Henry Jackson (to whom Laura was distantly related), photographed the West as a place of inviolate, pristine beauty, untouched by human habitation. For Laura the southwestern desert was not an unpolished jewel either awaiting or resisting the intrusion of human development, but a populated land rich with history and tradition inextricably bound up with the people who lived there. As Ansel Adams said after her death, she had "a highly individualistic eye. I don't have the sense that she was influenced except by the land itself."

Laura Gilpin's view of the landscapes she photographed take into account the human and emotional elements invoked by nature and, in so doing, have created a uniquely feminine vision of the terrain. Although she worked in a field traditionally dominated by men and in her own life insisted that her work was genderless, Gilpin's interpretations of the natural world, like some women writers of her day such as Willa Cather, give a highly personal and human account of the landscape.

Despite her reputation as a "feminine" photographer, Laura Gilpin was intimately connected to the male tradition of western landscape photography. American landscape photography grew as a natural extension of the government survey teams that went west in the 1860s and 1870s to capture accurate images of the undeveloped American frontier. Photography was a physically challenging business in those days, not only because of the remoteness of the areas but because of the equipment the art required.

A person needed hundreds of pounds of equipment, gallons of chemicals and fresh water for development, and fragile glass-plate negatives to create a photograph. All of this had to be hauled up mountains and across vast, arid desert expanses to capture an image. It was a difficult and lonely profession, requiring a good deal of grit and a thirst for adventure that was stronger than the need for human companionship. Most early explorer/photographers were spirited and independent men who were willing to spend many months away from their families and the comforts of home. A veteran of two decades of exploration photography, Carleton Watkins, complained to his wife in 1882, "I have never had the time seem so long to me on any trip I ever made from home, and I am not half done with my work. . . . It drags along awful slow, between the smoke and the rain and the wind, and as if the elements were not enough to worry me, a spark from an engine set fire to my . . . tent last week and burned it half up."

Survey photographers like Jackson or Watkins who photographed the West did not think of themselves as artists. They were surveyors, recording accurate photographic data that reflected what their government and railroad employers wanted to see: an expansive and inviting new land, unpopulated, and welcoming commercial development. Although these photographers made pictures of great beauty, their chief purpose was to document the land in the interests of American settlement.

All of this isolation and backbreaking enterprise would have seemed a strange path indeed for a young woman of Laura's generation to choose. But Laura was not an average young woman. Laura Gilpin grew up appreciating the rough and ready splendor of the West, and throughout her life remained a cowgirl at heart. She could camp out in the woods for days on end or lean out of an airplane at eighty-eight years of age if it meant getting the picture that she wanted. And she was a woman who could tolerate solitude. Laura worked for most of her life in virtual isolation, waiting in the silent, remote regions of the Southwest to hear the desert whisper its secrets to her.

Laura Gilpin was born in 1891 just outside Colorado Springs. She was distantly related to William Gilpin, the visionary expansionist and explorer who became Colorado's first territorial governor, and to the photographer William Henry Jackson. So she had, embedded in her genealogical history, the combination of pioneer and photographer that would steer her course.

As a girl, she knew Dr. William A. Bell, who had photographed along the thirty-second parallel for the Kansas Pacific Railroad in 1867. She was also a friend of General William Jackson Palmer, founder of the Denver and Rio Grande Railroad and to whom she herself accredited her lifelong love affair with the geography of the West.

Laura Gilpin's father, Frank, was a scion of Baltimore society with a misplaced love of the open range. He, like a lot of young men of his generation, went west, moving to Colorado in 1880 to seek his fortune. He tried his hand at ranching, mining, and investing before settling down to a career as a fine furniture maker in the late 1920s.

Laura's mother, Emma Miller Gilpin, did not share her husband's enthusiasm for the unwashed and, as far as she was concerned, uncivilized Southwest. Emma was from a prominent St. Louis family, and although she followed her husband west, she always tried to bring her love of Eastern refinement and culture into the family's rustic home life. She encouraged Laura to study music and art and insisted that her daughter be educated at the finest East Coast boarding schools. But Laura, who was much more in tune with her father's wide-ranging sensibilities, felt out of place in the traditional Eastern boarding-school setting that formed a backdrop to her life from 1905 until 1909, and she was rumored to have asserted her unique spirit by showing up at cotillions in cowboy outfits. Eventually she was allowed to come back to the West that she loved.

In 1916, after experimenting with photography for more than a decade, Laura Gilpin left the West once more and moved to New York to study photographic pictorialism at the Clarence H. White School. Rather like the impressionists' influence upon painting as a medium, pictorialists emphasized feeling and emotion rather than accurate physical description. Pictorialism was characterized by soft-focus-lens views of a hazy, romanticized world that appealed to Laura, and negatives and prints were manipulated to produce a more atmospheric and evocative image. They were an important step away from the work of survey photographers and toward a more artistic vision of photography.

Laura returned to the Southwest a year later, profoundly influenced by White's pictorial style. Her own creative inclinations had been radicalized by White's idea of photography as an art form. Years after, Laura recalled White's influence on her: "Many enter the field of photography with the impulse to record a scene. They often fail to realize that what they wish to do is to record the emotion felt upon viewing that scene. . . . a mere record photograph in no way reflects that emotion."

Shortly after her return to Colorado, Laura opened a commercial studio specializing in portraiture and began taking pictures of the nearby mountains and prairies of eastern Colorado. Her work won some early accolades in the press, most notably her picture of the Colorado prairie, which New York critics praised as giving "most successfully the sense of the vastness of the plains." Whereas a single tree or outcropping might represent an entire mountain range for documentary photographers, Laura focused on the big picture. Laura wanted to suggest the vast and mythic expanse of the place—the majestic scale of nature—so that she could better suggest the sweep of human history and the impact of the environment on patterns of human settlement.

Guided by this vision, in the 1920s Laura became increasingly interested in the rich historical legacy of the Southwest. She made her first trip to Mesa Verde in 1924 and tried to express through her photographs the tentative but enduring culture of the ancient cliff dwellers. The spare simplicity of their lives intrigued Laura, and the pictures she took at this time were soft-focus, evocative images that suggested the romantic spirit of the place.

As Martha Sandweiss, in her essay "Laura Gilpin and the Tradition of American Landscape Photography," explains it:

> Gilpin's broad, emotional response to Mesa Verde [she returned
> in 1925] was much like that of Willa Cather, whose story
> about the discovery of the ruins, The Professor's House, came
> out in 1925. Cather's hero, Tom Outland, lamented the fact
> that "we had only a small Kodak, and these pictures didn't
> make much show—looked, indeed, like scrubby little 'dobe ruins
> such as one can find almost anywhere. They gave no idea of the
> beauty and vastness of the setting." Gilpin thought her pictures
> of the majestic, sculptural ruins compensated for Outland's
> shortcomings. Some of Cather's writings even seemed to describe
> her own photographs. "Far above me," Cather had written, "a
> thousand feet or so, set in a great cavern in the face of the cliff,

*I saw a little city of stone, asleep. It was still as sculpture—
and something like that. It all hung together, seemed to have
a kind of composition." Gilpin hoped to interest Cather in
collaborating on an illustrated edition of The Professor's House;
unfortunately, her efforts to contact the author failed.*

Laura Gilpin self-published her Mesa Verde photographs in 1927 in the book *The Mesa Verde National Park: Reproductions from a Series of Photographs.*

Laura first encountered the subject that was to dominate the rest of her artistic life in 1930. While driving on the Navajo Indian reservation in remote southwestern New Mexico with her friend Elizabeth Forster, Laura ran out of gas. Laura, always a sturdy traveler, hiked more than ten miles to the nearest trading post to get more fuel. When she returned, she found her friend playing rummy with a group of Navajo Indians who had arrived to keep her company. A lifelong kinship between Laura and the Navajos was born in that moment, and throughout the rest of her life, Laura photographed the Navajos, lovingly creating an intelligent and compassionate record of a beleaguered Pueblo culture.

In 1930 she was elected an associate of the Royal Photographic Society of Great Britain, and in that same year the Library of Congress purchased a small collection of her photographs, but the Depression threatened the survival of her tiny gallery, and she was forced to focus on earning money. Laura published her own postcards and lantern slides and, in 1941, her first major book, *The Pueblos: A Camera Chronicle.* In the text of this book, Gilpin expressed her reverence for the ancient history of the Southwest, which was as "old as Egypt." Laura felt a connection with the rich history of the Pueblo and claimed it as her own. "There is something infinitely appealing in this land which contains our oldest history," she wrote, "something which once known will linger in one's memory with a haunting tenacity."

The photographs were a critical but not a financial success, and so, during the Second World War, Laura worked part-time as a photographer for Boeing to make ends meet. After the war she resettled in Santa Fe. In 1948 she published *Temples in the Yucatán: A Camera Chronicle of Chichen Itza.*

Laura's next book, *The Rio Grande: River of Destiny,* published in 1949, introduced a more mature and self-confident Laura Gilpin to the world. She placed a much greater emphasis, in this book, on cultural geography, a theme that was to also dominate the rest of her creative life.

Laura began work on the Rio Grande book in 1945, and during the next four years, she traveled more than 27,000 miles on borrowed gas ration coupons to make photographs for this ambitious project. Because the region was largely inaccessible by car, Laura packed in on horseback to photograph the river's source in Colorado, and she chartered a small plane to fly her over the river's confluence with the Gulf of Mexico. Author Martha Sandweiss describes Laura's book this way:

> *Her plan for the book dictated the content of her pictures: The people—the Spanish Americans, the Mexicans and the Anglos are important but are subservient to the river. The people come and go—the river flows on forever. Thus she made few portraits, focusing instead on landscapes and pictures that showed the people in the context of their environment. She organized the book geographically, following the river down through the Colorado mountains and the fertile San Luis Valley, into the Indian and Hispanic regions of northern New Mexico, and out through the ranching areas of west Texas and the Mexican borderlands.*

John Brinkerhoff Jackson, himself a student of the American landscape, reviewed the book as a "human geographical study," noting that Gilpin

> *has seen the river from its source to its end and permits us to see it through her eyes, not merely as a photogenic natural phenomenon, but as a force that has created a whole pattern of living, that has created farms and villages and towns and that conditions its future their growth. . . . Miss Gilpin is undoubtedly the first photographer to introduce us to the pueblos, the Spanish-American communities, the whole countryside of farms, as something more than picturesque.*

Laura's interest in cultural context, though less prominent in her photographs, was now expressed in text. She lovingly describes the region in human terms, citing the river's mineral wealth, its use in growing food and nurturing livestock, and its value as an oasis for weary travelers looking for a place to settle.

The final page of the book, featuring a picture called "Rio Grande Yields Its Surplus to the Sea (1947)," makes an evocative statement, in text and image, about Laura Gilpin's feelings regarding the beauty and fragility of the relationship between humanity and the natural world. The text reads:

> *Since the earliest-known existence of human life in the Western world, all manner of men have trod the river's banks. With his progressing knowledge and experience, man has turned these life-giving waters upon the soil, magically evoking an increasing bounty from the arid land. But through misuse of*

*its vast drainage area—the denuding of forest lands and the
destruction of soil-binding grasses—the volume of the river
has been diminished, as once generous tributaries have become
parched arroyos. Will present and future generations have the
vision and wisdom to correct these abuses, protect this heritage,
and permit a mighty river to fulfill its highest destiny?*

Almost immediately upon finishing *The Rio Grande: River of Destiny,* Laura returned to the Navajo reservation with Elizabeth Forster, resolved to do another book on Navajo life. This time she wanted to emphasize Navajo tradition and cultural continuity, so she rephotographed many of the people she had photographed years before, paying special attention to those who had preserved their ancient culture. She organized her book into four sections, corresponding to the importance of the number four in the Navajo religion. Laura wanted the book, which would be called *The Enduring Navaho,* to be written and photographed from a purely Navajo perspective.

The Navajo considered themselves the Dinéh, "the People of the Earth." As Laura wrote,

*they moved about in loneliness, though never lonely, in dignity
and happiness, with song in their heart and on their lips,
in harmony with the great forces of nature. The two salient
qualities of the people were their dignity and their happiness.
Both spring from their vital traditional faith, faith in nature,
faith in themselves as a part of nature, faith in their place in
the universe, deep-rooted faith born of their Oriental origin,
molded and strengthened by the land in which they live.*

The most important theme at work in *The Enduring Navaho* is the word *enduring.* Laura, like Elsie Clews Parsons, believed that Pueblo culture was alive and thriving in constant combination with new influences—remaining connected to the past, yet moving forward.

In 1972 Laura Gilpin published a book on the Canyon de Chelly. She was eighty-one years old. In this book she closely followed the lives of a small number of Navajo families that lived in this New Mexico canyon, which is accessible only on horseback, led by a Navajo guide.

Laura Gilpin created a pictorial portrait of the entire historical and geological landscape of the Southwest. As Martha Sandweiss put it, Gilpin communicated

*a landscape with a past measured not just in geological
or evolutionary time but in human time, as evidenced by*

*architectural ruins, ancient trails, and living settlements. It*
*was a landscape with intrinsic beauty, but one whose greatest*
*meaning derived from its potential to change and be changed by*
*humankind. Gilpin did not dislike the idea of a wilderness, but*
*for her there was no true wilderness in the Southwest, no area*
*that had remained untouched by more than a thousand years of*
*human settlement.*

Laura never considered herself an artist. She was simply a photographer, who for more than a half a century practiced her profession with consummate craftsmanship and a great love for the world she captured with her camera.

Laura Gilpin knew that the Southwest sometimes provided a nurturing landscape, sometimes a hostile one. She knew that the landscape could be modified by human action, but she also believed that the landscape should and would remain the dominant force shaping and molding human culture.

# OKLAHOMA WOMEN

# CATHERINE "KATE" ANN BARNARD

## (1875–1930)

### Child Advocate and Voice for the Poor

"I want to feel that the world is better because I have lived in it," Kate wrote in an article for *Sturm's Oklahoma Magazine* on the eve of the first Oklahoma Legislature's meeting. "I am especially interested in that class of legislation that will best protect the tiniest and frailest bit of humanity that is entrusted to our care. I am especially interested in child-life, because our fathers represent the past, we the present, and the children represent the future. I am interested in the passage of laws that will make it possible for the poorest child to receive an education—not only of letters and of books, but of lands."

Diminutive Catherine Ann Barnard, whom everyone from the homeless to governors called Kate, had three goals: to help the downtrodden, enrich children's lives, and give hope to those living in despair. She knew the loneliness of being motherless, yet managed to fill that emptiness with outstanding achievements that nurtured her own spirit and certainly nurtured others. She believed in the goodness of people. Even when politicians, newspapers, and friends turned on her for doing what she thought was right and good for the state, she pressed on. When she became so ill she couldn't get out of bed, she still pressed on. Not for herself, but for others.

Catherine Ann Barnard was born in Alexandria, Nebraska, on May 23, 1875, to John Barnard and Rachel Shiell Mason. Her father had come to America from Ireland when he was eight months old. He had a strong work ethic, which he instilled in Kate, and worked as a civil engineer, lawyer, surveyor, and railroad worker. Kate's mother, Rachel, had been married before she met John and had two sons. The couple married in 1873 in Geneva, Nebraska.

In January 1877, when Kate was just over a year and a half old, her mother and week-old brother died. Even though Kate wasn't old enough to know what was happening, this event would shape the rest of her life.

Soon after, her father sent the three children to live with his wife's parents while he left town to seek work. As he traveled from one position to another, Kate went from relative to relative. She seldom saw her father, but she idolized him. "My love for my father and a desire to help the poor became the two great dominant factors of my life. His example provided the moral strength behind every sacrifice for principle, every struggle for liberty, and every achievement recorded," she said later in life. He remained her constant. Her maternal grandmother decided she would raise Kate's two stepbrothers, but not her, so they were never a part of Kate's life.

In 1881, four-year-old Kate moved back in with her father and his new wife, Anna Teresa Rose. They settled in Kensington, Kansas. Kate was excited about her new life and time as a family, but two years into the marriage, Anna divorced Kate's father, leaving her motherless again. The couple had a son together, but Kate never knew her baby brother either.

This time, John took Kate with him in his search for work. The pair stayed with strangers and was never in one place long enough for Kate to get along in school or make friends. When Kate was thirteen, her father suffered financial setbacks that left them penniless, and they almost starved in their struggle to survive. A year later, Kate's father left her again and headed to the Oklahoma Territory, where he participated in the Land Run of 1889. After he had built a two-room dwelling, he sent for Kate. Their first stake was in a little town to the east of Oklahoma City called Newalla. Kate lived on the property by herself while her father worked in Oklahoma City as an attorney. It was a lonely time for Kate, and on days she despaired. However, when she turned eighteen, she moved to Oklahoma City at 209 West Reno, where her father had purchased property and built them a small house.

After she settled in with her father, her next order of business was to finish her schooling, which she did at St. Joseph's Parochial School. Although she couldn't afford to go to college, Kate was smart enough to pass the teacher's test and get her certificate from the Oklahoma State Board of Education. Kate's teaching career was destined to be a short one. In fact she had decided long ago on those lonely nights in Newalla what she wanted to do with her life: She wanted to help alleviate the suffering of the unfortunate. Now she became more committed, as she saw daily the sufferings of the poor in the area where she and her father lived, which was the red light district, a dilapidated Oklahoma City slum. She especially grieved for the children, and set her goal to become "a voice for those who suffered in the gutter of humanity."

There didn't seem to be enough happening with Kate's teaching to keep her energy bridled, and it certainly wasn't helping her reach her goals. So she decided to study stenography and gain secretarial skills so she could get a more challenging job. She found it when she took on a job as a stenographer and clerk in Guthrie, Oklahoma, for the Republican minority in the territorial legislature. It was here that she got a small glimpse of what politics was all about.

After working for several months in the legislature, an opportunity arose that she couldn't pass up. She competed with 498 other participants to represent

Oklahoma at the World's Fair in St. Louis, Missouri. She was chosen, and in 1904, at the age of twenty-nine, went to St. Louis as secretary and hostess of the Oklahoma Territory exhibit. While there, she spoke to exhibition leaders, did interviews, and talked about Oklahoma to visitors in general. She loved Oklahoma and wanted others to see the state in a favorable light. She also was able to attend meetings of humanitarian organizations where she heard not only about the plight of the poor, but also about reforms being made to help them. She wrote impassioned letters about what she was learning to the *Daily Oklahoman*. She also took her information to a local St. Louis paper. The editor at that paper assigned a reporter to Kate, and the pair went to every slum in the city. Kate got a view of life she couldn't have imagined existed.

After the World's Fair the *Daily Oklahoman* paid for her to attend Graham Taylor's Chicago School of Civics and Philanthropy so that she could write a series of articles. While she was *seeing* the problem, she traveled to Chicago and Denver to find *answers* to it.

She had made a strong ally in the *Daily Oklahoman* and became known and respected by its readership. So when she returned to Oklahoma, and wrote articles asking those who had an abundance to give to the less fortunate, or when she ran an advertisement asking for food and clothing, the community responded generously.

While she continued this humanitarian work, she also briefly held a job as stenographer for a city attorney, but was fired because she wouldn't work on Sunday and seemed more interested in the plights of the poor than her job. That only spurred her on. In December 1905, she took over and reorganized the United Provident Association. From 1905 to 1907 the group served over two thousand families in need. She joined labor organizations, fought for higher wages, and became a voice for those she felt would not only advance her causes but also help those in need.

Kate took her mission statewide. She traveled and made forty-four speeches before the November 1906 election. With statehood and a new state constitution on the way, she wanted to make sure that the reforms she championed would be guaranteed in the new constitution and that Oklahoma would become an example for other states. She campaigned for those who agreed with her. And while Kate's ideas were considered progressive and new to most Oklahomans, people listened to her.

Most important, the delegates listened to her, and when she was allowed to address the constitutional convention, she emphasized three proposals for the new constitution. First was a ban on child labor; second, a proposal for compulsory education; and third, a plan to create an office of Commissioner of Charities and Corrections. Because of Kate's immense popularity, lawmakers took notice of her suggestions. Oklahoma, in fact, became the first state to have a child labor plank included in its constitution. In the end, Kate got everything she asked for. The delegates had adopted a child labor ban, which determined the age at which a child could work and how many hours per day, set up a plan of education for children, required children ages eight to sixteen to attend school, and created the office of Commissioner of Charities and Corrections. This office would oversee charitable organizations and the state's prison system.

Kate was elated, especially so when she was chosen to run for the new office of Commissioner of Charities and Corrections. She saw it as an opportunity to safeguard newly won reforms and to bring further reforms to her new state. When the dust settled and the votes were counted on September 17, 1907, Kate had won by a landslide. She was not only the top vote-getter in Oklahoma's first election, but the only woman elected to a state office when women did not even have the right to vote yet.

After the election, lawmakers and state officers set to work implementing the new constitution. Within their ranks now, Kate began the job of overseeing 325 jails, poorhouses, orphanages, rescue homes, and institutions for the care of children, the blind, deaf, and insane on a local, city, and statewide level.

At first, her department received enough money to do the job for which it was commissioned. But Kate had made enemies, and one of the biggest was "Alfalfa" Bill Murray. He fought her on her reforms because he didn't feel they were needed, but mostly because she was a woman. She was successful—some say instrumental—in one of his election bid losses, and he would be back with more venom than Kate could handle.

While she was happy in her legislative success, her father's death on May 5, 1909, overshadowed that contentment. "He was the one being for whom I hoped to share my ambitions and my successes. It was to bring credit on his name that I strove so hard," she said after his death. Even though, his death hit her hard mentally and physically, it did leave her financially well off.

During her two terms in office, she was instrumental in getting children out of mines, harmful factories, and sweatshops, and into schools. She helped reform penal housing and had hundreds of prisoners held in Kansas prisons returned to Oklahoma. She helped institute eight-hour workdays and set limitations on where and when children could work when they were not in school. Kate also championed children convicted of crimes by reforming the juvenile justice system.

Her greatest fight and perhaps the one that brought about her demise was when she began reforms to recover and return Indian lands and monies to orphaned Indian children. When Indian lands were opened to white settlers, the government claimed the right to govern the Indians' finances as well. The government gave the Indians, children and adults alike, a certain amount of money for the land whites were now settling. In the case of Indian orphans, a guardian was placed in charge of them and their monies.

The whole business came to Kate's attention when some citizens in the eastern part of the state reported seeing fairies in the woods. Upon investigating, Kate discovered the "fairies" were three orphaned Indian children, starving, wearing rags, and living among the trees. Upon further inquiry, she found that the guardian was living off the children's allotment and not taking care of their welfare. Not only that, but she discovered this wasn't the only case. With the help of a newly hired attorney, her office began exposing cases like these as well as other types of corruption, exposing not only well-to-do Oklahoma citizens, but politicians as well.

The more she fought for reform and legislation, the more the politicians fought back. The more corruption she found and the harder she fought, the more her office was whittled down, until only Kate and one stenographer were left. She informed one of her supporters that she would not campaign for re-election of a third term. Instead, she would devote the rest of her time and energy on Indian issues and securing the protection of Indian property rights.

By 1914 Kate had been fighting an illness she couldn't recover from. She had contracted a severe form of type one herpes simplex virus that undermined her health. As her political influence was fading because of her health, Bill Murray launched a vicious campaign against her Indian rights work. It was a regrettably successful venture, resulting in the press's dissemination of false information about not only her personally, but her work. On January 12, 1915, she acknowledged defeat, packed up her belongings, and moved out of the office of Charities and Corrections. In the seven years she served, she had found her place and identity, but now it was time to move on.

Kate left the state, traveling to Colorado and Hot Springs, Arkansas, in an attempt to recover her health. She was so removed now from the centers of Oklahoma power that people began hearing rumors that she was dead. Yet from her sick bed she still wrote letters to people she thought could further the Indian cause and assist in helping the poor. By now, though, politicians considered her a joke. The bill that had been drafted at her request in regard to the Indian issue was not adopted. She realized all hope of ever getting it through the state legislature was lost.

At the end of October 1915, she had recuperated enough to go on a speaking tour in the east. She thought if Oklahoma wouldn't tackle the Indian issue, the federal government might, if she could generate enough interest. It was not to be. Totally exhausted after she could get no support, she had a relapse. Her heart was broken, and she gave up.

"I love my state, my father is buried in its soil. I love every tree and flower and I could scream my agony as I am compelled to pen these lines to you. But God knows there is no justice for Indians in Oklahoma. The only hope lies in Washington," Kate wrote in a letter to her friend and supporter, Walter L.

Fisher, Illinois Republican and secretary of the interior under President Taft. "Truly, I don't know why I was born. This battle is too much for me. It would kill a strong man."

Depressed and still battling her incurable illness, she closed the door on public life in 1916 and left Oklahoma City. She made a new home in Denver, but traveled frequently in the next ten years in an effort to find a cure or some relief from her disease, which was worsening. Her stress-induced herpes blisters, once confined to her mouth, were now breaking out all over her body.

She returned to Oklahoma City in 1926, but she lived as a recluse, seldom venturing from her room at the Egbert Hotel. Though isolated, she was still focused on improving the lives of others, this time working on a book about women and politics. At night, guests complained about the click of her typewriter. By 1929 both her physical and mental health had rapidly deteriorated. She became paranoid, imagining conspiracies threatening her and the Department of Charities and Corrections.

In February 1930 on a cold Sunday afternoon, a hotel maid found Kate in the bathtub of her living quarters. She was dead. The coroner pronounced her cause of death as heart failure. Her body was removed to the coroner's office and her relatives were notified. They refused any involvement in funeral arrangements. Finally, a friend stepped in and took care of the service. Fourteen hundred people showed up at her service, which was held at St. Joseph's Catholic Church. Former governors were honorary pall bearers and the flag at the Capitol was flown at half-mast in her honor. The funeral procession traveled to Fairlawn Cemetery where Kate was laid to rest beside her father.

Kate reached the pinnacle of popularity and success in her short political career helping the unfortunate. She was truly "Oklahoma's Angel." Through her reform ideas and a connection with a new state legislature, she saw what Oklahoma could be and she wanted the best for "her" state. She would be proud of the work that has been accomplished in the name of reform over the last decades, but she also would know there is a lot more work to be done as there always is in any civilized society.

# RACHEL CAROLINE EATON

## (1869–1938)

### Champion for the Cherokee

What does it take for one to be remembered through history? Must one become president or be involved in a great war? What great feats must be accomplished for one's life to be acknowledged? Perhaps it's not the big things that set people apart, but the small things steadily done over a lifetime. While many may not know who Rachel Caroline Eaton is, those researching the Cherokee nation will have come across her work. For those she encouraged to become educated or to continue their education, there is a deep appreciation of her achievements and influence.

Rachel Caroline Eaton was an educator and through her written work will continue to be one through generations. Whether for her classroom teaching or her work educating people about her Cherokee Nation, even in today's modern society, she is and will be remembered.

Rachel Caroline Eaton, affectionately known as "Callie" by friends and family, was born on July 7, 1869, four years after the Civil War ended, near Flint Creek in the Cherokee Nation. The location is just west of Maysville, Arkansas. Callie was the oldest child of George Washington Eaton and Nancy Elizabeth Ward Williams. She had three brothers and a sister, Martha "Mattie" Pauline, whom she remained close to her entire life. Her father, who was born in Texas, served in the Confederate Army during the Civil War. Her mother, who was part Cherokee, was named after Callie's grandmother, who had been removed from her ancestral homeland and came to Oklahoma on the Trail of Tears.

Callie's family settled in Claremore Mound, near Claremore, Oklahoma, in Rogers County in 1874. That is where she spent time as a little girl. Here, she learned about her ancestors, the struggles of the Cherokee Nation, and learned firsthand the cruelty and unfair practices of the US government. While she was always loyal to her country, she knew not to trust the men who ran it.

Her parents came to the Cherokee Nation in Indian Territory and home-steaded an area of over a thousand acres. By the time's standard, the family was well off. They had cattle, raised crops to sell, had bees for honey, and lived a comfortable life in their big two-story house with a large front porch. When the government decided they wanted more land for white settlers, the family's land allotment was cut down to 120 acres. The Eaton family was luckier than most. They got to keep the land where the big house sat, and their land still had the stream that ran along the edge of their new property line. The family never starved, but their assets were cut down to only twelve percent of what they were and they never could recover what was lost.

Growing up, she had heard the stories of her ancestors, and her interest in history, particularly Cherokee history, began at an early age. It probably seemed strange that the heritage her family and friends wanted to preserve wasn't talked about in the school she attended.

Callie began her formal early education in the Cherokee Nation's tribal schools, and then when she was old enough, she attended the Cherokee Female Seminary at Park Hill, Oklahoma. She wasn't a straight-A student, but she adopted the culture of the seminary early on and continued to live in its new ways. In other words, she learned to be white. Cherokee leaders felt their people had a lot to make up and strive for if they were to keep pace with the white man. Because they felt they had been cheated by the white man because of their ignorance in many areas, their goals were to educate their children so they wouldn't be taken advantage of like so many before them.

"While our neighboring Tribes and Nations are pressing forward in the pursuit of knowledge, let not the Cherokee . . . be second in the race," former Chief William Potter Ross said in a speech at the opening of the tribe's seminaries. "The last thing our tribe needs is lazy and useless men and slouchy and slip shod women."

To make sure this didn't happen, the seminaries were given a mandate not only to educate, but to make students well-rounded citizens by requiring that chores be done, a dress code followed, and that manners and etiquette be taught and used. Each grade had its own curriculum, and students were held to high standards. Younger children studied arithmetic, composition, grammar, geography, penmanship, phonics, and reading. Older students learned botany, chemistry, English history, French, German, and philosophy, and also read the works of Homer, Goethe, and Julius Caesar. Even though the school was Cherokee, the school taught no classes in Cherokee history, language, religion, nor any other aspects of Cherokee culture. The Cherokee language was not spoken, and the English language was not only spoken, but also taught.

Classes began in August and ran through the end of May. Callie and the other students began their day at 5:30 a.m. and ended it at 9:15 p.m. They were busy attending classes, praying in chapel, and preparing recitations. At mealtimes, the girls dressed in appropriate attire, filed into the dining room, and ate under the careful and watchful eyes of teachers or upper class women.

Callie lived and thrived in this type of environment. Always involved in church activities, she and a classmate, Bluie Adair, founded a branch of the

Young Women's Christian Association. In addition to the other chapel services and devotionals, this group offered an extra weekly prayer meeting at the school. Even from an early age, Callie was a member of the Presbyterian Church. Her loyalty and devotion came from the example her grandmother, Lucy Ward Williams, who became deeply involved with the Presbyterian Church. Callie's devotion was so deep, in fact, that her friends and family thought she might become a missionary.

Perhaps she considered it. As graduation grew near she was undoubtedly assessing her skills and planning her future. She now knew how to speak, read, dress, and carry herself like a lady, and make the Cherokee nation proud. While she and the two other girls who made up her graduating class were excited about their last year, an incident happened that dampened their spirits and affected the future life that Callie was so eagerly awaiting.

In 1887, Easter Sunday morning, a fire burned the girls' seminary building to the ground. A man by the name of Louis McLain often visited the seminary. He tried repeatedly to get the girls to go into the woods with him, so he could allegedly "preach the gospel" to them and save their souls. On this particular morning, on one of his strange visits, embers lifted from his pipe and drifted toward an open window, where they lighted on the curtains and caught fire. When the boys from the male seminary and the townspeople saw the smoke, they immediately came to help, but high winds and lack of nearby water made their efforts futile, and the building burned to the ground, along with most of its records. Callie understood that all the history of her beloved institution was gone, and she learned that day what it was like to experience true loss. She would later vow to preserve Cherokee Nation history so that it might avoid a similar fate.

That night, the girls were put up in the homes of residents from surrounding towns and in available rooms in the male seminary. The next morning, Callie began her hour-and-a-half trek home. While many of the female students had to enroll in other schools to continue their education, Callie and her two classmates were lucky enough to receive their diplomas with ten male graduates on June 28, 1888.

A new seminary was built at Tahlequah and opened a year after Callie graduated. She would return years later to teach at this new school under someone she admired.

After graduation, Callie headed east to Drury College in Springfield, Missouri, where she received her bachelor of science degree. It wasn't unusual for the girls from the seminary to attend the college. Many students from the Indian Territories wound up going to Drury. While she had always had a penchant for history, it was Professor Edward M. Sheppard who encouraged her to study Indian history, a field of study that would engage her longtime interest. She then went on to the University of Chicago, where she received her master's and doctorate in history.

When Callie finished her education, she taught in the Cherokee Nation public schools. One place that was near and dear to her heart was the Cherokee Female Seminary, now located in Tahlequah, Oklahoma. Even though the location had changed, the seminary still instilled the same moral and ethical values Callie had been brought up with and the educational standards she had come to respect. She served there for two years: 1896 through 1897. Through the years, she would be head of the history department for the State College for Women in Columbia, Missouri; history professor in Painesville, Ohio, at Lake Erie College; and dean of women at Trinity University in San Antonio, Texas.

Besides teaching, Callie had another love—writing. She knew that to preserve her love and respect for the Cherokee Nation, its stories needed to be written down. For her dissertation topic she chose Cherokee history; it was entitled "John Ross and the Cherokee Indians."

"The aim of this historical sketch is to trace the evolution from barbarism to civilization of one of the most progressive tribes of North American Indians; to give a sympathetic interpretation of their struggle to maintain their tribal identity and ancestral domains against the overwhelming tide of economic development advancing from the Atlantic seaboard westward." Another aim of the work, as Callie wrote in the forward of her paper, was "to relate the story of their forcible removal to the western wilderness where in the midst of hard-won prosperity they were plunged into the horrors of the Civil War."

Later, her dissertation was expanded into a manuscript that was published in 1914 by the George Banta Publishing Company of Menasha, Wisconsin. It was a huge success. Used frequently as a history book for schools and colleges, it continues to be the authoritative text for researchers, who respect the research that produced it and know that its historical content is priceless because Callie had access to people others didn't.

The book covered not only the history of the Cherokee Nation, and its importance to the United States, but also the history of how John Ross became the Cherokee's chief. That story began in the early eighteenth century when the white man began encroaching on the continent and Indians struggled to hold their people together. When the Civil War broke out, Chief Ross tried to keep his people neutral in the conflict, thinking it would save them grief in the future. But it was not to be. The young men of the tribe were drawn into the conflict, and another dark period in the Cherokee Nation.

"Miss Carolyn Eaton's book is a history of the Cherokee Nation from the beginning of the 18th century to the end of the 19th," a supporter, Mrs. Sam, wrote to James Thoburn in regards to getting the book added to the Oklahoma historical collection. "It is social, economic, and political in nature stressing the rapid advancement [the Cherokee] made in the arts of civilization and the phenomenal effect upon the tribe of Sequoyah's alphabet. It is *not* biographical in the sense that Emmet Starr's book is nor does it give lengthy quotations from source material as some Oklahoma authors do. She has gleaned much material, firsthand, from many prominent men and women of the Cherokee tribe of which she is a member. She has had the privilege of seeing and hearing all of the principal chiefs of the nation since the Civil War."

After the book was published in the 1920s, she served two consecutive terms as superintendent of public instruction of Rogers County in northeastern Oklahoma. As her education role continued, so did her research and writing; however, she wasn't able to devote the time she wanted to her writing until her retirement.

In 1930 she wrote an essay for the General Federation of Women's Clubs titled "The Legend of the Battle of Claremore Mound, Oklahoma." It was published in the Federation's booklet in October 1930 as *Traditional Background of the Indians*. Callie was an excellent source for the piece as her family's property backed up to Claremore Mound, and as a youngster Callie would have played around the site and visited it often. The family told stories about tourists coming through the area asking permission to visit the mound and hunt for arrowheads.

Callie was married for a brief time, but no children came of the union. The marriage was so short-lived, as a matter of fact, that even though her husband's name is known, nothing else is known about James Alexander Burns. The year of her marriage is also a mystery, although some believe the couple married shortly after she graduated from Drury College and were separated before she started studies for her master's degree. Callie remained single for the rest of her life, devoting herself to the educational field and her writing.

She kept herself busy in her community through clubs and organizations such as the Tulsa Indian Women's Club, a branch of the Oklahoma Federation of Women's Clubs, and Eastern Star. She also became involved with her sister's children, taking a nephew under her wing and making sure he had a place to stay in Tulsa while he completed his education.

Life never was easy for her. After she retired, she began work on another manuscript, *The History of the Cherokee Indians*. She was also diagnosed with breast cancer. While she worked feverishly on the manuscript, her one desire was to live long enough to finish it. She called her nephew to her on her deathbed and asked one favor, that he guard the manuscript and make sure it got published. Callie believed in exposing truths in her work, so she knew there would be opposition to what she had written. But she wanted the truth to be known. Through the years, the manuscript has been mailed out and rejected and passed down through generations. Almost eighty years later, the family is pursuing publication again.

In 1936, Callie was inducted into the Oklahoma Memorial Association's Hall of Fame as one of Oklahoma's most outstanding women. She died in Claremore, Oklahoma, on September 20, 1938, after a long but brave battle with breast cancer.

Although she is gone, her legacy lives on in the form of her books and articles. Anyone who wants to really understand Oklahoma and its Indians has but to pick up Callie's books and read them. She and her work will not be forgotten.

# DOROTHY K. BARRACK PRESSLER MORGAN

(1896–1978)

Pioneering Pilot

At the beginning of the twentieth century, aviation was coming into its own. The Wright Brothers had made history with their flying machine in 1903, and other men had made strides in the aviation field in the following years. While women may have been fascinated, not many were up to the challenge. There were a few, however, who threw caution to the clouds, and Dorothy Pressler Morgan was one.

"I really couldn't say how I got interested in flying," she said in an article in the *Oklahoma Times* in 1969, "but at the time I didn't have much else to do. A friend thought I'd like to learn to fly—and I did."

Dorothy Barrack Pressler Morgan was born on May 19, 1896, in Parkersburg, West Virginia. She came to Oklahoma in the 1920s with her husband, Howard Pressler, and they settled in Perry, Oklahoma. While Howard worked away from home doing field work for the Magnolia Petroleum Company, Dorothy filled her time playing bridge.

For the adventurous Dorothy, card games grew old quickly. For a change of pace, she decided to take flying lessons. Each week, she drove from Perry to Oklahoma City to attend flying class at the Graham Flying School, where classes cost twenty-one dollars an hour, which in the twenties was a lot of money. She started in 1929. Her first plane was a single-engine, open-cockpit OX5 American Eagle. In the early days of flying, it wasn't glamorous or all fun.

"It was lots of hard, hard work with no limits on hours," Dorothy said in an interview for the *Sunday Oklahoman* in 1963. "You'd have to love what you were doing to spend long hours in the open, in wind and dust, to clear runways and do all kinds of manual labor."

When Dorothy started flying, flying schools used open-cockpit planes for instruction. They had no instrumentation or navigational equipment. One learned to fly with a compass, good eyesight, and lots of luck.

"I have always thought it was a good thing I didn't know much about flying when I got started. I didn't know enough to be afraid. We just killed people off right and left. You couldn't open a paper without seeing where someone got cracked up."

Fear never fazed Dorothy. She was doing what she loved, and nothing was going to stop her. Curiosity had gotten her started, but she had always been interested in transportation, and how things moved. Her father had been a railroad engineer, and she guessed that's where her interest really started.

She had twelve hours and thirty-five minutes fly time when she had her first solo flight in April 1929. "That was not too few or too many for a woman." There was a lot of debate among the boys about whether Dorothy could or would fly, but she had the last laugh. Dorothy described her experience in a 1977 interview with Mary Roberts for the Oklahoma Historical Society.

> *I worried them considerably on my first solo. I was learning to fly off the Southwest Twenty-Ninth Street Airport just off May Avenue. They had just one runway that could be called a runway, and of course it was not paved. We had to come in over Wilson and Company, and over high lines where the stockyards were. I took off and went around the field to land. When I did, I pulled the knob off the stick, and it fell on the floor. That did excite me considerably because I really didn't know what to do.*

There was a slot in the floor where the controls were, and she was afraid the knob had fallen in there.

> *I did remember that they said if you run into difficulty trying to land, go around the field again until you collect your wits and come in. I went around and came back in again, and by that time I had my fingers in the top of the stick and I could hold on to it real good. I landed and bounced a little, of course, and came on in. Clint Johnson was one of the Graham Flying Service executives. I told him, "Well, I got down all right." They told me afterwards that he bit the stem off his pipe, he was so worried. I said, "Yes, he was worried about his ten-thousand-dollar airplane, not me."*

Dorothy got her pilot's license in 1931. It was a big day for not only her, but women in general. There was only one other female pilot flying in Oklahoma, May Haizlip. Her husband, Jim, was a flight instructor in Norman and taught her to fly. May was a race pilot. She and Dorothy became good friends. Through the years and their careers, they kept in touch.

It was around this time that Curtis Wright, a large national firm, bought out and then expanded the Graham Flying School. They put in a large hangar and brought in a lot of planes. Dorothy went around trying to get students for the school. She especially wanted to recruit women, but mostly just men signed up, and that disappointed her. "I was preaching to every woman I could talk to, but there was a real block there," Dorothy continued in her interview with Roberts. "You came into the difficulty of their husbands didn't want them to fly, their fathers didn't want them to fly, nobody wanted them to fly, but me."

Even for the women who were encouraged to fly, money was an obstacle. It was expensive. Dorothy finally went to work for Curtis Wright as a clerk so she could continue her flying lessons. "I went to work and turned my check over to them to pay for my flying."

During the Depression and when money was hard to come by, Dorothy did some acrobatic flying. She taught herself to do flying tricks by watching "the boys." The first stunts she did were barnstorming and doing loops over towns like Lawton, Enid, Chandler, and Geary. These tricks were meant to attract attention so the men, Ted Colbert and Clyde Knuckles, could go in and carry passengers. They'd pick up passengers, take them up over town, and then bring them back for five dollars. Business was pretty good as people were fascinated with flying.

Dorothy finally joined the Curtiss-Wright Flying Circus and debuted in a Commandaire airplane. She was considered Oklahoma City's best stunt flyer and those who saw her perform agreed. Her performance included six loops, the roll, wingovers, and the spin of death. Her spin of death was what caught people's attention. She'd fly up to an altitude of two thousand feet, go into a tailspin, level off, cut the motor, and then finally land to the crowd's explosion of applause. Dorothy also entered air races and performed in air programs. That's how she met Wiley Post and Amelia Earhart.

"I knew her well," Dorothy said of Amelia. "She was a very nice person who never threw her weight around."

Wiley Post was a close friend of Dorothy's and considered her a capable pilot. In her interview with Roberts, Dorothy said,

> One thing I always felt was a feather in my cap was when Wiley came back from his trip around the world. He had a Bird Airplane. He came into the field where we were, on his way to his home in Maysville, Oklahoma. As was customary when you got a new airplane, you let your friends fly it—just test hop it around the field. Several of the boys flew the plane. When he got through with them, he asked if I wanted to go for a ride. He said, "Go out and get in." I thought he was going to take me for a hop. I got in, fastened down; he came back and showed me several things on the plane including something new called a starter. I waited for him to get in and he said, "Well, go ahead."

*I said, "By myself?" His reply was, "Of course. You can fly as well as those fellows can."*

Dorothy had learned to fly by using her good judgment. Because flying was so new, she learned to fly like "the boys" learned, through trial and error. On her first solo cross-country flight, she flew from Oklahoma City to Tulsa. At the time, they didn't file flight plans and didn't have charts; pilots just flew by what they knew of the land. Dorothy wasn't very worried. She had handled maps when she had worked for the Magnolia Petroleum Company Land Department.

On this particular day, she was flying a Challenger Fledgling and following a plane. The weather wasn't very good. They were supposed to land in Bristow and wait until the weather cleared before they continued on, but when the plane in front of Dorothy flew right into the clouds, she knew that wasn't for her. She didn't believe in flying into disorienting clouds, so she decided to turn around and go back to Oklahoma City.

"I, of course, got lost," Dorothy said in her interview. "Then I remembered that if you didn't know where you were, get low and follow a road out until you came to something you could recognize."

Dorothy did find her way to Bristow, and they finally all made it to Tulsa. After that, Dorothy flew cross country to Dallas; Wichita; Garden City, Kansas; and back to Oklahoma City.

In 1934, Dorothy received her transport pilot license. "I was thrilled to death," she remembered. In 1932, there were only five thousand licensed pilots in the United States and only twenty transport-rated women pilots. To get a transport license, pilots needed two hundred flying hours and had to take three tests. The first two tests were for private and limited commercial, which allowed pilots to transport passengers; another was for transport, which allowed pilots to transport anything their plane was big enough to carry. It was at this time that Dorothy developed a cataract in one eye. "I had to take a test every time I turned around so that I could prove I could fly with only one eye, like Wiley Post."

Dorothy was involved in only one air accident, and she wasn't even the pilot when the incident occurred. She and the pilot were taking pictures of oil wells for a client when they ran out of gas. They landed in a cornfield near Binger, where they got gas, but when they tried to take off, the plane flipped upside down. Dorothy was afraid of fire, as gas was leaking all over her pink dress and black stockings and shoes. People came and cut her out of her seatbelt. She fell out of the plane with a thud and banged up her thumb when the Fairchild camera she was holding fell and hit it. Despite the accident, Dorothy was determined to continue flying. She was one of a handful of women pilots, and she wanted to see more women become involved in flying. To do so meant she had to bring attention to what then was considered the sport of flying. Part of that job was to test planes and see what each new one could do and to set records if possible.

On August 4, 1931, Dorothy and Captain Bill Bleakley were assigned to test a new plane, the Curtiss-Wright Junior. Dorothy had been flying the open-cockpit, light plane, and they wanted to see how high an altitude the plane would reach. The record at the time for planes of that weight was around fifteen thousand feet. Dorothy recalled,

> It was in August when we have buildups of clouds. We took off with full tanks, wearing heavy clothes, boots, and prepared for zero weather. The fur-lined flying suit I wore weighed more than I do. We flew and I took advantage of every cloud and the updrafts. I got boosted to 16,091 feet when I ran out of gas, which was supposed to be done. I started down and ran through two snowstorms at various altitudes, but came on in. As soon as we landed, they ran out and grabbed our wings to keep us from getting blown off the field.
>
> Bill had gotten the barograph from Fort Sill and the Federal Aeronautical Institute to monitor our flight. Unfortunately, the barograph uses India ink, which is based on water, and it froze. After the freezing point as we went up, it did not register and we had no verification. This made it unofficial and I never did try it again. I don't know whether I would have ever gotten that high again since it was the weather that boosted me.

Dorothy and others were clearing a path for women in aviation in the 1930s, partially through the efforts of the Ninety-Nines club. This international women pilots organization, which officially began in 1929, offered support for women pilots and worked to change legislation if needed so that aviation would be more accessible to women. Dorothy was a founding member of the group, one of the original "ninety-nine" charter members, though bad weather prevented her from attending a group meeting until 1939.

While Amelia Earhart was serving as president of the Ninety-Nines, Dorothy continued her membership, but was also on the board of directors and was secretary for the Oklahoma Aviation Service. She was a member of the Aviation Committee of Oklahoma City Chamber of Commerce, the National Aeronautical Association, the Betsy Ross Air Corps, and the Oklahoma City Altrusa Club.

In 1933 she became the nation's first woman municipal airport manager after she was appointed interim manager of the Oklahoma City Municipal Airport, which is now Will Rogers World Airport. Most people might believe that this was a cushy appointment, but it was not. It was a twenty-four-hour job, and Dorothy learned quickly that she could be called at any time of the day or night for anything. In October of that year, she was called in to manage her airport as the FBI escorted "Machine Gun" George Kelly and Kathryn Kelly through its corridors. They had been involved with four others in the kidnapping of Charles Urschel, an oilman and one of the richest men in Oklahoma City.

Dorothy also had to alert pilots of cows on the runway, and she was also called in frequently in the middle of the night to clear birds, particularly ducks, off the tarmac. She got pretty good with a shotgun.

Dorothy married her second husband, Merrill Morgan, in 1937. She'd met him years earlier while they were both taking flying lessons, though Dorothy soloed before he did. After their wedding they took a whistle-stop flying tour around the United States. Merrill worked for the Federal Aviation Agency. Dorothy loved flying, and flying with her husband was all the sweeter. But when Dorothy got pregnant, all that changed.

"They had a rule that if you were pregnant, you could not fly," Dorothy said. "They cancelled your license." For those women who did want children and wanted to fly, this was a double hardship. Dorothy was outraged. It took her a long time to get her license and it cost her a lot of money. She couldn't afford to take all those classes again. She spoke to the Ninety-Nines and the president of that organization, who backed Dorothy up. She told her to write down what she thought about the rule, and she said she would see if she couldn't get something done about it. The rule was in effect for two years, but finally the pilots associations got involved, took it up with Washington, and got the rule cancelled.

For Dorothy though, flying was out of the cards. Having her daughter, Sharon, was a factor, but so was her deteriorating eyesight. Even though she couldn't pilot a plane, she still continued to stay in the business. She got a job as secretary at Tinker Air Force Base.

During World War II, the couple moved temporarily to Houston, while Merrill trained the Air Transport Command to do instrument flying. The stay wasn't long, and they came back to Oklahoma City. Merrill died in 1955.

"I had to hurry and get back to work," Dorothy said in her recorded interview. She took a job at the Federal Aviation Administration herself until she retired in June of 1967.

When asked before her death about the changes she'd seen in aviation, she mentioned higher speeds and more reliable equipment. Dorothy knew pilots no longer had to fly by the seat of their pants, be their own weathermen, and that women made as many contributions to flight as men.

Dorothy passed away in Oklahoma City at St. Anthony's Hospital on January 31, 1978, after a long illness. In her obituary they called her a pioneer woman aviator. She became known nationwide in the 1930s as being one of only five women in the United States who held a transport pilot license.

She would have been pleased to know that in 1992 the Oklahoma Aviation and Space Hall of Fame honored her by giving her its Pioneer Award. She was a pioneer, the first female pilot in Oklahoma, and the first female in the United States to be rated as an airline transport pilot. And even though she was lesser known than Amelia Earhart, Dorothy Pressler Morgan cleared a path for all the women who fly today.

# LUCILLE MULHALL

⚜

(1885–1940)

## QUEEN OF COWGIRLS

Lucille Mulhall was known by many titles. When she rode out on Governor, her trick horse, during her father's shows, she was America's Greatest Horsewoman. When she rode wildly and roped steers in competition with the men, she was World's Champion Roper. When she rode in parades and opening ceremonies she was Queen of the Range. Crowds paid money to see her ride and cheered enthusiastically as she exhibited her skills. Cowboys respected her. The press loved her. Yet, when she was home, she was Lucille, America's First Cowgirl, who loved horses, roping, and ranch life.

Lucille Mulhall was born in St. Louis, Missouri, on October 21, 1885, to Zack and Agnes Mulhall. Her father was born Zachariah P. Vandeveer in 1847. His mother died when he was young and at the age of eight, in 1855, his father died of yellow fever. He was sent to live with his aunt and her husband, Mr. and Mrs. Joseph Mulhall, in St. Louis. While there are no records stating that he was adopted by the Mulhalls, Zack took the name of the couple who raised him. Another orphan came to live with the couple as well, Mary Agnes Locke. She was related to Joseph Mulhall. Mary Agnes, after receiving her college degree from Notre Dame in 1870, married Zack in 1875. They had eight children, but only two, Agnes and Lucille, survived to adulthood. Lucille also had two half-siblings, Charley and Mildred, son and daughter born to her father and his mistress, Georgia.

Lucille's father's early business consisted of contracting cattle shipments from the ranchers in Texas and Indian Territory for the Santa Fe Railroad. On one of the trips into the territory, he found a piece of land he wanted, so in true Mulhall style, when the land was opened for homesteading in the run of 1889, Zack Mulhall staked his claim. A year later he moved his family down to his eighty-two-thousand-acre ranch, forty miles north of Oklahoma City, and a fifteen-room house he had built for them. It was here that Lucille would become the horsewoman people across the world would come to know. She was only five.

Already at this young age, Lucille loved the ranch. Her family may have had an inkling of the horsewoman she would become when they sat two-year-old

Lucy on a horse, and she cried when taken off. Now, the ranch offered her all kinds of time with horses. She spent most of her days outdoors, roping steers or riding horses, the wilder the better.

When her older brother, Logan, died of diphtheria in 1895, Lucille took his place in helping run the ranch. All the cowhands came to respect her skill and accepted her, as she could cut any cow from the herd as well as the next man. With all the work she was doing, she decided she wanted to have a ranch and cattle of her own. She begged her father for a herd and he told her she could have as many of the calves as she could catch and brand. He called a halt to her activities, however, when *all* the calves he started seeing had her brand on them.

It was around this same time that Lucille and her brother, Charley, became local celebrities—Lucille for her roping and Charley for his bucking bronc riding. They not only put on shows for the hands at their father's ranch, but were invited to Guthrie by the mayor to entertain his guests.

Lucille's mother had worried for her safety for a number of years. She didn't think a young girl should be out roping wild steers. Her worry increased tenfold when Lucille was hurt roping a steer and ended up bruised and in bed for a week nursing her injuries. Her mother wanted to send her off to St. Louis to boarding school. Her father stood up for her, and the crisis was momentarily averted when Lucille promised she wouldn't rope steers again. That promise was broken some months later when Lucille rode out and attempted to rope the largest steer on the ranch. Not only did the steer die, but so almost did Lucille. The matter was then settled. Lucille was packed up and shipped off to boarding school as soon as arrangements could be made.

The following year was not a happy time for her. The convent sisters wrote to her parents telling them that while Lucille's grades were good, she was homesick for the ranch. There seemed to be no amount of work or activity that could snap Lucille out of her malaise.

After getting that report, Lucille's parents decided perhaps schooling closer to home might be the best thing for her. They decided that in the fall, Lucille would attend St. Joseph's Convent School in Guthrie, Oklahoma. It was a boarding school, so she would stay at school through the week and come home to the ranch on the weekend. This suited Lucille just fine.

When Zack went to pick Lucille up in St. Louis to bring her home, he took a riding outfit he had commissioned for her. They also visited the fairgrounds there before heading back to Mulhall. While there the pair saw a horse, Governor, doing simple tricks. Lucille fell in love with him, so her father bought him for her. This horse would become as famous as Lucille and carried her to many events, showing off his skills as well as helping her with hers.

The Mulhall Ranch had many visitors through the years. Teddy Roosevelt, Will Rogers, and Tom Mix were only a few of the men to come through and stay awhile. The Mulhalls first met Teddy Roosevelt when he came to Oklahoma City for a reunion of his Rough Riders in 1900. The Colonel and the Mulhalls were asked to put on a show for the Rough Riders and they did. Roosevelt was especially taken with Lucille's horsemanship and her ability with a rope. Colonel Zack and Colonel Roosevelt hit it off, and Roosevelt was invited back to the ranch.

One day, as the two of them stood watching Lucille rope and tie a large range steer, Roosevelt turned to Mulhall and smiled. "Zack, before that girl dies or gets married, or cuts up some other caper, you ought to put her on the stage and let the world see what she can do," Roosevelt said. "She's simply great!" And Roosevelt at that time should have known. He was a rancher himself in the Dakota Territory.

In later years, Zack would tell people that it was Roosevelt who gave him the idea for the show, when in truth, Mulhall had already started down the show path. Roosevelt just fed his ego and gave him the confidence to continue. When Theodore Roosevelt was elected president in 1904, Lucille, her father, and the show's band went to Washington and rode in Roosevelt's inaugural parade. Lucille's career and her popularity began a meteoric rise.

Will Rogers and Tom Mix got their start in shows on the Mulhall Ranch. Rogers and Lucille worked together, practicing their acts. Rogers showed Lucille his fancy tricks, and he was impressed with her roping and riding abilities.

In 1900, Colonel Zack took Lucille, her horse Governor, Rogers, Mix, Charley, the band, and several other ranch hands to the Louisiana Purchase Exposition in St. Louis to put on a Wild West Show. The show was a success and opened up opportunities for them to appear in exhibitions, contests, and shows

"Lucille was just a little kid when we were in St. Louis that year, but she was running and riding, her ponytail all over the place and that was incidentally her start too," Rogers wrote in an article in the *Daily Oklahoman* on Sunday, October 11, 1931. "It was not only her start, but it was the direct start of what has since come to be known as the cowgirl. As Colonel Mulhall from that date drifted into the professional end of the contest and show business, Lucille gradually came to the front, and you can go tell the world that his youngest daughter was the first well-known cowgirl.

"She became a very expert roper and was the first girl that could rope and tie a steer, not only do it but do it in such a time that it would make a good roper hustle to beat her."

The troop traveled across the country showing what they could do. Charley was becoming known for his bucking animal riding, be it steers, wild horses, or anything else that could be caught and held until he could get on. Lucille was a draw because of her riding and roping abilities. Audiences may have been skeptical about Lucille's skills when the group arrived, but by the time they left, everyone respected her talents.

One such town was El Paso, Texas. No one believed Zack's comments that his daughter could rope and tie a steer, least of all the local saloon owner. He posted odds that not only could she *not* rope and tie, but that she couldn't even rope. Zack bet on Lucille at ten-to-one odds.

When she first rode out, she missed the steer's horns, but on the second round, she not only roped the steer, but she tied it. The crowd went crazy. Not only that, they stormed the field and started tearing off her clothes. In a world where men had always been at the top of the barn ladder, they didn't believe Lucille was a girl. Charlie rode out and rescued her while Colonel Zack collected ten thousand dollars off the whole affair.

Lest people think her horsemanship abilities made her any less a woman, it did not. Her schooling had trained her to be a lady, and she was a beautiful one at that. She could read, sing, sew, and write; after all, she had attended finishing school and could rub shoulders with any other debutante of that day, as she was a cultured young woman. She could hold her own in society. The only difference was that she could rope, throw, and tie a steer in twenty-eight and one-half seconds.

As one can imagine, injuries came with the riding, roping, and steer tying. Lucille had her share of mishaps. One year in St. Louis, Lucille broke her ankle while roping a steer in a steer-roping contest. On another occasion while putting Governor through his paces, as she reached down to pick up a handkerchief as part of a trick, she reached over too far, got stuck in the stirrup and Governor dragged her across the arena. While people ran to assist her, she shook off, caught up with Governor, remounted, and continued with the trick. The crowd saw her resilience and loved it.

Her father's legal problems followed the troop after he shot three men at the 1904 St. Louis World's Fair, was charged with assault and intent to kill, and many years later was sued by the plaintiffs. While Lucille loved the contest and the roar of the crowd, those times cannot have been happy ones. In 1906, Mulhall shut the troop down. The Mulhalls went back to their ranch where they spent a year quietly recovering from the circuit they had been on.

In 1907, her father secured several contracts that would literally put Lucille on the stage, a vaudeville stage. Her brother, Charley, and several of the cowboys from the ranch appeared in the show. It was called "Lucille Mulhall and Her Ranch Boys." The *St. Louis Republic* was the first to announce the show.

> *Miss Lucille Mulhall of 4643 Washington Boulevard, fearless young horsewoman, well known throughout the United States because of her appearance in her father's Wild West shows in many cities, is to go into vaudeville.*

*Her engagements will begin January 20 in the Orpheum
in Kansas City, where her father has completed a contract for
her appearance in a number of shows for the rest of the season.
The vaudeville act will be modeled after the wild west shows in
which she has taken part so often.*

The tour was composed of one- to two-week stands in towns such as Omaha, Minneapolis, Pittsburgh, Cleveland, Chicago, Memphis, Louisville, Cincinnati, Philadelphia, and Brooklyn. The Mulhalls' part of the show lasted about thirty minutes. A young man, Martin Van Bergen, who sang for the show, was paired with Lucille for the opening set. After the song, Lucille performed tricks and maneuvers with Governor and then riding stunts. The stages she performed on were not very large, so she rapidly learned how to get her horse to stop quickly, lest she be thrown off his back and the stage and be injured.

In late 1907, rumors began to circulate that Lucille had married Van Bergen. She denied this at first, but by 1908, while in Kansas, she announced in an interview that they had been married in Brooklyn, New York, on September 14, 1907.

The following year the couple had a son, William Logan Van Bergen. Lucille took off through 1908 and most of 1909 to be a wife and mother. It is reported that Lucille made an appearance at the 101 Ranch Rodeo in 1909. It isn't known whether that show is what sparked Lucille's ambitions to return to the show circuit or if that is what she had planned all along. What is known is that in the fall of that year, she left her son in the care of Van Bergen's parents, and the Mulhalls went on the road again, this time as Lucille Mulhall's Broncho Busting Company. Their first stop was in St. Joseph, Missouri, for the Horse and Interstate Livestock Show. Lucille and Mildred did their horse and roping tricks, while Charley performed riding bucking broncos. Since Van Bergen is not mentioned in the act, it is likely he returned to vaudeville.

In the following year, Lucille's father put together one of the most ambitious shows to date. Besides starring Lucille, Mildred, and Charley doing their acts, he included several skits like the Pony Express and a stage coach hold-up. There were races, a trapeze act, tribal dances, and a Mexican bull fight. While there was a lot of excitement about the show, there was also a lot of controversy. The first was over the Mexican bull fight; the second over an accident that occurred in the stagecoach skit in which three female passengers, including Mildred, Lucille's sister, were injured; and the third over the way animals, particularly steers, were treated in such shows. Lucille was front and center in the steer incident.

The show had traveled to Chicago. Lucille was giving an exhibition of steer roping. A Chicago newspaper shared the story with those who were not able to attend.

*Several hundred men, women, and children saw a badly*
*frightened steer killed yesterday at the Coliseum by the woman*
*roper, Lucille Mulhall. When the animal, struggling feebly*
*as it was dragged about the ring by the young woman, gave a*
*compulsive gasp and became unconscious, a cry of disgust and*
*horror arose from the audience and a dozen cowboys rushed*
*forward and dragged the carcass from the arena.*

At that time, steers were roped around the neck. But after that things began to change. The Society for the Prevention of Cruelty to Animals (SPCA) stepped in, bringing charges against the Mulhalls and even though nothing much came out of the action except for some fines, the SPCA started getting legislation passed in states prohibiting steer roping.

In November of 1910, Lucille and Martin Van Bergen appeared one last time together in Arkansas. Not long afterward, perhaps reflecting how they had gone in different directions, they divorced.

Lucille had a difficult private life. Her life consisted of being on the road and pleasing her father. Lucille's father had not wanted her to marry. Being known as the "World's Greatest Horsewoman" had an image that demanded a certain reputation be lived up to, like being tough and as rough as the West itself.

Financial woes soon caused the big show to disband. Lucille and Charley formed their own show, but eventually Charley went his own way. Lucille formed her own company, Lucille Mulhall and Company. She continued to perform not only in Wild West shows, but in theater settings as well. One week would find her in Montana, the next in Texas, Kansas, or Iowa.

Other cowgirls were entering the scene by 1915, and Lucille competed against them in the rodeos. She was still a draw, but her times were slowing down in competitions with other women. When she helped manage a stock show in Texas, Lucille got an idea that would still keep her involved in shows: She would become her own rodeo promoter. In addition to promoting rodeos, where other cowboys and cowgirls came to compete, Lucille performed at these events and gave exhibitions.

World War I brought a lull in performing in 1917 and 1918. Lucille continued to attend cattlemen's conventions, and at one of these she met and befriended Tom L. Burnett. He was a well-known Texas rancher who came from a family with oil money. The couple was married on April 14, 1919. Lucille got involved in rodeos again briefly. By April 1922, the couple was divorced, and Lucille headed back to Oklahoma and the Mulhall Ranch.

Lucille settled into life on the ranch with her parents. She didn't go back on the road or perform again. On January 30, 1931, her mother died of cancer, which had been diagnosed a year earlier. Her father, Zack Mulhall, died the same year, on September 19, at the ranch.

Mildred and Charley came back to the ranch to live with Lucille after their divorces. Lucille rode in parades, and Charley put on amateur rodeos at the ranch. In September 1940, Lucille rode as an honored guest in the Cherokee Strip Parade. It was held in Ponca City and was to celebrate the land run of 1893. The parade would be Lucille's last public appearance.

Two months after her fifty-fifth birthday, Lucille, her brother, and his new wife were coming home from a visit in Orlanda, Oklahoma, a town six miles from Mulhall, when their vehicle was struck by a truck. Lucille was killed a mile from her beloved ranch. The date was December 21, 1940. The *Daily Oklahoman* included an article about her funeral, and in it was a line that conveyed the irony of her death: "As a cold rain whipped across the bleak eroded homestead that once measured its range in thousands of acres, Lucille Mulhall, the world's first and most famous cowgirl, was buried Thursday. . . . A machine killed Lucille Mulhall, but horses brought her to her final resting place."

Lucille was inducted into the Rodeo Hall of Fame in December 1975, the National Cowgirl Hall of Fame in 1977, and in April 1985, the Eighty-Niner Celebration in Guthrie, Oklahoma, honored her by dedicating their all-day event to Lucille.

Today, when one speaks of cowgirls, Lucille's name is always brought into the conversation, as well it should be. She paved the way for women to compete and be known for their skills in the Western arena. Today's cowgirls know this. Lucille would be happy to know many still remember her for her horsewoman skills and abilities, and that she still lives in the hearts of many horsewomen and is known as a pioneer in their field.

# OREGON WOMEN

# ABIGAIL SCOTT DUNIWAY

❦

(1834–1915)

## Path Breaker

Twelve-year-old Jenny Scott's heart ached as she stood at her mother's bedside. She had just watched the weary woman give birth for the tenth time in sixteen years. Now Mrs. Scott cradled her newborn daughter in her arms and wept tears not of joy but of anguish. "Poor baby!" she moaned. "She'll be a woman someday. Poor baby! A woman's lot is so hard!"

The scene reminded Jenny of her tenth birthday, when her mother had confided that Jenny's own birth in 1834 had been a sorrow "almost too grievous to be borne." Anne Roelofson Scott had wept then, too. The birth of a girl, in her mind, was no cause for celebration. She had lost her own vitality to the endless toil of frontier life and the strain of frequent pregnancies. She assumed her daughters were destined to suffer similar fates.

Jenny never forgot her mother's hopeless words, nor her mother's helplessness to improve her lot in life. Haunted by these memories, she committed herself to the fight for women's rights—and in doing so became one of the most important women in the history of Oregon.

Abigail Jane Scott—friends and relatives called her Jenny—was born on October 22, 1834, in a humble farmhouse on the Illinois frontier. She was the third of a dozen children born to Anne and John Tucker Scott. Her father was a strong, generous, and adventurous man who believed wholeheartedly in the motto "Hard work never hurt anybody." Her mother was a self-sacrificing, sweet-tempered woman whose early death disproved his belief.

Abigail's first year of life was especially difficult for the Scotts. Torrential rains and flooding followed by severe drought destroyed their crops. So the family had to rely more than usual on the money Anne Scott earned selling eggs, butter, and needlework. With her mother "worn . . . to a frazzle with such drudgery," baby Jenny got little attention. She spent her first summer, she later wrote, sitting on the floor "complaining and neglected, soothed only by a piece of bacon, attached by a string to a bed-post."

Abigail had to assume some of the burden of frontier farming when she was still very young. One of her earliest memories was of standing on a chair to wash dirty dishes with harsh, handmade soap. She picked and spun wool and peeled and quartered apples for drying. As she grew older, she churned butter, chopped wood, milked cows, hoed fields, and scrubbed clothes on a washboard. At the age of nine, while resodding a lawn that had been damaged by drought, she suffered a back injury that would plague her for the rest of her life.

Abigail grew quickly into a tall, spindly, awkward child with a strong will but a fragile constitution. She was often ill and, as a result, managed to attend school for only a few scattered months. Her busy mother somehow found time to teach her to read, spell, and recite rhymes. Abigail began to write "poesy," some of which was published in the local newspaper.

In 1852, when Abigail was seventeen, John Scott succumbed to "Oregon fever." The bug had bitten him more than a decade earlier, when he had attended a speech by Jason Lee, the enthusiastic Methodist missionary to the Pacific Northwest. Lee had extolled the beauty of the Oregon Territory and stressed the importance of American settlers laying claim to it before the British. Although Anne Scott was weak from caring for her nine surviving children and slaving dawn to dusk at her countless household tasks, her husband decreed that the family would make the long and dangerous journey west over the Oregon Trail. Amid tears and protests, the family set out on April 2 in five covered wagons packed with only their most essential belongings. Abigail smuggled a treasured spelling book in the bottom of her sewing bag.

For six months, the family crawled 2,400 miles across the plains and mountains with a train of other emigrants. At first, Abigail thought the trip was fun. After all, it offered a release from the drudgery of farm life. Her father had assigned her the job of keeping a travel diary. So while her mother and sisters cooked the evening meal, she sat with pen and paper, recording the day's events. She dutifully noted the forts they passed, the rivers they forded, and the condition of the grass for the cattle and horses, but she was especially impressed by the scenery, which she found "grand," "romantic," "picturesque and sublime."

It wasn't long before tears stained the pages of Abigail's journal. On June 20, as the caravan neared Fort Laramie, Wyoming, she wrote, "How mysterious are the works of an all-wise and overruling Providence! We little thought when last Sabbath's pleasant sun shed upon us his congenial rays that when the next should come it would find us mourning over the sickness and death of our beloved Mother!"

Poor, work-worn Anne Scott had been too frail to resist an outbreak of cholera among the emigrants. One day she was well; the next she was gone. The family scratched a shallow grave in a hillside ablaze with wildflowers, and then covered it with stones to protect the body from hungry wolves. Abigail's younger sister Harriet later recalled that they "heaped and covered mother's grave with beautiful wild roses, so the cruel stones were hid from view."

On August 28, near what is now Durkee, Oregon, tragedy struck yet again. This time its victim was Abigail's three-year-old brother, Willie. "The ruthless monster death not yet content, has once more entered our fold & taken in his icy grasp the treasure of our hearts!" Abigail wrote. "Last night our darling Willie was called from earth, to vie with angels around the throne of God." He had died, she said, of "cholera infantum, or dropsy of the brain."

During the final month of the journey, as the family crossed the Cascades, Abigail's diary was tinged with disenchantment. She wrote of hunger, lost cattle, worn-out shoes, and crippled wagons. Finally, on September 28—penniless, exhausted, and grieving—the Scotts reached the Willamette Valley and the home of maternal relatives. "We found them all in good health and well satisfied," she noted in her last journal entry. "They were of course glad to see us."

Despite her lack of formal education, Abigail soon managed to get a job as a teacher in what is now Eola, a tiny community six miles west of Salem. The spelling book she'd smuggled across two-thirds of the continent came in handy as she crammed to learn what she would teach her students the next day.

As Abigail's career blossomed, so too did her social life. One of the main attractions of the Oregon Territory was the Donation Land Act of 1850, which entitled every married man to a sizable tract of free land. He could claim an equal amount in his wife's name, so unattached women—what few there were in the region—were coveted prizes. Ranchers, lumberjacks, and teamsters scoured the countryside for brides in what one historian referred to as "the most serious epidemic of marriage fever in American history."

Suddenly besieged by suitors, Abigail had no intention of becoming a "land bride," wooed only for the acreage she could bring to a union. She had nothing but scorn for those shameless men who proposed indiscriminately "to tearful widows of a fortnight and little girls dirty with mud pies." Cautiously, she favored Benjamin Duniway, a tall, good-natured rancher four years her senior. When they married in August 1853, she recalled so vividly her mother's servile existence that she purged the wedding ceremony of the word "obey."

Since Ben had not married within a year of reaching Oregon, he wasn't eligible for a land claim in his wife's name, but he did own 320 acres in untamed Clackamas County. So now, little more than a year after leaving the grind of the Scott farm, Abigail found herself stuck on her husband's meager homestead. For the next four years, she washed, scrubbed, churned, cooked, and nursed her first two babies, Clara and Willis. Bachelors in the neighborhood—and there were many—got in the habit of flocking to her home at mealtime, hoping for a good home-cooked stew or a slice of fresh-baked pie. Hospitable Ben always invited them to pull up an extra chair and stay awhile.

Abigail resented the extra work these freeloaders created and derisively dubbed her cabin "Free Hotel." Decades later, in her autobiography *Path Breaking*, she wrote bitterly of those "monotonous years":

> *To bear two children in two and a half years from my*
> *marriage day, to make thousands of pounds of butter every*
> *year for market; . . . to sew and cook and wash and iron; to*
> *bake and clean and stew and fry; to be, in short, a general*
> *pioneer drudge, with never a penny of my own, was not*
> *pleasant business for an erstwhile school teacher, who had*
> *earned a salary that had not gone before marriage, as did her*
> *butter and eggs and chickens afterwards, for groceries, and*
> *to pay taxes or keep up the wear and tear of horseshoeing,*
> *plow-sharpening and harness-mending. My recreation during*
> *those monotonous years was wearing out my wedding clothes,*
> *or making over for my cherished babies the bridal outfit I had*
> *earned as a school teacher.*

Eventually, Ben abandoned his barren acreage on the fringe of the wilderness. In 1857, he acquired a more fertile tract in Yamhill County, where he hoped to establish a fruit orchard. Abigail found herself cooking and cleaning for a batch of hired hands. She could barely afford to take time out to give birth to two more sons, Hubert and Willis. To her dismay, she was following in her mother's weary footsteps, but she took some comfort from the fact that her husband was "sober, industrious, and kind" and her marriage "more than usually harmonious."

Besides, Abigail had grown up with the idea that a woman's lot was, in her words, to "engage in a lifetime of unpaid servitude and personal sacrifice."

"I was filling my Heaven-appointed sphere," she later wrote, "for which final recompense awaited me in the land of souls."

Desperate for intellectual stimulation, Abigail again turned to writing. She began with lively letters and articles for the weekly *Oregon Argus.* In 1859, when she was twenty-five, she had a book published. Entitled *Captain Gray's Company, or Crossing the Plains and Living in Oregon,* it was a novel based on her own experiences on the Oregon Trail. Reviewers called it "silly" and scoffed at its bad grammar. One critic was "hugely disgusted with its general lack of good taste." But for all its faults, it gave Abigail her first claim to fame: It was the first novel ever printed commercially in Oregon.

Two years after Abigail's plunge into the literary world, Ben made a decision that pitched his family into crisis. Abigail was busy plucking ducks one day with the intention of making feather pillows when she saw an acquaintance approach Ben as he was working at the woodpile. She overheard the man ask Ben to co-sign a business loan. The arrangement would make Ben responsible for repaying the loan if the man could not.

Abigail cringed. A transaction like that could spell financial ruin for the Duniways! Shouldn't she have a say in something that could affect her family so adversely? But this was business, and business was the domain of men. She bit her lip and hoped for the best.

This time the best was not to be. The fledgling business was destroyed in a flood, and the sheriff soon came knocking at the Duniways' door, demanding repayment of the loan. There was nothing they could do but sell the farm and use the proceeds to pay off the debt. In 1863, devastated by their bad luck, they moved to a small house they owned in the nearby town of Lafayette.

With four children now to provide for, Ben went to work hauling freight with his team and wagon. Abigail tried to do her part by operating a small school, but fate had not yet finished with the Duniways. Soon after their move, Ben's team of horses bolted, knocked him to the ground, and dragged a heavy wagon over him. He spent the rest of his life as an invalid, incapable of supporting his family.

Suddenly, Abigail was forced to be the family breadwinner as well as homemaker. She enlarged her school and converted the loft of their home into a dormitory for female boarders. The workload was overwhelming, as she later recalled:

> *I would rise from my bed at 3 o'clock in Summer and 4 o'clock in Winter, to do a day's work before school time. Then, repairing to my school room I would teach the primer classes while resting at my desk. For two hours afterwards I would occupy the time with the older students. . . .*
>
> *I would prepare the table for luncheon in the dining room before repairing to the school room; and, returning to lessons at 1 o'clock p.m., would resume school work until 4 o'clock, before taking up my household duties again in the home. And yet, notwithstanding all this effort, I led an easier life than I had known on a pioneer farm. . . .*

After about a year, Abigail had saved enough money to move her family to Albany, a larger and livelier town on the Willamette River. She sold her school at a profit and opened a millinery shop. It was the only profession other than teaching that was considered "respectable" for a woman.

It was as a storekeeper that Abigail learned how unjustly the law treated women. As she fitted hats, she offered a sympathetic ear to customers down on their luck. On one occasion, the wife of a well-to-do farmer begged her for sewing work because her husband had bought a racehorse with the money she'd saved selling butter. Now she couldn't afford coats for her daughters to wear to Sunday school.

On another occasion, a "faded little over-worked mother of half a dozen children" came to Abigail in distress. Her husband had just sold their household belongings and vanished with the money. The desperate woman knew of a family about to leave town who would rent her their house and sell her their furniture for a reasonable price.

"If I could borrow the money in a lump sum," she pleaded, "I could repay it in installments. Then I could keep my children together, with the aid of a few boarders."

Abigail arranged for a charitable friend to loan the woman the money. All was well until, one day, the derelict husband returned. He refused to acknowledge his wife's debt and sold all the new furniture. In the eyes of the law, he had every right. His wife couldn't borrow money legally without his consent, and any property she owned was his to do with as he pleased. The couple eventually divorced, and the woman lost custody of her children.

On yet another occasion, Abigail loaned a woman the supplies she needed to open a millinery shop in another town. The woman's husband, Abigail explained, was a "well-meaning but irresponsible fellow, noted chiefly for poverty."

One day a stranger came to collect on a debt the woman's husband had incurred before their marriage. Since her husband was unable to pay, the creditor seized all of the woman's merchandise, forcing her to close her business.

Abigail brooded over these injustices. With laws as they were, women were at the mercy of their husbands. One evening, after dinner, she poured out her frustration.

"Ben," she complained, "one-half of the women are dolls, the rest of them are drudges, and we're all fools!"

Idly stroking her hair, he replied, "Don't you know it will never be any better for women until they vote?"

Abigail felt as if someone had lit a fire inside her. "The light permeated the very marrow of my bones," she later recalled, "filling me with such hope, courage, and determination as no obstacle could conquer and nothing but death could overcome."

Abigail was ready to take on the world as a crusader for women's suffrage. She began in November 1870 by joining with two friends to form the Oregon State Equal Suffrage Association. Next, she moved her family to Portland and founded the *New Northwest,* a weekly newspaper that, for the next sixteen years, would serve as a forum for her feminist views.

She was able to get some journalistic guidance from her younger brother, Harvey, who was editor of the Portland-based newspaper, the *Oregonian.* She also had the blessing of her husband and the support of her children, whom she one day would describe as her "highest achievement and principal asset." While her older sons helped set type and print the newspaper, daughter Clara kept house and managed the millinery shop. Ben returned to work as a part-time clerk with the Portland customs house, a humble and undemanding job he got with the help of his brother-in-law. He also tended the youngest boys, Clyde and Ralph, who had been born in Albany during the late 1860s. It was he who nursed them when they were ill, gave them their baths, and entertained them at bedtime with stories and songs. His children adored him for his tenderness. Their feelings for their mother were more ambivalent. Certainly they respected her for her ambition and accomplishments, but they resented the lack of maternal attention. One of her sons, when he was grown, complained that Abigail "lacked the calmness and patience to deal with the personal needs of ailing children."

Abigail was careful not to use the *New Northwest* as a grindstone for too many axes. To attract readers throughout Oregon, Washington, and Idaho, she served up a lively mix of crime reports, political exposés, advice columns, fashion hints, and serial fiction. Still, from the outset she let her readers know exactly where she stood. In her debut issue of May 5, 1871, she wrote:

> *We started out in business with strong prejudices against*
> *"strong-minded women." Experience and common sense have*
> *conquered those prejudices. We see, under the existing customs*
> *of society, one half of the women over-taxed and underpaid;*
> *hopeless yet struggling toilers in the world's drudgery; while*
> *the other half are frivolous, idle and expensive. Both of these*
> *conditions of society are wrong. Both have resulted from*
> *women's lack of political and consequent pecuniary and moral*
> *responsibility. To prove this, and to elevate women, that*
> *thereby herself and son and brother man may be benefitted*
> *and the world made better, purer, and happier, is the aim of*
> *this publication.*

A few months after founding her newspaper, Abigail launched in earnest her campaign for suffrage. She invited Susan B. Anthony to travel to Portland from San Francisco, where the nation's foremost feminist had lately been stumping for women's rights. Anthony agreed to a two-month lecture tour of Oregon and Washington, with Abigail as her manager and publicist. The pair crisscrossed the region by stagecoach and steamer, stopping to speak in churches, schools, saloons, barns, private homes—anywhere they could gather an audience for their message. When Anthony finished the tour and returned to the East Coast, Abigail continued on her own to carry "the gospel of equal rights" throughout the Pacific Northwest.

For the next several years, Abigail traveled three to five days a week, penning articles and editorials while on the move and mailing them back to the *New Northwest*. She was a persistent crusader. In 1886 alone, she gave 181 lectures; traveled 3,000 miles by stage, rail, steamer, buggy, buckboard, and on foot; and wrote 400 columns for her paper—all the while soliciting new subscriptions in every town she visited. In her spare time, she scribbled novels, at least one of which was published, featuring downtrodden women who either succumbed to overbearing men or asserted their independence.

Often Abigail's equal-rights message was not well-received. Many men were threatened by the idea of sharing political power with women, while some society dames, content upon their pedestals, were reluctant to tinker with the status quo. But Abigail believed that equality for women was important to the welfare of both sexes.

"Women who seek the ballot for liberty's sake are not proposing to govern men," she explained. "We are seeking for an opportunity to govern ourselves. We ask nothing but our right to use our voices, as [men's] companions and co-workers, in making the laws which we are taxed to maintain, to which we, equally with [men], are held amenable."

Abigail counted on logic, passion, and wit to convert people to her cause. Once, when she was traveling by stage to Yakima, Washington, a fellow passenger taunted her about suffrage to the amusement of his traveling companions.

"Madam," he said, "you ought to be at home enjoying yourself, like my wife's doing. I want to bear all the hardships of life myself and let her sit by the fire toasting her footsies."

When the stage reached Yakima, the driver stopped to let the man off at his own front gate. There, in his snow-covered yard, stood his wife, busily chopping firewood. As the man climbed from the coach, Abigail called after him, "I see your wife is toasting her footsies!" From then on, the man was known to his chums as "Old Footsie Toaster."

Sometimes Abigail allowed her quick temper to get the best of her. She could be tactless and combative when responding to opponents. Once, she described a California man who had voted against women's suffrage as "California's greatest curse and deepest shame," a "blatant blatherskite," a "worthless alien cur," a "truckling coward," and a "brazen braggart" with a "following of corner loafers, midnight ruffians, sand-bag garroters, flannel-mouthed bog-trotters and adulterous political preachers."

When the editor of a Pacific Northwest newspaper claimed that his "estimate of womanhood [was] too high to . . . aid in an effort to drag her down to the filthy pool of party politics," Abigail shot back with a militant response:

*We have waited long for our brothers, who have made the filth,*
*to arise in their boasted might and cleanse and purify their*
*politics. . . . The reeking political slime in which they daily*
*writhe calls aloud to us for purification. Women have harkened*
*to the call, and . . . woman, with her scrubbing brushes, her*
*dustpan, her soap suds and her ready-waiting raiment of*
*cleanliness, is baring her arms and fortifying her "constitution"*
*to come to the rescue.*

In 1872, Abigail persuaded the Oregon legislature to consider suffrage legislation for the first time. The bill was defeated by a narrow margin, but as a consolation prize lawmakers passed the Sole Trader Bill. It protected the holdings of businesswomen from seizure by their husbands' creditors. In 1878—with the grand prize of suffrage still eluding her—Abigail helped secure passage of the Married Woman's Property Act, which permitted wives to hold property and earn wages of their own.

As the suffrage movement continued to sweep the Pacific Northwest, another movement spearheaded by women was also gaining a foothold. In 1874, a group of angry Midwestern wives and mothers had formed the Women's Christian Temperance Union (WCTU). Their goal originally was to encourage self-control and the moderate use of liquor, but some were beginning to call for its prohibition.

A teetotaler herself, Abigail at first welcomed an alliance with the WCTU. But she soon became alarmed by talk of prohibition, which represented a loss of individual rights—the very antithesis of what the suffrage movement was all about. In her opinion, prohibition was "intolerance and quackery." She believed in discouraging the use of liquor through taxation, education, regulation, and ridicule—not by banning the sale of liquor altogether.

Women's suffrage, she said, "will prove in time the magic key to . . . enable women to rear a race of men who will be voluntarily free from drunkenness, because a race of free, enlightened mothers will naturally produce a race of free, enlightened sons."

Meanwhile, she argued, let's not alienate men—who, after all, hold the power to grant women the right to vote—by threatening to use that vote to deprive them of their whiskey. To do so, she said, would be like "driving nails into the closed coffin lid of . . . women's liberties."

Abigail withdrew her support from the temperance movement, infuriating her former allies in the WCTU. They accused her of selling out to liquor, of being a closet drinker, and of disgracing the cause of women's suffrage. When she tried to speak against prohibition at a national convention, she was rebuked even by her colleague Susan B. Anthony. Oregon suffragists urged her to withdraw from the campaign because she had become too controversial.

Life on the home front had become equally distressing. In January 1886, Abigail's beloved daughter Clara died of tuberculosis at the age of thirty-one. Ben's health, too, had taken a turn for the worse. He decided, along with several of their sons, to buy a cattle ranch in Idaho, in the hope that outdoor living and country air would be more invigorating.

Grief-stricken and discouraged, Abigail sold the *New Northwest* and followed her family to Idaho. It was "like parting with a loved and trusted child," she later said. She helped cope with her sorrow by immersing herself for the next seven years in the battle for suffrage in Idaho. Her impassioned speeches helped to make it, in 1896, the first of the three Pacific Northwest states to enfranchise women.

Abigail's first big victory was tarnished by the death that same year of her husband, Ben. Ailing and alone, but inspired by her experience in Idaho, she threw herself back into the fight for suffrage in Oregon, having returned with Ben to Portland in 1894. The state legislature had defeated suffrage bills in every session since 1872, and Abigail watched in frustration as they continued to do the same in the first decade of the new century. Some blamed the record number of defeats on Abigail's antagonistic ways and "errors in judgment." Abigail blamed them, at least in part, on her brother Harvey and his powerful newspaper, the *Oregonian,* which had been the only major paper in the state to oppose women's suffrage, on the grounds that ignorant voters were dangerous and most women were uneducated. When Harvey died in 1910, the *Oregonian* withdrew its opposition, and the path to victory lay clear at last.

In November 1912, a few days after Abigail's seventy-eighth birthday, Oregon by a narrow margin became the ninth state to recognize the right of women to vote. Governor Oswald West invited Abigail, as the "architect of woman's suffrage in Oregon," to sign the official proclamation. She also had the honor of being the first woman to register to vote. Deaf, overweight, crippled with arthritis, and confined to a wheelchair, the fiery crusader, once hated and feared, had become the "Grand Old Woman of Oregon."

Abigail died at the age of eighty on October 11, 1915—five years before ratification of a national suffrage amendment. After a lifetime of "toil, hardship, privation, ridicule, sneers, and vituperation," she was able, as she had always wished, to "enter heaven a free angel."

# LOLA GREENE BALDWIN

(1860–1957)

Premier Policewoman

Lola Baldwin surveyed the small, dingy room in the Portland lodging house with horror. Its only furnishings were a rickety chair and a flimsy, narrow bed. On that bed lay the bodies of two destitute young women who, in Lola's words, had "chosen a death by suicide rather than a life of discouragement, misery, and sin." The girls' meager possessions were stashed in a pair of baking-powder tins. In their closet hung several cheap dresses and "crepe paper gew-gaws" they had worn to local dance halls in the evenings.

This was just the sort of grisly incident that had prompted the Portland police department to hire Lola in 1908—a move that gave her the distinction of being the first policewoman in the nation. Her job was to protect the moral welfare of young women and girls, and for the next dozen years she would do so with exceptional zeal and skill.

Lola envisioned her job as much more than cracking down on female law-breakers. She was one of the country's first proponents of preventive policing. In her opinion, government and social organizations had a responsibility to "weed out the evil environments that lead to crime" and, in particular, to steer vulnerable women away from trouble. This maternal approach would earn her the nickname "Municipal Mother."

In the course of her career, Lola would lobby for laws to protect women's health and welfare, hound state officials into opening a home for troubled women, advise other states and cities on women's law-enforcement issues, and crusade vigorously against vice and corruption. She also would prove through her own accomplishments that women could play a valuable role in law enforcement.

"Baldwin's true legacy survives in the thousands of women who have followed in her professional footsteps," according to Gloria E. Myers, who wrote a comprehensive biography of Lola entitled *A Municipal Mother*. "Although Baldwin herself would probably have preferred that [female officers] remain 'separate but equal' [from male officers], the complete integration of women into modern law enforcement is a living monument to the efforts of Portland's pioneering female 'cop.'"

Prim and proper Lola certainly didn't seem destined for a job in law enforcement, although the foundation for her unusual career choice was laid early in life. Born in 1860 in Elmira, New York, she soon moved with her family to Rochester, where she attended the Christ Church Episcopal School for Girls. There, in addition to mastering reading, writing, and arithmetic, she absorbed the high moral standards needed to avoid life's "highways and resorts of dissipation."

When her father suddenly died in 1877, Lola had to quit high school and find a way to make a living. She taught school for several years in New York and Nebraska. Then, in 1884, she married LeGrand Baldwin, a Lincoln dry-goods merchant. Eventually, she quit working to stay home with their two sons.

Because she had been forced to venture out on her own at an early age, Lola empathized with young women struggling to make their way in the world. She began to do volunteer work to help "wayward" girls. When her husband took a job in Portland in 1904, Lola volunteered at the local Florence Crittenton Home, a refuge for young, unwed mothers.

Portland was scheduled to host the Lewis and Clark Centennial Exposition in 1905, and the city expected an influx of more than a million visitors. Unfortunately, some of them would be pickpockets, con men, and shysters, but there would also be legions of young women, lured to the city by its bright lights and the prospect of finding a temporary job at the fair. Concerned that some of these vulnerable young women might be led astray, members of the local Young Women's Christian Association decided to establish a Travelers' Aid program.

The notion that society should provide guidance and protection for young women was a product of the Progressive movement that was sweeping the nation. Women's roles were being redefined. Many women believed that, in addition to their duties at home, they had a responsibility to help cure the ills of urban America. This conviction had led to a burgeoning "social hygiene" movement that aimed to make cities safer, both morally and physically, for families, children, and working single women. Reformers sought to improve public-health programs, aid impoverished immigrants, ensure education for all children, and combat vice. As this reform effort gathered steam, America was shaking off the shackles of the Victorian Age and entering a "ragtime" era of more relaxed social mores.

Lola marched in the front lines of the social hygiene reformers, and her volunteer work so impressed YWCA officials that they offered her seventy-five dollars a month to run their Travelers' Aid program. Lola leaped at the chance to protect young women from moral pitfalls. In her new role, she helped newcomers find safe housing, checked out job offerings, arranged free medical care and temporary shelter, and exposed massage parlors that were really fronts for brothels.

Lola and her workers helped more than 1,500 young women and girls during the exposition. Writing in *Sunset* magazine in 1912, Louise Bryant attributed Lola's success to

*the fact that she is on good terms with the girls with whom she
deals. She is a Big Mother to them all. She develops in them
a sense of companionship that invites their confidence. In a
tawdry, foolish, self-conscious girl she sees qualities upon which
to build for her future as a good citizen and perhaps a mother.*

The case of an unwed and impoverished pregnant girl named Caroline was
typical of the lengths to which Lola would go to help her charges. She arranged
to get food, baby clothes, and shelter from various charities and found a doctor
willing to examine the girl for free. The doctor discovered that Caroline had
tuberculosis and would need a cesarean section.

Undaunted, Lola persuaded Good Samaritan Hospital to admit Caroline
free of charge. Then she marched the girl to the district attorney's office and
demanded that officials press charges against the irresponsible father. After the
baby's birth, Lola persuaded the Florence Crittenton Home to shelter the young
mother and child. And when Caroline developed medical complications, Lola
made sure she was treated at the county hospital. Lola even found the girl a job
and arranged child care for the infant.

Lola was shrewd enough to recognize the public-relations value of cases such
as Caroline's. She kept meticulous records and, from them, compiled disturbing
statistics. She alerted the press to an increase in vice in the city and pointed out
that most of the victims were local girls and women, not outsiders.

The problems actually multiplied after the closure of the fair. As the temporary jobs disappeared, many young women could find no suitable employment.
Desperate as they were, they were easy prey for procurers.

Lola's findings alarmed city officials, particularly Mayor Harry Lane, a physician who had made a campaign promise to curtail vice, promote public health,
and make Portland "America's healthiest city." Lola had little trouble convincing
him that he should add a woman to the city's police force in order to combat vice
crimes involving women. Lola applied for the new job, got a high score on the
civil-service exam, and was hired at the age of forty-eight.

Lola performed her new job from her old office at the YWCA. She argued
that troubled women wouldn't seek help if they had to visit the station house.
Her monthly salary was $150—about $35 more than most male detectives
made—but she quelled any criticism by noting that her position required special
training and that she had accomplished more in her three years with the YWCA
than a dozen regular patrolmen could possibly have done.

In her first monthly report to the police chief, Lola hinted at her novel
approach to police work. Rather than tout arrests and investigations, she noted
that her "chief aim and purpose was to prevent downfall and crime among

women and girls by investigation, timely aid, and admonition." This emphasis on preventive policing would become a hallmark of her career.

Lola believed that young women who moved to Portland to find work were particularly susceptible to temptation and exploitation. She estimated there were ten thousand such women in the city.

"The average working girl is lamentably ignorant and innocent of the ways of the tempter, whether he appears clothed in a dress suit or rough homespun," she once said.

Often, other police officers and health workers brought such girls to Lola's attention. She would find them jobs or places to live, enroll them in job-training courses, and help them deal with abusive bosses or customers.

When fortune-tellers in Portland began using attractive girls to lure customers, Lola led a movement to run the fortune-tellers out of town. She also targeted massage parlors, shooting galleries, dance halls, and saloons—any business that exploited pretty young women.

Once, Lola sent an investigator to several of the more notorious shooting galleries. He reported that female employees were performing "can-can" dances, hugging and kissing drunken men, and otherwise acting in a "disreputable manner." These shooting galleries, he believed, were "mere blinds for houses of prostitution."

Lola confirmed his suspicion with her own investigation. Armed with her findings, she pressured city officials to stop amusement businesses from hiring young women and dooming them "inexorably to moral ruin."

Next, Lola targeted the local dance halls, which were scandalizing Portland by offering jazz and ragtime music and featuring sexually suggestive dances. She discovered that innocent girls were being plied with liquor and thrust into the arms of lecherous men. "The great majority of women and girls owe their downfall to the dance hall," she declared.

She campaigned for a crackdown on these places of "unmitigated evil" and was a key proponent of a plan to license and inspect them. She also wanted to prevent them from serving liquor, to ban dancing on Sunday, and to prohibit unseemly dance steps. With a few modifications, the city adopted the new restrictions in 1913.

As the cultural climate of the nation evolved in the early 1900s, so did Lola's targets. She spoke out against vaudeville acts, movies, literature, and even clothing that she considered too racy. Her attempts at censorship may seem oppressive today, but at the time there was strong sentiment for policing morality.

Likewise, many Portland residents backed Lola's efforts to crack down on abortion practitioners. She used decoys to gather evidence and then prosecuted abortionists, and she campaigned against newspaper ads that touted abortion or birth control.

Lola also took aim against venereal disease, pulling into custody infected young women and requiring them to get treatment. She arrested young women who wore men's clothing and were thought to be lesbians, and she led raids that she hoped would shut down Portland's sex trade.

Although Lola was aggressive in her pursuit of unmarried mothers and the men who impregnated them, she didn't consider jail the best solution to the problem. Instead, she arranged social services for single mothers and insisted that they reveal the identities of the delinquent fathers. Many men decided it was more prudent to marry than to face prosecution for seduction.

Lola believed that crime-prevention programs were at least as important as corrective measures. "A fence around the top of the cliff is better than an ambulance down in the valley," she once said. One of her strategies was to persuade city officials to banish women from saloons. Another was to establish an after-care program that monitored delinquent girls to make sure they stayed out of further trouble. Still another was to lobby for creation of a state home for delinquent girls. The Oregon legislature approved funding for such a home in 1913. It became known as Hillcrest.

Word spread of Lola's aggressive and progressive programs to curb vice. She began to travel around the country to explain her tactics, and in 1917 she was appointed regional field secretary of the national Committee on Protective Work for Women and Girls. The goal of the committee was to police prostitutes infected with venereal diseases so that they would not threaten the health of World War I troops headed for Europe. Lola supervised the development of "war emergency" moral standards, as well as venereal disease treatment and prevention services in the Northwest. A year later she was promoted to oversee the program for the entire Pacific Coast and Arizona.

True to form, Lola was a zealous pursuer of her cause. She had strong public support because of the widespread fear that prostitution was exposing soldiers to serious health risks. Few people cared about the concern of some civil libertarians that Lola's program violated the rights of innocent women.

Lola considered her wartime job the highlight of her career, but it soon ended. In 1920, at age sixty, Lola returned to her old post with the city of Portland. She recognized that times had changed and her influence was waning, so she retired from the police force on May 1, 1922. After seventeen years of influencing local, regional, and national women's safety, she was tired of fighting the good fight. According to author Myers:

> *Her writings at the time of her retirement indicate a certain*
> *weariness of spirit which seemed compounded by societal*
> *changes around her. She appeared to have a difficult time*
> *readjusting to postwar civilian duty once she shed her federal*

*authority. As if her years of vigilance had had no effect*
*whatever, the "Ragtime Era" had slipped unhindered into*
*the "Jazz Age." The removal of wartime restrictions bared a*
*Portland with drastically transformed social and cultural mores.*

Even in retirement, Lola resisted societal changes of which she didn't approve. She complained bitterly of the "new woman" who smoked cigarettes, drank liquor, and otherwise "carried on." She wrote letters to newspapers and worked with women's groups, remaining active until her death in Portland on June 22, 1957. But her influence continues to live on in such forms as the Lola Greene Baldwin Foundation, which was created in Portland in 1999 to help victims escape and recover from lives of prostitution.

While Lola often bemoaned changes that she thought would prove harmful to women, she herself was part of a major shift in the attitude of society toward the role of women. With energy and compassion, she had demonstrated that women were capable of working in a profession traditionally limited to men. Myers put it this way:

> *[H]er strength of character, insistence on relative employment*
> *equality, and strict standards of investigation and professional*
> *behavior reserve an honored place for her in both law*
> *enforcement and women's history. . . . Portland's "Municipal*
> *Mother" . . . should be remembered with genuine respect, and*
> *given her due as the nation's premier policewoman.*

# ALICE DAY PRATT

❧

(1872–1963)

## Dry-Land Homesteader

Alice Day Pratt shivered inside her canvas tent as the slate-gray sky spit snow-flakes the size of dimes. For more than a month, temperatures had hovered near zero at her marginal homestead in central Oregon. Her supply of firewood was perilously low, and she could hardly find even slivers of juniper under the deepening snow.

Desperate for warmth, Alice split into kindling her large chopping block, the last relic of a wagonload of firewood that friends had delivered several months ago. It flared into a welcome blaze, but the comforting heat didn't last long.

Years later, she recalled her growing desperation as she struggled to survive single-handedly:

> *On the next day—the blizzard continuing—I burned my*
> *ladder, and on the next would have sacrificed my steps, had not*
> *a blessed chinook blown up in the night, carried the snow away*
> *in foaming torrents, and laid bare many a rich and unsuspected*
> *treasure of fuel.*

The serendipitous chinook wind helped Alice to endure that grueling winter of 1913, but at least as significant were her own hard work, grit, and resourcefulness. She summoned those traits time and time again as she tried to tame an unforgiving land, or at least to reach some kind of compromise with it. Although she eventually had to abandon her "homesteading dream," she managed to outlast many a fellow dreamer.

Later in life, Alice looked back on her homestead years with mixed feelings:

> *I have known lean years and leaner years, hope and*
> *discouragement, good fortune and disaster, friendship and*
> *malice, righteousness, generosity, and double dealing. . . .*
> *Now and then I have known burdens—most often physical*
> *burdens—too heavy for mortals to bear. I have been cold and*

*hungry and ragged and penniless. I have been free and strong and buoyant and glad.*

Alice Day Pratt was part of the last wave of homesteaders who flooded the West in the early twentieth century—spurred on by passage of the Enlarged Homestead Act of 1909. Earlier emigrants to Oregon had already snatched most of the moist and fertile acreage in the western part of the state, so the latecomers had to settle for vast expanses of semiarid uplands east of the Cascades.

The new homesteaders often were unaware of how unforgiving and unprofitable this dry land could be. Pamphlets published by the railroads and other promoters had convinced them that the land was fecund and plentiful, just waiting to reward with riches those who got there first. The homesteaders also believed that the West offered adventure and independence. Here was one last chance to grab a piece of the quintessential American dream.

Alice herself had imagined being "afar on the prairies with the wind in my hair and the smell of new-plowed earth in every breath I drew." By heading west, she expected to put behind her a life of competition, high pressure, and "extremes of gayety and misery." Ahead, she envisioned hope, freedom, opportunity, and limitless spaces.

While Alice shared the same dreams and hopes of many homesteaders, she differed from most of them in an obvious way: She was a single woman in what was predominantly a man's world. Of the tens of thousands of people who filed homestead claims in the early 1900s, only about 10 to 13 percent were unmarried women, according to some historians.

Alice was unique in yet another way. She was one of only a few women who left behind an extensive firsthand account of her homesteading experience. In her book *A Homesteader's Portfolio,* published in 1922, she described how she moved to Oregon at the age of thirty-nine and "proved up" a homestead some sixty miles east of Bend. In engaging detail, she told of enduring drought and dust, hostile neighbors and hungry hawks, loneliness and larcenous rabbits. Although she presented the book as a work of fiction, the account is obviously autobiographical.

Author Molly Glass, in her introduction to the book, described it as "an especially significant work" because it presented "not only a rare but an extraordinarily complete report of the life of a single-handed woman homesteader on a landscape fraught with peril and difficulty—a woman not the victim of her circumstances but taking her place as a part of history, and a maker of history."

Over the years, Alice wrote other articles and books, including a self-published memoir, *Three Frontiers,* which delved into her Minnesota childhood. She was born in June 1872 to William and Sophie Pratt at the family's cottage near Mankato. Her father, a native of Connecticut, thrived on adventure but wasn't particularly adept at business. When his lumber company began to fail in 1877, he set off for the Black Hills of South Dakota, hoping to establish a prosperous lumber business among the hordes of miners lured there by the discovery of gold. He left his young family behind and returned home only for brief visits. Not until 1886 was the family reunited on a remote homestead in Little Elk Canyon, fifteen miles north of Rapid City and twenty-five miles from William Pratt's business in Deadwood.

Alice's father continued to spend much of his time away from home, so many of the heavy chores fell to her. She helped care for two younger siblings and an ailing grandfather, toted heavy pails of water up a steep slope from a spring, tended the garden, looked after the horses, and trekked two miles to a small country store when the family needed supplies.

Alice's only schooling took place at home. She pored over books about plants and animals and hiked the Black Hills collecting specimens for her studies. Her interest in natural history became a lifelong pursuit. She wrote essays about flora and fauna for various magazines, and she published a children's book, *Animal Babies,* in 1941.

Although Alice's childhood in South Dakota was stark and demanding, she later would remember those years fondly. "We were always warm in the house and no fears beset us," she wrote. "Life was so simple that not much could happen to it."

Eventually, Alice left home to become a teacher. But, after working at schools in North Carolina and Arkansas, she pined for a more adventurous life. She began thinking seriously about her childhood desire to acquire her own "portion of the earth's crust" on the Western frontier. She had very little money and couldn't afford to buy land, but she knew she could get some free if she homesteaded. She decided to take a teaching job in northeastern Oregon where she could begin scouting for promising property.

Once in Oregon, Alice hired a "locator," who identified 160 acres in the middle of the state, near a tiny town called Post. As soon as Alice heard about the parcel in the fall of 1911, she dashed off to inspect it. She was smitten at first sight. Standing at the foot of Friar Butte amid sagebrush and junipers, she envisioned the butte as her upland pasture. The deep wash at its foot she saw planted in grain. Off in the distance, she spotted timbered mountains and a cleft cut by the Crooked River. She could see no houses or other signs of human habitation.

Alice knew she was home. She selected a handsome, cone-shaped juniper and decided it would stand in her dooryard. As she turned and looked over the sweeping valley, she picked a name for her homestead: Broadview.

Alice's first order of business was to file the proper papers at the local land office. Under the Enlarged Homestead Act, she got title to the land, but she couldn't sell or mortgage it until she had lived there and made improvements for three years.

Her second order of business was to return to northeastern Oregon to complete the school year and pack her belongings. She arrived back at her dry-land homestead on June 20, 1912, pitched a tent, and set to work. Homestead law required her to cultivate five of every forty acres within three years of taking possession. She had equipment to assemble, fields to plow, seed to buy, shelters to erect, firewood to collect, water to haul—so many chores they were nearly overwhelming.

Alice realized she would need help. When some of her new neighbors stopped by to say hello, she asked about the availability of hired hands. A few of the neighbors volunteered assistance, but rarely did they commit to a specific task and time. Once, neighbors offered to haul wood to help her construct a tent house, but they postponed the job week after week, even as fall approached.

Early one August, another neighbor agreed to plow forty acres so Alice could plant a wheat crop, but by mid-October the sod still lay undisturbed. Finally, the ground froze so hard it would no longer yield to the plow. An irate Alice later learned that the man had taken other jobs and had been leaving hers for last. As a result, she would have no wheat crop the following spring.

"My difficulties have been far oftener with the human element than with the rigors of the climate or the hardships of labor," she wrote in *A Homesteader's Portfolio.*

Alice had most of her problems with "Old Oregonians"—longtime ranchers who disdained the new homesteaders. One of them once bluntly told her, "The only way to deal with them homesteaders is to starve 'em out."

Fortunately, Alice also had a handful of good, caring, helpful friends, most of them newly arrived homesteaders like herself. With them, she enjoyed basket socials, dances, picnics, pageants, and other pleasant gatherings. These were welcome diversions from the physical and psychological hardships of her life.

Being a single woman, Alice occasionally found herself deflecting the advances of local bachelors. She feared "the life-long bond" of marriage, but, to her own surprise, she found some men appealing. After an evening walk with one young friend and neighbor, she confessed, "What sort of old maid am I anyway that I can't walk home in the moonlight with an attractive boy without tingling from head to foot! Good reason why devoted hermits segregate themselves. In the peace of Broadview I haven't felt this way for lo these many moons."

With few friends and neighbors on whom she could rely, Alice often turned to animal companions to help her combat the loneliness of her solitary life. She kept cats, horses, dogs, and chickens. The latter, she wrote, would "gather in little groups about me as I work here and there, engaging me in cheery conversation, essaying little familiarities and friendly overtures, even performing certain stunts with self-conscious gravity, delighting in personal attention."

Alice also felt a special attachment to her milk cow, Bossy, and Bossy's calf, Psalmmy. The calf resisted Alice's efforts to wean it, but she badly needed Bossy's milk for her own consumption and to earn extra income. When Alice confined Bossy to pasture, Psalmmy would follow Alice around the yard, suck the door-knob of her house, and roll his eyes to express his hunger. The calf was clever enough to circumvent Alice's many creative attempts to restrain him. When she tried muzzles, Psalmmy simply nuzzled them aside. When she smeared red-pep-per paste on Bossy's teats, Psalmmy smacked his lips but then ignored the fiery sauce. When Alice built a fence to corral Bossy, Psalmmy found a gap. Years later, Alice described her frustrations:

> *I tried another fence. I tried another pasture. I tried the government reserve twenty miles distant. Always sundown of a day sooner or later arrived that brought Bossy and Psalmmy peacefully home together, Bossy released of her rich and ample load, Psalmmy rolling in his gait and stupid to inebriety.*
> *No wires were too closely set, no gate too high, no location too distant for the ingenuity or the valor of his ruling passion.*

Neighbors counseled Alice to butcher Psalmmy, but she couldn't do it; she had become too attached to the clever calf. Instead, she finally erected a fence tall enough to complete the job of weaning.

Domestic critters were not Alice's only worries. She battled coyotes that harassed her stock, rabbits that munched her crops, and hawks that snatched her chickens. She scared away some of the hawks with well-timed shotgun blasts but failed to hit any. She tried poisoning the rabbits but had limited success.

In truth, Alice did not have the heart to try more lethal weapons. In her writ-ings, she lamented the cruelty that was needed to keep the pests under control. She also worried about upsetting the balance of nature—a decidedly progressive sentiment for an early-twentieth-century homesteader. She wrote:

> *For a thousand years, presumably, this vast plateau which is now my home has been covered with sagebrush and bunch grass and sprinkled with juniper trees, and has supported a normal population of jack rabbits and sage rats. Then suddenly comes man with his alien stock, his dogs and his cats, his new and succulent crops, with their admixture of weed seeds and germs of insect life. And lo, this quiet and harmonious state of nature is all in turmoil.*

Alice's own existence on her dry-land homestead was always tenuous. She spent several years living in a tent house, which would shake "like a rat" in storms and heat up like an oven on blistering summer days. It was cozy in the winter only if she had plenty of firewood.

Eventually, neighbors helped her to build a barn and a rickety twenty-by-twelve-foot wooden house. It had a single room with a kitchen and shelves at one end and a table, cot, and bookshelves at the other.

Alice could not afford a sturdier home or more household conveniences. She had to horde her money for necessities, such as seeds and plowing. She sold chickens, eggs, alfalfa, hay, grain, and vegetables, but her earnings never amounted to much. At times, she had to take teaching jobs to make ends meet.

As soon as Alice proved up her homestead by meeting the residency requirement, she traveled to the East to visit her family and earn some money. She returned to Broadview two years later, in 1918, but funds were still short and she had to take another teaching job ten miles away at Conant Basin. It enabled her to cling to her "homesteading dream" despite the drought, bad weather, and poor commodity prices that had driven so many others off the land. In 1921, she wrote:

> *Over my six hundred and forty acres—thus increased by a second beneficent allowance—roams a beautiful little Jersey herd. A group of dear white ponies call me mistress. White biddies still dot my hill slopes and cackle ceaselessly. Pax, an ᴀ̶ᴍᴏᴜᴍᴀɪɴ Day puppy, and El Dorado, son of Kitty Kat, have succeeded those earlier friends whose gentle spirits still wander with me on the sagebrush slopes. There is a mortgage. There is still necessity to teach. My little flock of orphan citizens still beckons from the future. Yet, for me, the wilderness and the solitary place have been glad, and nature has not betrayed the heart that loved her.*

Alice held onto her homestead even as drought persisted into the 1920s. The good topsoil blew away, wells dried up, and the soil grew more alkaline. To make things worse, prices for grain and dairy products were dropping, and harsh winters battered the plains. The winter of 1924–1925 was ruthless. One day a blinding storm dumped enough snow to reach the upper sashes of the school where Alice was teaching. Two days later, temperatures plummeted to thirty-three degrees below zero—the lowest Alice had ever experienced. She had to kick her way through deep snow to check on her chickens. As she later recalled:

> *Twenty young cocks, as white as the snow drifts, sat starkly upon their perches as if enchanted. There was a statuesqueness*

*about them that sent a chill over me, cold as I was. No, they were not dead, but thos [sic] wattles that characterize their breed were as hard and stiff as plaster. Their feet were not frozen. It was the evening dip in the water that had done the mischief. Dabbling in the water had started the freezing before the night's cold had found them. Full-feeding was all that had saved the flock from death.*

On her way back to her house, Alice was struck by its appearance, "lost in the wilderness of snow, and fringed with icicles almost to the ground." Later in her life, as she lay in bed in a comfortably warm apartment, she sometimes wondered if the little house still stood "in a wilderness of snow, and whether little calves are crying in the willows."

After that frigid winter, Alice enjoyed a few years of better weather, but it was not to last. Another drought struck in 1928. Alice was forced to take out a large loan, and a year later she had to sell her dairy herd to repay it. In 1930, she gave her chickens and horses to neighbors, shuttered her little house on the prairie, and climbed on the train for one last trip to the East. She must have held out hope of seeing Broadview again, because she didn't sell it until 1950.

Most dry-land settlers had packed up and fled long before Alice. By 1920, only half of the original homestead population remained. By 1940, two-thirds of the land allotted under the Enlarged Homestead Act had reverted to the federal government.

After moving back to the East, Alice lived with her mother and her sister Marjorie, first in Niagara Falls and then in New York City. She continued to teach and write magazine articles and books. Some of her manuscripts were published, while others gathered dust on a shelf. Late in life, Alice suffered from crippling arthritis and was confined to her apartment, though her intellect and spirit remained strong to the end. Alice died on January 11, 1963, at the age of ninety.

What was left of Pratt's homestead cabin stood until 2009, when nature finally reclaimed it. The building's remarkable resilience symbolized Alice's own stamina and resourcefulness in an age when women's capabilities were underestimated. After she turned eighty, Alice herself talked about the valuable lesson she had learned facing such adversity on the Oregon frontier:

*Success may be the smallest and least important of the fruits of endeavor; it is the endeavor itself, the opportunity to use one's whole self completely—initiative, creativity, and physical strength—that is its own reward: and it may well be that one looks back upon the times of greatest strain and anxiety as the high points in [one's] pilgrimage.*

# TEXAS WOMEN

# LEONOR VILLEGAS DE MAGNÓN

(1876-1955)

### The Laredo Rebel

Imminent change was afoot roughly one month after the revolutionary hero and Mexican president, Francisco Madero, had been arrested by a military junta at the National Palace, taken to the state penitentiary, and summarily shot to death in the back. The progressive press in the border town of Laredo, Texas, churned out copy decrying the new dictator, Victoriano Huerta. Meanwhile, in various Mexico towns along the Rio Grande, revolutionary forces assembled under several anti-Huerta generals, hoping to conquer the Mexican frontier and work their way south toward the capital. None in Laredo followed the news more closely than Leonor Villegas de Magnón, whose heart burned with revolutionary fervor. She knew that her fellow revolutionaries were descending on Nuevo Laredo, just across the river in Mexico.

In the early dawn of March 17, 1913, Leonor was awakened by the exchange of gunshot across the river. She telephoned her friends who lived in Nuevo Laredo to hear the news. No response. Undeterred, she dressed hastily and hailed a large sedan in the street, driven by someone else's chauffeur. "Take me to the offices of *El Progreso,*" she ordered. There, at the newspaper building where her friend Jovita Idar worked as a journalist, she plastered a drawing of a red cross on the window of the sedan, saying only, "Wait here." With Jovita, she rounded up four other young women to join her mission. The town pharmacist brought her some medical supplies, including a bottle of whiskey wrapped in a white towel.

Seated directly behind the bewildered chauffeur, she then asked him to do the unthinkable: to drive across the bridge into the battle zone. When he balked, she pressed the top of the bottle to his neck, as if it were a gun, and repeated her order: "Drive on." This worked. The car arrived in Nuevo Laredo, with Leonor waving the towel out the window as a white flag. The other women were dropped off with supplies at the Nuevo Laredo hospital while Leonor proceeded to the outskirts of town, where the battle had taken place.

Getting the wounded to the hospital and treating them was relatively easy. Getting them out of the hospital and back with their units was more challenging. The *federales* guarded every door of the hospital. But Leonor had a plan.

Reinforcements from the Mexican army had been dispatched to Nuevo Laredo. She knew that they never arrived anywhere without a good deal of fanfare and pageantry. She enlisted her lifelong friend, the family servant Pancho, to wait on the river in his skiff the day the troops arrived. Amid the noise and excitement, the forty imprisoned revolutionaries were able to escape to the overgrown river bank, and were ferried over to Laredo in the dark.

After this triumph, Leonor proudly renamed her team the White Cross, La Cruz Blanca. She wanted no association with the Mexican National Red Cross, which was not dispensing its aid neutrally, but rather aiding the Mexican forces. Not that Leonor aspired to neutrality! She wished to serve the other side, the revolutionaries—or Constitutionalists, as they were called—because they favored the rule of law and equality rather than the dictator Huerta's rule by might. She began spreading word of her mission and enlisting local doctors in her cause.

It seemed inevitable, then, that her home at 811 Flores Avenue in Laredo, Texas, already a hub of intellectual fervor and revolutionary activity, became the hospital for Constitutionalists wounded in the second major battle of Nuevo Laredo, on January 1 of the following year, 1914. She and her assistants raided her brother's home for bed linens and converted the tables where she taught kindergarten into beds. Through her connections she was given the use of four other buildings to accommodate the nearly 150 wounded rebels who eventually showed up. American doctors and Mexican doctors worked side by side in the operating room that had been set up in her living room.

Once again, politics complicated her efforts, as American authorities questioned the harboring of Mexican combatants on Texas soil. This was especially true because the American ambassador to Mexico, Henry Lane Wilson, had acted in support of Huerta's coup. Although Woodrow Wilson denounced Huerta when he had taken office the previous year, he did not immediately throw his support behind the Constitutionalist revolution, working rather for a diplomatic solution. Meanwhile, Leonor's hospital was surrounded by American soldiers. It was the same problem all over again: As the soldiers' wounds healed, they could not simply return to fight for the revolution. Instead, they faced arrest.

However, Leonor slyly noted that the federal forces, who hailed from all over the country, would not know the difference between Laredo's Hispanic citizens and the Mexican soldiers. So, she arranged to have one or two citizens enter the facility to deliver milk; then, one or two soldiers dressed in milkmen's clothes would exit with the empty pails. Or, three or four soldiers would be pronounced dead and solemnly carried out in caskets, only to be driven to a place where they could be released and return to the battle lines. One suspicious guard actually opened a coffin lid. The soldier in it remained still, but the guard questioned why the dead man was being buried with a pair of shoes. Leonor improvised: "It is a Spanish custom," she lied.

Leonor's quick-wittedness was matched only by her steely resolve. After a while the disappearance of the men could no longer be ignored, and the soldiers doubled down on their security. Leonor hired a lawyer to fight for their freedom. She personally wrote letters to the governor of Texas and a US senator from Texas decrying the injustice of the detainment. Her arguments finally found purchase with US Secretary of State William Jennings Bryan, who summarily ordered the soldiers' release.

As Leonor tells it in her fictionalized memoir, her very birth prefigured her destiny as a revolutionary figure. On the day of her birth, June 12, 1876, all of Nuevo Laredo was in disarray due to stormy weather and the cresting floodwaters of the Rio Grande. For the townspeople, this event capped a year of chaos from the efforts of General Porfirio Díaz to take leadership of Mexico by force.

Among Diaz's rebels in the streets of Nuevo Laredo were men seeking only profit for themselves. In this time of chaos from the flood, there was loot to be had! One group of rebels arrived at the manor and warehouses of Leonor's father, a Spaniard and prominent trader. Understanding the danger of armed men, Don Joaquin Villegas coolly invited the bandits in and led them through the courtyard to the wine cellar. Urgent pounding at the door indicated that federal forces had spied them and followed. The rebels scaled the courtyard walls and scattered, while a second group of men, these in uniform, burst into the Villegas home. "We know the rebels are here!" shouted the commander.

Don Joaquin rose to the occasion with grace. "I am hiding one rebel," he admitted with a smile, turned, and walked down a dark hallway and opened the door to the chamber where his wife was recuperating from childbirth. Baby Leonor's squalling burst through the open door. "My rebel is a girl." The soldiers laughed and forgot their mission, leaving the residence peacefully.

Though she spent much of her life north of the Rio Grande, Leonor identified strongly with Mexico and its political struggles. She also embraced the "rebel" moniker, titling her memoir *The Rebel* and referring to herself in third person as "The Rebel" or "the Little Rebel" (in girlhood) throughout its pages.

In *The Rebel,* the heroine's destiny is burned into the palm of her hand one fateful night when she is still a toddler. This incident would have occurred in the late 1870s near the north Mexican town of Cuatro Ciénegas, later dubbed Cuatro Ciénegas de Carranza, after the town's most famous son, Venustiano Carranza, the leader of the revolutionary Constitutionalist Movement, and later President of Mexico from 1915 to 1920. To foreshadow Carranza's leading role in her life's work, Leonor weaves him into this childhood memory.

The Villegas family, servants, and guards—even the family doctor and his young family—had been on a long caravan trek from their family's Cuahillo ranch, Hacienda de San Francisco, to their Nuevo Laredo home. Winter was coming, and Leonor's delicate mother was pregnant: two good reasons to move the family closer to the comforts of town. There, on the Mexican side of the Rio Grande, Leonor's father conducted a thriving import-export business, in addition to his ranching enterprise. From the towns along the trek, he would gather more goods to sell.

For young Leonor, about three years old, the three-month trek was all excitement. This excitement peaked when the Villegas' ensemble encountered a band of Comanche Indians. Although the Comanches' reign over the plains of northern Mexico had ended, their reputation for cruelty was still alive. Don Joaquin smoothed over their differences with proffers of wine, blankets, and food, and executed a trade for Comanche hides on quite favorable terms for the Indians. Nonetheless, when the Comanches pitched camp within sight of their caravan, lit fires, and began drumming, Leonor's mother was shaken to the core, and her need for medical care seemed imminent. Messengers were dispatched to Cuatro Ciénegas, a day's travel away, and a local patron invited the Villegas family to stay at his empty villa.

In fact the villa was quite luxurious, a home outfitted for the patron's newly-wed daughter, who had just begun her honeymoon with her husband and would not be back for several weeks. While the family doctor attended at the mother's bedside, the Villegas family and their servants waited by the fireplace, roasting chestnuts. Leonor, sleepy from the eventful day, found her way into the lap of the doctor's wife—to the displeasure of the woman's son, about her same age. When the doctor, his father, entered to announce the birth, this boy stole his pearl-handled knife and held it to the fire. The luminous pearl and shiny metal entranced the young girl, and before she knew it, the boy had pressed it into the palm of her left hand. The peaceful scene exploded with Leonor's cries of pain from the burn.

According to Leonor's account, just as the doctor had finished wrapping her wound, a messenger arrived at the door, calling him to come treat the left-hand burn wound of another young person. It may be true that Venustiano Carranza sustained such a burn in young adulthood, but surely some liberty as to the timing must be inferred on behalf of our memoirist. Her scar, she noted, formed a "V," the same letter she had seen branded into the Villegas family cattle. But more important, it was the initial of the man whose military campaign drew her into the world of action, when many years later, she joined Carranza's forces as chief nurse and sometime-adviser to the general himself.

The caravan continued on after her brother Lorenzo's birth at the Cuatro Ciénegas villa, but it did not end in Nuevo Laredo. Don Joaquin, worried about his wife's health, decided to move the family across the river and north by train to San Antonio. The family was soon ensconced in a modest house near St. Paul Square while Don Joaquin traveled to and from Nuevo Laredo on business.

Leonor's mother was the first to notice the cosmopolitan family who moved in across the street: a Presbyterian minister from Spain, his Swiss wife, and their well-educated multilingual children. Doña Valeriana had hardly recovered from the birth of Lorenzo before her frail body had been taxed with another pregnancy. With her condition and worsening health, she was not at liberty to visit, but asked her husband to put himself at their service. He set the Ramón family's boys up in business while Leopold and Leonor were charged with visiting the Ramón home every day, sending their mother's good wishes. Her dying insistence on this bond between the families seems remarkable given the events that followed.

Doña Valeriana asked to return home to her mother in Nuevo Laredo for what she knew would be her last days. Leonor's father arranged for her and Leopold to remain in San Antonio at the Ramón house, with the Ramón daughters providing their schooling. One year later, after the ordeal of his wife's passing, her father would marry one of those daughters, young Eloise Ramón, who devoted herself to raising Lorenzo and little Lina, who had managed to be born after all. Under Eloise's influence, Don Joaquin established a new home and business headquarters on the American side of the Rio Grande, in Laredo. This would be Leonor's "home city" as an adult.

Meanwhile, Leonor attended boarding school at the Ursuline convent in San Antonio, where she lived up to the nickname of "Rebel," then on to the Academy of the Holy Cross in Austin and the Academy of Mount St. Ursula in New York City. She graduated in 1895 with vague wishes of being a nun. Her father knew better for his strong-willed girl, and urged her to come home to Laredo.

A handsome, dark-haired man makes mysterious, electrifying appearances at this point in Leonor's memoir: once on the train station platform on her return to Texas, again in the parade of "Laredo boys" who returned victorious from the Spanish American War. The man was Alphonso Magnón, a man of American and French nationality, and through the agency of her younger brother Lorenzo—now "Lawrence"—romantic notes were exchanged between the two. It was a perfectly romantic courtship, complete with serenades rising up to Leonor's balcony. The handsome suitor finally wrote to Don Joaquin, who promptly whisked his family off to a two-year tour of Europe, including his ancestral lands in Spain. Alphonso spent those two years building a solid reputation, and, as their passion was still keen on Leonor's return, wedding plans were promptly made. The mayor of Laredo served as best man, and the town's shops all closed for the morning of the wedding. After the wedding feast, the newlyweds boarded the train for Mexico City, where Alphonso had work as a steamship company agent.

One could skip several pages of Leonor's memoir and never know she married Magnón, or had three children, two boys and a girl. Nonetheless, their passions coincided for a time. They lived in Mexico City at the "zenith of the nation's glory and wealth" under Porfirio Díaz. But wealth and opulence interested her romantic sensibilities less than the revolutionary talk of Francisco Madero and his supporters at the Café Colon, which was owned by a friend of the family. Little did she suspect how powerful this movement was, until one afternoon she found herself amidst a "moving sea of humanity" at a 1910 Madero rally to protest the dictator Díaz's rigged "reelection." When Alphonso returned home that night, she thrilled to hear him reveal that he had been at the rally as well, and was equally moved by the revolutionary fervor.

Stimulated by what she heard, Leonor began writing articles for *La Crónica,* a progressive Laredo Spanish-language newspaper owned by family friends, the Idar family. In them she decried the oppression of Mexico's peonage system, which made the country's peasants virtual slaves of the landed class, as well as the takeover of the country's resources by foreign interests—and she boldly signed her full name to the articles.

Later the same year, in 1910, her father's grave health called her to Laredo. Though her activism had jeopardized his assets in Mexico—the dictator Díaz confiscated much of this property at will—he gave her his blessing. After his death, she decided not to return to her husband in Mexico City but remain where she had the most connections and could accomplish the most for the revolution. Her friends started a second progressive newspaper in Laredo, *El Progreso,* which eventually reported on all the war fronts. The first issue sponsored a food and clothing drive for victims of a flood in León, and spurred Leonor to form a beneficent society that helped the local poor as well as flood victims in Mexico. She also started a bilingual kindergarten in her home. Laredo had become a hotbed of activism, and women like Leonor and her friend Jovita Idar were at its center.

Meanwhile, Mexican politics had begun a rollercoaster ride that would ultimately amount to a twenty-year revolutionary period. Díaz was deposed, and the moderate leader Leonor had championed, Francisco Madero, became president in 1911. His ineffectiveness led to several coup attempts with the joint efforts of Huerta, Ambassador Wilson, and Bernardo Reyes, who was killed in the 1913 battle that finally succeeded in deposing Madero. Reyes had begun his reactionary campaign in Nuevo Laredo, Leonor's "back yard."

It appears that revolutionary politics came between Leonor and her husband. Alphonso's brother Antonio was among Reyes' chief supporters—even imposing on Leonor to make her home their Laredo headquarters—despite the fact that Leonor supported Madero and the Constitutional cause. It has been conjectured that Alphonso, despite his initial enthusiasm for Madero, hewed closer to his brother's line, or at least made insufficient efforts to deter him from using Leonor this way. Not until Carranza's death in 1920 was the couple reunited. Completely consumed by her revolutionary work, Leonor placed her three children under the care of her brother Leopold's wife in Laredo.

As American soldiers guarded her home and the Mexican revolutionaries it harbored, Leonor was working quickly to secure funding and authority to expand the operation of the White Cross. Shortly after the first battle of Nuevo Laredo, Venustiano Carranza had announced the Plan of Guadalupe, declaring Huerta and his administration illegitimate, and demanding a return of constitutional rule and free and fair elections to Mexico. This statuesque, fastidious, and somewhat old-fashioned aristocrat had emerged as the leader—*El Jéfe*—of the Constitutionalist movement. He, along with Generals Obregón, Villa, and others, were continuing their military campaigns in the north of Mexico. Leonor dearly wished for her White Cross to have a role. Together with thirty-three of the soldiers she had treated, she took a train to El Paso to meet *El Jéfe*.

Leonor brought with her a white American woman, Lily Long, who served as her secretary. Later, the journalist Jovita Idar would serve as her secretary. Several nurses accompanied her as well. The organization's activities ranged from finding donors to outfit their hospitals, often on confiscated estates, finding local women to help nurse, and caring for the wounded on the battlefield, to wiring news back to Laredo and other border towns and writing, printing, and distributing Constitutionalist propaganda to the locals. Leonor spoke often with Carranza and met many of the major players of the Constitutionalist revolution; indeed, she once scolded Pancho Villa, the hugely popular peasant general, for his insubordination to *El Jéfe*. With her many contacts and steadfast loyalty, she became a reliable conduit for intelligence about the war. Even the love stories and intrigues of her nurses seemed to hinge upon her actions. As described in her autobiography, it was the role of a lifetime.

The revolutionary generals began their campaigns at the northernmost parts of Mexico, then, victory after victory, worked their way down to the capital to take power, with more than a little jockeying for power amongst each other. Thus, from April 1914, when she traveled to El Paso, to August of the same year, when Huerta finally resigned, Leonor followed the revolution deeper and deeper into Mexico—to Chihuahua, Torreón, Durango, Saltillo, and San Luis Potosí, organizing brigades and temporary hospitals, then leaving them in capable hands as she moved on. Finally, on August 20, 1914, Carranza made his triumphal entrance into Mexico City.

There were several disappointments to follow. Carranza failed to assign Leonor a post in a Mexico City hospital; she turned in her resignation, saying that the work of the White Cross was over. All her hard work seemed forgotten, unrecognized. Even in 1939, when the Mexican government established the Medal of Revolutionary Merit for veterans of the revolution, she—along with other women revolutionaries—had to fight for the recognition that came much easier to men. Having published her memoirs in Spanish, she rewrote and reworked the book in English for an American audience. However, this version remained unpublished during her lifetime.

Perhaps most devastating, the war in Mexico continued on for fifteen years after Carranza's assumption of power. While he oversaw the drafting of the country's current constitution and became the first elected president in 1917, the country was in ruins from the fighting, Mexico's people continued to suffer, and dissension was rife. There was only so much Carranza could do to improve the situation, and he was assassinated in 1920.

In the face of these disappointments, Leonor returned to more traditional female roles, albeit roles of leadership. After dissolving the White Cross in 1914, she returned to her home and children in Laredo, and then traveled with them to live in New York City, where she enrolled them in private Catholic schools. She served as a volunteer nurse in World War I, and eventually established a private school for girls in Laredo. One can only imagine the stories of former glory she shared with her students, never forgetting to remind them that they, too, could be heroines in the great dramas of history.

# JESSIE DANIEL AMES

(1883–1972)

Antilynching Crusader

In April 1924 forty-one-year-old Jessie Daniel Ames faced the most challenging speaking engagement of her life. As a volunteer for the Commission on Inter-racial Cooperation (CIC), Jessie had talked to countless people—starting with her female friends from the suffrage movement—about the problem of racism in Texas. Her dedication and competence could not be ignored, and in January the CIC had rewarded her with a salaried job as regional women's organizer.

But a lot of people in the South weren't ready to hear Jessie's message. People in her hometown of Georgetown had called her names and sent her ugly hate mail. Her most virulent opponents were members of the Ku Klux Klan, a white supremacist organization that used violence to keep African Americans demoralized. After World War I this group had surged into power all across the South and had a lot of sway over the Democratic Party. Texas was no exception. Later in 1924, at the National Democratic Convention, the Texas delegation supported the Klan's candidate for president.

Jessie was going to speak in Mississippi, one of the most Klan-dominated states of them all. She knew her audience of Mississippi Women's Club members included more than a couple Klan supporters. To add to the pressure, the woman who had invited Jessie to speak was her older sister, Lulu Daniel Hardy. During their youth Lulu had been their father's obvious favorite. She was now the happy and influential wife of the president of a Mississippi military academy and mistress to a large staff of servants. In stark contrast Jessie's adult life had been filled with hardship; her husband's early death had left her strapped for cash and a single mother of three.

No record exists of the words Jessie spoke to the elite white women of Mississippi that day. By her own account worried sick, she had prepared extensively, but when the time came, "I discarded my three speeches, rose up when I was introduced and spoke for thirty-five minutes." Her talk probably stressed how the fates of blacks and whites were intertwined. Many of these women had domestic servants. As tactfully as possible, Jessie would have asserted that

Negroes—as black Americans were called at the time—needed improved education and living conditions if they were to become effective members of society.
She would have implied that these ladies could improve their households by
improving the lot of their servants.

Later in Jessie's career she told her followers to "tie up" any speech they
gave with the subject of lynching. In Mississippi alone hundreds of black men
had been savagely killed by mobs claiming to defend white women's virtue and
honor. Jessie looked coldly on the idea that women needed this protection, even
as she recognized its sway among Southern women. Though Jessie might not
have broached this topic in 1924, her message of interracial cooperation that day
was persuasive. She received hearty applause, and after her visit, the women of
Mississippi formed an interracial committee of their own.

The region in which Jessie grew up was no stranger to racial. violence, either.
She was born in rural East Texas in 1883 and later moved with her family to
Overton, near Tyler. When Jessie was eleven, and again when she was thirteen,
black men accused of crimes were executed by local mobs before the court could
try their cases. Jessie later would recall listening in confused horror while the
family's hired hands spoke of a victim blinded by a red-hot iron.

Jessie's childhood in Overton was stressful for other, more immediate
reasons. Her parents had come to Texas without money or family ties. Both of
them worked, her mother as a nurse for the town doctor, her father as a railroad
dispatcher. Together they earned a modest income, but they never really joined
the life of the small town. Her father, James Daniel, took a special pride in his
"Yankee" outsider status, proclaiming atheism in a place where religious revivals
were the summer's high point. Thus, Jessie's childhood friends were among the
poorest of the poor. That itself would have been fine with her, she later said,
except that they sometimes died from diphtheria, smallpox, or typhoid.

Worst of all for the introspective child was her role in the family drama.
Both parents were high strung and argued frequently. The third of four children,
Jessie felt especially unloved by her domineering father. When Lulu, the eldest,
enrolled at Southwestern College, her father insisted that the whole family move
to Georgetown to be near her. Later, when Jessie entered the college, she was
forced to wear Lulu's discarded clothes and was kept from attending parties. Still,
Jessie admired her father and aimed to please him. Indeed, her lifelong distance
from religion (both her mother and sister were unapologetically Methodist) was
probably attributable to him. Jessie graduated from Southwestern College in
1902 with a Bachelor of Art degree.

Jessie's marriage to Roger Ames, a respectable army surgeon, might have
seemed to Jessie a way to escape from her family. Unfortunately, Roger did
little to persuade his family to accept his "socially inferior" bride. He may have

had second thoughts himself. Jessie's visits to his overseas posts were brief; she often left with a feeling of rejection. She and her growing brood found refuge in Lulu's home during this time, but her sister's happiness probably added to her silent rancor.

By 1914, when Roger Ames passed away, Jessie's mother was also a widow. Jessie and her three children moved into the Georgetown household. Together she and her mother managed the telephone business James Daniel had left behind. Jessie found it more socially acceptable to be a widow than a rejected wife. Even more important, her role as office manager gave her a new self-assurance. A secretary described the time an irate customer came to the telephone company's office to complain. "If you were a man," he said to Jessie, "I would like to cuss you out." Jessie replied with cool condescension, "Now don't let that stop you. You just come in here and get it off your chest."

Jessie's interest in women's rights had taken root the first year of her marriage, when she found that she could not open a bank account without her husband's permission. Now, with her newfound financial independence, Jessie looked again at the status of women. Women who didn't have husbands were controlled by their bosses or by public opinion; women with husbands were controlled by them or by social custom.

Jessie herself didn't face either dilemma; she had no husband, she had no boss, and she didn't much care for public opinion. No one was better situated to speak up on the behalf of women than she. In 1916, when the Texas Equal Suffrage Association (ESA) called for local organizers, Jessie was the first in Georgetown to respond.

Jessie hosted the first Georgetown suffrage meeting in her house and was unanimously elected president of the local ESA organization. When the state ESA president, Minnie Fisher Cunningham, came to speak at a Georgetown meeting, Jessie immediately found a mentor. A political maven with her own place in Texas history, "Minnie Fish" encouraged Jessie to broaden her efforts. Jessie began a weekly newspaper column and agreed to speak at statewide gatherings. Within a short time she was the third most influential woman in the state movement, behind Cunningham and Jane Y. McCallum, a lifelong rival.

The story of Texas women's first vote is one Jessie Ames loved to tell. After the suffragettes had helped impeach the crooked Governor James Ferguson in 1916, the stage was set for a bill enabling women to vote in Texas primaries. At that time Texas was a one-party state; voting in the Democratic primary was more important than voting in the general election.

The bill passed in the state legislature and was signed into law by the new governor, William P. Hobby. The catch was that the law did not take effect for ninety days, leaving the women only two weeks to register to vote before the deadline. Complicating matters was the deceitful promise by county officials to send representatives to the precincts to register women. The law plainly stated that women must register "in their own hand" at the county courthouse.

Jessie and her fellow suffragettes knew the law word for word. They organized a "get-out-the-vote drive to end all drives." Nearly four thousand women in Jessie's home county came "by wagon, by hack, by foot" to register. Jessie exulted at seeing women get together to "compare ideas on politics and candidates not clothes or recipes." She then helped to coordinate the intensive voter education that followed. With the women's vote firmly aligned on primary day, a slate of progressive Democrats swept out the reactionary candidates.

Then came the week in June 1919 when the Texas legislature was poised to ratify the Nineteenth Amendment. Because most members of the senate were in favor of women's suffrage, the opposing senators decided to leave town to deny a quorum—the number of legislators required for a binding vote. Catching wind of this plan, the suffragettes and their friends in the senate were waiting at the Austin train station to send the deserters back to work. The vote was cast, and Texas ratified the amendment—the first state in the South to do so.

Throughout the years the fundamental opposition to female suffrage had centered around "the cult of true womanhood," which said that women should not soil their hems in the cesspools of business and politics; their true force should be felt in the home. This Victorian ideal was eroding as more and more women entered the workforce, but another objection to suffrage had arisen in the South. If white women could vote, then why not black women? This was unthinkable to many of those whose daily needs and wants were carried out by low-paid black women servants.

In its final phase, when Jessie joined it, the suffrage movement understood the conservative nature of public opinion. It had long since ceased being the equal rights movement founded by Susan B. Anthony and Elizabeth Cady Stanton—a movement of high ideals and noble convictions. Now, more than seventy years later, it was focused on a single goal: women's suffrage. Jessie's ideals matched those of the movement's founders, but she was competitive and wanted to win, by whatever strategy worked, so she adopted the more conservative approach prevalent in the South. Jessie had truly found her niche in politics.

Thus, she was part of the latter-day suffrage campaign, led by Carrie Chapman Catt, which suggested that whites had nothing to fear from women's suffrage because there "were more of us than them." In Texas the ESA had also promoted a poll tax to keep "undesirables" from voting, and in 1918 the Texas legislature enacted such a tax "in the event of the ratification of the Nineteenth Amendment." After ratification, Jessie helped organize a drive to help middle-class women to pay this poll tax so that they could vote. She kept to herself her dislike for its racist objectives; it was all part of her job as the president of the newly formed Texas League of Women Voters (TLWV).

Jessie was simply following the lead of the National League of Women Voters, organized by Catt to continue the cause of women's participation in the political system. The organization's stance was squarely middle-class, non-partisan, and anti-immigration; it promoted such measures as English-only ballots and refrained from entering campaigns, even when one of the candidates represented the Klan. Serving as the president of the Texas branch gave Jessie a chance to lead a statewide organization, something she had desperately wanted to do, and it helped define her lifelong mission of educating white, middle-class women for full and responsible citizenship. Soon, however, she would find other educational issues that reached far beyond the league's middle-class concerns.

Jessie's work branched out when the TLWV joined other Texas women's organizations to form a joint legislative council focused on issues such as maternity health, prison reform, school improvement, and Prohibition. The group of women reformers became known in Austin as the "Petticoat Lobby"; despite this not-so-subtle mockery, many of their measures were adopted.

Jessie's reform efforts with this group exposed her to shocking racial inequity. When touring the state's prisons, she found the conditions of black women so deplorable that she lobbied effectively for a state-funded center to train delinquent black girls. When touring the black schools in her county, she found them to be little more than shacks, with an average class size of ninety students. Immediately she set to work raising private funds to improve the schools' finances.

These were problems Jessie could address, and did. But the real problem was in people's attitudes, the same racial attitudes that had stood in the way of women's suffrage in the South. Jessie saw with growing discomfort how the progressive agenda excluded blacks to gain the support of more conservative voters. She concluded that "someone with enough background to do it" was going to have to address these attitudes head-on.

The CIC was an organization created to bring blacks and whites together to address the "peculiar situation" of the South. It was based in Atlanta, also a major headquarters for the Ku Klux Klan. In 1922 Jessie became the chair of the women's committee for the CIC's newly formed Texas branch. Galvanized at a meeting where three prominent black women exposed the injustice they suffered, Jessie dove into her work, acquiring a library of books on race relations and enrolling in University of Chicago extension courses to develop her thinking.

Although Jessie founded the Association of Southern Women to Prevent Lynching (ASWPL) and remained its sole paid officer from 1930 to 1942, she did not author the critical analysis that became its hallmark. Decades earlier, Ida B. Wells had collected the data on lynchings that proved only a fraction were motivated by rape accusations, despite all the rhetoric about upholding white women's honor. In more recent times the black leaders of the National Association for the Advancement of Colored People (NAACP) had called on white women to condemn this travesty. But the moment for this mass protest had not yet come.

What Jessie did was to lay the groundwork necessary to make the most of the moment when it did gain popularity. As a state and regional organizer, she contacted and met hundreds of local officers of the Young Women's Christian Association (YWCA) and the Methodist Women's Missionary Council, the two legs of the women's interracial movement. These contacts generated countless speaking invitations. All of her life's experiences contributed to her skills as a speaker. Even the fact that she had heard about—if not attended—religious revivals caused her to speak in rousing sentences. At the same time she was aware of each group's ideological limits. Jessie wrote that her new job called for "all the tact, the brains, the training and the mentality which I have been accumulating. . . . My years of working with wild-eyed women and suave politicians have stood me in good stead."

In 1929 Jessie and her family moved to Atlanta so that she could accept a national position with the CIC. In October of that year, the stock market crash ushered in a period of extreme racial tension, especially among the rural poor. The number of lynching incidents spiked. Jessie asked the CIC director if she could devote all of her time to forming a women's organization focused solely on lynching. He agreed, and the ASWPL was born.

From her self-education Jessie knew that lynching was as much a means of intimidation as it was anything else. Disputes over wages or economic conditions were the hidden cause of many lynchings. For many sharecroppers summer was the season of fear, not just because passions ran hot, but also because the cotton crop was planted and the harvest yet to come. A murmur of an accusation was enough to drive hardworking families away, leaving the spoils to the landowners. The ASWPL's literature highlighted these aspects of the dreadful crime. These facts helped change the minds of whites who had always assumed that lynchings were the result of righteous anger at crimes committed by blacks.

Lynchings were most common in rural regions, where Jessie's grassroots organizing proved her greatest strength: She reached out to women on a county-by-county basis. The organization kept a tight watch on potential eruptions of violence and contacted nearby ASWPL women when action was needed. The women spoke out for law and order. They worked with local sheriffs, encouraging them to do their jobs. As elected officers, these men often felt pressured to comply with the will of the voters, including the men who wanted to take punishment into their own hands. The women made sure to remind them that they, too, were voters.

Jessie also trained women to use their pens against lynching. She empowered them to conduct on-the-scene investigations of vigilante acts. She encouraged them to correspond closely with newspaper editors. Jessie herself addressed a convention of the Southern newspaper publishers, asking them to tone down their sensationalist language in reporting race-related crimes. A single inflammatory word could undo all the editorials the paper ever printed advocating due process of law.

By the end of the 1930s, Jessie's all-volunteer group had won national recognition and acclaim. She had collected endorsements from every major religious and civic women's group in the South. Her petitions had garnered almost 45,000 signatures, including some 1,300 from peace officers. The rest were the signatures of white women. Though she corresponded with black leaders like Mary McLeod Bethune, Jessie insisted from the start that her organization be whites-only. Her political instincts told her to take on one fight at a time.

In the end Jessie's caution failed her. In 1938 Jessie made national news by opposing a proposed bill to make lynching a federal crime. She feared such a law would only increase racial hostility in the "states' rights" South. But times had changed; the New Deal had made openly liberal views more acceptable. Many of her members disagreed with her, and the organization quietly crumbled. Jessie retreated to the hills of North Carolina; she later returned to Texas to live with her daughter.

Jessie Daniel Ames successfully raised three children, one of whom had infantile paralysis. After her prominent career ended, she lived on to witness the struggles and successes of the civil rights movement. But according to her biographer, Jacqueline Dowd Hall, her just recognition did not come until the women's movement of the 1960s and 1970s. Jessie had led women in rejecting the "crown of chivalry that has pressed upon us like a crown of thorns" and in taking up more empowering battles in the real world. And she had taught them to look beyond their self-interest, as well, to fight the battles that most needed to be fought.

Jessie Daniel Ames died in Austin, Texas, in 1972.

# BESSIE COLEMAN

✿

(1893–1926)

## Flying for the Race

Three girls sat at the feet of their older sister, who was reading a book under the light of an oil lamp. Ten-year-old Bessie Coleman read with the dramatic tones of the black Baptist preacher at the Waxahachie church the girls attended every Sunday. A natural performer, she often made her sisters laugh. But just as often—for instance, when she read about Harriet Tubman, who led so many slaves to freedom—Bessie's emotional voice made them tingle with awe.

Tonight Bessie was reading *Uncle Tom's Cabin*. Every day she looked forward to the story's continuation during the evening reading ritual. After all, she spent those days washing, cooking, gardening, and looking after Nilus and Georgia, her two youngest sisters. It had been only three years since her father, part Native American, had left for Oklahoma and the promise of full citizenship. Bessie's mother, Susan, an African American, had not wished to follow him into Indian country. Instead, she found a full-time housekeeping job to support her family, leaving the home chores to her eldest daughter.

Bessie had received only scant instruction in the local one-room school. She had learned more from Susan, who never missed an opportunity to educate her children. Gradually, Bessie had taken over the night reading, and now was her moment of triumph. All eyes were turned toward her. She read the part where George Shelby tells his slaves how Uncle Tom has died, beaten to death by the cruel overseer. The book concludes with his announcement:

> *It was on his grave, my friends, that I resolved, before God, that I would never own another slave, while it was possible to free him. . . . So, when you rejoice in your freedom, think that you owe it to that good old soul. . . . Think of your freedom, every time you see Uncle Tom's cabin; and let it be a memorial to put you all in mind to follow in his steps, and be honest and faithful and Christian as he was.*

Bessie closed the book in a display of solemn piety. She scanned the faces of her captive audience. Then she broke the spell. "I'll never be a Topsy or an Uncle Tom!" she snorted.

It is part of slave folklore that Africans could fly—a glorious symbol for escaping life's harsh realities. In her role as the first black aviator, Bessie would come to symbolize just this kind of freedom for African Americans. Throughout her barnstorming career, Bessie constantly worked to "uplift the Negro race." Her ultimate goal was to open a flying school for people of color, who were categorically banned from US aviation schools. As she once told a Houston newspaper, she wanted "to make Uncle Tom's cabin into a hangar."

Bessie was born in a dirt-floor cabin in Atlanta, Texas, on the Arkansas border, where her father, George Coleman, worked as a day laborer. She had five older siblings, but three had already moved away. When Bessie was two, her father brought the family to Waxahachie, the county seat of "the largest cotton-producing county in the United States." They lived on a quarter acre of land on Mustang Creek, four miles from the town center, in a house George Coleman built himself.

For the poor folk of Waxahachie, Texas, harvest time meant long days in the hot sun with raw, bleeding fingers and a sack strapped to one's back. Young Bessie knew that she was destined for greater things than picking cotton. She lagged behind the rest of the family; once or twice she was even caught riding the sack of the picker in front of her. But she was spared discipline; as the one Coleman who could add, she had the important job of watching the foreman weigh their pick and calculate their pay. And, when she had the chance, she pressed her foot on the scale.

At seventeen Bessie left to attend college in Oklahoma. But after just one semester, the family's funds were depleted, and Bessie was forced to return home and work as a self-employed laundress. Every day for four years, the petite young woman would walk into town carrying a load of clean laundry and walk home with another load to wash. Along her endless rounds she was sometimes given a newspaper. Her favorite was the *Chicago Defender,* an African-American newspaper brought to town by the porters on the trains.

Increasingly, the papers contained news of World War I. Another country had entered the war; another spy had been caught. Beside the headlines of U-boat attacks and the Battle of the Marne, there were reports of amazing new flying machines: the British and their Sopwith Camels, the "Red Baron" and his Fokker Triplane. In the *Defender* the opinion pages always attracted Bessie's attention. There, the editors boosted the South Side scene, boasting that in Chicago, one could find a decent-paying job among one's own people. Bessie's brothers had moved to Chicago years ago, and in 1915, she joined them. Within several years her mother and sisters followed.

After a brief course at a beauty school, Bessie was hired as a manicurist in the White Sox barbershop along State Street, the stretch where prominent African Americans went to see and be seen. With her copper-colored skin, high cheekbones, and vivacious laugh, Bessie herself was seen and noticed in the shop's front window, where she worked. Confident of her charms, Bessie was soon strolling State Street arm in arm with well-heeled gentlemen and dreaming of her prospects.

When the United States entered the war, Bessie's brothers Walter and John enlisted with the Eighth Army National Guard, an African-American regiment. Two years later they returned from the front lines with a hoard of observations, one of their favorites being "the liberated French." The French, they said, didn't even know the meaning of racism. In France women had careers; French women even flew planes!

One fateful day John entered the barbershop intoxicated and proceeded to reminisce about his time in the service with anyone who cared to listen. As usual, the conversation turned to French women, with an invidious comparison to the women of the South Side. John turned to Bessie: "You nigger women ain't never goin' to fly. Not like those women I saw in France."

The barbershop customers might have guffawed, but Bessie was not to be put down. "That's it!" she said with rigid determination. "You just called it for me." She had decided to fly.

For advice about achieving this goal, Bessie contacted her friend Robert Abbott, the editor of the *Defender*. He was especially interested in how her story would boost race morale—and his newspaper's circulation. He recommended she go to France for instruction and promised to help any way he could. While Bessie took a hasty course in the French language, she buttonholed other well-off male friends, asking them to contribute to her cause. According to her family her suitors at this time included white and black, young and old, even a gentleman from Spain. Bessie must have been very persuasive, because in November 1920 she sailed for France.

Flying was then far more dangerous than it is at present. Bessie was turned away from a Paris aviation school because two women had recently fallen to their deaths. At the school where she finally enrolled, she witnessed an accident in which a male student pilot was killed. The open-cockpit Nieuport and Curtiss JN planes she flew were constructed of wood, canvas, wire, aluminum, steel, and glue. In her seven-month course, Bessie learned basic maneuvers and tricks such as "looping the loop." During this stunt the only thing keeping the flyer in the cockpit is a fastened seatbelt and centrifugal force.

In 1921 Bessie graduated from the school, the only woman in her class. She received an international flying license. This was two years before Amelia Earhart learned to fly. Only one African American, Eugene Bullard, already had a flying career; originally from Alabama, he had flown for France in the war.

Reporters from black newspapers greeted Bessie as a celebrity when she returned to the United States. She declared, "You have never lived until you have flown," and expressed her hope that young men of "the Race" would learn to fly. She exaggerated her own youth by five years or so and said she had ordered a plane from France, when in fact she could not afford one. The reporters were too taken with her dynamic beauty to doubt her veracity.

In the breathless months that followed, Bessie flew in a few air shows, gave any number of specious interviews, and continued to seek financial backers. Few were ready for her headstrong attitude, and she alienated many of those who could have created opportunities for her. In the most dramatic of these debacles, she walked out of a contract as lead actress in a film when she learned that her character started out as a ragged country girl arriving in the big city. Remembering with pain her cotton-picking past, she swore, "No Uncle Tom stuff for me!"

Bessie's aborted foray into film was a natural digression. In the 1920s pilots were part of a self-made entertainment industry. It would be a decade before passenger flights would become common; in the meantime, ex–World War I aviators who had found their life's passion in the sky found work in "flying circuses." Enterprising barnstormers arranged their own gigs by landing in pastures, negotiating with farmers, and pulling together audiences of a few dozen townspeople. Engine failure was not uncommon; many pilots crashed before their shocked spectators.

Bessie was at a disadvantage because she lacked the capital needed to purchase and maintain her own airplane. She also faced prejudice from the white press, which was reluctant to cover her despite the anomaly she posed as the world's only "Negro aviatrix." Hence, she lived on hope and half-truths, spreading sensational rumors about her accomplishments and future plans.

Her most celebrated triumph during this time came at a 1922 air show in Chicago's Checkerboard airdrome. Thousands turned out to see the local heroine so ballyhooed in Abbott's *Defender*. In a borrowed plane Bessie soared through a figure eight in honor of Chicago's Eighth Regiment. At the apex of the loop, she dove into a free fall, righting the plane at the last instant to circle the field for a final landing. While free falls were common barnstormer stunts, in this case the engine of her plane had actually stalled, and only luck had saved her. Wearing a dashing leather outfit, she walked off the field dazed and jubilant, into the arms of her family and friends from Chicago's South Side. Four months later, her secondhand Jenny failed over Santa Monica as fans in Los Angeles awaited her arrival. Strangely, the disappointed crowd wasn't sympathetic; they were enraged! Bessie telegrammed from the hospital, "My faith in aviation and the [use] it will serve in fulfilling the destiny of my people isn't shaken at all."

Two years later, in May of 1925, Bessie commenced her most successful stretch of shows, a summer tour in her home state of Texas. Everything about this tour seemed providential, including the date of the opening show, June 19, or "Juneteenth," the day black Texans celebrate their freedom from slavery. Bessie inspired the Houston crowd with her free falls and barrel rolls. Afterward she took about seventy-five of Houston's bravest souls, mostly women, for bird's-eye views of their city. The same people who were not allowed to ride the morning train flew in an open cockpit plane! The local black newspaper, *Houston Informer,* proudly noted that this was "the first time the colored public of the South had been given the opportunity to fly." It was for moments like these that Bessie risked her life.

She was immediately booked to fly at Richmond for a Baptist Association meeting and back at Houston for a picnic of the railroad's African-American employees. Then, on July 12, she flew again for the Houston public, this time charging for rides afterward. Between her show dates Bessie gave lectures encouraging black women in their struggles for equal rights and access to politics and education.

Bessie performed in San Antonio and Galveston and many towns too small to record the event. Everywhere she went, black families opened their houses to her. Back in Houston a woman scheduled to parachute from Bessie's plane lost her nerve; unwilling to disappoint the loyal Houston crowd, Bessie hired a friend to pilot the plane and jumped herself. In her hometown of Waxahachie, Bessie scored a victory against Jim Crow laws by refusing to perform unless blacks entered the same gate as whites. And the people of Wharton, Texas, loved her act so much that they raised money to help her buy her own plane.

Bessie went to Dallas's Love Field to shop for a used aircraft. There she found a Jenny that suited her, but, more important, she caught a brief glimpse of a world where race made no difference. Those who lived and worked at the airfield treated the black mechanic, Louis Manning, as one of the guys. They ate and socialized together, and whenever a stranger questioned the arrangement, they'd say, "We're all black people here!"

Bessie followed this Texas tour with a series of lectures in Georgia. She accompanied her lectures with film clips of her shows, always lamenting that African Americans were "so far behind the white Race" in aviation. She moved on to Florida, continuing to lecture at theaters. The Orlando Chamber of Commerce booked Bessie for a parachute jump, planning it as a show for whites. Here she scored yet another victory over Jim Crow. She not only demanded that blacks be allowed to attend as well, she insisted that planes fly over the city's African-American neighborhoods to drop printed invitations.

In Orlando, too, Bessie glimpsed a peace she had rarely known. The Baptist Reverend and Mrs. Hezekiah Hill had met her at a lecture and invited her for a prolonged stay at their parsonage. The Hills kept an open dinner invitation for members of their congregation; at their table Bessie met dedicated church workers and school board members of the community, people so very different from her friends in Chicago. During her days in Orlando, Bessie happily entertained the neighborhood children, hoping that they, too, would become "air-minded" or at least "uplift the Race." The faith of her childhood was renewed and, with it, her dream of an aviation school for blacks in the United States. She left for her last show in Jacksonville with the promise that she would return to Orlando to build on that dream.

Bessie's friendship with a white Orlando millionaire made it possible for her to pay the balance on the Love Field Jenny she had selected. A Dallas man, William D. Wills, was to deliver the plane, which needed some mechanical work before it would be ready to fly. Wills arrived in Jacksonville with the plane three days before the show.

The next day, by a stunning coincidence, Bessie's entourage entered a Jacksonville restaurant where Robert Abbott, the *Chicago Defender* editor, was dining. With great fanfare she introduced him to her friends as "the man who gave me my chance." According to Bessie's sister Eloise, Abbott expressed an instant distrust of Wills. If he did, Bessie shrugged it off.

On April 30, 1926, Wills took Bessie for a test ride in her plane above the field where she would perform. At 3,500 feet the plane suddenly accelerated, then took a nosedive. Witnesses said the plane began a tailspin at 1,000 feet. Bessie had left her seatbelt unfastened so that she could lean over and see the field. She had also neglected to wear a parachute, something she always did when she was at the helm of a plane. At five hundred feet the plane flipped upside down, and Bessie's body hurtled to the ground. The plane landed on top of Wills and was ignited when Bessie's distraught manager lit a cigarette.

From the burned wreckage it was determined that whoever had serviced the plane had accidentally left a wrench in the engine. When the airplane climbed, the wrench had wedged against the controls. It was a typical accident for early-model planes. It was a tragic end for Bessie Coleman.

Bessie's life had been a chaotic drama of will and improvisation. She had seized on a purpose and pursued it in every way available to her. Eclipsing her unrealized dream of teaching African Americans to fly was her very capacity to dream so boldly. More than five thousand people turned out for her funeral. She likely inspired thousands more to rise above the cotton fields and "fly" for the race.

# UTAH WOMEN

# PATTY SESSIONS

(1795–1892)

Pioneer Midwife

Read just a few entries in Patty Sessions's diary and you'll get a good idea of how she lived. Take, for example, a few days in the winter of 1855. Working as a midwife, she helped a woman through a difficult delivery of twin babies. She hired a man to build a fence around her prized fruit orchards. She knitted a pair of mittens, a rug, a dress, and two pairs of stockings. She conducted a meeting of the charity she headed, then gave another group an educational lecture on raising children.

She visited friends, took care of a sick woman who was brought to her house, and distributed some vegetables she had preserved from her garden. A few days later, she was called to care for another pregnant woman—and that evening she attended dance lessons.

At the time, Patty was a vibrant sixty years old.

Patty Sessions lived for nearly a century during some of the most tumultuous times in Utah and American history. More than forty years of her life survive through her meticulous diary, now preserved in archives of the Church of Jesus Christ of Latter-day Saints, commonly known as the Mormon church. But she was famous in Utah long before anyone read her diaries, and they would not have been interesting to historians or admirers if she hadn't been such an inspiring woman.

All her life Patty never waited or asked for help from anyone: If something had to be done, she did it herself, whether that meant delivering a woman's baby or driving a wagon across the plains on the trek to Utah. Her life embodies the can-do spirit that fueled all pioneers to make the arduous journey westward and create new lives for themselves and later generations.

Patty was born in Maine in 1795, when much of the present-day United States was still a forested wilderness. Her father was a cobbler and her mother a seamstress. Married at seventeen to David Sessions, she almost immediately started to help her mother-in-law, who worked as a midwife. She didn't get much schooling but loved to write and was always curious about the world around her.

That curiosity may have been one reason she listened to missionaries preaching about modern-day revelations from God to a young man named Joseph Smith from upstate New York. Already a devout Christian, Patty was baptized into the Mormon church in 1834, four years after Smith founded it, and persuaded other family members to join the next year. In 1837 they moved to Missouri, where the Latter-day Saints hoped to form a community of believers.

By this time Patty had already given birth to seven children, four of whom had died; she was pregnant again when the family made the difficult trip by foot and wagon to Missouri. At forty-two she was showing the stamina that would serve her in busy decades to come.

A year later, violence erupted between Latter-day Saints and Missourians, and more than two dozen people were killed in bloody skirmishes. Upon hearing about the fighting, Missouri's Governor Lilburn Boggs issued an "extermination order," giving the Mormons a choice between death and exile. Running from mobs of suspicious residents as well as the state militia, families quickly packed up what they could carry and moved to Illinois, leaving their new homes and farms behind.

It was winter and no one was prepared for such a journey. Patty Sessions trudged through deep snow, ice-encrusted rivers, and mud that sucked at her boots and skirts. She did all this without enough food, carrying her young daughter, Amanda, in her arms as she walked. Sometimes she had no shelter but a tent. At night she would try to keep herself and her baby warm. But the baby was sick for much of the journey. Amanda would die soon after Patty's family reached the new settlement of Nauvoo, Illinois.

By the early 1840s Nauvoo was a thriving town with 15,000 residents, Mormon and otherwise—about three times the number of people living in Chicago. As one of the church's early converts, Patty Sessions was close to Joseph Smith and considered him a modern-day prophet.

Joseph Smith was spiritually married to a number of women, including Patty. Mormons believed being "sealed" in their temple formed a bond that lasted beyond death. Since women who were sealed to church leaders anticipated living in the afterlife with the men chosen by God to lead His people on Earth, it was a great honor to be chosen as one of them. Both Joseph Smith and Brigham Young married women who were already married to other men, which meant men like Patty's husband might be blessed with multiple wives—but one of his wives could also be "sealed" to a church president.

Patty formed a lifelong circle of friends with a group of elite Mormon women she would later call "Brigham's girls" or "Heber's girls" (many of the women were married to church leaders, including presidents Brigham Young and Heber C. Kimball).

It was while they lived in Illinois that Patty Sessions began keeping a diary, in a simple notebook a friend had given her. She was fifty-one years old and had already established herself as a vital member of her community. Spelling, punctuation, and clarity were not Patty's top priorities. Her diaries were filled with smeared ink, crossed-out words, and crammed handwriting. It was an account she wrote for herself, not for posterity.

She wrote things as they happened, giving the account a lively sense of immediacy. In brief stream-of-consciousness daily entries, she recorded even the most mundane details of her life, including the time she spent washing, sewing, or gardening. Those details, together with more thoughtful commentary and items about the people she knew, make for an engaging record of one well-known woman's life and times.

Mormons' happiness in Nauvoo was short-lived. In 1844 violence erupted again between Mormons and residents of surrounding communities. In retaliation, the Mormon militia tore down the presses of an anti-Mormon newspaper. Joseph Smith and his brother Hyrum were arrested and killed by a mob while in jail, and Brigham Young took over as head of the church.

The Mormon pioneers knew they were not safe in Illinois or any place where they could incite an unsympathetic local population. They decided to head west, across the Rocky Mountains and into the Great Basin. They didn't know much about their new home, except that other pioneers hadn't deemed the arid, mountain-ringed valley worthy of settling. What is now Utah was then part of Mexico (it would become part of the United States in 1848, after the Mexican War). "We started for a resting place, we knew not where," Patty wrote.

Patty Sessions and her family helped form the "Big Company," which arrived in the Salt Lake valley shortly after the first group of settlers in July of 1847. As the family's leader (several of her children and their families came west with her), she drove and maintained her own wagon—evidence of her independent and tough-minded spirit.

She slogged up to twelve miles or more a day through prairie grass and over rocky hills in a region with no roads or towns. Sometimes, at the end of the day, she had to turn around and retrace her steps to minister to a sick traveler or help a woman give birth. She once delivered three babies in six hours while the convoy moved westward. Sometimes the women had babies after walking or riding for miles earlier in the day. She records one instance where a woman continued on the trek for thirteen slow miles *after* she went into labor.

Sometimes Patty went for days without sleep. When she did, it was often with aching muscles and raw hands. On her fifty-second birthday, she helped a woman give birth, went to a small party her friends had for her, then tended to another two women that same night.

Patty worked under difficult circumstances, with almost no equipment or medication. She didn't even have access to the fresh herbs that were the foundation of her treatments. Sometimes, the most she could do was keep patients clean and warm—and pray they would get better. She and her own children were often sick. "I have never felt so bad as now, but I am not discouraged yet," she wrote, laid up in the back of the wagon during one long illness. But she pushed forward in her typical determined fashion. "My health is poor, my mind weighed down, but my trust is in God."

"Mother Sessions" was known not only as a skilled midwife but as a healer with the ability to minister to both physical and spiritual needs of the sick. She would do a "laying on of hands" for healing and give religious blessings. Her diaries record many instances of "speaking in tongues," which was common for healers in many religions at the time. Joseph Smith had encouraged this role, quoting the biblical book of Mark: "Signs follow all who believe." He felt this applied to women as well as men.

It was also common for women to preside over their own church meetings, which were a mixture of religion and socializing. In one women's meeting, organized by her friend Eliza R. Snow, "they spoke in tongues, I interpreted, some prophesied—it was a feast," Patty wrote, with obvious satisfaction. At another meeting Patty "blessed Sister Christeen by laying my hands upon her head and the Lord spoke through me to her great and marvelous things." Many of those roles would later be designated specifically as men's responsibilities, but Patty's acts show how powerful women were in the church's early years.

Though she was one of Joseph Smith's many "celestial" wives, Patty was less happy about the idea of her husband taking other wives. When David married his second wife, Rosilla, the two strong-willed women fought often. Their sour relationship drove a wedge between Patty and her husband.

Months of Patty's diary entries complain about Rosilla and tell of Patty's sadness when her husband seemed to be favoring his other wife. Writing was an outlet for this woman who wasn't used to feeling helpless. Patty detailed Rosilla's "saucy tongue," her refusal to do chores, and her threats to take David for herself. "Have had another long talk with Rosilla. She says she will not receive any advice from me, she will do as she pleases," Patty wrote in October of 1846. Her diaries make it clear how hard it was for this whirlwind of a woman to share her life and her husband with someone she disliked so much. Then again, Patty's forceful personality probably would have made it hard for her to back down to any sister wife.

Rosilla eventually gave up and returned to Nauvoo. Even though David was angry that Patty had driven Rosilla away, Patty must have been secretly pleased at her victory. When David Sessions took a third wife, Harriet, Patty tried to make peace with the arrangement, drawing on her deep well of inner strength. Like other women of her time, she believed that polygamy was a commandment of God, and she relied on her faith to get past the heartache.

She also turned her energy toward her many outside enterprises—always a source of satisfaction and self-confidence. When she arrived in Salt Lake City, she set up a home surrounded by fenced orchards she carefully tended (people in Utah still grow the Sessions plum, which she first cultivated). She sold fruit most of her life; she also grew herbs for the poultices and emetics she used for healing. She kept notes on payments from her patients—as well as the times when they couldn't afford to pay and she didn't ask them to. She kept meticulous records of her finances, including money owed and repaid on loans to family, friends, and the church.

She was shrewd in many areas, but she was most famous throughout the territory for her skill as a midwife. Midwives were often the only medical practitioners around, male or female. The importance of children and families, along with the support of male church leadership, made them high-profile members of Mormon society.

And Patty Sessions was, so to speak, the mother of all Mormon midwives. During Utah's early years, Patty helped many of the state's women give birth, delivering about 250 babies in her first year in Utah alone and a lifelong total of 3,977. Her gnarled and calloused but powerful hands were the first things many babies felt in their new world. Her friendly face—with weathered skin, long nose, and broad forehead often topped by an old-fashioned bonnet—was the first thing they saw.

Like most midwives, she learned her trade mostly through observation and trial and error, but she also attended medical lectures whenever she could. She was a member and later president of the Council of Health, a group dedicated to educating health professionals. She also presided over the Mormon women's group dedicated to helping the less fortunate, including both settlers and native people, which would later become the church-wide Relief Society. "Much good done in both societies over which I presided," she wrote in her diary. "The squaws were cloked [sic] the sick and poor were visitet [sic] and administered to and their wants relieved [sic]."

After David died in 1850, Patty, then in her mid-fifties, maintained her own home, alone—but not for long. In 1851 John Parry, a musician and the first conductor of the Mormon Tabernacle Choir, asked her to marry him. In her journal she wrote, in her usual pragmatic tone: "I feel to thank the Lord that I have some one to cut my wood for me."

John took a second wife, but by this time little could faze Patty. She didn't hold it against him—even though, as in her first marriage, she ended up taking on most of the household responsibilities. That included earning much of the family's income through her orchards and work as a midwife. She was one of the early investors in Zions Cooperative Mercantile Institution (ZCMI); by 1883 she owned $16,000 worth of shares in the store—an incredible amount of wealth for a woman with such modest beginnings.

Always looking for extra income, she took in boarders and did the cooking, cleaning, and bookkeeping that entailed. Her hands never stopped moving; she was constantly making gifts for people by hand or on her loom, even into very old age—though by then, she was nearly blind and the recipients often had to redo them. Apparently, doing something poorly wasn't enough to stop her from doing it. She also frequently gave to charity, dutifully paying her church tithing and adding extra funds to help pay others' passage to Utah.

All the while Patty kept teaching and learning—including those dance lessons—well into very old age.

John Parry died in 1868, and Patty once again settled into running her own household and affairs. In 1870 she moved to Bountiful, a town her son helped found north of Salt Lake City. Building on a lifelong love of education, she used proceeds from the ZCMI mercantile to create the Patty Sessions Academy, housed in an attractive brick building, where all were welcome to send their children for a free education. Of course, she taught the classes. This was in 1883, when she was eighty-eight years old.

Patty continued tending the sick as well as her orchard into her nineties. A diary entry in 1886, when she was ninety-one, reads, "We have got the corn hauled here & stacked." When she was ninety-three, she recorded going for sleigh rides almost every day and clearing snow off her house after a storm. Patty Sessions wrote her last known diary entry in 1888. She died in 1892, when she was ninety-seven.

Patty Sessions's diaries are a detailed and invaluable record of life in the early days of the Church of Jesus Christ of Latter-day Saints. But they are also a look into the mind of a particularly strong-willed powerhouse. In her homespun language she expressed her feelings later in life: "I have been reading my journal and I feel to thank the Lord that I have passed through what I have," she wrote. "I have gained an experience I could not have gained no other way."

# REVA BECK BOSONE

(1895–1983)

### Lawyer, Judge, Congresswoman

Reva Beck Bosone had her first memorable run-in with authority when she ran for student body president in high school. As election day drew nearer, she was on track to become the first girl in state history to win that office.

Then one day the school principal called her into his office and suggested she run for vice president instead. It just didn't seem right for a girl to win, he said. Bowing to his wishes, she dropped out of the race for president and agreed to be vice president. As something of a consolation prize, she was selected the town's "Goddess of Liberty" later that year—something the principal no doubt thought was more suitable.

That was the last time Reva would ever let someone convince her to hold back based on her gender. From then on, if there was an office she wanted, she would run for it. And chances were that she would win. One of Utah's most successful politicians, she served two terms in the state legislature, twelve years as the state's first woman judge, and two terms in the US House of Representatives.

Reva Zilpha Beck was born in 1895 to Christian M. Beck and Zilpha Chipman Beck. They were descended from some of Utah's earliest Mormon arrivals, but the family had left the church over polygamy. Reva was a fighter—and a handful—from the start. In her unpublished memoirs, she wrote: "A thirteen-pound baby is enough to kill any mother. Part of my thirteen pounds at birth must have been a wrought-iron jaw. Otherwise I would have been knocked out of politics long ago."

Although it wasn't common for women to become lawyers in her day, law was in her DNA. The Beck family held to a saying: "If you want to do good, go where the laws are made." She and two of her three brothers would practice law, and one of her brothers also became a judge.

Reva grew up in American Fork, a medium-size town between Salt Lake City and Provo, where her family owned the town's best hotel. At first, her body was not quite as strong as her intellect. She had a heart condition and was kept out of any strenuous activity until she was a teenager. But there was plenty at home to keep her mind occupied.

The family loved debating over government and current affairs. Reva was the only girl, but she could hold her own. She later credited those many discussions with not only igniting her passion for making a difference in the world but also for giving her a lot of practice at getting along with men.

Reva's parents eventually made enough money to buy the town's opera house, where she acted in local productions. Tall, with green eyes and red hair, she thought about making a living on the stage. "It was decided long before I was grown up that I would graduate from college, then go to New York City and attend a dramatic art school," she later recalled. But her mother talked her out of becoming a professional actor, and Reva lost interest.

Her vibrant personality didn't come naturally at first. As a student, she was inclined to be shy and self-conscious. She was keenly aware of her above-average height and red hair, which she thought made her stand out a little too much. But by the time she was in high school, with her family's encouragement, she had worked to overcome her insecurities and built an armor of competence around herself that she would later use to brush off criticism.

She was a good student, with a special talent when it came to memorizing information and reciting it later. Not surprisingly, she was on her high school debate team.

She always knew she would go to college. She attended Westminster College in Salt Lake City, then a two-year school, and graduated in 1917.

While her brothers went off for further study at the University of Utah, Reva headed for the University of California at Berkeley, where her mother had always wanted one of her children to study. Reva studied English and graduated in 1919 after having won the admiration of her teachers and peers—and survived a severe bout of influenza during the epidemic of 1918.

Although she knew she wanted to become a lawyer, one of her brothers suggested she might want to wait until she was a bit older. It would be hard enough for a woman to be taken seriously as a lawyer, but it might be impossible for a young one. She returned to American Fork to live at home, work as a teacher for a few years, and save up for law school.

At twenty-five she married Harold G. Cutler, but it wasn't a good match, and they were divorced within a year. Over the next few years, she moved through a series of jobs that each paid a little better and gave her more of the freedom and authority she wanted. She taught in the eastern Utah town of Delta before moving to Ogden.

At the time, Ogden was the state's second-largest city, a thriving railroad town with cultural aspirations that matched Reva's. She taught English, speech, drama, and debate, becoming the head of Ogden High School's speech and drama department. She directed school plays and coached the debate team.

What could have been a fallback career flourished into a passion, and everyone at school loved Reva. Her magnetic personality and engaging speaking style urged students to work harder even as they were having fun. After school "Miss Beck" became "Reva," as students hung around her classroom to tell her stories and ask her advice on subjects they didn't dare discuss with their parents.

Reva's life outside school activities was as austere as her professional life was crowded. She wore only two dresses, both simple and black (she wore one while the other got cleaned), and while her colleagues spent their summers traveling, she returned home to help clean the family hotel. By 1926 she had saved enough to take the big trip she had always wanted: a three-month, nine-country tour of Europe.

She returned happy but exhausted, only to get into a dispute with the school superintendent over her salary. He told her that although her performance was as good as ever, he couldn't keep giving her the same raises he had been. The event was a catalyst that steered her back to her original plan. She resigned and signed up for law school at the University of Utah, where she was one of two women in her law school class and the only one who graduated.

Years later, when she was making a speech, she saw the superintendent in the audience. "I introduced him as a man who had done me a tremendous favor. He really beamed," she recalled. "And then I proceeded to relate the event that had hastened my study of law—much to his discomfiture, I believe."

Some people were mystified at why a woman would want to give up a successful teaching career to go back to school. But for Reva, it was a logical next step. She wanted to be a lawyer for the same reason she did almost everything in her life: to make a difference in the world. And she decided the best way to do that was to get into politics. She knew law was a traditional route to becoming a legislator. That, on top of the chance to help average people fight their legal battles, made her decision.

She would never entirely give up teaching, nor her view of herself as a teacher. During law school she taught a freshman English class and was so popular that during one term, fifty students signed up for her class—and that was far too many. The department asked for ten volunteers to drop the class and got no takers, no matter how much she or the department chair begged. "Way down deep, I glowed!" Reva wrote in her memoirs. "Does anyone wonder why I'd like to wind up my life teaching?"

During law school she also met Joseph Bosone, a fellow student. He was a devout Catholic, but she didn't want her children raised in a strict Italian Catholic household. They tried to break up, but they couldn't bear being apart. When they got back together, he took her to meet his parents in the small town of Helper, near Price in eastern Utah. In this rough-and-tumble mining town at the base of yellow, coal-filled cliffs, she fell in love with his family and their close-knit immigrant community. The couple quietly married in 1929.

In 1930 Reva's oldest brother, Clarence, made the motion to admit her to the bar; she was the eleventh woman in the state to be accepted. She decided to practice law under her maiden name as a sign of her independence but eventually added her married name, partly to placate her hurt mother-in-law.

Reva practiced law with her brother, then took time off to have a baby daughter she named Zilpha after her mother. But Reva was soon back at work, though she stayed in Helper so Joe's mother could watch the baby while he and Reva practiced law. Reva wasn't sure the diverse populace in this mining region would accept her, but she quickly made herself a visible figure on the local scene.

She didn't back down from challenges. As a lawyer who worked in a some-what gritty mining town and was sympathetic to the working class, she represented some unsavory clients, including a couple of prostitutes. In one of her first cases, she defended two boys accused of rape in a highly publicized trial and won the case after pointing out holes in the accusers' stories. Her victory broke the prosecutor's two-year winning streak.

In 1932, less than two years after moving to Helper, she ran for the state legislature. Her desire to help working-class people led her to become a Democrat, though she grew up in a family of Republicans. She canvassed door-to-door to introduce herself, sometimes with her two-year-old daughter in tow, impressing the people she met with her self-assured but unassuming manner. She won as part of a statewide Democratic landslide and was one of six female legislators heading to the state capitol in 1933.

It was the height of the Great Depression, and everyone was concerned about economic and labor issues. Reva was chosen to be a member of eight committees in the state legislature and focused on labor laws dealing with minimum wage and child labor.

Hoping to make a better living from their practice, Reva and Joe moved to Salt Lake City, where they continued to take all kinds of cases. Since she was no longer a resident of Carbon County, she resigned from her seat in the legislature. Even though she had just moved to a new and much bigger city, she was confident she would be elected again from her new district—and she was.

She ran for speaker of the state house of representatives; though she lost that by a few votes, she was chosen as the House Democratic majority leader.

In 1936 a distinguished judge encouraged her to run for the office herself. Never one to back down from a challenge or a good idea, Reva agreed. She won, and was elected Utah's first female judge. In Salt Lake City's Police and Traffic court, she heard all kinds of cases. She was known as fair and unflappable, although she was nervous at first, knowing a spotlight was on her.

She was known for impatience with bad drivers and raised the fines for drunken and reckless driving to deter offenders. Tired of levying so many fines and hearing so many stories about bad drivers, she instituted the state's first traffic school. (Once, a *Deseret News* reporter offered to get rid of any unflattering photos of her that the newspaper had on file if she would dismiss his traffic ticket. She declined the offer and said he was lucky to get away with just his fine.)

She also had a weekly radio show, where she talked in general about her experiences and warned people about the consequences of breaking the law.

She tried to treat everyone fairly, from well-known figures to the prostitutes, drunks, and hardscrabble thieves who showed up in her court. She was one of the first judges to order psychiatric evaluations of defendants, in case extenuating circumstances could help her make a better decision. She looked for ways to rehabilitate those who could be helped, and she was one of the first judges in Utah to send people with drinking problems to Alcoholics Anonymous. She helped found the Utah State Board for Education on Alcoholism and accepted a position as its chairwoman, approaching alcoholism as a disease and education as one of its cures.

The office had a fun side, too. The first marriage ceremony she presided over, at the elegant Hotel Utah, joined starlet Marla Shelton and Jack Dawn, an MGM makeup man. They later divorced.

Reva's own marriage hit rocky times by 1940, when she found evidence that Joe was having affairs. She was heartbroken, but she couldn't go along with his pleas to stay together. Always a woman of principle, she asked for a divorce.

Reva kept busy as a member of several political, social, and business organizations. She also recruited for the Women's Army Corps, which helped on the "home front" during World War II. After the war she was an official observer at the founding of the United Nations and helped write a women's equality clause for its charter.

Through the 1940s Reva's associates urged her to run for national office. She joined the Democratic race in 1948 and campaigned with Harry Truman. Even she was pretty sure she wouldn't make it—after all, she was not only a woman but a single parent, and she was running against an incumbent, William A. Dawson. She also wasn't Mormon. To many people's surprise, both she and Truman won.

Reva and Zilpha, by this time a college student but always close to her mother, moved together to Washington and explored the new city. Zilpha always agreed with her mother that gender shouldn't be an impediment, and a couple of years later she joined the Air Force (Reva spoke at her graduation). She went on to be the first woman intelligence officer ever for an American air force squadron.

Reva wanted to be on the Interior Committee, an important one for Utah since it deals with land use and natural resources. When she inquired about the possibility, she heard back that no woman had ever been on it and no woman should—because the committee might at some point have to discuss "animal breeding." A bemused Reva responded that after hearing so much as a judge about human sex, animal breeding would be nothing. She won the appointment . . . and never heard a discussion of animal breeding. She used her post on the committee as a springboard to help resolve water and soil conservation issues in the West.

As she had everywhere, she made many friends in Washington and was known for being a conscientious and principled legislator. She also used her speaking skills to her advantage. Early in her tenure, she was invited to speak at the Women's National Press Club Dinner. She didn't know she would be asked to speak first, and she walked to the stage not knowing what she was going to say. She saved herself by doing an impersonation of the many men who had appeared before her while still drunk. "Jedge, you here again?" she slurred. It was a memorable performance that made her some immediate friends who would come in handy later.

She continued to feel she shouldn't be treated any differently because she was a woman. A vote in Congress was worth the same whether cast by a man or a woman, was it not?

Once, the US Navy invited members of Congress to spend a weekend aboard a naval carrier. She happily accepted—but the navy withdrew its invitation when it learned she was a woman. The ship, it said, didn't have "facilities" for women.

Reva argued that since any family's "facilities" are used by all members of the family, that shouldn't be a problem. Not only did they let her, another congresswoman, and a female reporter go on the trip, they let the women sleep in the admiral's quarters.

For the 1950 campaign, the Republicans chose a woman, Ivy Baker Priest, to run against Reva (Priest would later become the US treasurer). The women respected each other too much to fight a dirty campaign, though Priest attacked Reva for her efforts to reform the health-care system. The "socialized medicine" charge didn't work, and Reva was reelected.

Things were more difficult the next time around. In 1952, in the middle of the McCarthyist anti-communism crusade, Reva's opponents called her a communist. That was partly based on Reva's opposition to a bill that made it illegal for the federal government to hire anyone with communist sympathies. She had also voted against the creation of the CIA. She thought those measures threatened civil liberties and could hurt innocent people, and she didn't like the idea of the government covertly keeping tabs on its citizens.

William Dawson, the man whose seat she took in 1948, not only brought up the "socialized medicine" charge but also said she had engaged in "unladylike conduct" and reminded voters that she was divorced. The most damning charge, considering the time and place, implied Reva was a communist. One piece of campaign literature proclaimed, "You, Reva Beck Bosone, have sold your heritage to the Kremlin."

Dawson won, part of a wave of Republicans swept in during the Eisenhower years. The campaign wounded Reva deeply, and Dawson was the only opponent she was never interested in befriending. Utah wouldn't get its next female congresswoman until Karen Shepherd won in 1992.

Reva returned to Salt Lake City and busied herself with a new television show discussing current events. Afraid she might run for Congress again in the next election, her political opponents called her advertisers to complain.

Reva did run in 1954, and this time the race was dirtier than ever, with opponents spreading rumors that she was a drunk (a strange charge, considering her career—and the fact that she rarely drank). She felt her opponents were trying to swing women voters against her by attacking her character even as they took advantage of national hysteria over the communist threat. At the same time, the old "New Deal" Democratic party was losing its appeal in Utah, where voters were turning more conservative in general.

She lost the election. More devastating, she was treated as something of a pariah in Utah's political circles, and for a while she had a hard time finding another job.

She decided to go back to Washington, where she was hired as legal counsel for a congressional subcommittee on education in 1958. In 1961 she took a job as the highest-ranking judicial officer in the US Post Office—which required her to look into everything from fraud to obscenity.

She retired in 1968, spending her time traveling, visiting friends, writing many letters, giving advice, and accepting awards. Those included an honorary Ph.D. from the University of Utah and the UC Berkeley Distinguished Service in Government Award in 1970. Irving Stone included her among thirty-nine distinguished alumni in the history he compiled of UC Berkeley. Reva died in Virginia in 1983.

When Reva Beck Bosone retired from her postal service job, the *Salt Lake Tribune* wrote, "Retirement is a difficult step to take when the person involved is being nagged by apprehensions of things being left uncompleted. Fortunately for Reva Beck Bosone, who leaves public office Saturday after 40 years of service, there need be no such anxiety." That was an apt summary of a life spent making a difference for other people—which is exactly what Reva set out to do.

# JUANITA BROOKS

✦

(1898–1989)

Historian Who Sought the Truth

When Juanita Brooks first stood on a hill and looked out over the valley called Mountain Meadows, she pondered what she knew about this mysterious place—and what she didn't.

She grew up hearing that many years earlier, this quiet place was the site of a horrific massacre. She had been told that Indians had raided a convoy of white immigrants and slaughtered most of them. But she and others were starting to suspect the place held dark secrets that implicated some of her neighbors' ancestors. Overlooking the slopes of Mountain Meadows and into the vast Great Basin desert beyond, the young schoolteacher had a feeling many of those who committed the crime were never held accountable.

In her memoirs she recalled the moment the thought struck her. "Men did not gather here by chance or mere hearsay. If they were here, they had come because they were ordered to come. And whatever went on was done because it had been ordered, not because individuals had acted upon impulse."

Moments like this convinced her she must find the truth about Mountain Meadows and tell it to the world.

Juanita Brooks was driven by a desire to find and tell truths about history, and she was determined to bring a clear-eyed perspective to it. Although she lived her whole life as a faithful Mormon, she wrote about the church's warts as well as its positives. She was one of the first Utah historians to take a critical look at her homeland's history—an aim that didn't endear her to those who preferred that the past be left sleeping.

She was already well known as a historian and a teacher when she tackled the Mountain Meadows Massacre, one of the most controversial subjects in Mormon history. But as much as a historian, she was a biographer, seeking to humanize history and tell the life stories of regular people.

Juanita Leone Leavitt was born in 1898 in Bunkerville, Nevada, a desert Mormon settlement just southwest of the Utah border. She got her effervescent energy from her mother, who did much of the work on their small homestead, which was surrounded by jagged mountain ranges, high mesas, and miles of vast, open desert. As the oldest child, she helped her father with his mail route, capturing fresh horses to bring to him. The family also rented out half of the house to the local school, which gave Juanita a chance to listen in on lessons before she was old enough to attend.

She was always a little self-conscious about her appearance—thin, with a large nose and crooked teeth (her teeth only got worse until she finally got dentures decades later). Juanita was an excellent student and skipped first grade but was held back in the sixth because she looked so sickly the teacher refused to accept her in his class. As an adult, she tended to keep her hair pulled back and wore practical clothes. She overcame lifelong insecurities about her appearance with a gregarious personality and witty conversation.

After graduating from high school and spending a year helping out at her cousins' farm, she went to a nearby "normal school" to become a teacher. Her teacher, a Columbia University graduate, inspired Juanita and opened her eyes to the way people outside Mormonism viewed the world.

After graduating she taught at the elementary school in Bunkerville, then in nearby Mesquite. While she was working as a teacher, she got to know many of the residents and earned their respect.

One of those she befriended was the local patriarch, an elderly man tasked with giving special blessings to young church members. One day the old man asked her to help him write something important, but she was busy and put him off. Shortly thereafter, she heard that he was calling for her from his deathbed. By the time she got to him, he was too far gone.

As she recalled in her memoirs: "He seemed troubled; he rambled in delirium—he prayed, he yelled, he preached, and once his eyes opened wide to the ceiling and he yelled, 'BLOOD! BLOOD! BLOOD!'"

Juanita was alarmed. "What is the matter with him?" she asked a relative. "He acts like he is haunted."

"Maybe he is," the man replied. "He was at the Mountain Meadows Massacre, you know."

Juanita was shocked. She blasted herself for not immediately grabbing a chance to hear a firsthand account of the massacre that happened sixty years before. It was the first time she began asking questions about the event that would become a major focus in her life.

She married Ernest Pulsipher at age twenty-one, but he died of cancer soon afterward, leaving her and a baby son. With dreams of higher education, she helped work her in-laws' farm and took odd jobs to save money for college. She graduated from Brigham Young University in Provo after excelling as a debater and taking summer courses in writing. She took classes in everything from economics to English to education, but her degree was in food and nutrition because those were the classes she could take while neighbors and housemates watched her son.

She moved to St. George in southwestern Utah to teach English, public speaking, and debate at Dixie College. St. George was like an oasis in the desert, a cultural center near where she grew up. It was far from any major city: Salt Lake City was 300 miles away, Las Vegas was then little more than a rest stop in the desert, and Los Angeles was nearly 400 miles distant. It was founded when Brigham Young sent settlers to the Southwest, hoping they could grow cotton and other warm-weather crops (thus the nickname "Dixie").

In 1928 Juanita used a paid sabbatical to make the long trip to New York City, where, inspired by her former teacher, she earned a master's degree at Columbia University. It was a big challenge, at a time when women—and especially single mothers—weren't expected to try for such things. Jumping into a thesis about American literature gave her invaluable experience in doing in-depth research, and living in a cosmopolitan eastern city gave her a whole new perspective on the world outside of Utah and Mormonism.

She returned to St. George, where she was appointed dean of women at Dixie College. She had a huge impact on the sleepy town, helping it mature into an independent city with its own cultural assets. Long before she was nationally famous, she was a powerful force for historical preservation and documentation. She wanted to tell the history of "Utah's Dixie," which wasn't well known to those outside the region.

Like other Mormons who settled the West, the settlers here kept detailed diaries. Few outsiders could make much of an inroads into the region's collective psyche, but Juanita could. During her long and busy career, the region would give her plenty of untapped history to mine—and her status as a local helped her win the trust of those who had the information she needed.

The church had founded the college that later became Dixie State in 1911. By 1933, when Juanita left to raise children with her second husband, it had become an official state college. She would return again several times, spending much of her adult life as a teacher there. She was known as a hard grader and rarely gave A's. She could both inspire students with wry, funny stories and terrify them with red-ink comments on their essays.

In 1931 she had her first long conversation with Will Brooks, a local sheriff (he later worked as the regional postmaster) as he was giving her a ride to the other side of southern Utah. After his wife died in 1932, he courted her, and they were married in 1933. He was seventeen years her senior and had four sons.

Although Juanita loved her professional life, she was ready to move beyond being everyone's favorite sister, aunt, or cousin and become a full-fledged wife. She felt responsible for making the merged household work, and she loved family more than anything else—and very quickly, she discovered she was pregnant. She and Will would go on to have four more children over the next five years, adding to their already boisterous family.

Juanita was also called by the church to be the regional president for the Relief Society, a demanding job in itself that required organizing everything from big ceremonies to visits with local congregations she supervised.

She had always loved and doted on everyone in her family, giving help and serving as a second mother to her younger siblings. She handled her home life with the enthusiasm she applied to everything. She was a multitasker, always keeping ironing handy in case guests dropped by so she could have something to do while they conversed.

There was no time for major academic pursuits. Instead, Juanita focused her intellect on writing freelance articles. She earned a reputation for approaching her historical accounts of southern Utah in a balanced, thoroughly researched yet entertaining way. One of her first articles, about polygamy, was published in *Harper's Magazine.* It was a major triumph that got people talking.

Most readers, including many who had never heard of Juanita Brooks, thought she did an admirable job with a tough subject. One elderly polygamist wrote to her: "The theme is a delicate one for some of us, and such abhorrence for others of us, that to discuss it frankly and freely and to do it with a grace and such supreme good-taste that no one can fail to be pleased is a real achievement."

She began traveling throughout the state and the West speaking, lecturing, serving on panels, and helping other scholars with their research—activities she would squeeze into her schedule throughout her life. She was well regarded enough to write for both the *Salt Lake Tribune,* which had never defended Mormons, and the Relief Society's official magazine.

She took charge of several major projects for the Utah State Historical Society, for which she was assistant state supervisor. During the Great Depression she oversaw collection and transcription of diaries and oral histories under the Works Progress Administration. She reserved space in a back room of her house where women came in to type the reminiscences of their forebears, copies of which eventually made it into the Library of Congress's collection in Washington, DC.

As Relief Society president, Juanita had access to historical documents stored in the St. George temple; only church officials had full access to the sacred building. She pored over them, developing an even deeper knowledge of the people who had settled the region over the previous few decades. Never one to get much sleep, she often stayed up late to make typed copies of their diaries.

After writing a few more history-oriented articles for regional and national magazines, Juanita wanted to pursue a bigger project. Writers were starting to use scholarly tools to reexamine Mormon history, sometimes causing controversy in the process. They included Fawn Brodie, a church member whose *No Man Knows My History* delved into the life of the church's founder, Joseph Smith. When she portrayed him as a charlatan, the church excommunicated her.

Juanita wanted to write a book about frontiersman Jacob Hamblin, one of St. George's most important founders. While researching the Hamblin book, she took some time out to write a biography of her grandfather, Dudley Leavitt, a hearty pioneer who had forty-eight children by five wives and who became the forebear of a significant segment of southern Utah's population.

During her research she soon realized Jacob Hamblin had somehow been involved in the Mountain Meadows Massacre—a subject no one in southern Utah wanted to talk about.

St. George's early years were marked not only by the usual pioneer hardships but by an event that historian and Juanita Brooks biographer Levi S. Peterson says caused "a guilt as devastating and ineradicable as that which afflicted the participants in the Salem witch trials in the late seventeenth century": the Mountain Meadows Massacre.

At the time of the massacre, the US government was growing increasingly suspicious of Mormons—and vice versa. As distrust grew, the federal government sent troops to keep an eye on the Mormons and remind them that they were still subject to US authority. Mormons feared that war would erupt at any moment and they would have nowhere to go. They mustered a statewide militia that stood ready to fight the army if necessary.

Mountain Meadows is a high-elevation mountain valley north of St. George where immigrants en route to California watered and rested their convoys before the trip across the bone-dry desert. In 1857 a group of about 120 immigrants passing through from Arkansas to California were attacked by a group of Paiute Indians, who killed all the men and women and most of the children.

Shortly before the massacre, members of the Fancher party had circled their wagons and defended themselves during a five-day initial siege by the Paiutes, during which several immigrants were killed.

A short time later, militia leader John D. Lee went to Mountain Meadows and offered the Fancher group peaceful passage. When the immigrants uncircled their wagons, the Indians killed everyone old enough to identify them, took the youngest children with them, and left the bodies scattered all over the hillsides. Local Mormons took in the surviving children to raise as their own.

That was the original story. But details emerged after the event, and it grew clear to Juanita and others that someone had recruited the Indians to attack the immigrants.

For one thing, the travelers known as the Fancher party had clashed with Mormon settlers in the area before the massacre. The Fancher party had asked the Mormons to sell them food; the Mormons refused. Mormons were still upset over the way they had been treated in Missouri twenty years earlier, before the flight to Utah. Some members of the Fancher party were from Missouri—and personally opposed to Mormonism. The rest of the group was from Arkansas.

As Mormons geared up for a possible war with the US government, Mormon apostle Parley P. Pratt was killed in Arkansas by a man whose wife had left him to join the Mormons and become one of Pratt's wives.

After the Civil War, federal investigators looked into the matter and indicted nine men but convicted only John D. Lee, who was hanged in 1877. When Juanita interviewed descendants of Jacob Hamblin, a local Mormon leader at the time of the massacre, they still reacted angrily to any mention of Lee. Lee's descendants reacted the same way to mentions of Hamblin, whom they saw as one of many who used their ancestor as a scapegoat. It seemed everyone was trying to paint the other side's forebear as villain and theirs as hero.

In the years following the massacre, bits and pieces of the story had trickled out (Ann Eliza Webb Young had written about it in her memoir, for example), but no one had done a thorough, scholarly investigation into what exactly happened or written it into one comprehensive account. To anyone who reviewed the evidence—and many journalists and historians had—it was clear that Lee wasn't the only one orchestrating the attack. Some speculated Brigham Young knew about it or even ordered it.

Juanita realized she was in a unique position: She knew how to do historical research. She knew how to write. She already knew people who might have evidence about what happened. And she was one of few people who didn't have an ax to grind for or against the Mormon church. Someone should tell the truth about Mountain Meadows. And no one could tell it the way she could.

In 1945 she got a grant from the Huntington Library in California, which had the original transcripts of John D. Lee's trial, and used part of it to hire others to do her domestic chores while she traveled around the West, looking for sources for the book and other research. She fought for access to the Mormon church archives, which included early documents relating to the massacre.

To write the book, she had to gather information no one had ever compiled. And it wasn't easy. For a long time, Dixie residents had tried to forget the brutal tragedy, and when Juanita started to investigate it, they felt she was reopening old wounds that should stay closed. Why publicize the details of such an ugly event, since doing so could embarrass her own church?

That resolve to uncover the truth, whatever it may be, took a lot of bravery. She faced ostracism from church leaders (who banned her from publishing any work in official church publications when they found out what she was doing) and even her local congregation. She knew she risked not only disapproval but possibly excommunication, no small threat to a believer. She initially hid some of her fact-finding activities from the church leadership in Salt Lake City, fearing they would try to stop her.

But she persevered, showing the determination that had propelled her all her life.

She hoped her fellow Mormons would see her not as a gadfly but as a sincere member of their congregation. If their faith was as strong as her own, she felt, nothing she wrote could harm it. She wrote to her editor at Stanford University Press: "I do not wish to be excommunicated from my church for many reasons. But if that is the price that I must pay for my intellectual honesty, I shall pay it—I hope without bitterness."

That perspective made her the model for other faithful but questioning Mormon scholars, today as well as in her own time.

*The Mountain Meadows Massacre* appeared in 1950. Juanita retold the story, saying the local Mormon leadership had initiated the first attack on the convoy. Then, they and their Indian collaborators returned to kill every adult in the Fancher party. She determined that Brigham Young had probably not known about the massacre in advance and may have tried to prevent it. But she also found that he and others, including his counselor George A. Smith (ironically, St. George's namesake), had inflamed the Mormon militia before the massacre and helped cover up its involvement after the fact.

Juanita also took some of the blame and accompanying shame away from John D. Lee, who she said was unfairly blamed after the event. She wanted everyone to know that the massacre was not just the work of one or even a few crazed men. Rather, it arose from an atmosphere of distrust and vengeance that everyone in the church, not just those in far-flung southern outposts, were responsible for creating. She also told how her own Mormon leaders denied her access to records in an attempt to bury ugly truths.

The book got mostly good reviews from within and outside the Mormon community—though some of the Mormon hierarchy either were angry or refused to talk about it at all. She won praise not so much for her conclusions as her nuanced approach to the story. She wrote with trademark humanity and a sense of narrative, which went a long way toward helping heal, rather than inflame, old wounds.

The book made her something of a celebrity throughout the West, and she was a popular speaker for all kinds of audiences, retelling the details of her book and her own part in investigating it. She returned to teaching at Dixie and continued writing freelance articles.

At any given time she was working on many things at once. She edited John D. Lee's diaries for publication and then wrote a detailed biography of him, reminding the world that before he was blamed and exiled for the massacre, he had been a respected and influential explorer, pioneer, healer, and leader. She was thrilled and his descendants vindicated when his church membership was posthumously reinstated.

All this time she continued to run a household and help her children with everything from housing to cars to education. She and Will were a cheerful, hardworking team with many friends and a packed social life. They loved hosting friends, family, or even casual acquaintances, many of whom shared Juanita's interest in history.

Juanita had a vast network of friends and colleagues, including many of the West's foremost historians. By the 1950s and 1960s, she was the center of a circle of Mormon scholars who openly questioned certain church decisions, past and present. They hoped the church wouldn't excommunicate them for their efforts, but some of them eventually were forced to leave it. Juanita feared she would be but never was; maybe her decades of service to the church outweighed her criticisms of it. She felt telling the truth was her highest calling. She was also just never very good at bowing to authority.

As well as her work with the Utah Historical Society, which spanned several decades, she was a member of the Utah Folklore Society. In 1964 Utah State University awarded Juanita an honorary doctorate degree. The College of Southern Utah and the University of Utah would also award her honorary degrees.

In 1965 she won praise for her work on editing the diaries of Hosea Stout, an early Mormon convert and eventual speaker of the Utah territorial legislature who was part of or close to many significant events in the church's history. She acted as a reader and editor for several other writers' books, including Wallace Stegner's *The Gathering of Zion*. Throughout her life she collected diaries of as many southern Utah settlers as she could, typing them up and giving the originals back to their families.

Juanita and Will kept busy well into old age, working on one of their houses, traveling, and socializing. Living in St. George but still doing a lot of work in Salt Lake City, Juanita took night buses back and forth to save time. She didn't get a driver's license until she was seventy-one, when Will could no longer drive. He died in 1970. Shortly thereafter, tired of the commute, Juanita moved to Salt Lake City.

By the late 1970s Juanita had started suffering from memory loss—much to her frustration. Over the next ten years, her dementia worsened, and she went to live in a nursing home, where she died in 1989.

Juanita Brooks explored the faith that brought her forebears to Utah, and explained it to those who had come for other reasons. Her work was a sign of hope for better relations between the state's Mormon residents and gentiles. She shaped the way people in Utah see their history and helped start a dialogue about history that continues today—as she felt it should.

# WASHINGTON WOMEN

# MARY ANN BOREN DENNY

❧

(1822–1910)

## Mother of Seattle

In preparation for the journey north from Portland to Puget Sound country, the young mother, Mary Ann Denny, laundered her family's clothing and washed and starched her sun bonnet until the brim was properly stiff. She laid a cloth on the grassy ground and ironed her bonnet and dress so that she would appear well groomed for the trip.

Mary Ann, her husband Arthur, two young daughters—Louisa (seven) and Lenora (four)—and her newborn son, Rolland, who had been born in Portland just twelve days after her arduous four months of travel across the country by wagon train, set sail on the schooner *Exact* on November 5, 1851. Bound for Puget Sound with the Dennys were Mary's brother, Carson Boren, and his family; her sister, Louisa Boren; Arthur's brother, David Denny; the Low family, whom they had joined on the Oregon Trail; the Bell family, with whom they had become acquainted in Portland; and Charles and Lee Terry from New York by way of Olympia. With the twelve adults on the excursion were twelve children, all under the age of nine. The *Exact* was taking gold prospectors north to the Queen Charlotte Islands and settlers to Olympia, which was one of the few "settled" towns north of Portland.

As they waited to board the *Exact,* Mary bought salmon from local Indian vendors. There was a small cookstove aboard the ship, so the wives took turns cooking the fish for their family meals. Before they could even finish cooking, the women began to feel ill. One by one, men, women, and children became incapacitated by seasickness. Whole families took to their bunks below deck as the ship was tossed and turned by the rolling sea.

The wind, which caused so much discomfort to the passengers of the tiny schooner, was a great boon in sailing up the Pacific coastline; just eight days after leaving Portland, the ship sailed into Puget Sound. The captain dropped anchor in the middle of the sound and sent his passengers ashore in rowboats. Mrs. Alexander, a passenger aboard the *Exact* headed for Olympia, described the women of the landing party in a newspaper interview:

*I can't never forget when the folks landed at Alki Point. I was*
*sorry for Mrs. Denny with her baby and the rest of the women.*
*You see, it was this way. Mr. Alexander and me went on to*
*Olympia, but the rest stopped there. I remember it rained awful*
*hard that last day—and the starch got took out of our bonnets*
*and the wind blew, and every one of 'em, and their sun bonnets*
*with the starch took out of them went flip flap, flip flap, as they*
*rowed off for shore, and the last glimpse I had of them was the*
*women standing under the trees with their wet bonnets all*
*lopping down over their faces and their aprons to their eyes.*

It was 8:00 a.m. on the morning of November 13, 1851, when the Denny party landed at Alki Point amid a typical Puget Sound winter storm. Winds howled and rain poured. The women and children of the party huddled on the rocky beach. Shivering with cold and drenched to the skin, their long calico frocks were plastered to their forms. The ship had already been partly shrouded by a curtain of driving rain, and they found themselves on a rocky shore at the base of a high sandy bank, with an endless expanse of dark, forbidding forests beyond that.

Mary Denny hugged her baby to her chest in a futile attempt to keep him warm and dry. The rain ran in rivulets from her limp bonnet. She and the other women sought shelter for their children as the men secured their household goods from the incoming tide.

Surely Arthur's brother, David, who had gone ahead to explore the Puget Sound region and had stayed there to build cabins for the families would have completed several homes for the group. Mary and the others were dismayed to find just one partially constructed log cabin, sans roof. They watched forlornly as the *Exact* sailed out of Puget Sound and out of sight. Baby in arms and daughters at her side, Mary Denny sat down on a soggy, fallen, old log and began to cry. Arthur Denny described the scene as he found his wife upon returning to Alki Beach:

*We were landed in the ship's boat when the tide was well out,*
*and while the men of the party were all actively engaged in*
*removing our goods to a point above high tide, the women*
*and children had crawled into the brush, made a fire, and*
*spread a cloth to shelter them from the rain. When the goods*
*were secured I went to look after the women, and found on*
*my approach, that their faces were concealed. On a closer*
*inspection I found that they were in tears, having already*

*discovered the gravity of the situation. . . . My motto in life*
*was never to go backward and in fact if I had wished to retrace*
*my steps it was about as nearly impossible as if I had taken up*
*my bridge behind me. I had brought my family from a good*
*home, surrounded by comforts and luxuries and landed them*
*in a wilderness, and I did not think it at all strange that a*
*woman who had, without complaint, endured all the dangers*
*and hardships of a trip across the great plains, should be found*
*shedding tears when contemplating the hard prospects then so*
*plainly in view.*

Noted University of Washington history professor Edmond S. Meany aptly stated, "The foundation of Seattle was laid in a mother's tears," regarding Mary Denny's welcome to the area.

Members of Chief Seattle's[1] tribes—the Duwamish and Suquamish—witnessed the landing of the Denny party. They peered curiously from the woods, and some ventured cautiously onto the beach. An Indian mother showed Mary how to extract milk from the clams that were profuse on Alki Beach and how to nurse the baby with clam's milk. Mary Denny had been so sick during the trip from Portland, as well as stricken with fever in Portland, that she could not produce milk to feed her baby. Indian babies were often fed with the nectar of clams, on which they thrived, as it provided excellent nutrients. The baby, Rolland, was fed with clam nectar and broth until the party was able to bring its cattle north early the next year. The cattle had been left to winter in the Willamette Valley with Arthur Denny's father, who settled in Portland while the Dennys traveled north to the Puget Sound region.

The local Duwamish women were fascinated with the baby, Rolland. They stared intently at this tiny white-skinned child, with light curly hair atop his head. Then they would shake their heads at the pale, fragile child and cluck their tongues, "Acha-da! Acha-da! Memaloose—memaloose!" which is translated, "Too bad! Too bad! He die! He die!" In fact, Rolland lived well into old age as the last living member of the Denny party.

That night on Alki Point, twenty-four people and their belongings took cover from the pounding rain within the confines of the roofless cabin. Indian mats provided some shelter from the downpour. The Denny party's introductory night on Puget Sound left them wet, cold, and miserable by morning's light. This scene could not have been imagined by Mary Denny when she agreed to move west.

---

1. Denny's granddaughter, Roberta Frye Watt, reports that Chief Seattle himself was present when the Denny party first arrived at Alki. Other sources, including Arthur Denny's book, *Pioneer Days on Puget Sound*, do not mention Chief Seattle's presence on that day.

Mary Ann Boren was born November 25, 1822, in Nashville, Tennessee. In 1843, at the age of twenty, she married a young civil engineer, Arthur Armstrong Denny, and the couple settled in Illinois. Letters from friends who had ventured into the vast Oregon Territory enticed Arthur Denny to move his family west. Arthur had a good position as the county supervisor for Knox County, Illinois. Still, when the word came east of the Oregon Territory's virgin forests, majestic mountains, mild year-round climate, and fertile soil, Arthur Denny got the bug. However, Arthur would not uproot his wife and two young daughters unless Mary Ann would consent to the move. When he finally summoned up the courage to ask her, Mary agreed to go west.

As Mary and Arthur told family of their plans, the size of their traveling party increased. On April 10, 1851, Mary and Arthur, along with many in their extended families, left their home in Cherry Grove, Illinois. The Denny-Boren party included Arthur and Mary Denny with their two little daughters; Arthur's father, John Denny (a widower who had married Mary's mother, Sarah), wife, Sarah, and their baby daughter, Loretta; Arthur's four unmarried brothers, James, Samuel, Wiley, and David; Mary's unmarried sister, Louisa Boren; and Mary's brother, Carson Boren with his wife and child. The group left Illinois in four wagons pulled by teams of horses and accompanied by a few head of cattle and two dogs. These brave pioneers left behind comfortable homes to venture west into the new Northwest territory.

In an attempt to retain some of the refinement of her home in Illinois while on the trail, Mary set the table properly for supper each evening, made up the beds with linen sheets for her family, and changed into nightclothes before retiring. One ferocious storm changed all of this by drenching their linens, bedding, and clothing thoroughly. From then on, the pioneers were so fatigued at the end of a day's travel that they gratefully fell into their bedrolls wearing whatever they had on at the time.

Conventions were often lost on the Oregon Trail. Mary's shoes soon wore out, and she finished the journey wearing buckskin moccasins. One of her daughters lost her only pair of shoes, so the two little girls were forced to share a single pair. They took turns wearing the shoes—one going barefoot, as the other went shod.

The small wagon train endured many hardships and dangers while crossing the barren plains, climbing winding mountain trails, and traveling through hostile Indian territory. The women bravely bore their travails. Mary Ann Denny was pregnant with her third child throughout the journey and not long after leaving Illinois, her two daughters came down with whooping cough. In addition to her trailside duties, Mary now had two children to nurse. The young mother worried about the lack of clean water and fresh fruits and vegetables to feed her little girls. Biscuits cooked over campfires and wild game were their staples.

The Denny party encountered additional hazards along the Oregon Trail: scorching deserts, sudden storms, droughts, rattlesnakes, wild animals, quicksand, stampeding of their own livestock, and an attack by a warring tribe. After four months of such grueling overland travel and a treacherous ride down the Columbia River, the party arrived in Portland on August 22, 1851. Once in Portland, members of the party, including Arthur and Mary, became gravely ill with malaria.

While on the trail, Arthur heard tales of the Puget Sound region from another traveler. When they arrived at their original destination in the Willamette Valley around Portland, they found it to be already inhabited by settlers. The members of the Denny-Boren party decided that John Low and David Denny would go north and explore the region. Along the route they were joined by Lee Terry in Olympia and while there, met Captain Robert Fay, who took them by boat to Puget Sound.

When Low, Denny, and Terry arrived on the shores of Elliott Bay on September 25, 1851, they found an encampment of Indians on the beach, fishing for salmon. By some accounts, Chief Seattle was among those camped there that day. David Denny was reported to have been greeted by the chief and resolved then to learn the language of the native people of the region. Low, Denny, and Terry slept near this camp their second night on Puget Sound. Two of Chief Seattle's men were hired the next day to take the men exploring. After their excursion, the men decided the gently sloping beaches of gravel and sand, surrounded by tall fir timbers on a peninsula the Indians called Smaquamox, was the place to start their settlement. Smaquamox was the southwest point of land, across Elliott Bay from Seattle's present site.

Terry, who was from New York, gave their town the name "New York." The three men envisioned a great city at this site, as great as any on the Atlantic seaboard. Since their vision was still far in the future, the name "Alki" was suggested. This was the Chinook term for "bye-and-bye." The town then was known as "New York Alki." The name Alki remained with the peninsula after the pioneers later moved north along the bay.

Low returned to Portland to bring his family north; he brought with him a letter from David Denny to his brother, Arthur, urging him to come up as well. The two remaining men cleared the land to lay foundations for cabins. Terry and Denny notched the logs, and began to build the walls of the first log home. When Terry went in search of needed tools, David Denny stayed behind to build shelters so the families would be safe from the elements when they arrived.

Local Indians, curious as to the source of the fires, began to paddle by in canoes. Chief Seattle's daughter, Princess Angeline, paddled her canoe to see what the huge fire was all about. They were surprised to see the outline of just one log cabin in the clearing, with such an enormous fire beside it. Princess Angeline and her party were told that the land was being cleared for other settlers, and that a boatload of people was expected, including a baby. Word of the new arrivals quickly spread among the local tribes, and many of them were on shore to greet the boat when it arrived from Portland.

Unfortunately, David Denny, left alone to finish the cabin, cut his leg and became ill before the rest of the Denny party arrived. For this reason, twenty-four wet and miserable men, women, and children found themselves attempting to keep dry in a single, roofless dwelling.

After the rest of the party had arrived, the men's first order of business was to finish construction of their shelter's roof. With a new roof now over their heads, Mrs. Denny and the other women suddenly realized that Christmas was fast approaching. Although they were surrounded by evergreens and could have easily found a perfect Christmas tree, the women decided that they did not have room for a wet tree in the crowded cabin. Improvising, the ladies put a ladder against the wall and draped it with a sheet.

Christmas Eve, while the children slept, Mary and the others scoured their possessions for materials to use in making presents. The women sewed bits of lace, velvet, and ribbon into decorative collars for the little girls. The mittens and scarves the pioneer wives had knit while traveling west were pinned to the sheet so that each child had a present on Christmas morning. The party said prayers and sung hymns in celebration of the Christmas holiday. Christmas dinner consisted of a roasted goose, prepared on Mary's cookstove, and a native Northwest salmon side dish.

The first business enterprise for the new settlement was initiated by the arrival of the ship *Leonesa,* which dropped anchor off of Alki Point several months after the Denny party had settled there. The ship's captain requested the pioneers supply him with logs for market in San Francisco. In exchange for sorely needed cash and provisions, the settlers and their Indian friends began the task of logging. While the captain waited for the logs to be harvested, he entertained the women and children of the Denny party with stories of his high seas adventures. The Denny women, in turn, told tales of their adventures in crossing the plains to Oregon. When the ship had been loaded with lumber, the captain paid the settlers and Indians in provisions he could spare and the balance in cash. The settlers also placed orders for merchandise and provisions with the captain for his return voyage.

More ships followed in search of timber and exchanged compensation with the settlers and their Indian friends. The women looked forward to the conversation and provisions that the captains of the ships would bring. The ladies wondered about current fashions and complained that the clothes they had brought had become shabby and full of holes. Mary and her friends urged the captains to bring fabric with them from San Francisco on their next trip north.

One captain, upon bringing a bolt of fabric with him to Elliott Bay, bet his crew that before the ship was loaded with logs for return to California, all of the women in the settlement would be dressed alike. The captain won his bet, but as more ships ventured north to trade with the new settlement, a variety of dress material and other provisions became available. The ships became busy markets when they dropped anchor in Puget Sound, as the settlers were eager for provisions and news from the outside world.

When the new citizens of the Northwest weren't trading with docked ships, they prepared to construct a cabin for each family. Before long, many local Indian families were moving tepees onto the lots the pioneers had staked out for themselves. The Indians explained that they wanted to be close to the settlers for protection from enemy tribes. The Denny party was soon surrounded by an encampment of up to one thousand Indians who were extremely curious about their neighbors. Cultural differences caused some misunderstandings, as the natives felt free to enter the cabins and help themselves to what they found. On one occasion, an Indian man entered Mary Denny's cabin as she was frying up a large fish. As the man reached into Mary's frying pan, she was forced to defend her dinner by striking the man on the hand with a spoon.

Another custom that caused confusion was that of young Indian men placing their tepee poles so that they obstructed the doorways of the cabins. It was their custom that if a woman touched the poles to move them aside, then she must become the pole owner's wife. Several of the native men had designs on Louisa Boren. Once informed of the plan by a tribal elder who had learned Chinook (the language of trade among early trappers and various Northwest tribes) from the Hudson's Bay men, the settlers quashed the matrimonial plan. Louisa, the Sweetbriar Bride (she brought sweetbriar seeds with her from Illinois), later married David Denny in a ceremony that caused great intrigue among the local Indians.

Confrontations sometimes occurred between natives and settlers. Mary Denny, while outside the family cabin, was confronted by Nisqually Jim, who, without saying a word, leveled his rifle directly at her. He got no response from the brave pioneer woman, as she stood unflinchingly, returning his stare. He then lowered the gun and retreated. Mary's explanation for the incident was to say that, "I suppose he did it to show that he could shoot me if he wanted to."

Certainly, the new settlers to the area and the natives were not always at odds. Mary and the women of the settlement formed valuable friendships with native women who showed them how best to obtain and use the Puget Sound region's bounty of edible goods. Indian women often came to visit bearing gifts of food, such as baskets full of ripe blackberries.

After the first winter in Alki, Chief Seattle reportedly pointed out to the Denny party that the land to the northeast, sheltered within Elliott Bay, would be a more desirable location to build a town. Arthur Denny explored the area, noting the deep water harbor, which he used Mary's clothesline to measure, and nearby trail over the Cascade Mountains. In 1852, the Denny, Boren, and Bell families moved to that site, where downtown Seattle is located today. This new location provided far better shelter from the wind and winter storms.

Within the next year, many more pioneer families moved to the area. In 1853, the territorial legislature selected the name "Duwamps" for the new town, and mail was addressed to "Duwamps via Olympia, Oregon." Later, the town's name was changed to "Seattle," and after a conflict with its namesake was resolved, the name stuck and the town prospered.

In 1855, warring tribes from east of the Cascade Mountains incited violence against the settlers in the Puget Sound region. The year before, Washington territorial governor Issac Stevens had begun organizing treaties with Indian tribes within the territory. In exchange for cash and trinkets, the tribes were moved to reservations and their original lands were opened to settlers. In protest, some eastern Washington Indians from various tribes rebelled against prospectors and pioneers. As the warring tribes moved west, settlers in the Duwamish Valley were killed, along with two young men killed in Seattle during the fighting. Cabins were ransacked, and some burned to the ground. Mary Denny's treasured wedding dress was taken from her cabin, and she often wondered who wore it through the woods after that. The Denny families and Seattle's settlers took refuge in the old blockhouse that stood at the corner of the present-day streets of First Avenue and Cherry Street. The war, known as the Battle of Seattle, was ended rather abruptly by the presence of the warship *Decatur* in Puget Sound. When she saw the ship, Mary Denny's daughter, Louisa Catherine, remembers her mother exclaiming, "Thank God! Our prayers are answered!"

Mary and Arthur Denny became wealthy, well-respected members of Seattle society. In addition to bringing the first non-Indian baby to Seattle from Portland, Mary Ann Denny also gave birth to the second non-Indian baby, and first male child in Seattle. The baby boy, Orion Orvil, was born to them in July of 1853. The Denny's homestead fronted First Avenue and covered several present-day city blocks north to Union Street. Arthur used his civil engineering skills to survey and lay out Seattle's streets. He was instrumental in governing the young city and territory—serving in the first Territorial Legislature[2] and being elected as a delegate to the US Congress. Building the city's economic foundation, Arthur helped to bring a road across the Cascades, shipping to Puget Sound, and the railroad to Seattle. Without Mary's support, Arthur would never have made the journey west.

---

2. The Washington Territory was officially formed from the Oregon Territory in 1853.

Mary Denny was known for her benevolence—giving anonymous gifts to poor families and generously buying presents for children in need. Mary's memories kept alive the pioneer spirit. She told of making the trip between Seattle and Olympia (the nearest real town) in Indian canoes, sailing vessels, steamships, trains, and automobiles, and it was her ambition to make the journey by "flying machine." She recalled Secretary of the Interior William Seward visiting Seattle in 1869 on his way to inspect his purchase of Alaska. Seattle at that time had approximately one thousand residents, but Seward predicted future greatness for the city, calling Puget Sound the "Mediterranean of the Pacific."

Mary Ann Boren Denny passed away on December 30, 1910, at the age of eighty-eight. On the day of her death, boldface headlines in the *Seattle Daily Times* proclaimed, "Woman Founder of City Passes Away." The article stated:

> *[W]ith the demise of Mrs. Denny there passed one of the oldest*
> *human landmarks in the history of the city. She was the first*
> *white woman to land on the shores of Puget Sound and together*
> *with her husband played a prominent part in the upbuilding*
> *of this city. Her death took from Seattle not only one of its most*
> *interesting characters, but one of its noblest women.*

A group of descendants of the Dennys and Seattle's other founding families was formed in 2004 to thank the Duwamish Tribe for helping the settlers survive their first winter on Alki. The "Descendants Committee" organized the "Coming Full Circle" ceremony at the Museum of History and Industry to acknowledge the tribe's contributions. The committee went on to raise funds to help build the Duwamish Longhouse, a tribal cultural center and the only property owned by the tribe since ceding the land under the city of Seattle to the federal government. The group of first families continued their work to raise awareness of the Duwamish Tribe's fight to gain federal recognition. Ironically, the tribe of Chief Seattle has struggled to be recognized by the US government since signing the treaty that gave away their land.

# MOTHER JOSEPH

✧

(1823–1902)

### Chief of the Lady Black Robes

Clouds of dust erupted as the stagecoach wheels ground to a halt on the narrow mountain road. Four masked gunmen greeted the startled passengers with the cold steel barrels of their revolvers. "Get out of the stage, and throw your bags to the side of the road! Now!" barked the gang leader. Pistols were trained on the terrified travelers as they disembarked. A middle-aged nun among the passengers whispered to the others, "Pray, pray!"

Once the luggage had been deposited by the roadside, the people were herded back into the stagecoach as the robbers began to rifle through the baggage. The nun looked up from her praying as if seized by a sudden impulse. She jumped to her feet and called out, "Mister . . . Mister. . . ." Her co-passengers, thinking they might all be killed any minute, urged to her to be quiet.

The sister was undaunted and spoke more authoritatively, addressing the youngest member of the gang with a thick French accent, "Mister . . . my boy." The young thief started, as if no one had ever spoken to him in such a manner. For a moment, he stopped his pilfering.

"My boy, please give me that black bag!"

While the other passengers, cowering in the stage, looked on in horror, the young man asked, "Which?"

"That one—the black one over there."

The boy searched through the pile of luggage, then held one up with a questioning look toward the sister.

"No, no."

He continued to sort through the bags, eventually coming upon a large carpetbag, and held it up for the nun's approval.

"Yes, my man. Give it to me. There is nothing in it you would want."

Stunned by the nun's audacity, the bandit brought her the bag.

"Thank you. God bless you," commended the sister graciously. The boy then returned to looting with his gang, and the nun rejoined her companions in the stage. She winked at the petrified young nun traveling with her and patted her bag. Several hundred dollars the sisters had collected that day from miners had been saved from the bandits.

The two nuns, Sister Mary Augustine and her bold superior, Mother Joseph of the Sacred Heart, continued on this begging tour through the mines of Oregon, Idaho, and Colorado for another sixteen months. The Sisters of Providence sought contributions from generous miners to fund the building of an orphanage in Vancouver, Washington Territory. The stagecoach robbery was but one of many adventures and hardships that Mother Joseph endured while on her begging tours throughout the West to raise money for her charitable endeavors.

She was born Esther Pariseau in French-speaking Saint Elzear, Quebec, on April 16, 1823. Esther was the third of twelve children of Joseph and Francoise Pariseau. During the snowy winter months when he could not farm, Joseph Pariseau worked as a coach maker, a talent he became well known for throughout the region. As a young girl, Esther worked beside her father in his shop, learning to love the tools and wood crafting at which her father was so skilled.

Madame Pariseau, educated by the Sisters of Notre Dame in Montreal, taught her children to read and write. When she was seventeen, Esther entered the Saint Martin de Laval boarding school run by Mademoiselle Elizabeth Bruyere in 1840. Strong and direct, Esther had a dignified presence and a natural capacity for organization and leadership. She loved school and adored her instructor, Mademoiselle Bruyere, but it did not surprise Esther when her teacher announced she was leaving the school to become a nun.

Shortly after her instructor left, Esther felt her own calling. She was inspired to work for the poor and infirm by a visit from Monseigneur Bourget to her family's farm. Father Bourget told of a new order of nuns, the Sisters of Providence, who were serving the poor with wonderful works of charity for the sick and destitute in Montreal. The priest sought money to construct a convent, the Asile of Providence, for the new order of nuns.

Joseph Pariseau brought his young daughter to this newly built convent, the Asile, on December 26, 1843. As Joseph respectfully approached the dignified Mother Superior Gamelin, he stated his purpose and introduced his daughter.

> *Madame, my daughter, Esther, wishes to dedicate herself to the religious life. She is now twenty years of age, and for some time she has prayed with the family for enlightenment as to the decision she is about to make. . . It is a great sacrifice for me to part with Esther, but if you will accept her into your company, she will be a real acquisition. She has had all the education that her mother and I could give her, besides what the Parish school could offer. My daughter can read, write, figure accurately, sew,*

*cook, spin, and do all manner of housework. She can even do*
*carpentering, handle a hammer and saw as well as her father.*
*She can also plan for others, and succeeds in all she undertakes.*
*I assure you, Madame, she will make a good superior some day.*

Esther cried out in embarrassment, "Oh, Father, please! *Pour l'amour de Mon Dieu!* Must you tell all my accomplishments, my talents, and the work my mother taught me?"

"Let your father speak, child," interrupted the mother superior, "What he says interests me very much."

Joseph continued, "Only twenty now, Esther is healthy and strong, has never been ill. She is clever and knows her mind. She is very well determined to give herself to God in the Providence to answer the appeal of Monseigneur Bourget for helpers."

"And you, Monsieur Pariseau, are you willing to make the sacrifice of your daughter?"

"Certainly, Madame, that is why I brought her today. This is her Christmas offering to the Divine Child, the gift of herself."

After arranging Esther's dowry and a hug goodbye, Joseph was gone. Esther now entered into a new life. She took her vows in 1845 and with them the name Sister Joseph in honor of her father.

When, in April of 1852, Father Francis Norbert Blanchet (Archbishop of Oregon City) and his brother, Father Magloire Blanchet (Bishop of Nisqually) visited the Asile, the direction of Sister Joseph's life changed again. Father Magloire Blanchet had spent six years in a remote wilderness called the "Oregon Territory," most recently as the Bishop of the Nisqually Diocese. Father Francis Norbert Blanchet had been in the territory since 1838. All at the Asile were intrigued with tales of the Oregon Territory, including Sister Joseph, who had dreams of going west and working with native people.

The Fathers Blanchet had been well received by the Hudson's Bay Company, the entity that controlled the Oregon/Washington Territory for Great Britain. The Hudson's Bay enclave Fort Vancouver was the dominant settlement in the Washington Territory at that time. Catholics were welcomed by Dr. McLoughlin, the head of the Hudson's Bay Company, and the trappers who were mostly Catholic. The priests had a huge job in covering all of this territory and were in need of sisters to help them. Upon this return to the Asile in 1852, the Bishop of Nisqually spoke of this need for sisters to serve in the new land. Sister Joseph volunteered, but the council in Montreal refused to let her go, as she was much needed there.

In November of 1856, after a previous expedition of nuns had failed, Sister Joseph was allowed to be part of a new expedition. Frightened and confused by the wild country, winter storms, and floods, the first group of nuns had sailed for home, only to end up settling in Chile. The new party of five mostly French-speaking nuns was led by Father Magloire Blanchet. The priest appointed Sister Joseph as their mother superior, a job she reluctantly accepted. She was given the title, "Sister Joseph of the Sacred Heart."

Due to strong anti-Catholic sentiments of the time, the nuns were advised not to wear their habits when traveling, especially not in New York City, where they were to embark upon their journey. Having borrowed and purchased used clothing for their travels, the women, in their unfashionable attire, attracted far more attention than a few habits would have drawn. While riding cabs through the streets of the city they heard cries such as, "Look at the Quaker ladies!" The waiters at the Catholic-owned hotel where they stayed could hardly contain their laughter when the women first entered their dining room. Following dinner, the maître d' tipped the sisters that they had nothing to fear were they to wear their habits in the hotel, on the boats, or even in the city itself. The sisters must have breathed a collective sigh of relief. From this time on, Mother Joseph was never without her habit.

On November 6, 1856, the party sailed from New York to Panama, where they crossed the Isthmus of Panama by train. The sisters were lucky to have a train in 1855, as the expedition of nuns in 1852 had crossed Panama on mules. Even so, this train ride of forty-seven miles took them five hours.

Once at the Pacific Ocean, the nuns boarded a ship to San Francisco. Then, after a few days' rest, they transferred to a steamer bound for Vancouver. This was to be the hardest part of the trip. Winter storms made for turbulent seas. Ferocious waves tossed the ship like a toy boat, and trunks and baggage were thrown about by the violent lurching of the boat. Everything not tied down flew around the cabins as the vessel creaked and groaned. The main mast was blown over. It was impossible for the passengers to leave their bunks, as they could not stand without being heaved through the air. The nuns were chilled to the bone and seasick—so much so that Mother Joseph thought she might die.

When the seas finally calmed, the captain announced they were entering a place known as the "Grave Yard," due to its hidden shoals and shifting sands. Many ships had been lost crossing the sandbars at the mouth of the Columbia River. Landing safely at Astoria, Oregon, they traveled on the Columbia to Vancouver.

Along the Columbia, the nuns saw dense forests with trees so tall they disappeared into the fog. They saw little civilization, but for a few log cabins. At Fort Vancouver, the party was greeted by a small crowd of what seemed to be all young soldiers. Fort Vancouver, once run by the British Hudson's Bay Company, was now an American military post where there were only a few women and no Indians.

At the Vancouver Mission, the women found no housing and a priest who opposed their staying at Vancouver. Vicar General Brouillet thought it more appropriate that the sisters reside in Olympia, the new capital of the Washington Territory. The vicar argued with Bishop Blanchet that the women would be better provided for in Olympia. Here they had only a shed to give them for quarters. Mother Joseph, overhearing the conversation, offered to stay in the shed.

The nuns spent their first night in Father Blanchet's dusty attic, which they first had to clean! Their bedding consisted of dirty old quilts used by settlers and Indians who took refuge at the mission during the Indian Wars. The following months were also spent with Father Blanchet, crowded into his simple board house over which the nuns assumed care. Mother Joseph constructed a dormitory-refectory-community room. Using the skills acquired from her father, she built bunk beds, a table hinged to the wall, and cupboards.

The sisters spent the unfamiliar rainy winter planning for a convent and a school. On Ash Wednesday, February 22, 1857, the nuns moved to their own small, wood-frame house. In it Mother Joseph had constructed an attic dormitory and chapel complete with an altar and tabernacle.

Prior to the school's opening, the nuns received their first little pupil. Three-year-old Emily Lake arrived at the convent with a mother eager to leave her behind with the nuns. The child was fatherless, of mixed race, and appeared dirty and neglected. Mother Joseph was delighted to take the girl; she held the tiny, grimy hand tightly and assured the mother they would care for Emily. The mother showed no emotion, just relief, and made a quick exit, never to be seen again. Mother Joseph adored little Emily, and for the first time in her life, Emily was wanted and protected. She could often be seen following Mother Joseph around in the garden and in the chapel.

Before long, a baby boy named William was placed with the sisters. Mother Joseph pitied the little orphans, often placed with guardians who mistreated them and raised them without morals. Such guardians sometimes traveled hundreds of miles to the mission to abandon these poor children.

Next, an eighty-five-year-old man, feeble and poor, asked to be taken in. There was so little room at the tiny convent that the old man's bed was put next to the stove in the kitchen.

On April 15, 1857, the first Catholic school in the Northwest opened its doors to seven little girls. The school was small and plain, but impeccably clean. A language barrier impeded the teaching of these American pupils as only two of the nuns spoke English. Mother Joseph, who spoke very little English, often wrote to her mother superior in Montreal of the need for more English-speaking nuns. She particularly hoped that the mother superior might send a music teacher west.

Mother Joseph found Vancouver to be a town full of sin. She was aghast at the lifestyles of her fellow French Canadians. In her letters to her mother superior, she noted that Vancouver's population was a mixture of people from everywhere, and that both the Catholics and Protestants had been poorly schooled in religion, although the Protestants welcomed religious instruction for their children.

Initially, the sisters' mission was to create schools and orphanages. Mother Joseph had hoped to work and live among Indian people but, to her dismay, she learned that "these poor unfortunates" had been driven to the mountains by an increasing number of white settlers. She longed to establish Indian schools, but the Indian Wars of the mid-1800s made for turbulent times. Bishop Blanchet, on occasion, brought orphaned Indian children to the convent from east of the Cascade Mountains.

From the time they arrived, the sisters had visited Vancouver's sick and infirm. In the spring of 1858, they were called to take in a young man named John Lloyd who was afflicted with tuberculosis. Though they wanted to help the poor, sick, homeless man, they had no place to house him. The vicar proposed building a hospital. The ladies of the town—Catholic, Protestant, and Jewish alike—assembled to assist in the endeavor.

Mother Joseph had built a tiny clapboard cabin, which she intended to be used for a laundry and bakery. The town's ladies offered to complete the interior and furnish the small building if Mother Joseph would allow them to use it as their hospital. Mother Joseph agreed, and Saint Joseph's, the first hospital in the Northwest, opened in April of 1858, with only four beds. Before long, young John, the waiting patient, was admitted to Saint Joseph's and was soon followed by many sick and injured Northwesterners. Thus, the nuns had created the first official school, orphanage, and hospital in the Northwest.

In the spring of 1861, a mentally ill woman was placed in the sisters' care. They then devoted two small buildings to housing the "mentally deranged." By 1866, there were twenty-five patients cared for under a contract with the Washington Territory. The patients later moved to a more spacious house, but when the territorial government revoked their contract to care for the insane over a dispute resulting from Mother Joseph's insistence on being paid in gold coin rather than "greenbacks," the home to Saint John of God Asylum became the new Saint Joseph's Hospital.

At the urging of priests, the sisters founded Saint Vincent's in Portland, Oregon, in 1875 and Providence Hospital in Seattle in 1877. These were the first of twenty-nine institutions Mother Joseph established during her forty-six years in the Pacific Northwest. Although high mortality rates in the logging camps around Seattle were creating an urgent need for hospitals, the sisters often met with less than enthusiastic welcomes from the citizens they came to serve. At the time, Seattle was a rough, muddy, sparsely populated, Protestant or atheist, logging and seaport town. The people were suspicious of the French-speaking nuns and of Catholics in general. However, the sisters persisted, and the people came to depend upon them.

In 1881, after the hospital had outgrown two buildings, Mother Joseph designed a new elaborate Providence Hospital in Seattle. This stately building was like nothing the city had ever seen, with its gas-lighting system and steam-driven elevators. Mother Joseph conducted the final inspection of Providence Hospital in a sawdust-covered habit with her hammer swinging from her tool belt.

Although Mother Joseph's first preference was to work with a hammer and saw, she recognized the need to raise money to build and run these institutions. Asking for financial support from the community flew in the face of tradition, but the industrious sister would do what was necessary to get the job done and then later pray for forgiveness. Mother Joseph and her nuns traveled on begging tours throughout the West, appealing to miners to fund their charitable works. To Westerners they were known as the "Lady Black Robes," with Mother Joseph designated, by the Indians, as their chief.

Mother Joseph's description of one such begging tour can be found in the annals of the Sisters of Providence for July of 1866. Mother Joseph and Sister Catherine had traveled by boat to Wallula, near Walla Walla, and then by stagecoach to Walla Walla and on to Idaho City where they collected $3,000 from the miners. During their six-week begging tour in Idaho, they met with varied reactions from those they appealed to for alms. In Idaho City, the nuns were received cordially even by "Infidels and Protestants who marveled at [their] daring, and commended [their] perseverance." Often in the mining camps the sisters encountered cold indifference, and even abuse. In her habit, Mother Joseph made perilous descents into the black mines, hundreds of feet below the earth's surface, in order to contact the many miners who worked underground.

Encouraged by good fortune in Idaho, the two nuns set out for Montana. The miners of Montana were not as enthusiastic as those in Idaho, yet the sisters still collected $2,000. Following a visit with four, lonely sisters at the Saint Ignatius Mission forty miles north of Missoula, the women set off for home on horseback. They would no longer have the luxury of traveling by boat or stagecoach. Only on horseback could they pass through the forests that lay between them and the lower Columbia country. The sisters at Saint Ignatius loaned them saddles and riding habits—the Jesuit Fathers provided the horses.

"In the last days of September our little caravan set out. It was composed of Father Louis Saint-Onge, an Indian named Sapiel from the mission, Father Joseph Giorda, S.J., who went with us as far as Missoula, Sister Catherine and myself." With them were two pack horses with provisions and a tent. They traveled through dark forests and steep, precipitous mountains on narrow Indian trails. Except for some lone miners, the party met no one.

Every evening they looked for a clearing, with water and grass for the animals, in which to make camp. Father Saint-Onge hunted for game, Sapiel cared for the horses and collected firewood, and the sisters took charge of cooking crêpes and fresh meat. They ate, conversed, sang hymns, and prayed before the light of the fire. In preparation for bed, they pitched their tent, wrapped themselves in blankets, and with saddles for pillows, retired for the night.

One day while riding on steep Rocky Mountain trails, a fierce storm broke upon them. Low, dark clouds hung overhead menacingly. When the clouds broke, the gradually increasing rainstorm gave way to a relentless downpour, thunder, and lightning. Traveling in the deep mud was challenging, as was building a fire in the driving rain. By the time camp was set up, all were soaked to the skin. With great difficulty, Sapiel was able to set a small fire inside the tent. They lay down that night in the mud, as near to the fire as possible. Several nights later, an enormous tree fell just three feet from the tent in which the two nuns were sleeping.

Traveling through dense forests over an animal trail, they would often lose sight of each other on the winding paths. On the ninth day of travel, the party, overcome with fatigue, camped in a ravine between two mountain ranges. They were jolted awake by a terrifying howl that, according to Mother Joseph's account, "froze the blood in our veins." Sapiel quickly cut wood and circled the camp with fire, since wolves do not ordinarily cross a line of fire. Soon the woods were full of the horrible howls. The travelers knew wolves, which hunt in packs, were now all around them. The horses, tethered inside the ring of fire, were lathered to a frenzy. Trees surrounding the area had been dried by a prior fire, and soon the flames, meant to protect the party, were a serious threat to their safety. Branches and brush around them began to burn, embers cracked and popped menacingly, and great limbs burned and crashed to the ground. The whole night was spent battling burning cinders and blinding smoke, while surrounded by an increasing number of howling wolves. Some provisions were destroyed, the tent had caught fire several times, and the saddles were singed. The dawn's light chased away the wolves, ending a night of trauma and prayer. Exhausted, they fell to the ground with fatigue.

Suddenly, a new sound was heard, that of horses tramping up the trail. Before they could react, a party of Indian warriors with painted faces surrounded the camp. The Indian braves noticed the crosses around their necks and recognized Father Saint-Onge. They immediately offered hand signs of friendship and respect. The Indian people were drawn to Catholicism, the long, dark robes of the priests and nuns, and the symbols of the faith. They trusted the priests far more than the rugged frontiersmen they met in the territory, and the priests often acted as envoys between the tribes and the settlers. The party shared a meal with the Indians, but "cringed before the scalping knives" that hung at their sides.

Another evening while still in the Coeur d'Alene forests of Idaho, Father Saint-Onge spotted tracks while raising the tent. Sapiel identified the tracks as those of a grizzly bear, known to his people as the most dangerous creature in the forest. The only arms the men had against the massive beast were a six-shooter and an ax. The two did not mention the danger to the others, and the night passed without incident.

Early the next morning, Sapiel went to check on the horses. He was horrified to find an enormous grizzly bear attacking one of the horses. The bear, spying Sapiel, jumped the log corral and made straight for him. Sapiel took off running with the grizzly in close pursuit. The bear's claws swiped at the man several times, and he could hear teeth grinding near his head. Sapiel somehow managed to elude the creature's great claws. Suddenly, the bear became distracted by the sound of tinkling bells. A pack train of mules came into sight and the cries of the Mexicans leading the mules, and those of Father Saint-Onge, scared the grizzly off.

"One more adventure before the curtain falls on this unforgettable tour of the Rocky Mountains," Mother Joseph wrote in her chronicles. On a quiet night on the trail, Father Saint-Onge, sleeping under the stars, was awakened by a sensation of something cold gliding up his trouser leg. He knew it was a rattlesnake. With extreme willpower he lay perfectly still so that the reptile would go to sleep near the warmth of his body. After several minutes, which must have seemed an eternity, Father leapt to his feet so the serpent slid away from him. The snake was seen slinking away leaving the poor priest shaken, but unscathed.

The weary travelers arrived back in Vancouver on October 16, 1866, exhausted by the long horseback journey fraught with dangers. The sisters were grateful for the financial success of their tour and for their safe return home.

Many years of contention between the United States and the British Hudson's Bay Company put the sisters' property claim in Vancouver in jeopardy. In 1869, the American government served the mission with an eviction notice, which was later rescinded under protest by the Bishop.

Mother Joseph saw that it was time to consolidate all of their scattered little buildings. Her dream was to construct a magnificent brick convent. With the help of the Bishop's nephew, Mother Joseph negotiated with local businesses for building materials. The nun had developed a reputation as a force with which to be reckoned, even among seasoned salesmen. She could not be pushed around by businessmen who sometimes saw the nuns' works as encroachment and their free labor as unfair competition. It was unusual at the time to find a woman with such will and determination. Her blunt, direct manner sometimes made her seem difficult, even among the sisters.

Mother Joseph's strong work ethic and love of construction made her a taskmaster. She was known to rip apart faulty construction with her own hands, only to rebuild the structures herself. Witnesses recall the black-habited Mother Joseph emerging from beneath a building after checking its foundation, or balancing on a high beam to test its strength. Stories grew of her skill as a carver and woodworker. Many of the convent's statues were carved by Mother Joseph herself.

In 1874, Mother Joseph moved the sisters, the boarders, and the orphans into the House of Providence on Tenth and Reserve Streets in Vancouver. The people of the Pacific Coast cities were amazed at the enormity of the convent, unlike any structure then found in Washington or Oregon. The sisters now had their grand convent; however, they also were in debt $20,000. Once again Mother Joseph set out on a begging tour, this time to the Frasier River country of Canada, raising $10,000, in just three weeks.

For nearly forty-seven years, Mother Joseph of the Sacred Heart continued her work throughout the Northwest. She built schools for Indian children at Tulalip, Colville, and Coeur d'Alene, along with dozens of hospitals and orphanages. Even at age seventy-seven, she answered a call to build an orphanage in British Columbia.

In her last years, Mother Joseph was nearly blinded by a brain tumor and mostly confined to the convent. She died January 19, 1902, of her condition. Her dying words were to remind the sisters to always attend to the care of the poor without regret.

In 1980, the state of Washington named Mother Joseph its most distinguished citizen. A bronze statue of the nun, hammer by her side, was constructed by Felix de Weldon for the Statuary Hall of the House of Representatives in Washington, DC Mother Joseph was only the fifth woman, first Catholic nun, and second Washingtonian (joining Dr. Marcus Whitman) to be so honored. Today, the West Coast Lumberman's Association acknowledges Mother Joseph as the first (non-Indian) Northwestern artist to work in the medium of wood. The American Institute of Architects named Mother Joseph the Pacific Northwest's first architect in 1953, fifty-one years after her death. In addition to her wonderful work on behalf of the poor, building schools, hospitals, and orphanages, she designed architecture far ahead of anything in the West at the time.

# THEA CHRISTIANSEN FOSS

༺❈༻

(1857–1927)

## The Original "Tugboat Annie"

"Creak, splash—creak, splash," the rhythmic sound of oars grinding against their locks, and then dipping into the waters of the sound caught her attention. The young woman, gutting a fish on the porch of her rough-hewn houseboat, looked up to see a lone rower approaching. Thea had just purchased a salmon from an Indian fisherman on Tacoma's waterfront and was busily at work preparing it for the evening meal. Usually her husband, Andrew, provided fish for the family, but he was across Puget Sound on a carpentry job.

"Hello there," the man called out as he drew near the floating home. "This boat's for sale, would you be interested?"

"How much?" asked the woman in her thick Norwegian accent.

"Ten dollars," came the reply.

Thea considered the offer carefully. Ten dollars was a lot of money to the Foss family. Money was scarce, but she was so tired of hauling heavy buckets of water on foot from the creek that emptied into the bay a quarter mile from her home. "I'll give you five dollars," countered the astute Thea Foss.

"Okay," the rower responded to her amazement, "I'm leaving town anyway and have no further use for the boat."

The rustic appearance of the houseboat must have tipped the seller that money was a rare commodity in the Foss household, and perhaps he took pity on Thea in accepting her offer.

When Andrew Foss returned home two months later, he proudly pulled out his earnings, pouring thirty-two dollars' worth of gold and silver coins onto the kitchen table. Without a word, Thea extracted the contents of her cookie jar, forty dollars. Then, to her dumbfounded husband she remarked in Norwegian, "I sell and rent rowboats. No matter what time of the day or night people come for them, I am always ready!"

That hot summer night in 1889, Thea's purchase of the rowboat gave birth to the Foss Maritime Company, the largest towing, barging, and marine transportation services operation in the Northwest and one of the largest in the United States. The company motto, coined by Thea Christiansen Foss, is "Always Ready!"

With a remarkably intuitive business sense, Thea knew that there would be a demand for rowboats. She adorned her five-dollar purchase with green and white paint, colors that would become well known in Northwest waters, and sold the boat for a profit. Next, she bought two more boats that she repainted and resold, allowing her to buy four boats. Soon Thea had her own fleet of rowboats, which she rented out to fishermen and duck hunters for 25 to 50 cents a day. Thea Foss's head for business, coupled with her husband's shipbuilding and maritime skills, soon built the Fosses a fleet of two hundred rowboats. Henry Foss, the couple's youngest son, described his parents in a 1966 interview: "Mother was absolutely honest but shrewd. Father was not strong physically, but he was always ready to help anyone out—day or night."

Thea Christiansen was born on June 8, 1857, in Eidsberg, Norway. While visiting her sister, Julia, and brother-in-law, Theodore, in Christiana (now Oslo), Thea met Andrew Olesen, the seafaring brother of Theodore, whose ship happened to be in port. Andrew was attracted to the proud young woman, with her golden braids coiled neatly upon her head. The young mariner could not read or write, but his strong goals and idealistic visions appealed to Thea.

Andrew's dream had always been to sail across the Atlantic Ocean. He and Thea made plans for a future home in the promised land of America. Andrew shipped out, working as a forecastle hand on a vessel bound for Quebec. From Canada, Andrew went south to Saint Paul, Minnesota, drawn by its large Norwegian community. Instead of working with his beloved boats, Andrew found a job building houses and saved every penny to send for his fiancée.

Finally, when he had saved enough for her passage, Andrew sent money to Thea. To his surprise, his brother, Iver, showed up in St. Paul instead. Andrew set to work earning more money to send for his intended. When he had again sent enough money for Thea's trip to America, he was greeted by his sister, Kristina. Frustrated, Andrew now intended to go to Norway and fetch Thea himself! Before he could do this, Thea arrived in Minnesota of her own volition. Determined to pay her own passage to America, she had given the money Andrew sent her to his family members. Thea had worked as an indentured servant to a wealthy family until she had earned enough for her way over. Andrew and Thea were married in St. Paul, Minnesota, in 1882.

St. Paul's Norwegian community already had so many Olesens that Andrew and Thea changed their last name to Olesen-Fossen, the latter meaning waterfall. As the family became more Americanized they shortened their surname to Foss.

During the eight years the Fosses lived in Minnesota, three children were added to the family: Arthur in 1885, Wedell in 1887, and Lillian in 1889. A daughter, Lilly Marie, was also born in Minnesota, but died at age four.

Andrew's love for the sea and strong dislike of cold winters would lead the family west to Tacoma, Washington, on the waters of Commencement Bay in Puget Sound. Leaving his young family, Andrew ventured into the Northwest in 1888. He worked his way west as a carpenter for the Northern Pacific Railroad and, once in Tacoma, became employed as a deck hand for the Tacoma Tugboat Company. In his spare time, Andrew combed beaches for cedar logs with which to build a floating house. Beached logs and salvaged timber were crafted into a simple, one-room floathouse for his family. When finished, the house contained a secondhand stove, beds, a table, and some crude furniture.

After being separated for eight months, Thea and the children traveled aboard an immigrant train to meet Andrew in Tacoma. The end of each railcar held a stove, and the air was thick with greasy smoke from cooking. The train was noisy, sooty, and packed full of immigrant families. Thea arrived in Tacoma in the spring of 1889, near exhaustion from caring for three children—all under the age of five (including one newborn baby)—aboard the crowded, grimy train.

With pride, Andrew brought his young family directly from the train station to their new floating home. A rough-slabbed, wooden structure with a tarpaper roof and stark furnishings floated before her, but seeing her husband's pride, Thea could show no disappointment. She viewed the situation as temporary and accepted her lot even though she would have to haul fresh water to the houseboat every day. Thea could not have imagined then that the family would live on Tacoma's waterfront for nearly a quarter of a century. That first day, both of her young boys added to her apprehension by falling into the bay. Though she harbored a fear of the water, which she never overcame, Andrew's enthusiasm and the natural beauty of their Puget Sound surroundings soon won over Thea Foss.

Once settled into her new home, the young wife's hands were full with housekeeping, washing, and caring for three small children aboard a floating home with no running water. Within three weeks of the family's arrival, Thea became very sick, and for three months she battled typhoid-pneumonia. Andrew begged a local doctor to come to the houseboat and treat his deathly ill wife. The kind doctor paid the houseboat call and provided Thea with medicine at no cost. Although the Fosses could not pay the doctor's fee then, they never forgot the kindness. In more prosperous years, they made substantial donations to Tacoma hospitals. As Thea recovered, Andrew's health began to falter, a fact he blamed on the cold Minnesota winters he had endured.

With Thea expecting a fourth child and Andrew beginning employment anew at a shipyard, the family was forced to move. The city of Tacoma was diverting the Puyallup River to promote industrial development. The Fosses moved their tiny wooden houseboat to "Hallelujah Harbor," named for the

Salvation Army shacks dotting the shoreline. Water would still have to be hauled into their home.

In search of more income for his family, Andrew took a construction job on the Kitsap Peninsula across Puget Sound. He would have to be away from his family for two months. It was during this time that Thea launched the family business with the purchase of the five-dollar rowboat. Thea's timing was impeccable; sport boating was extremely popular, thus the business flourished. A sign bearing the slogan "Always Ready," was posted on the roof of the floathouse. The floating home bustled with activity and thrived as a business. This enabled Andrew to enjoy his chosen vocation, boat building, to add to their fleet.

With the birth of another son, Henry, in 1891, the family now counted six members and had outgrown their tiny floathouse. Andrew and his two oldest sons built a larger houseboat in another saltwater location. This house had a modern amenity—running water! The Foss floating home became a center for Norwegian social activities, as well as for the Foss boating business. Thea was hospitable by nature and loved to entertain the local Norwegian community at "kaffe slaberas" (coffee klatches) in her spacious new home.

Although Thea loved her rowboat rental business, Andrew felt driven to create more. Using the old houseboat as a workshop, he and his brothers salvaged parts from a wrecked steamboat and built a fifty-foot steamer. They lost money on the unsuccessful venture but thought they were on to something.

The young Foss boys spent the majority of their time on the beach. Thea, still deathly afraid of the water, at first tried to keep them away from it. Later, she gave in and let them follow the lure of the sea. Soon the children were venturing forth on the sound by boat. The boys helped build the boats, bailed and cleaned the returned rentals, gave sailing lessons, and collected spilled bait from the rental boats and resold it to fishermen. Thea's enterprising sons even developed their own business by beginning a rescue operation with their powerboat. Using a telescope, they searched for boaters in distress. They did not charge to rescue their own customers, but if the boaters had not rented from the Fosses, they were charged 25 cents.

One day, it dawned on Thea that her boys could run an efficient ship-to-shore delivery service. She purchased a two-horsepower launch, reasoning that the ships anchored in the sound would be better served by the small powerboat than by the rowboats presently bringing them supplies. This acquisition became the first of many powerboats owned by the "Foss Launch Company." Andrew set to work building more boats, and before long they had Foss launches serving every ship in the harbor.

The Foss Launch Company did so well that they were able to buy a fleet of launches from a competitor and ultimately take on the bulk of the harbor service and ship docking on Puget Sound. The Fosses continued to service the anchored ships in Puget Sound, bringing supplies, fresh food, and a water-taxi service to the crews. The boys' tactic was to meet incoming ships with a box of Washington apples and pitch their company's services.

Thea's boys would go on to lifelong careers in boating with the family business. Her daughters would not live to see the family business at its peak. Thea's second to last child, Lela, was stillborn, and her four-year-old, Lilly Marie, had died in Minnesota. In 1914, Thea lost her lovely twenty-five-year-old daughter, Lillian, to tuberculosis. Always accepting, Thea endured Lillian's passing but never recovered fully from the loss. She poured her energy even more fervently into the Foss family business.

Many of Thea's relatives arrived from Norway and became involved in the family business. By the early 1900s, the company had outgrown its headquarters and staff of family members. The Fosses began hiring nonrelated, Scandinavian immigrants, plentiful in the Northwest at the time. Andrew built a dormitory for the growing crew. Thea cooked for twenty-five to thirty men, who dined with the family. She also served as counselor and surrogate mother to the crews. Andrew and Thea insisted the men study for their citizenship tests and become US citizens. The crews rewarded them with loyalty, calling them "Mother and Father Foss."

The Foss general store, run by Thea, supplied ships with food and gear. She stocked the store with fresh eggs, meat, and milk from her own animals, which were kept on an adjacent sandlot. The waterfront store was a popular gathering place among sailors, crews, and dock workers. People were drawn to Thea in spite of her quiet nature. A natural diplomat, this was a woman who had the ability to converse with all of those who frequented the waterfront. These abilities earned her the respect of sea captains, prominent businessmen, dignitaries, and domestic and foreign crews. She ran the boarding house, store, and company office and still had time for her beloved Norwegian Church, as well as for works of charity. She often provided comfort and shelter to young Norwegian immigrant girls. Her philosophy is evident in the following entry of January 19, 1907, from her diary:

> *The law imprinted in all men's hearts is to love one another. I will look on the whole world as my Country and all men as my brothers. We are made for cooperation and to act against one another is to act contrary to nature. Say not I will love the wise and hate the unwise, you should love all mankind. Let us not love in word and in tongue, but in deed and in truth.*

Thea Foss had endless stamina with which to perform the multitude of tasks and businesses she undertook. She also had the ability to organize those around her. Each member of the family had multiple chores—even the cow,

Annie, had extra duties. Thea kept forty chickens, several pigs, and the cow (which was fed pancakes through the kitchen window). In addition to providing milk, Annie guided boats in dense Pacific fog. When a captain had trouble navigating Puget Sound waters in the heavy fog, he would blow his horn until Annie met the ship at the end of the Fosses' pier with a resounding "Moooo!" She was then paid by the arriving sea captains who, once safely docked, rewarded her with bovine treats.

The turn of the century brought major changes to the Foss Launch Company. Bicycles became the rage, and pleasure rowing was suddenly out of fashion. Automobiles soon replaced travel by rowing and sailing on Puget Sound, and ships became self-propelled, relegating the Foss rowboats and launches to little use.

The Fosses saw the hills all around the Northwest booming with logging activities. These logs were rafted and towed to local mills around the sound. Seizing another opportunity, the Fosses had their launches begin towing rafts of logs, but they lacked the power to do so efficiently. They decided to invest in more powerful engines for their boats. Key to their success was the fact that Thea and Andrew never borrowed for these upgrades. They saved during prosperous times, for they knew their business was cyclical.

The improved boats were better, but Andrew set out to design a boat just for log towing. Andrew designed his tugs by hand carving prototypes. He fashioned a "teardrop"-shaped boat with a more balanced rudder. His concepts became industry standards, though he never patented any of his inventions, saying they were for the "common good." The tug business grew, along with charter hauling of landfill and war cargo during World War I.

In August of 1919, at the close of the war, Thea's sons sponsored a water sports carnival in her honor. August was chosen as the anniversary of her first rowboat purchase and the founding of Foss Launch and Tug Company. The carnival was held at the family's houseboat along Tacoma's waterfront and was attended by hundreds of spectators.

As Thea and Andrew aged, the boys took command of the company. Together, the family had decided that Arthur would leave school in the eighth grade to assist with the growing family business. They later decided that Wedell should attend law school, and Henry business college. Henry was eventually elected to office as a Washington state senator. Throughout her life, Thea worked tirelessly on behalf of the Foss company. In her later years, she continued to help with the business when she could, telling her children, "Ya, jeg har so mange ting ot gjore." ("Yes, I have so many things to do yet.") Her interest in Foss Launch and Tug never waned. By now, Andrew had built her a grand house on dry land, uptown where Tacoma's "better people" lived. Unfortunately, the new home was out of sight of the family's fleet of tugs and launches, but her boys always kept her up to date on the company. Thea Christiansen Foss passed away on June 7, 1927, one day before her seventieth birthday.

Thea's funeral procession was the largest ever seen in Tacoma. The Foss fleet flew their green and white flags at half-mast as they cruised up Tacoma's waterway. On September 15, 1989, sixty-two years after her death, the Tacoma City Waterway was renamed the Thea Foss Waterway in her honor.

With her son Wedell's assistance, Seattle native Norman Reilly Raine penned a series based on the life of Thea Foss for the *Saturday Evening Post*. Wedell provided the storyline for the first article, published in 1931. The series ran for some time until Raine began to write scripts for the movie industry. Inspired by Thea's life, Raine wrote the script for the film *Tugboat Annie*. The movie, starring Maureen O'Sullivan, Marie Dressler, and Wallace Beery, premiered in 1933. It was shot on Seattle's Lake Union, Elliott Bay, and throughout the Strait of Juan de Fuca. Although pleased by the tribute, Wedell was quick to point out that the raucous Irish character Tugboat Annie was nothing like his quiet, pious, Norwegian mother with her morbid fear of the water.

# Bibliography

## Alaska Women

### Nellie Neal Lawing

Allen, Lois Hudson. "Woman Unafraid." *Alaska Sportsman.* July 1939.
*Anchorage Times.* "Famed Alaska Nellie is Dead at Age of 84." May 11, 1956.
Capra, Douglas. Correspondence with author, January, February 2005.
———. Interview with author, December 2004.
———. *Into Alaska a Woman Came: A Play Based on the Life of Alaska Nellie.* Unpublished manuscript, 2003. First produced in Seward, Alaska, March 2003.
———. "Legend of Alaska Nellie as Big as the State Itself." Seward, Alaska: Seward Visitor Guide, 1996.
Jones, Grace C. "Christmas at Alaska Nellie's." *Alaska Sportsman.* December 1963.
Lawing, Nellie Neal. *Alaska Nellie.* Seattle: Chieftain Press. Seattle Printing and Publishing Co., 1940.
Olthius, Diane. Interview with author, September 7, 2004.
———. *Lawing: Alaska Nellie's Stabilization Plan.* Kenai Mountains–Turnagain Arm Corridor Communications Association: Alaska Nellie's Historical Society, 2003.
Pierce, Carrie Ida. "I Remember Nellie." *Alaska Sportsman.* January 1957.
Rhodes, Herb. "Alaska Nellie: A Florence Nightingale of the North." *Great Lander Shopping News.* August 27, 1975.

### Etta Eugenie Schureman Jones

Breu, Mary. Interview with author, May 2, 2011.
———. *Last Letters from Attu.* Portland, Oregon: Alaska Northwest Books, 2009.
———. "Pioneer and Prisoner: Etta Jones in Alaska." *Alaska History Journal.* Vol. 18, Nos. 1& 2, Spring/Fall 2003.
Jones, Etta. Personal correspondence to family members ("Dear Everybody"). Kipnuk, Alaska. August 30, 1932; January 25, May 7, June 4, and August 23, 1933; April 13, 1935.
———. Personal correspondence to Elinor Smith. Attu, Alaska. April 9, 1942.
———. Personal correspondence to Elinor Smith. Manila. September 6, 1945.

*Florence Barrett Willoughby*

Ferrell, Nancy Warren. *Barrett Willoughby: Alaska's Forgotten Lady*. Anchorage: University of Alaska Press, 1994.

Rockwell Kent papers (circa 1840–1993, bulk 1935–1961). Archives of American Art, Smithsonian Institution.

Willoughby, Barrett. *Alaskans All*. Freeport, New York: Books for Libraries Press, 1971.

———. *Alaska Holiday*. Boston: Little, Brown and Company, 1944.

———. *Gentlemen Afraid*. New York, London: G. P. Putnam's Sons, The Knickerbocker Press, 1928.

———. *River House*. New York: Triangle Books, 1942.

———. *Sitka: Portal to Romance*. Boston and New York: Houghton Mifflin Company, 1930.

———. *Spawn of the North*. New York: Grosset & Dunlap, 1932.

———. *Where the Sun Swings North*. New York and London: Putnam's; New York: A. L. Burt Co., 1922.

———. Letter to Wilma Lee Ury. December 1, 1935, Seward Community Library, Barrett Willoughby File.


*Anfesia Shapsnikoff*

Anfesia Shapsnikoff Collection. Box 1, Folders 15, 17, 18. Archives, Alaska and Polar Regions Department, Rasmuson Library, University of Alaska Fairbanks.

Baranov Museum website. "Attu Grass Basket Weaving with Hazel Jones." www.baranov.us/events.html.

Hudson, Ray. *Moments Rightly Placed: An Aleutian Memoir*. Kenmore, Washington: Epicenter Press, 1998.

———. Correspondence with author, July 25, 2005.

Letters from Anfesia Shapsnikoff, 1967. Margaret Hafemeister Collection, Archives and Manuscript Department, Consortium Library, University of Alaska Anchorage.

Neseth, Eunice. Transcript, Oral History Interview at interviewer's home, Kodiak, Alaska, May 21, 1971. Anfesia Shapsnikoff Collection, Archives and Manuscript Department, Consortium Library, University of Alaska Anchorage.

Oleksa, Rev. Michael. *Six Alaskan Native Women Leaders: Pre-Statehood*. Alaska State Department of Education, January 1991.

*Unugulux Tunusangin, Oldtime Stories*. Unalaska City School District, Unalaska, Alaska.

## Arizona Women

### Lozen

Aleshire, Peter. *Warrior Woman: The Story of Lozen, Apache Warrior and Sha-man.* New York: St. Martin's Press, 2001.

Ball, Eve. *In the Days of Victorio.* Tucson: University of Arizona Press, 1970.

Stockel, H. Henrietta. *Women of the Apache Nation: Voices of Truth.* Reno and Las Vegas: University of Nevada Press, 1991.

———. *Chiricahua Apache Women and Children: Safekeepers of the Heritage.* College Station: Texas A&M University Press, 2000.

———. Letter to author. August 6, 2002.

Sweeney, Edwin R. *From Cochise to Geronimo: The Chiricahua Apaches 1874–1886.* Norman: University of Oklahoma Press, 2010.

Thrapp, Dan L. *The Conquest of Apacheria.* Norman: University of Oklahoma Press, 1967.

———. *Victorio and the Mimbres Apaches.* Norman: University of Oklahoma Press, 1974.


### Sister Mary Fidelia McMahon

Ames, C.S.J., Sister Aloysia. *The St. Mary's I Knew.* Tucson: St. Mary's Hospital of Tucson, Inc., 1970.

Byrne, Leo G. and Sister Alberta Cammack C.S.J. *Heritage: The Story of St. Mary's Hospital, 1880–1980.* Tucson: St. Mary's Hospital and Health Center, 1981.

McMahon, Sister Thomas Marie, C.S.J., B.A. *The Sisters of St. Joseph of Caro-ndelet: Arizona's Pioneer Religious Congregation, 1870–1890.* Thesis presented to the Faculty of Graduate School of St. Louis University in Partial Fulfillment of the Requirements for the Degree of Master of Arts, OR, 1952. Accessed June 2, 2002, from www.library.arizona.edu/carondelet/thesis/thesis_title.html.

Quebbeman, Frances E. *Medicine in Territorial Arizona.* Tucson: Arizona Historical Foundation, 1966.


### Mary-Russell Ferrell Colton

Colton, Mary-Russell F. *Art for the Schools of the Southwest: An Outline for the Public and Indian Schools.* Museum of Northern Arizona Bulletin 6. Flagstaff: Museum of Northern Arizona, 1934.

Mangum, Richard K. and Sherry G. *One Woman's West: The Life of Mary-Russell Ferrell Colton.* Flagstaff, Arizona: Museum of Northern Arizona, Northland Publishing, 1997.

Miller, Jimmy H. *The Life of Harold Sellers Colton: A Philadelphia Brahmin in Flagstaff.* Tsaile, Arizona: Navajo Community College Press, 1991.

### Carmen Lee Ban

Ban, Edward, personal communication. August 20, 2002.

Editorial. *Arizona Bulletin,* July 6, 1906, 3.

Fong, Lawrence Michael. "Sojourners and Settlers: The Chinese Experience in Arizona." *Journal of Arizona History,* vol. 21, no. 3, Autumn 1980, 227–256.

Hatch, Heather (compiler). "The Chinese in the Southwest: A Photographic Record." *Journal of Arizona History,* vol. 21, no. 3, Autumn 1980, 257–274.

Hu-Dehart, Evelyn. "Immigrants to a Developing Society: The Chinese in Northern Mexico, 1875–1932." *Journal of Arizona History,* vol. 21, no. 3, Autumn 1980, 275–312.

Keane, Melissa, A.E. Rogge, Bradford Luckingham. *The Chinese in Arizona: 1870–1950 (A Component of the Arizona Historic Preservation Plan).* Phoenix: Arizona Historic Preservation Office, 1992.

*The Promise of Gold Mountain: Tucson's Chinese Heritage.* Accessed July 15, 2002, from www.library.arizona.edu/Images/chamer/railroad_041801.html.

Tom, Mike L. Personal communication. August 2002.

## California Women

### Mary Ellen Pleasant

Bennet Jr., Lerone. "The Mystery of Mary Ellen Pleasant." *Ebony.* April and May 1979.

Longstreet, Stephen. *The Wilder Shore: A History of the Gala Days of San Francisco.* Garden City, NY: Doubleday, 1968.

Ravage, John W. *Black Pioneers: Images of the Black Experience on the North American Frontier.* Salt Lake City: University of Utah Press, 1997.

### Toby Riddle

Bauer, Helen. *California Indian Days.* Garden City, NY: Doubleday, 1968.

Dillon, Richard. *Burnt-Out Fires: California's Modoc Indian War.* Englewood Cliffs, NJ: Prentice Hall, 1973.

Faulk, Odie B., and Laura E. Faulk. *The Modoc.* New York: Chelsea House Publishers, 1988.

Rawls, James J. *Indians of California: The Changing Image.* Norman, OK: University of Oklahoma Press, 1984

## Mary Austin

Austin, Mary. *Earth Horizon.* Albuquerque: University of New Mexico Press, 1991.

———. *The Land of Little Rain.* Boston and New York: Houghton Mifflin, 1903.

Church, Peggy Pond. *Wind's Trail: The Early Life of Mary Austin.* Santa Fe: The Museum of New Mexico Press, 1990.

Fink, Augusta. *I-Mary: A Biography of Mary Austin.* Tucson: University of Arizona Press, 1983.

Stineman, Esther Lanigan. *Mary Austin: Song of a Maverick.* New Haven: Yale University Press, 1989.

## Tye Leung Schulze

Goldberg, George. *East Meets West: The Story of the Chinese and Japanese in California.* New York: Harcourt, Brace, Jovanovich, 1970.

Weatherford, Doris. *Foreign and Female: Immigrant Women in America, 1840-1930.* New York: Facts on File, Inc., 1995.

Yung, Judy. *Unbound Feet: A Social History of Chinese Women in San Francisco.* Berkeley: University of California Press, 1995.

# Colorado Women

## "Aunt Clara" Brown

"Aunt Clara Brown Dead." *Denver Tribune Republican,* October 27, 1885, 8.

Bruyn, Kathleen. *Aunt Clara Brown: Story of a Black Pioneer.* Boulder, CO: Pruett Publishing, 1970.

Davidson, Levette J. "Colorado's Hall of Fame." *Colorado Magazine,* vol. 27, January 1950, 23–25.

Editorial. *Denver Republican,* March 17, 1890, 7.

Harvey, James R. "Negroes in Colorado." *Colorado Magazine,* vol. 26, 165–73.

Katz, William Loren. *Black Women of the Old West.* New York: Atheneum Books for Young Readers, 1995.

"Old Aunt Clara Brown, An Aged Colored Woman Who Crossed the Plains in 1859." *Denver Tribune Republican,* June 26, 1885, 2.

Painter, Nell Irvin. *Exodusters: Black Migration to Kansas after the Reconstruction.* New York: Alfred A. Knopf, 1977.

"Pioneers Who Have Gone." *Denver Tribune Republican,* October 28, 1885, 8.

Ravage, John W. *Black Pioneers: Images of the Black Experience on the North American Frontier.* Salt Lake City: University of Utah Press, 1997.

Rice, Arnold S., and John A. Krout. *United States History from 1865.* New York: HarperCollins, 1991.


### Florence Sabin

Bluemel, Elinor. *Florence Sabin, Colorado Woman of the Century.* Boulder: University of Colorado Press, 1959.

Flanagan, Mike. *Out West.* New York: Harry N. Abrams, 1987, 91–93.

"Florence Rena Sabin." *Current Biography.* New York: H. W. Wilson, 1945, 527–29.

"Florence Sabin 1871–1953." National Women's Hall of Fame, Seneca Falls, NY, www.greatwomen.org/sabin.htm.

Parkhurst, Genevieve. "Dr. Sabin, Scientist." *Pictorial Review,* January 1930, 2, 70–71.

Phelan, Mary Kay. *Probing the Unknown: The Story of Dr. Florence Sabin.* New York: Thomas Y. Crowell, 1969.

Stoddard, Hope. *Famous American Women.* New York: Thomas Y. Crowell, 1970.

Yost, Edna. *American Women of Science.* Philadelphia and New York: Frederick A. Stokes, 1943.


### Josephine Roche

Armstrong, Gerald R. "Miss Josephine Roche, President, The Rocky Mountain Fuel Company, 1927–1951." Report to Rocky Mountain Fuel Company shareholders, April 14, 1975.

Barrett, Marjorie. "Josephine Roche: She Fuels an Historic Era of Area History." *Rocky Mountain News,* April 20, 1975, 15.

Chernow, Ron. *Titan: The Life of John D. Rockefeller, Sr.* New York: Random House, 1998.

Fong, Tillie. "Capitalist and Humanitarian." From Colorado Millennium 2000 website. Sponsored by *Rocky Mountain News,* NEWS 4, and Colorado Historical Society. (Website no longer active.)

———. "Capitalist and Humanitarian." *Rocky Mountain News,* July 13, 1999. http://denver.rockymountainnews.com/millennium/0713mile.shtml.

Halaas, David Fridtjof. "Josephine Roche, 1886–1976: Social Reformer, Mine Operator." *Colorado Heritage News,* March 1985, 4.

"On Losing Side." *Business Week,* April 28, 1945, 72.

Rice, Arnold S., and John A. Krout. *United States History from 1865*. New York: HarperCollins, 1991.

"Roosevelt, Roche, and Recovery." *Literary Digest,* September 1, 1934, 8.

Vandenbusche, Duane, and Duane A. Smith. *A Land Alone: Colorado's Western Slope*. Boulder, CO: Pruett Publishing, 1981.


## Idaho Women

### *Louise Siuwheem*

Bradley, Rt. Rev. Cyprian, O.S.B. and Most Rev. Edward J. Kelly, D.D., Ph.D. *History of the Diocese of Boise 1863–1952*. Boise: Roman Catholic Diocese of Boise, Caldwell: The Caxton Printers, Ltd., 1953.

Chittenden, Hiram Martin and Alfred Talbot Richardson. *Life, Letters and Travels of Father Pierre-Jean De Smet, S.J. 1801–1873*. New York: Francis P. Harper, 1905.

De Smet, Rev. P. J., S. J. *New Indian Sketches*. New York: D. & J. Sadlier & Co., 1865.

Dozier, Jack. "The Light of the Coeur d'Alenes." *The Spokesman-Review*, 15 July 1962.

Hultner, Vi. "The Good Grandmother of the Coeur d'Alenes." *The Spokesman-Review*, 7 December 1952.

### *Kitty C. Wilkins*

Beal, Merrill D., Ph.D. and Merle W. Wells, Ph.D. *History of Idaho*. Vol. II. New York: Lewis Historical Publishing Company, Inc., 1959.

"Death Takes Colorful Pioneer Horsewoman." *The Idaho Statesman*, 11 October 1936.

Farner, Tom. "The Queen of Diamonds." *Western Horseman*, September (1992): 26–33.

Hart, Arthur A. "Idaho Yesterdays: Horse Queen of Idaho Reaped Much Publicity." *The Idaho Statesman*, 18 December 1972.

"Horse Queen of the West." *St. Louis Post-Dispatch*, 10 October 1895.

"Horses Are Her Delight." *Sioux City Journal*, 26 June 1891.

"Kitty Wilkins 'Horse Queen' Dies Suddenly." *The Idaho Statesman*, 9 October 1936

"Kitty Wilkins Tells Story of Lost Gold Mine Near Jarbidge." *The Idaho Statesman*, 10 January 1926.

"Parents of Idaho's Horse Queen Came West in 1853." *The Idaho Statesman*, 22 April 1928.

"Pioneer Stockman Called By Death." *The Idaho Statesman*, 24 September 1936.

St. John, Harvey. "The Golden Queen." *True West,* July–August (1964): 34–35, 64.

"Their Parents Visit Old Fort Boise in '53." *The Idaho Statesman,* 9 September 1934.

"Twenty Years Ago: The 'Horse Queen of Idaho.'" *The Idaho Statesman,* 18 December 1927.

### Emma Russell Yearian

Accola, John. "Grandson of Idaho's 'Sheep Queen' Bases Novel on His Family History." *The Idaho Statesman,* 13 November 1977.

Defenbach, Byron. *IDAHO The Place and Its People.* Chicago–New York: The American Historical Society, Inc., 1933.

"Mrs. Yearian, Idaho Wool Grower, Dies." *The Idaho Daily Statesman,* 26 December 1951.

Penson, Betty. "Emma Russell Yearian's Climb to Fame." *The Idaho Statesman,* 22 January 1978.

———. "The Story of Idaho's Amazing Sheep Queen." *The Idaho Statesman,* 29 January 1978.

Penson-Ward, Betty. *Idaho Women In History.* Boise, ID: Legendary Publishing Company, 1991.

Savage, Thomas. *I Heard My Sister Speak My Name.* Boston: Little, Brown and Company, 1977.

Swank, Gladys R, *Ladies of the House (and Senate) History of Idaho Women Legislators Since Statehood.* Lewiston, ID: private publisher 1978

## Kansas Women

### Lilla Day Monroe

Kleiman, Dena. "How Pioneer Women Lived." *New York Times,* October 17, 1975.

Monroe, Lilla Day. "Some Woman Suffrage History: Address of Mrs. Lilla Day Monroe of Topeka at Pike's Pawnee Village, September 26, 1906." *Transactions of the Kansas State Historical Society,* vol. 10. Topeka: Kansas State Historical Society, 1908.

Stratton, Joanna L. *Pioneer Women: Voices from the Kansas Frontier.* New York: Simon and Schuster, 1982.

### Ella Deloria

Boyer, Paul. *Native American Colleges, Progress and Prospects: An Ernest L. Boyer Project of the Carnegie Foundation for the Advancement of Teaching.* San Francisco: Jossey-Bass, 1997.

Deloria, Ella. Letter to Franz Boas, 1926. Ella Deloria Biographical File. Haskell Indian Nations University Museum and Cultural Center Archives, Lawrence, KS.

Deloria, Ella, and Raymond J. DeMillie. *Waterlily.* Lincoln: University of Nebraska Press, 1988.

Deloria, Ella, and Vine Deloria Jr. *Speaking of Indians.* Lincoln: University of Nebraska Press, 1998.

Erodes, Richard, and Alfonzo Ortiz, eds. *American Indian Myths and Legends.* New York: Pantheon, 1985.

Stille, Darlene R. *Extraordinary Women Scientists.* Chicago: Children's Press, 1995.

Vuckovic, Myriam. *Voices from Haskell: Indian Students between Two Worlds, 1884–1928.* Lawrence: University Press of Kansas, 2008.

### Peggy Hull

Beasley, Maurine H., and Sheila J. Gibbons. *Taking Their Place: A Documentary History of Women and Journalism.* Washington DC: American University Press in cooperation with the Women's Institute for Freedom of the Press, 1993.

Bogart, Eleanor A., and Wilda M. Smith. *The Wars of Peggy Hull: The Life and Times of a War Correspondent.* El Paso: Texas Western Press, 1991.

Kansas Historical Society. "Kansas Memory." Accessed July 12, 2011. www.kansasmemory.org.

Kroeger, Brooke. *Nellie Bly: Daredevil, Reporter, Feminist.* New York: Random House, 1994.

Peggy Hull Duell Collection. Kansas Collection, RH MS E66 (scrapbooks). Kenneth Spencer Research Library, University of Kansas Libraries, Lawrence, KS.

Peggy Hull Duell Collection. Kansas Collection, RH MS 130 (papers and miscellaneous items, 1916–66), Boxes 1 and 2. Kenneth Spencer Research Library, University of Kansas Libraries, Lawrence, KS.

### Missouri Women

#### Alice Berry Graham and Katharine Berry Richardson

Johns, Beatrice. *Women of Vision.* Wentzville, MO: ImagineInk Publishing Company, 2004.

*Kansas City Star Magazine.* "She Spells Success the Old-Fashioned Way," August 3, 1924.

Wenner, Herbert A. and Sydney F. Pakula. The History of the Children's Mercy Hospital in Kansas City, Missouri. Unpublished manuscript, 1984.

"Women in Health Sciences: Biographies: Alice Berry Graham (1850–1913) and Katherine Berry Richardson (1858–1933)." http://beckerexhibits .wustl.edu/mowihsp/bios/GrahamRichardson.htm

### Rose Cecil O'Neill

Brewster, Linda. *Rose O'Neill: The Girl Who Loved to Draw.* Princeton: Boxing Day Books, 2009.

Formanek-Brunell, Miriam, ed. *The Story of Rose O'Neill: An Autobiography.* Columbia: University of Missouri Press, 1997.

Scott, Susan K. "America's First Female Cartoonist Fought for Women's Suffrage," *The Ozark Mountaineer,* March/April 2010, pp. 5–10.

*The Story of Rose O'Neill* (DVD). Branson, MO: Bear Creek Productions, 2004.

### Nell Donnelly Reed

Ancel, Judy. "The Garment Workers," Talk for Kansas City Labor History Tour, October 17, 24, 1992. http://kclabor.org/garment_workers.htm.

McMillen, Margot Ford, and Heather Roberson. *Called to Courage: Four Women in Missouri History.* Columbia, MO: University of Missouri Press, 2002.

O'Dwyer, Tom. "Hot Cargo," *True Detective,* August 1943.

O'Malley, Terence Michael. *Nelly Don: A Stitch in Time.* Kansas City, MO: The Covington Group, 2006.

Snider, Amy, "Nell Donnelly Reed Is Dead at Age 102," *Kansas City Star,* September 9, 1991, A1:3, A1:9.

## Montana Women

### Lucia Darling Park

Darling, Lucia A. Manuscript Collection 145. Montana Historical Society Archives, Helena.

"Death Came to Mrs. S. W. Park Today," *Warren Daily Tribune,* August 18, 1905.

Faust, Homer. "Montana's First School Was Taught by Miss Lucy Darling at Bannack. . . ." Montana Newspaper Association, June 2, 1932.

"First Schools Were Missions." Montana Newspaper Association, November 8, 1937.

*Not in Precious Metals Alone.* Helena: Montana Historical Society Press, 1976.

Plassmann, Mrs. M. E. "First Schools in Montana Were Conducted in Private Homes." Montana Newspaper Association, April 5, 1934.

Sanders, W. F., II, and Robert T. Taylor. *Biscuits and Badmen: The Sanders Story in Their Own Words.* Butte, MT: Editorial Review Press, 1983.

"The Schools." *Fairfield Times,* February 17, 1927.

Thane, James L., Jr., ed. *A Governor's Wife on the Mining Frontier: The Letters of Mary Edgerton from Montana, 1863–1865.* Salt Lake City: University of Utah, Tanner Trust Fund, 1976.

Towle, Virginia Rowe. "Lucia Darling Park: Courage and Determination Behind a Demure Facade." In *Vigilante Women.* New York: A. S. Barnes & Co., 1966.

Upton, Harriet Taylor. *A Twentieth Century History of Trumbull County Ohio.* Vol. 2. Chicago: The Lewis Publishing Co., 1909.


*Mother Amadeus*

*Daily Yellowstone Journal,* Miles City, MT, January 19–26, 1884.

Dwyer, Sue. "Missionary Among the Indians: The Saga of Mother Amadeus." *Toledo Blade Magazine,* June 7, 1981.

"History of Religious Women in Montana." In *Religion in Montana: Pathways to the Present.* Vol. 1, ed. by Lawrence F. Small. Billings, MT: Rocky Mountain College, 1992.

Lincoln, Mother Angela. *Life of the Reverend Mother Amadeus of the Heart of Jesus.* New York: The Paulist Press, 1923.

McBride, Mother Clotilde. *Ursulines of the West.* Mount Angel, OR: Mount Angel Press, 1936.

McBride, Sister Genevieve. *The Bird Tail.* New York: Vantage Press, 1974.


*Nancy Cooper Russell*

Dippie, Brian W., ed. *"Paper Talk": Charlie Russell's American West.* New York: Alfred A. Knopf, in association with the Amon Carter Museum of Western Art, 1979.

McCracken, Harold. *The Charles M. Russell Book.* Garden City, NJ: Doubleday & Co., 1957.

"Mrs. Russell, Widow of Cowboy Artist, Passes in California." *Great Falls Tribune,* May 25, 1940.

Renner, Ginger K. "Charlie and the Ladies in His Life." *Montana, the Magazine of Western History,* Summer 1984.

Russell, Austin. *Charlie Russell, Cowboy Artist.* New York: Twayne Publishers, 1957.

Russell-Cooper marriage announcement. *Great Falls Tribune,* September 9, 1896.

Russell, Nancy C., ed. *Good Medicine: The Illustrated Letters of Charles M. Russell.* Garden City, NJ: Doubleday & Co., 1929.

Stauffer, Joan. *Behind Every Man: The Story of Nancy Cooper Russell.* Tulsa, OK: Daljo Publishing, 1990.

## Fannie Sperry Steele

Blakely, Reba Perry. "Wild West Shows, Rodeos and No Tears." *World of Rodeo and Western Heritage,* October 1981.

Clark, H. McDonald. "Women's Ex-Rodeo Champ Still Active at 67: Fannie Sperry Steele Operates Ranch in Blackfoot Valley." *Great Falls Tribune,* January 9, 1955.

Clark, Helen. "Fannie Sperry Steele Was a Rodeo Queen 50 Years Too Early." *Montana Farmer-Stockman,* January 21, 1965.

———. "Grand Old Lady of Rodeo: Fanny Sperry Steele." *Western Horseman,* September 1959.

———. "Montana's Lady Rider." *Inland Empire Magazine of Spokesman-Review,* January 25, 1959.

Henry, Olive. "Fanny Sperry Steele Lives Alone with Her Memories." *Independent Record,* December 10, 1961.

"Horsewoman Steele Dead at 95." *Great Falls Tribune,* February 12, 1983.

Marvine, Dee. "Fannie Sperry Wowed 'Em at First Calgary Stampede." *American West,* August 1987.

Steele, Fannie Sperry. "A Horse Beneath Me . . . Sometimes." *True West,* January/February 1976

Stiffler, Liz, and Tona Blake. "Fannie Sperry-Steele: Montana's Champion Bronc Rider." *Montana, the Magazine of Western History,* Spring 1982.

# Nevada Women

## Sarah Winnemucca Hopkins

Butruille, Susan G. *Women's Voices from the Western Frontier.* Boise: Tamarack Books, Inc., 1995.

Canfield, Gae Whitney. *Sarah Winnemucca of the Northern Paiutes.* Norman: University of Oklahoma Press, 1983.

Dunlap, Patricia Riley. *Riding Astride: The Frontier Women's History.* Denver: Arden Press, Inc., 1995.

Hopkins, Sarah Winnemucca. *Life Among the Paiutes: Their Wrongs and Claims.* Edited by Mrs. Horace Mann. Boston: Cupples, Upham & Company, 1883.

McClure, Andrews S. "Sarah Winnemucca: [Post] Indian Princess and Voice of the Paiutes" (critical essay). Published by The Society for the Study of the Multi-Ethics Literature in the United States (MELUS), 24.2

(1999), 29–51. Accessed November 2, 2002, from www.findarticles
.com/cf_0/m2278/2_24/59211506/print.jhtml.

Miller, Susan Cummins, ed. *A Sweet Separate Intimacy: Women Writers of the American Frontier, 1800–1922.* Salt Lake City: University of Utah Press, 2000.

Moynihan, Ruth B., Susan Armitage, and Christine Fisher Dichamp, eds. *So Much to Be Done: Women Settlers on the Mining and Ranching Frontier.* Lincoln: University of Nebraska Press, 1990.

Schlissel, Lilliam, and Catherine Lavender, eds. *The Western Women's Reader: The Remarkable Writings of Women Who Shaped the American West, Spanning 300 Years.* New York: Harper Perennial, 2000.

Stewart, Patricia. "Sarah Winnemucca." *Nevada Historical Society Quarterly* 14, no. 4 (winter 1971), 23–38.

Zanjani, Sally Springmeyer. *Sarah Winnemucca.* Lincoln: University of Nebraska Press, 2001.

*Eliza Cook*

Abram, Ruth J., ed. *"Send Us a Lady Physician": Women Doctors in America, 1835–1920.* New York: W. W. Norton & Company, 1985.

Cook, Eliza. "Outline of My Life." Original document found beside Dr. Cook at the time of her death, 1947.

Jones, Cherry. Personal correspondence. December 2003–January 2004. Luchetti, Cathy. *Medicine Women: The Story of Early-American Women Doctors.* New York: Crown Publishers, 1998.

Sohn, Anton P. *The Healers of 19th-Century Nevada.* Reno: Greasewood Press, 1997.

*Maude Frazier*

Cummings, Nancy R., and Dorothy Ritenour, compilers and writers. *County School Legacy: Humanities on the Frontier: Report from Southern Nevada,* 1981.

Davies, Richard O., ed. *The Maverick Spirit: Building the New Nevada.* Reno: University of Nevada Press, 1999.

Frazier, Maude. *Autobiography/Maude Frazier.* Las Vegas: University of Nevada, Las Vegas Special Collections, 1960.

Glass, Mary Ellen. *Maude Frazier.* Prepared for Notable American Women. Reno: University of Nevada, 1978.

Hulse, James W. *The Maverick Spirit: Building the New Nevada.* Reno: University of Nevada Press, 1999.

## New Mexico Women

*Mary Colter*

Grattan, Virginia L. *Mary Colter, Builder Upon the Red Earth.* Grand Canyon, AZ: Grand Canyon Association, 1992.

*Nina Otero-Warren*

Otero-Warren, Nina. *Old Spain in Our Southwest.* Santa Fe: Sunstone Press, 2006.
Whaley, Charlotte. *Nina Otero-Warren of Santa Fe.* Santa Fe: Sunstone Press, 2007.

*Laura Gilpin*

Gilpin, Laura. *The Enduring Navaho.* Austin: University of Texas Press, 1968.
———. *The Pueblos: A Camera Chronicle.* New York: Hastings, 1942.
———. *The Rio Grande: River of Destiny.* New York: Duell, Sloan, and Pearce, 1949.
Sandweiss, Martha A. *Laura Gilpin: An Enduring Grace.* Fort Worth, TX: Amon Carter, 1986.
———. "Laura Gilpin and the Tradition of American Landscape Photography." www.cla.purdue.edu/waaw/Sandweiss/.

## Oklahoma Women

*Catherine "Kate" Ann Barnard*

Barnard, Catherine. Personal Correspondence. R. L. Williams Collection. Oklahoma Historical Society, Oklahoma City.
Burke, Bob, and Carlille, Glenda. *Kate Barnard: Oklahoma's Good Angel.* Edmond: University of Central Oklahoma Press, 2001.
*Daily Oklahoman* (Oklahoma City). "Barnard Gift Will Be Taken." February 27, 1930.
———. "Kate Barnard to Be Honored." February 25, 1930.
———. "Kate Barnard: Unsung Heroine." February 23, 1941.
———. "Orphan's Home to Be Investigated." March 13, 1914.
Edmondson, Linda, and Larason, Margaret. "Kate Barnard: The Story of a Woman Politician." *Chronicles of Oklahoma* 78 (Summer 2000): 160.
Federal Writer's Project. "Kate Barnard." Oklahoma Historical Society, Oklahoma City.
FS Barde Collection. Oklahoma Historical Society, Oklahoma City.
Huson, Hobart. "Oklahoma's Juvenile Court Law Most Effective of All." *Daily Oklahoman* (Oklahoma City), January 28, 1912.

Jesse J. Dunn Collection. Oklahoma Historical Society, Oklahoma City.

Musselwhite, Lynn. *One Woman's Political Journey: Kate Barnard and Social Reform 1875–1930*. Norman: University of Oklahoma Press, 2003.

*New York Times*. "Miss Kate, Livest Wire in Prison Reform Visits Us." December 8, 1912.

Ropp, Mrs. "Human Ideals in State Government," *The Survey Magazine* 23 (October 1909–March 1910), 16.

Schrems, Suzanne H. *Who's Rocking the Cradle?* Norman, OK: Horse Creek Publications, 2004.

*St. Louis Post Dispatch*. "Barnard and 'Bill' Murray Clash Again." March 17, 1915.

———. "'Grafters After Me,' Says Kate Barnard: Oklahoma's Guardian Angel Hits Foes Appeals to Legislature for Hearing." February 16, 1913.

*St. Louis Republic*. "'Oklahoma Kate' Warns Her Enemies She'll Be Ready for Next Campaign." February 16, 1913.

*Sturm's Oklahoma Magazine* (Tulsa, Indian Territory). "Oklahoma's Child Labor Laws," February 1, 1908, 42.

*Weekly Chieftan* (Vinita, Oklahoma). "Kate Barnard," April 29, 1910, 8.

### Rachel Caroline Eaton

Bass, Althea, "A Cherokee Daughter of Mount Holyoke." Oklahoma City: Oklahoma Historical Society, 1937.

Berry, Christina. "Rachel Caroline Eaton—Cherokee Woman, Historian, and Educator." The All Things Cherokee website, www.allthingscherokee.com/articles_culture_people_010201.html.

Eaton, Rachel Caroline. *John Ross and the Cherokee Indians*. Menasha, WI: George Banta Publishing, 1914.

———. "The Legend of the Battle of Claremore Mound, Oklahoma." In *The Traditional Background of the Indians*. General Federations of Women's Clubs, October 1930.

Fite, Mrs. R.L. *Historical Statement*. An Illustrated Souvenir Catalog of the Cherokee National Female Seminary, Tahlequah, Indian Territory, 1850–1906. E97.6 .C35 C45. Oklahoma History Center Archives, Oklahoma City, Oklahoma.

———. Historical Statement on the Cherokee. Oklahoma Historical Society, Oklahoma City.

Foreman, Carolyn Thomas. *Park Hill*. Muskogee, OK: The Star Printery, 1948.

Mihesuah, Devon A. *Cultivating the Rosebuds*. Champaign: University of Illinois Press, 1998.

Price, Warren C. "Removal of the Indians From Southeast a Major Tragedy." Ragland Collection. Oklahoma Historical Society, Oklahoma City.

Wright, Muriel, H. "Rachel Caroline Eaton." *Chronicles of Oklahoma* 16 (December 1938): 510.

"Tahlequah and Park Hill Area." Ragland Collection, 82.100, Box 23, Folder 8, Oklahoma Historical Society, Oklahoma City, Oklahoma.

### Dorothy K. Barrack Pressler Morgan

*Betsy Ross Corps News.* "Dorothy Pressler." May 1932, 6.

Claypool, Dorothy. "City Woman Is Marking Her 34th Year in Aviation," *Sunday Oklahoman* (Oklahoma City), January 27, 1963, Section C, 2.

"History of the Ninety-Nines, Inc." Archives, 99s Museum of Women Pilots, Oklahoma City.

Hodgman, Ann and Djabbaroff, Rudy. *Skystars.* Harrisonburg, VA: RR Donnelley and Sons, 1981.

Holden, Henry M. and Griffith, Lori. *Ladybirds: The Untold Story of Women Pilots in America.* Mount Freedom, NJ: Black Hawk Publishing Company, 1991.

Jessen, Gene Nora. "The Ninety Nines, 1929–1979." In *The Ninety-Nines: Yesterday-Today-Tomorrow.* 10–21. Paducah, KY: Turner Publishing Company, 1996.

——. "Women with Wings Meet Dorothy Morgan." *Western Flyer.* November 1974, 6.

*Journal Record* (Oklahoma City). "Aviation, Space Hall of Fame Honors Cooper, Inductees." November 11, 1992, 2.

*Kansas City Journal Post.* "Noted Women Fliers of Middle West Here for Betsy Ross Corps Rally." April 8, 1932.

Morgan, Dorothy. Personal Letters, from American Eagle, May 27, 1930.

——. Personal Letters, from Oklahoma City, dated October 2, 1950.

*Oklahoma City Times.* "Dorothy Morgan." February 1, 1978, 27.

Ostrand, Phil Van. "Early Woman Aviator Still Spry at 73." *Oklahoma City Times,* May 23, 1969, 7.

Owens, Violet. "Echo 1 Brings Echo of Past." *Beacon,* November 1960.

Roberts, Mary B. "Dorothy Morgan." Living Legends Oral History Collection. June 9, 1977. Oklahoma Historical Society, Oklahoma City.

### Lucille Mulhall

Carlile, Glenda. "Lucille Mulhall—America's First Cowgirl." In *Buckskin, Calico and Lace: Oklahoma Territorial Women,* 129–142. Stillwater, OK: New Forums Press, 2008.

*Daily Oklahoman* (Oklahoma City). "Lucille Mulhall, World Famous Cowgirl and One-Time Toast of Royalty, Dies in Car Crash." December 23, 1940.

*Guthrie Daily Leader.* "Live Stock Convention." February 10, 1903, 5.

———. Society Page. February 27, 1903, 5.

"History of Mulhall." 83.213, Box 1, Folder 1. Oklahoma Historical Society Library Archives, Oklahoma City.

*Mulhall Enterprise.* "Three Shot by Mulhall," June 24, 1904.

Olds, Fred. "The Story of Lucille." *The War Chief: Official Publication of the Indian Territory Posse of Oklahoma Westerners* 8, no. 3 (Dec. 1974): 2–11.

Oral history given by Effie Strothman, *Oral History Tape #83.027,* February 7, 1983. 83.213.1. Oklahoma Historical Society Library, Oklahoma City, Oklahoma.

Rogers, Will. "Death of Mulhall Sends Will's Thoughts to Days When He Got Show Bug." *Daily Oklahoman* (Oklahoma City), October 11, 1931, 23.

Stanbury, Kathryn B. *Lucille Mulhall: Her Family, Her Life, Her Times.* Mulhall, OK: K.B. Stanbury, 1985.

Tompkins Collection Scrapbooks 6, 7, and 9. Tompkins Exhibit No. 2. Oklahoma Historical Society Archives, Oklahoma City.

## Oregon Women

### Abigail Scott Duniway

Duniway, Abigail Scott. "About Ourself." *The New Northwest.* May 5, 1871.

———. "A Few Recollections of a Busy Life," in *Souvenir of Western Women,* ed. Mary Osborn Douthit. Portland, OR: Anderson & Duniway Co., 1905.

———. *Path Breaking: An Autobiographical History of the Equal Suffrage Movement in Pacific Coast States.* Portland, OR: James, Kerns & Abbott Co., 1914.

———. "Personal Reminiscences of a Pioneer," in *Portland, Oregon: Its History and Builders,* ed. Joseph Gaston. Chicago: S. J. Clarke Publishing, 1911.

Duniway, David Cushing. "Abigail Scott Duniway, Path Breaker," in *With Her Own Wings,* ed. Helen Krebs Smith. Portland, OR: Beattie & Co., 1948.

Johnson, Jalmar. *Builders of the Northwest.* New York: Dodd, Mead & Co., 1963.

Morrison, Dorothy Nafus. *Ladies Were Not Expected: Abigail Scott Duniway and Women's Rights.* Portland, OR: Oregon Historical Society Press, 1985. Originally published in 1977.

Moynihan, Ruth Barnes. "Of Women's Rights and Freedom: Abigail Scott Duniway," in *Women in Pacific Northwest History,* ed. Karen J. Blair. Seattle: University of Washington Press, 1988.

———. *Rebel for Rights.* New Haven: Yale University Press, 1983.

Smith, Helen Krebs. *The Presumptuous Dreamers: A Sociological History of the Life and Times of Abigail Scott Duniway (1834–1915).* Lake Oswego, OR: Smith, Smith & Smith Publishing Co., 1974.

### Lola Greene Baldwin

Bryant, Louise. "A Municipal Mother," *Sunset,* September 1912.

Hills, Tim. *The Many Lives of the Crystal Ballroom.* Gresham, OR: McMenamins Publishers & Brewery, 1997.

Myers, Gloria E. *A Municipal Mother: Portland's Lola Greene Baldwin, America's First Policewoman.* Corvallis: Oregon State University Press, 1995.

### Alice Day Pratt

"Alice Day Pratt," in *The History of Crook County, Oregon.* Prineville: Crook County Historical Society, 1981.

Pratt, Alice Day. *A Homesteader's Portfolio,* with introduction by Molly Glass. Corvallis: Oregon State University Press, 1993. Originally published in 1922.

———. *Three Frontiers.* New York: Vantage Press, 1955.

Raban, Jonathan. *Bad Land: An American Romance.* New York: Pantheon, 1996.

Silver, Clarine. "Alice Day Pratt, early day homesteader at Post, wrote of harshness, challenge of life on the high desert." *Bend (OR) Bulletin.* February 10, 1973.

## Texas Women

### Leonor Villegas de Magnón

de Magnón, Leonor Villegas. *The Rebel,* ed. Clara Lomas. Houston: Arte Público Press, 1994.

Gibson, Karen Bush. *Jovita Idar.* Bear, Delaware: Mitchell Lane Publishers, 2003.

Lomas, Clara (ed.). "Revolutionary Women and the Alternative Press in the Borderlands." In *The Rebel,* de Magnón Leonor Villegas (pp. xi–lvi). Houston: Arte Público Press, 1994.

Rocha, Martha Eva. "The Faces of Rebellion: From Revolutionaries to Veterans in Nationalist Mexico." In *The Women's Revolution in Mexico, 1910–1953,* edited by Stephanie Mitchell and Patience A. Schell (pp. 15–35). Lanham, MD: Rowman & Littlefield Publishers, 2007.

Tinnemeyer, Andrea. "Mediating the Desire of the Reader in Villegas de Magnón's *The Rebel.* In *Recovering the US Hispanic Literary Heritage,* Volume 3, edited by María Herrera-Sobek (pp. 124–137). Houston: Arte Publico Press, 2000.

Wilkinson, J. B. *Laredo and the Rio Grande Frontier.* Austin, TX: Jenkins, 1975.


## Jessie Daniel Ames

Ames, Jessie Daniel. *The Changing Character of Lynching.* Atlanta: Commission on Interracial Cooperation, 1942.

Brewer, Anita. "Suffragette Recalls her 1918 Vote Fight." *Austin American* (May 24, 1965): 24

Crawford, Ann Fears, and Crystal Sasse Ragsdale. *Texas Women: Frontier to Future.* Austin, TX: State House Press, 1998.

Green, Elna. "'Ideals of Government, of Home, and of Women': The Ideology of Southern White Antisuffragism." In *Hidden Histories of Women in the New South,* edited by Virginia Bernhard et al. Columbia: University of Missouri Press, 1994.

Hall, Jacqueline Dowd. *Revolt Against Chivalry: Jessie Daniel Ames and the Women's Campaign against Lynching.* Revised edition. New York: Columbia University Press, 1993.

NAACP. *Thirty Years of Lynching in the United States, 1889–1918.* New York: Arno Press, 1969.

Nieuwenhuizen, Patricia B. "Minnie Fisher Cunningham and Jane Y. McCallum: Leaders of Texas Women." Senior thesis, University of Texas at Austin, 1982.

Texas State Library. File, Jessie Daniel Ames. Austin, Texas.

Winegarten, Ruthe, and Juding N. McArthur. *Citizens at Last: The Woman Suffrage Movement in Texas.* Austin, TX: Ellen C. Temple, Publisher, 1987.


## Bessie Coleman

Caidin, Martin. *Barnstorming.* New York: Duell, Sloan and Pearce, 1965.

Fisher, Lillian M. *Brave Bessie: Flying Free.* Dallas: Hendrick-Long Publishing Co., 1995.

Lomax, Judy. *Women of the Air.* London: John Murray, 1986.

Rich, Doris L. *Queen Bess: Daredevil Aviator.* Washington: Smithsonian Institution Press, 1993.

Robinson, P. J. "Queen Bess Flies Forever." *The Metro Herald* (Washington, DC) 6:16 (April 21, 1995): 1 ff.

## Utah Women

### Patty Sessions

Arrington, Chris Rigby, "Pioneer Midwives" in Bushman, Claudia L., ed. *Mormon Sisters: Women in Early Utah*. Logan: Utah State University Press, 1997, p. 43–66.

Black, Susan Easton. "My Heart Is in God" in Smith, Barbara B. and Thatcher, Blythe Darlyn. *Heroines of the Restoration*. Salt Lake City: Bookcraft, 1997, p. 34–45.

Derr, Jill Mulvay. "Strength in Our Union" in Beecher, Maureen Ursenbach and Anderson, Lavinia Fielding, eds. *Sisters in Spirit: Mormon Women in Historical and Cultural Perspective*. Urbana: University of Illinois Press, 1987.

Scadron, Arlene, ed. *On Their Own: Widows and Widowhood in the American Southwest, 1848–1939*. Urbana: University of Illinois Press, 1988.

Smart Donna T., ed. *Mormon Midwife: The 1846–1888 diaries of Patty Bartlett Sessions*. Logan: Utah State University Press, 1997.

Smart, Donna Toland. "Patty Bartlett Sessions: Pioneer Midwife" in Whitley, Colleen, ed., *Worth Their Salt: Notable but Often Unnoted Women of Utah*. Logan: Utah State University Press, 1996.

### Reva Beck Bosone

Abbott, Delia. *Women Legislators of Utah, 1896–1976*. Salt Lake City, Utah Chapter, Order of Women Legislators, 1976.

Clopton, Beverly B. *Her Honor, the Judge: the story of Reva Beck Bosone*. Ames: The Iowa State University Press, 1980.

Law Library, "Reva Beck Bosone," http://law.jrank.org/pages/4822/Bosone -Reva-Beck.html.

Stone, Irving, ed. *There Was Light: Autobiography of a University, Berkeley, 1868–1968*. Garden City, NY: Doubleday, 1970.

Walton, Juanita Irva Heath. "Reva Beck Bosone: Legislator, Judge, Congresswoman." Master of Arts thesis, Department of History, University of Utah, 1974.

### Juanita Brooks

Brooks, Juanita. *The Mountain Meadows Massacre* (3rd edition). Norman: University of Oklahoma Press, 1991.

——. *Quicksand and Cactus: A Memoir of the Southern Mormon Frontier*. Logan: Utah State University Press, 1992.

Bush, Laura L. *Faithful Transgressions in the American West: Six Twentieth-Century Mormon Women's Autobiographical Acts.* Logan: Utah State University Press, 2004.

Peterson, Levi S. *Juanita Brooks: Mormon Woman Historian.* Salt Lake City: University of Utah Press, 1988.

Sillito, John, and Susan Staker, eds. *Mormon Mavericks: Essays on Dissenters.* Salt Lake City: Signature Books, 2002.

## Washington Women

### Mary Ann Boren Denny

Atkins, Frank R. "Schooner 'Exact' Brought Settlers to Alki Landing." Costello Scrapbook. Seattle Public Library.

Bagley, Clarence B. *Pioneer Seattle and Its Pioneers.* Seattle: Argus Press, 1928.

Beaver, Lowell J. *Historic Memories from Monuments and Plaques of Western Washington.* Trademark Historic Memories, 1960.

Buerge, David M. "Seattle's Pioneer Women." In *Washingtonians.* Seattle: Sasquatch Publishing, 1989.

Crowley, Veryle Morehouse. "The First Christmas at Alki Point." In *Incidents in the Life of a Pioneer Woman.* The State Association of the Daughters of the Pioneers of Washington, 1976.

Denny, Arthur. *Pioneer Days on Puget Sound.* Seattle: C. B. Bagley Printer, 1888/Seattle: The Alice Harriman Company, 1908.

"Denny Family 'Stitch in Time' Is Historical." *The Seattle Times,* December 11, 1932.

"Dennys Celebrate: Its Wedding Day & Birthday Fete." *The Seattle Times,* September 2, 1933.

Hanford, Cornelius. *Seattle and Environs.* Seattle: Pioneer Historical Publishing Co., 1924.

Kamb, Lewis. "Aiding Seattle's First People." *Seattle Post-Intelligencer,* August 9, 2004.

"Mrs. Arthur A. Denny Dead: Woman Founder of City Passes Away." *The Seattle Daily Times,* December 30, 1910.

Newell, Gordon. *Westward to Alki: The Story of David and Louisa Denny.* Seattle: Superior Publishing Company, 1977.

"Rolland Denny's Life of Integrity Spanned Era of City's Development." *Seattle Star,* December 21, 1947.

*Sketches of Washingtonians.* Seattle: Wellington C. Wolfe & Co., 1906.

*A Volume of Memoirs and Genealogy of Representative Citizens of the City of Seattle and King County Washington.* New York and Chicago: The Lewis Publishing Company, 1903.

Watt, Roberta Frye. *Four Wagons West: The Story of Seattle.* Portland, OR: Binford & Mort, 1931.

Special thanks to Denny descendants Amy Johnson and Andrew Harris.

### Mother Joseph

Acceptance of the Statue of Mother Joseph. Presented by the state of Washington, May 1, 1980. Washington, D.C.: U.S. Government Printing Office, 1980.

Archives of the Sisters of Providence—Sacred Heart Province:

Letters from Mother Joseph to:

Mother Caron, November 16, 1856; Mother Caron, December 4, 1856; Mother Caron, December 21, 1856; Bishop Bourget, December 29, 1856; Father Truteau, April 19, 1857; Mother Caron, May 1857; Mother Caron, June 1857; Bishop Larocque, August 15, 1857; Bishop Bourget, December 27, 1857; Bishop Bourget, December 18, 1858; Bishop Bourget, January 30, 1861; Bishop Larocque, March 3, 1862; Father Brouillet, V.G., January 2, 1863.

Annals of Providence Academy: Mother Joseph—December 26, 1843—Entrance, p. 372

Annals of Sisters of Providence:

1861—pp. 142, 145, 147

Collections in The Mines of Idaho and Montana, 1866—pp. 207, 210, 222

Begging Tours: 1867—p. 224; 1873—p. 303

House of Providence Building: 1873—p. 327, 1874—pp. 329, 370–371; 1877—pp. 230, 235, 274

Diary written on The Sea Voyage, November 2, 1856—translated by Sister Martin, and Sister Mary Barbara.

"Chronicles of Saint Joseph Hospital," Vancouver, WA, Vol. 8, 1858–1952. Translated by Sister Dorothy Lentz, S.P., 1978.

"The Institute of Providence," Vol. 1—1800–1844

Letter of Chief Selstice of the Coeur d'Alenes to Sister Catherine, 1870.

Lucia, Ellis. *Seattle's Sisters of Providence.* Seattle: Providence Medical Center, Sisters of Providence, 1978.

McCrosson, Sister Mary. *The Bell and the River.* Seattle: Sisters of Charity of Providence, 1957 and 1986.

Tucker, Joan Pinkerton. "Beggar/Builder," videotape produced by KWSU Productions, written and narrated by Joan Pinkerton Tucker, 1993.

Special thanks to Sisters of Providence Archives, Sacred Heart Province, Seattle: Loretta Zwolak Greene, Archivist; Sister Rita Bergamini, S.P., Archivist Assistant.

*Thea Christiansen Foss*

"Andrew Foss." Obituary. *The Seattle Times,* March 14, 1937.

"City Makes It Official: Thea Foss Waterway." *The Morning News Tribune,* October 18, 1989.

Evans, Walter. "Thea Foss: Lasting Wake on Sound." *Seattle Post-Intelligencer,* June 4, 1976.

Foss, Henry. "A Mother Molds the Character of a Boy." *Tacoma News Tribune,* May 14, 1967.

"From the Crow's Nest." *The Seattle Times,* September 12, 1935.

Green, Frank L. "Thea Foss—A Gallery of 100 Eminent Washingtonians." Tacoma, WA: Washington State Historical Society, 1989.

Johnson, Bruce, and Michael Skalley. *Foss: a Living Legend.* Printed for Foss Maritime Company, 1990.

Michener, Charles T. "A Remarkable Saga of Tugs and Towing." *Seattle Magazine,* 1966: 39–43.

Skalley, Michael. "Foss: Ninety Years of Towboating." August 23, 1982.

"'Tugboat Annie' Continues Run." *Seattle Post-Intelligencer,* August 4, 1933.

"Tugboat Annie Picture to Be Sold." *Seattle Post-Intelligencer,* June 4, 1976.

Whitney, Marci. "Thea Foss Was No 'Tugboat Annie.'" *Tacoma News Tribune,* September 19, 1976.

Special thanks to Kae Paterson, Commencement Bay Maritime Center; Tim Brewer, Vice President, and Michael Skalley, Historian, Foss Maritime Company.

# Sources

*More than Petticoats: Remarkable Alaska Women*, 2nd edition, by Cherry Lyon Jones
    Nellie Neal Lawing
    Etta Eugenie Schureman Jones
    Florence Barrett Willoughby
    Anfesia Shapsnikoff

*More than Petticoats: Remarkable Arizona Women*, 2nd edition, by Wynne Brown
    Lozen
    Sister Mary Fidelia McMahon
    Mary-Russell Ferrell Colton
    Carmen Lee Ban

*More than Petticoats: Remarkable California Women*, 2nd edition, by Erin H. Turner
    Mary Ellen Pleasant
    Toby Riddle
    Mary Austin
    Tye Leung Schulze

*More than Petticoats: Remarkable Colorado Women*, 2nd edition, by Gayle C. Shirley
    "Aunt Clara" Brown
    Florence Sabin
    Josephine Roche

*More than Petticoats: Remarkable Idaho Women*, 2nd edition, by Lynn Bragg
    Louise Siuwheem
    Kitty C. Wilkins
    Emma Russell Yearian

*More than Petticoats: Remarkable Kansas Women*, by Gina Kaufmann
    Lilla Day Monroe
    Ella Deloria
    Peggy Hull

*More than Petticoats: Remarkable Missouri Women*, by Elaine Warner
    Alice Berry Graham and
        Katherine Berry Richardson
    Rose Cecil O'Neill
    Nelly Donnelly Reed

*More than Petticoats: Remarkable Montana Women*, 2nd edition, by Gayle C. Shirley
    Lucia Darling Park
    Mother Amadeus
    Nancy Cooper Russell
    Fannie Sperry Steele

*More than Petticoats: Remarkable Nevada Women*, 2nd edition, by Jan Cleere
    Sarah Winnemucca Hopkins
    Eliza Cook
    Maude Frazier

*More than Petticoats: Remarkable New Mexico Women*, 2nd edition, by Beverly West
    Mary Colter
    Nina Otero-Warren
    Laura Gilpin

*More than Petticoats: Remarkable Oklahoma Women*, 2nd edition, by Deborah Bouziden
    Catherine "Kate" Ann Barnard
    Rachel Caroline Eaton
    Dorothy K. Barrack Pressler Morgan
    Lucille Mulhall

*More than Petticoats: Remarkable Oregon Women*, 2nd edition, by Gayle C. Shirley
    Abigail Scott Duniway
    Lola Greene Baldwin
    Alice Day Pratt

*More than Petticoats: Remarkable Texas Women*, 2nd edition, by Greta Anderson
    Leonor Villegas de Magnón
    Jessie Daniel Ames
    Bessie Coleman

*More than Petticoats: Remarkable Utah Women*, by Christy Karras
    Patty Sessions
    Reva Beck Bosone
    Juanita Brooks

*More than Petticoats: Remarkable Washington Women*, 2nd edition, by L.E. Bragg
    Mary Ann Boren Denny
    Mother Joseph
    Thea Christiansen Foss

# Index